GREEN

ISLANDS

GUIDE

YOUR PASSPORT TO GREAT TRAVEL!

CRITICAL ACCLAIM FOR
OPEN ROAD TRAVEL GUIDES!

Whether you're going abroad or planning a trip in the United States, take Open Road along on your journey. Our books have been praised by **Travel & Leisure, The Los Angeles Times, Newsday, Booklist, US News & World Report, Endless Vacation, American Bookseller, Coast to Coast,** *and many other magazines and newspapers!*

Don't just see the world – experience it with Open Road!

ABOUT THE AUTHOR

George McDonald, a native of Scotland, is a professional travel writer who now makes his home in Brussels, Belgium. George has written numerous travel articles, and is the author of UK Automobile Association/Thomas Cook guides to China, Cyprus, and Belgium; the Insight Pocket Guide to Brussels; and several chapters of the Insight Guide to the Netherlands.

HIT THE OPEN ROAD - WITH OPEN ROAD PUBLISHING!

Open Road Publishing now has guide books to exciting, fun destinations on four continents. As veteran travelers, our goal is to bring you the best travel guides available anywhere!

No small task, but here's what we offer:

• All Open Road travel guides are written by authors with a distinct, opinionated point of view – not some sterile committee or team of writers. Our authors are experts in the areas covered and are polished writers.

• Our guides are geared to people who want great vacations, great value, and great tips for both standard tourist sights *and* fun, unique alternatives.

• We're strong on the basics, but we also provide terrific choices for those looking to get off the beaten path and *experience* the country or city – not just *see* it or pass through it.

• We give you the best, but we also tell you about the worst and what to avoid. Nobody should waste their time and money on their hard-earned vacation because of bad or inadequate travel advice.

• Our guides assume nothing. We tell you everything you need to know to have the trip of a lifetime – presented in a fun, literate, no-nonsense style.

• And, above all, we welcome your input, ideas, and suggestions to help us put out the best travel guides possible.

GREEK ISLANDS GUIDE

YOUR PASSPORT TO GREAT TRAVEL!

GEORGE McDONALD

OPEN ROAD PUBLISHING

1st Edition

To my mother, who would have loved Greece

Text Copyright ©1997 by Geroge McDonald
Maps Copyright ©1997 by Open Road Publishing
- All Rights Reserved -

Library of Congress Catalog Card No. 96-68659
ISBN 1-883323-40-1

TABLE OF CONTENTS

CONTENTS

CONTENTS

CONTENTS

MAPS

CONTENTS

SIDEBARS

1. INTRODUCTION

I'd like to say that I've been fascinated with Greece ever since I first read Aristotle, but it's truer to say that the fascination began with my first sip of retsina a long time ago in a restaurant far, far away. No ordinary wine, retsina somehow manages to combine the tan of the goatpen with a startling clarity and freshness that is peculiarly Greek. Like Greece itself, it's a very easily acquired taste, and once acquired is rarely given up.

Some fear that Greece is losing its soul, but it hasn't done so yet. The magic and mystique of the Greek Islands are still there to be discovered and experienced. Sure, you can go for the beaches alone, or for the wild nightlife of some resorts. You'll be missing a lot, though, if you don't dig a little deeper, to see where the people and the country have come from, and to wonder about where they might be going. If you are the kind of traveler who wants to miss nothing of the sensual (in the widest sense of the term) delights of this warm-hearted land, you'll find that this book is aimed squarely at you.

In addition to basic travel planning information and the necessary cultural and historical background, I've selected a wide swath of the wondrous and many Greek Islands for you to consider visiting. All the information you need to move around easily between islands is here, and each destination is covered in depth: where to stay, where to eat, ruins, seeing the sights, fun activities, nightlife and cultural offerings are featured throughout. As most of you will arrive and depart from Athens, and will no doubt spend at least a few days there, I've included a detailed chapter on Greece's capital city as well.

This guide's starting point is the love of the country; its intention is to accompany you with affectionate yet unclouded eyes through the reality of modern Greece and the wonders of its past – and, of course, to help you have some fun along the way!

2. EXCITING GREEK ISLANDS! - OVERVIEW

Overview

Surely the first thing you will notice when you arrive in Greece is the light. It seems almost hypernaturally clear, a limpid curtain hanging from a cerulean sky.

The pure Aegean light that so dazzles the eye shines too like a beacon of hope through the roiling darks of history. It illuminates not only a particular time and place and a particular people, but the whole of humanity, showing what *can* be when intelligence and love of beauty combine to move the human drama forward. Images take shape: graceful columns in Pentelic marble, gray-bearded sages whose words are received with solemn respect, the mystic blue of that ever-present, island-strewn sea.

We have come to recognize that other cultures also shone their lamps into the night, and that not all was fair in Periclean Athens. But something draws us back ever and again to the glories of ancient Greece. Myth and reality swirl around each other in the luminous mists, as though, while sitting on the terrace of some seafront taverna, sipping our chilled *retsina*, we might easily expect a triple-banked galley to come sliding out of history and tie up alongside.

There is no easy separating these images from the truth, even though the latter can sometimes be as harsh as the noonday sun. Classical Greece is gone, of course, no matter how much of it still resides in the landscape and in the minds of men. Slow waves of history have washed over the land since then, taking much away and leaving a far different imprint to the one Plato would have recognized. Gods there are in abundance though, and your fellow travelers join the pilgrimages to their temples in numberless hordes. Don't blame them: they are doing no more than you and for exactly the same reasons. In any case, the scene at such places may not have been too different in antiquity.

Greece exists in the imagination as much as in the real world, but it is in the real world where you will spend your vacation. No one should be too surprised that the 20th century – and in particular its last few decades – has drastically changed the landscape, both human and natural. Much of what has been done is ugly by any standards. Yet it seems especially cruel that Greece, where for so long an easy beauty at one with the landscape was second nature, should succumb to the "charms" of concrete and the lure of a quick drachma. There are Greeks who, in the midst of the tourist-swamped high season, let slip their grip on the high standards of hospitality that once were more first nature than second.

Overdevelopment has its costs, and these are some of them.

One of many idyllic Greek images is that of life on the islands scattered like seeds thrown across Homer's wine-dark sea. Altogether there are 9,835 islands, islets, and scraps of rock in the archipelago, only 115 of which are inhabited, covering a land area of 25,000 square kilometers (19 percent of the national territory), and supporting 15 percent of the population. There is something about them, each one a little private kingdom of the mind, something about even just being on a Greek island that makes otherwise well-adjusted people long for the life of the Lotus-Eaters.

That is not to say that romance is an unfailing commodity. Some islands have all but sold their souls for the fool's gold of tourist bucks. Yet even on the most heavily exploited islands, you usually need do no more than move a few kilometers inland from the hard commercial carapace along the shore and you are back in the timeless Greece of an earlier – and poorer – era.

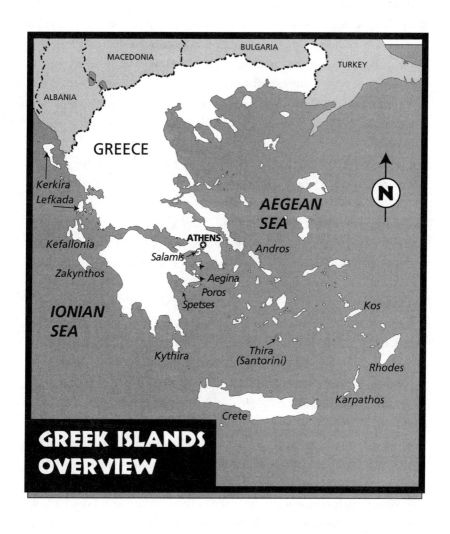

GREEK ISLANDS
OVERVIEW

As always in the Greek islands, the regrets that runaway tourist development engenders must be balanced to an extent against the wealth and jobs such tourism has brought to what were once poor and isolated places. It is surely not being too patronizing or carping, however, to wish the process could have been managed with more grace and less greed. It is especially galling to see earlier and often disastrous mistakes repeated constantly in new places, as though the Greek love of learning has no room for learning from experience. More importantly, the consequent environmental degradation threatens rare species and, in the long run, may drive away the very tourists who brought the resorts into being in the first place.

Still, when all the necessary provisos have been made, there is nowhere in Europe where visitors receive a better welcome. And the deep currents of the Greek character are still there, running strongly a little way below the jaded surface of a busy July day. You won't need to embark upon too big a flight of fancy to feel that some of the magic of gods and heroes survives and that you have been touched by it in your soul.

ATHENS

Let's start with Athens, your likely starting point for any holiday in the Greek islands. Take the time to see the major sights like the **Acropolis**, the **Agora**, and the **National Archaeological Museum**; wander around the taverna-and-shops enclave of **Plaka**, the flea market in **Monastiraki**, and Cyclades-style **Anafiotika** below the Acropolis; move on to **Exarhia**, **Omonia**, and **Koukaki**; get your greens in the **National Garden** and **Areos Park**; climb the **Filopapou** and **Likavitos Hills** for the fresh air and the view; catch the bus or trolley at **Plateia Syntagma**; and if you feel the need to go upmarket, start out around **Kolonaki** then head out to **Kifissia**.

When you leave for the islands, if you're smart you won't depart from Piraeus. Leave instead from **Rafina**, a much smaller harbor east of the capital.

THE SARONIC GULF

The islands of **Aegina, Poros, Hydra,** and **Spetses** are layed out like stepping stones down through the Saronic Gulf from Athens. All are within range of a daytrip from Athens, although the farthest, Spetses, is a bit of a stretch. Despite being so close to the big city and being mostly overrun with Greek and foreign tourists come summer, they are still genuine Greek islands. You have to get to them by boat, for one thing, and once there the traditional magic of being on a Greek island asserts itself.

Highlights include the **Temple of Aphaia**, one of the most remarkable surviving ancient temples in Greece, on Aegina; **Eginitiko Arkhontiko**, a historic mansion that has been converted into a hotel, also on Aegina; **Trireme**, a replica of the wooden galleys with three banks of oars that gave the ancient Greeks command of the seas in Poros; and **Hydra town** on the island of Hydra, one of the most charming of all Greek towns, with its stonebuilt mansions set on a scenic location around a steep-sided bay.

CRETE

Crete, the largest Greek island, has terrific beaches, but don't spend all your time burning your flesh. Crete's mountains are quickly reached from **Heraklion** and the coastal resorts. Their cool air is a benediction in summer, as you pass through pretty mountain villages and take the opportunity to get closer to nature along hiking trails.

But you didn't come to Crete just to hit the beaches or hike in the mountains, splendid as these experiences are. Superlatives cannot do justice to the ruins and museums of Crete. In **Heraklion**, don't miss the **National Archaeological Museum**, where you can see artifacts from the ancient Minoan culture and some of the most important historical collections, and **Knossos**, the great palace complex of the Minoans, now partially and beautifully reconstructed, giving visitors a unique insight into a vanished civilization.

In western Crete, visit **Rethimno** and **Hania**. The old centers of these two towns retain enough of their original Venetian and Ottoman graces to make them among the most handsome towns in Greece. Another marvelous sight in western Crete is the **Samaria Gorge**, a deep fissure 14 kilometers long in the Lefka Mountains, traversing which has become an essential rite-of-passage for fit and healthy nature lovers on the island.

In eastern Crete, stop by the **Lassithi Plateau**, where some 5,000 windmills spin their canvas blades on this fertile plateau overlooked by the great mass of Mount Dikti. While in this corner of the island, visit **Kato Zakros**, an unspoiled little village where Minoan remains mark the site of one of their important harbors.

KYTHIRA

Kythira is a geographical nuisance that nobody knows what to do with. It lies off the south Peloponnese coast, just about where the Ionian Sea, the Aegean Sea, and the Sea of Crete mix their waters. There is an embarrassment of riches in terms of beaches on Kythira, most of them deserted and only a few offering tourist facilities. The best beaches are around **Diakofti,** sheltered by the offshore islet of Makronissi. Other good bets are those at **Platia Amos**, north of Agia Pelagia.

There are sights here worth discovering, but the main activity is relaxation and escape.

THE IONIAN SEA

There are about 40 islands in the **Ionian** archipelago, stretching from off the Albanian coast in the north to the Peloponnese in the south, but some of them are no more than chunks of rock. The three biggies geographically and touristically are **Corfu**, **Kefallonia**, and **Zakynthos**; occupying a middle-sized position are **Ithaca** and **Lefkada**; while two of the more notable smaller islands are **Paxos** and **Meganissi**.

Highlights include **Corfu Old Town**, a warren of narrow streets, shaded arcades, little squares, crumbling houses with shutters closed against the sun, and genuine Greek charm – even though most of it dates from the Venetian period; the Sweet Red Wine of **Antipaxos** on Paxos; **Porto Katsiki**, a powerful contender for the best beach in Greece on the island of Lefkada; and **Smuggler's Cove** in the northwest corner of Zakynthos.

THE CYCLADES

There are some 56 islands, big and small, in the **Cyclades** group, which lies off the southeast coast of Attica and stretches southwards towards Crete. One of the early centers of European civilization, the Cyclades Islands hosted a flourishing culture as early as 3200 BC, which has left behind a rich legacy of art, and which merges with the Minoan culture of Crete by around 2100 BC, a fusion that produced the marvellous **Thira** frescoes to be seen at the National Archeological Museum in Athens.

Nowadays they are the most popular Aegean islands with tourists. This is partly due to their proximity to Athens and its ports of Piraeus and Rafina, to the extensive ferry links between them, which make getting around in summer fairly easy (if you ignore the crowded ferries), and partly due to their own fascination, which keeps the crowds coming back time after time.

Three of my favorites in this group are: **Ano Mera**, a tiny inland village on **Mykonos** that has escaped, at least partly, the tidal wave of touristic hype; **Mount Knythos**, a 112-meter hill on Delos with superb views from the top of the ancient religious zone and the islands beyond; and the excavations at **Akrotiri** in the south of **Thira**, perhaps better known as **Santorini**, which may be uncovering the real Atlantis. The dig here is uncovering a Minoan town whose houses were decorated with fabulous mosaics and which was abandoned just before the cataclysmic eruption of the island's volcano in about 1470 BC.

RHODES

Rhodes fully deserves to be one of the most popular islands of the Mediterranean, and it is. A beautiful, scented, green, diamond-shaped jewel of an island, it is the fourth biggest in Greece, and is possessed of a climate, scenery, and historical fascination matched by few others. It has superlative beaches, and the backing of Helios, the sun god himself. These attractions add up to a floodtide of summertime visitors, who all but overwhelm the island's hotel space, beach space, and inner space.

Don't miss **Rhodes Old Town**, as marvelous a medieval spectacle as you will see anywhere in Europe; the **Statue of Helios** (more accurately, where did the great colossal statue of the sun god that was one of the seven wonders of the ancient world stand?); and **Prassonissi Lighthouse** on the marvelously isolated southern tip of Rhodes.

CYPRUS

Cyprus is "Aphrodite's Island" because it is where in Greek mythology Aphrodite, the goddess of love, was born, drifting ashore on a seashell from the wine-dark sea. Sunshine, blue skies, beaches, fields of grapes ripening in the sun, orange and lemon groves, a multicolored carpet of flowers in spring, wild mountain ranges, cedar forests, remote villages, Stone Age tombs, Persian palaces, Greek temples, Roman mosaics, Byzantine monasteries, Crusader castles, Gothic abbeys, Arab mosques, Turkish bath-houses, Imperial British hill stations – where else but Cyprus?

Cyprus is not Greece, although many of its people are of Greek origin and consider themselves to be Greek – kind of. The Republic of Cyprus is an independent country and has a seat at the United Nations. However, more than one-third of the island's territory has been occupied by Turkey since 1974 in contravention of UN resolutions, and the UN Peacekeeping Force in Cyprus (UNFICYP) mans a thin blue line across the island between the Turkish and Cypriot armies. But Cypus is a safe destination, and you should not let the political division of the island affect your vacation plans.

Among Cyprus's great finds are **Akamas Peninsula**, a wild and scenic area almost untouched by the hand of man; the **Greek Theatre** in Kourion, where you can still see plays performed; **Lefkara**, where you can watch the women sitting outdoors creating their superb handmade lace; **Panagia tou Kykkou**, a mountaintop monastery in the Troodos Mountains); **Panagia Angeloktistos**, for its spellbindingly beautiful and rare early Byzantine mosaic of the Virgin and Child in Larnaka; and **Kolossi Castle** in Limassol, where you can pretend to be a Crusader knight at this Commandery of the Knights of the Order of the Hospital of St John of Jerusalem.

3. SUGGESTED ITINERARIES

Suggested Itineraries

How to get to all those fragments of paradise? Do you really want to spend all your time jumping on and off airplanes? That is the only way to see a lot of islands in a short time. Simply "collecting" islands is not experiencing them. To do that you must travel at the sea's pace and strike a balance between time afloat and meaningful time ashore.

In two weeks you won't be able to do much. Yet the Greek islands are one of Europe's most delectable treats. Whatever you can manage is a whole lot better than nothing. Remember: there is no point in scurrying backing and forth all over the Aegean, cherry-picking. You'd do better to choose one island group and do it some kind of justice.

This is an idealized itinerary. Do what you can of it and head back to Athens when your time or endurance runs out.

DOING THE CYCLADES

Don't leave from the madhouse port of Piraeus near Athens. Instead begin from **Rafina**, a much smaller harbor lying east of the capital. Take the ferry to wooded **Andros**, which is less obviously touristic than some other islands of the Cyclades group, and whose slower pace is a restful introduction.

From here the boat goes to neighboring **Tinos**, also slow-paced, and noted for its dovecotes and Italianate towers. A sidetrip to **Syros** is a worthwhile excursion, especially for lovers of plants and flowers, and its main town, Ermoupoli, is big enough to have reasonabe shopping.

Next stop **Mykonos**. It's like this: you'll either love it or hate it. Fun-lovers can't get enough of it and although its cachet may be tarnished it's still the hippest place in the Aegean. The gay beaches would probably have been fine by the ancient Greeks, but can't sit too easily with Byzantine Orthodoxy. You'll certainly want to make a sidetrip to nearby **Delos**, an astonishing archeological preserve.

Moving on to **Paros** gives you a whole stack of options, as it is the major ferry interchange point in the Cyclades. From here you can cover an outer arc running from **Naxos**, back to Paros, then onwards to **Sifnos** and **Milos**, before moving to the inner arc of **Folegandros**, **Sikinos**, and **Ios**. Or you can just slice straight through from Paros to **Ios** then on to **Thira**, better known as **Santorini**. Historians have long speculated about what brought the Minoan civilization of ancient Crete to it knees. The volcanic eruption on Thira around 1470 BC could be the smoking gun – one that for good measure may have given rise to the legend of Atlantis. Thira, with its black sand beaches and sheer volcanic cliffs, is a sight to see.

On a two week vacation, the itinerary so far described can easily have used up all your available time. If so: bye-bye. If not, you can do no better than move on to **Crete**.

CRETE & RHODES

The island has taken some heavy hits from mass tourism and some of its finest places are no longer as fine as they used to be. Yet Crete is big enough to absorb most of the blows without being too heavily damaged. While the obvious approach is to go around the coast and make sidetrips into the mountains, taking in magical Minoan **Knossos** on the way, Crete is so big that you could easily spend two weeks doing it alone.

Much the same applies to **Rhodes**, which can be reached from Crete via a seasonal ferry to **Karpathos**, an almost unspoiled island to Rhodes's southwest. Rhodes itself is heavily touristed and Rhodes town can often seem overrun. The island has fascinating Venetian and Crusader remains, as well as inland villages that have escaped the worst effects.

THE DODECANESE ISLANDS

This is the point to divert east to Cyprus, but it might have been better to have done this direct from Athens by airplane. Instead, make a northward swing though the Dodecanese Islands, most of which are a breath of tranquil air after Rhodes. You can take in beautiful **Symi**, then **Tilos** and **Nissiros**, on the way to **Cos**, which takes you back into the realm of mass tourism, particularly in July and August. **Kalimnos**, **Leros**, and **Patmos** are a lot quieter and put you in range of little hideaways like **Lipsi**, **Arki**, and **Agathonissi**, before moving on to "civilizaton" on **Samos**.

CENTRAL & NORTHERN AEGEAN

At this point it would be understandable if you never wanted to consult a ferry timetable ever again in you life. But you may have caught the bug of sailing the wine-dark sea and be thirsting for more. If you're still with the program you'll find that, like a well-crafted play, the Greek islands retain their invention to the final scene. Now, however, the distance between islands becomes greater as you head further north.

Chios is next on the agenda. Like all the islands in this area it is close to Turkey and a good place from where to make a sidetrip there. Chios itself has enough to keep you occupied, though scarcely busy, and hasn't yet been swamped by mid-season tourists.

Beautiful, langurous, seductive **Lesbos** (**Mytilini**) is next up. There are those who would go no further, ever, than this soft, gentle island, where the poet Sappho sang the praises of her fellow women. From here you can go by ferry direct to Thessalonika on the mainland. If you've come this far though, why not continue to the bittersweet end?

Doing so will take you into the northern Aegean, through wild and rugged **Limnos** and **Samothrace**, to the mainland at **Alexandroupoli**. From here you can either fly, drive or go by train back to Athens.

CYPRUS

Cyprus is worth a separate trip by air from Athens, but you can certainly do it as part of an Aegean cruise. **Nicosia** is the capital, a city divided between Greek Cypriots and Turkish Cypriots, and a city with good nightlife, hotels, and restaurants.

The south coast around **Agia Napa** and **Protaras** is where you'll find great holiday resorts. Further west, **Larnaka** and **Limassol** have sprouted "wings" in the hotel strips that reach out either side of them along the coast. **Pafos** is fast developing as a big resort area but has some way to go before it gets as "spoiled" as the others, or you can head to the coast east of Polis for a remote and almost untouched vacation escape

Just a little way back from the hard commercial carapace along the shore you enter a different Cyprus, a place of timeless villages and rugged scenery, reaching up to the windy heights of the **Troodos Mountains** in the west and the **Pentadaktylos Mountains** in the north. There are Byzantine monasteries and churches, Crusader castles, and hard-working farmers who turn out a cornucopia of fruits, vegetables, and grapes for wine.

4. A SHORT HISTORY

A Short History

BEGINNINGS

(Prehistory-2500 BC)

Greek prehistory begins in the Stone Age, and it was to be quite a few thousand years before the stone of choice became marble. A Neolithic people that later Greeks would call the **Pelasgians** were established on the peninsula from the seventh to the third millennium BC. By the start of the third millennium BC they were being joined by colonists from Anatolia who knew how to make bronze from copper and tin. The Stone Age gave way to the Bronze Age.

MINOANS

(2500 BC-1500 BC)

The story of Greek civilization, which is the story of Greece, begins on the island of **Crete**. Whatever else you could say about the ancient Cretans, they certainly weren't cretins. Almost 5,000 years ago they were getting together a neat little civilization, right up there with the bright lights of Mesopotamia and Egypt, at a time when most of the human race was still dressing poorly and washing never. By 2500 BC, they were living in towns and villages around the coast and were trading with the Aegean islands, Anatolia, and Egypt.

From about 1900 BC things took a big jump forward with the building of the superb **Knossos Palace**, from where the kings of this "**Minoan**" civilization ruled. They talked a lot of bull at Knossos, where the legendary **King Minos** married **Pasiphae**, the daughter of the sun, who left him holding the horns while she dallied with a bull and became the doting mother of a right little monster, the **Minotaur**. Half man and half bull, this creature lived in a labyrinth and ate up all the nice boys and girls the Greeks sent to visit him.

But it was the Greeks who told all that a thousand years later. The Minoans themselves seem to have been an almost childishly naive and charming people, who loved dolphins and flowers, dancing, collecting fine pottery and leaping acrobatically over the backs of bulls, perhaps from sheer joie de vivre. Their women dressed elegantly in long skirts with open bodices that exposed their breasts. Compared to their Egyptian neighbors, who were obsessed with death, the Minoans reveled in life. For their time, they were affluent, optimistic, and cosmopolitan.

Minoan civilization reached the height of its powers around 1600 BC. Little more than a century later it was tumbling into ruins. One theory suggests a disaster of biblical proportions. In 1470 BC, the volcanic island of **Thira** (aka **Santorini**) blew itself apart in a titanic explosion, dropping a cloud of ash and dust on Crete 105 kilometers to the south, and destroying its agriculture. Far worse, a tsunami that may have reached a height of 50 meters slammed into Crete's northern coast, wiping out towns and fleets, while subsequent earthquakes took care of whatever buildings remained standing.

Meanwhile, back at Knossos, Greek invaders from the mainland moved in and civilized life continued for another hundred years or so, before the great palace and other urban centers were destroyed – whether by earthquakes or war is unknown. Minoan civilization disappeared, only to be rediscovered in the 19th century and gradually brought to light by archaeology. Its writing, called **Linear A**, remains undeciphered, yet the Minoans speak to us still across the millennia and their love of beauty shines through clearly.

MYCENAEANS
(1500 BC-1100 BC)

Compared with the Minoans, the early **Mycenaean** Greeks of the mainland were a rough and uncivilized lot. They did a lot of strutting around, crowing about how heroic they were. In a word: macho. If a foreigner interfered with one of their womenfolk they were ready, at the drop of a spear, to sail after the upstart and besiege his city for ten years, then burn it to the ground. Which is what they did when **Paris**, the son of **King Priam** of **Troy**, kidnapped **Helen**, the wife of **Menelaus**, brother of **King Agamemnon** of Mycenae. Or at any rate that's what **Homer** said happened in one of the enduring works of world literature, *The Iliad.*

Archaeologists place the destruction of Troy, or Ilium, a fortified town on the northwest coast of present-day Turkey, at around 1200 BC. It seems that Homer's tale, written 400 years after the event, may be a magnificently distorted version of a raid by Mycenaean sea rovers who were ravaging the eastern Mediterranean at that time, as Greece dissolved into anarchy and invaders flooded in from the north. On the other hand it may be perfectly true. Thanks to the Wooden Horse, the unlucky Trojans were the first to learn to "beware of Greeks bearing gifts."

The ancestors of the Mycenaean warrior aristocracy – Homer called them "**Achaeans**" – had begun arriving in Greece from about 2500 BC. By 1600 BC their kings ruled from the palace at Mycenae in the Peloponnese and there were other palaces at Tiryns and Pylos. Their script was influenced by the Minoans and is known as **Linear B**, a recognizable precursor of Greek. Many of the familiar gods of the Homeric pantheon made their appearance with the Mycenaeans, and lecherous old **Zeus** was already behaving badly.

Considering that they fancied themselves as heroes, the Mycenaeans let themselves down when barbarian raiders swept into Greece from about 1200 BC onwards. They ran away.

THE DARK AGE
(1100 BC-750 BC)

These new invaders, the **Dorians**, cheated by bringing fancy new iron weapons with them. So you can't really blame the bronze-armed Mycenaeans. There was an archaic missile gap and they were on the wrong side of it.

Anyway, the Dorians were also Greeks, though not very civilized ones. It is not recorded whether they washed their hands before eating, or after killing, but the Mycenaean accomplishments and palaces were swept away. The Greeks even forgot how to write, possibly in the very middle of a sentence. Being Greek they didn't forget how to talk, however, and oral traditions in the mouths of traveling bards and minstrels carried the epic tales of the Heroic Age forward.

Dark Ages don't seem to be much fun for anyone. The Greeks probably couldn't wait for the lights to come on again and the run-up to the Classical Age to begin. It was, however, during the Dark Age that the first **Olympic Games** took place, in 776 BC.

THE ARCHAIC PERIOD

(750 BC-600 BC)

There are a lot of theories about **Homer** – even one that the epic poems *The Iliad* and *The Odyssey* were not written by Homer, but by another man of the same name – yet not many facts. If he lived at all he probably lived around 750 BC, and was born in Asia Minor or on one of the Aegean islands. He probably did write down the two great tales, although his may not have been the only hand in them, and they were probably based on stories from the earlier oral tradition and had been much modified in the course of more than four centuries.

So what? They are magnificent. *The Iliad* is based on an episode from the ten-year Siege of Troy. While **Achilles** sulks in his tent his buddy **Patroclus** gets himself killed by **Hector**. **Agamemnon** gets pretty irritated at everybody, and finally Achilles goes off and kills Hector then drags his body around the walls behind his chariot, to the great distress of Hector's dad, King Priam, who goes to Achilles and... And so it goes. Homer would have made a great Hollywood scriptwriter – except that *The Iliad* would probably have been put into redevelopment and turnaround, and a slew of hired guns called in to punch it up and add a happy ending.

In *The Iliad* there is no happy ending. The fine young heroes die one after the other, pierced by the glittering bronze, beside the fast ships or before the windy walls. Their strength collapses and they sink down sorrowfully into Hades. The gods are everywhere, working overtime on both sides of the street: urging, betraying, protecting, destroying, pleading, avenging, and occasionally wading into the mess themselves.

The Odyssey is more of an adventure story, telling the tale of **Odysseus'** action-packed ten-year voyage home from Troy to Ithaca across the wine-dark sea. He encounters a giant called the Cyclops, makes a sidetrip to the underworld, escapes from the monsters Scylla and Charybdis, gets taken in by two-faced Circe and Calypso, and finally arrives home in time for dinner, alone, bedraggled and the worse for 20 years wear and tear, to find would-be usurpers making free with his wine and his wife quite as if he had no intention of ever returning. So he slaughters them.

Greek tradition depicted Homer as being blind. His sightless gaze turns towards us down the centuries and his epics still seem as fresh and vibrant – and every bit as complex – as they must have done to his first readers when the world was a younger and maybe a more innocent place.

During this period the Greeks spread their wings – or more accurately their sails – and ventured out to establish colonies not only across the Aegean and along the coast of Asia Minor, but westwards across the Mediterranean to Italy, France, Spain and Libya, and northwards to the Black Sea. So many Greek cities were founded in Sicily and southern Italy that the area became known as **Magna Graecia** (Great Greece). Among them were Syracuse, Messene (Messina), Sybaris, Neapolis (Naples). Massilia in southern France is the present-day Marseilles.

CITY-STATES
(600 BC-338 BC)

The geography of Greece, its isolated valley and island communities, favored the development of the *polis*, or city-state. There was more to it than geography. As all-powerful kings gave way to a more committee-based system of government, citizens came to have more say in how they were ruled. At first, many of these governments may not have been too different from Mafia families, but gradually they acquired the trappings of legality and civic life. Some even developed democracy, most notably Athens, although that took time.

Changing methods of war also called for better organization. While the warriors of the Heroic Age had each fought on his own hook, seeking death or glory, the new iron weapons encouraged the establishment of disciplined formations composed of heavily armed infantrymen called **hoplites** (you had to be tough to hop lite in all that armor). Victories were now won by superior control and shock tactics.

Citizenship of a polis was a prized status. Citizens had more fun than slaves or women, but they had to earn it by paying taxes, taking part in civic life and, if needs be, donning armor to fight and die for the polis. Athens, Sparta, Thebes, and Corinth were all city-states. There were many others, on the mainland, on the Aegean islands, across the sea in Asia Minor and the Black Sea coast, and westwards in Italy, France, and Spain as colonies spread.

There existed about as many forms of government as there were city-states. One was unique: **Sparta**. It seems to have been the perfect totalitarian state, even though all citizens could vote from the age of 30. The Spartans reckoned the best way to survive in a hostile world was to be better at hostilities than anyone else. They spent all their lives as soldiers, living in barracks from age 18-60, honed by a harsh discipline that instilled a will to victory or death. It was said that Spartans were happy to die in battle because life at home was so bad – but probably nobody said so to their faces.

The **Athenians** were the exact opposite. Undisciplined, argumentative, irrational, and vain, they were also open, enquiring, and moved by ideas and ideals. They could be every bit as valiant in battle as the Spartans, or they might decide that discretion was the better part of valor and run away. In either case they preferred to do so through their own good choice, as free men contending for what they held dear.

Greeks belonged first and foremost to their polis and only secondly to **Hellas**, which was more a shared cultural identity than a political unit. The city-states squabbled and fought with each other as if there was no tomorrow and no external enemies ready to step in and pick up the pieces if they ever fought themselves to exhaustion. Only rarely did the Hellenes combine, more or less, to face an outside threat. When it came down to it they usually preferred to hang separately than to hang together.

And that was what they finally did when **Philip II** of Macedon smashed the last Greek coalition at the Battle of Chaeronea in 338 BC, and brought the city-states under his heel.

GREEKS VS. PERSIANS

(499 BC-479 BC)

An expanding Persian Empire first bumped its sharp elbows against the Ionian Greeks along the coast of Asia Minor, where there were several well-established city-states. It didn't take long for the independent-minded Greeks to rebel against Persian interference in the sacred internal affairs of the polis, nor for the Greeks to find out that the Persians had a sharp way of dealing with rebels.

The rebellion began in 499 BC. By 494 BC it was all over. Miletus, the most cultured Greek city of the time, was a smoking ruin and the other rebel cities had been taught a lesson that shocked them into line (Greeks vs. Persians: Love-15). Mainland Greeks had helped the Ionians in their plight so **Darius**, the Persian King of Kings, decided to extend the lesson to them. Instead it was Darius who learned things the hard way when an Athenian army thrashed his own superior force at **Marathon** in 490 BC (15-All).

His son and successor, **King Xerxes**, tried again ten years later and determined not only to punish Greece but to conquer and occupy it as well. The Greeks had other ideas. At least some of them had: only 31 cities joined the Persians-Go-Home Coalition; others preferred to give Xerxes the "earth and water" that signified surrender. **Leonidas** and his **300 Spartans** earned eternal glory by being wiped out at the **Pass of Thermopylae** by Xerxes' 300,000 invaders (15-30). Xerxes then advanced to Attica, captured Athens and razed it to the ground (15-40).

The Greek fleet under **Themistocles** attacked the Persian fleet unexpectedly at Salamis near Athens and routed it (30-40). Xerxes personally witnessed the loss of his fleet and ordered a retreat by the army (Deuce). Next year at the Battle of Plataea the Greek army smashed the Persians and drove them back to Asia Minor (Advantage Greeks). It was not until **Alexander the Great** invaded Persia in 334 BC that the final result could be declared (Game, Set, and Match to the Greeks).

THE GOLDEN AGE OF ATHENS
(489 BC-406 BC)

Athens emerged from the war with Persia with its power and prestige greatly strengthened. Democracy was on a roll, as the Spartan army returned to its barracks. **Pericles** emerged as the Athenian leader and he was a champion of democracy as was no other statesman, perhaps, until Thomas Jefferson. He championed democracy for Athenian citizens alone, however, not for the slaves who kept democracy running (also like Jefferson). In promoting Athens' interests he promoted democracy in other city-states too, which began to rankle with more oligarchically inclined rulers, and always with Sparta and its fearsome military machine lurking in the background.

Pericles beautified Athens as well. The magnificent temples on the Acropolis, including the **Parthenon**, were built under his direction and mostly with money "donated" by Athens's allies in the **Delian League**. This alliance of some 150 city-states against Persia rapidly took on the character of an Athenian Empire, as was shown after 449 BC when peace with Persia was signed and some of the allies tried to leave. Athens kept them on her team by force, using the big Athenian navy to do it.

In 431 BC, it came to war between Athens and Sparta for mastery of the Greek world. The **Peloponnesian War** lasted for 26 years, with only a brief time-out for a couple of years from 421 BC. Athens couldn't match Sparta's army and Sparta couldn't face Athens's navy. The advantage swung back and forth until in 415 BC an Athenian naval expedition sent to conquer Sparta's ally Syracuse in Sicily was annihilated. Finally, with Persian help Athens was blockaded and starved into submission.

Sparta didn't have long to enjoy its victory. The Spartans tried their hand at dominating Greece and were defeated by **Thebes** at Leuctra in

371 BC. Theban power was shattered in its turn in 362 BC. By this time, after 70 years of internecine warfare, Greece was on its knees.

THE HELLENISTIC WORLD
(338 BC-146 BC)

On its knees was precisely the position in which **King Philip II** of Macedon, a half Hellenized and half barbarian kingdom to the north of Greece, wanted to see the Greeks. His victory over them at **Chaeronea** in 338 BC confirmed the death of the polis system and began the Hellenistic Age, when Greek culture was spread throughout much of the civilized world and in turn was colored by the older cultures of the Near East.

Philip's son **Alexander the Great** was the standard-bearer of this great drive as he led his combined Macedonian-Greek army to victory over Persia and to the gates of India. Alexander died in Babylon at the age of 33 and his newly won empire was divided between his top generals. Mainland Greece and the Aegean islands gained a measure of independence because of all this, and promptly went back to fighting among each other. Eventually a new power stepped into the vacuum, one that would tolerate no dissension: imperial Rome.

PAX ROMANA
(146 BC-395AD)

The **Romans** came, liked what they saw, conquered it, and took what they liked. They may not have liked the Greeks much but they liked what the Greeks had achieved and created. So they packed up the best of it and shipped it back to Rome.

This was a compliment of sorts from the boorish masters of the world to their new and nimble-minded servants, many of whom likewise found themselves going west to the Eternal City as tutors, doctors (quacks mostly), philosophers (who set up such a din of competing ideas there that the exasperated Romans occasionally expelled them en masse), artists, poets, sculptors, architects and the like. Even the Greek gods were exported to fill out the limp Roman pantheon with the kind of exploits that real soap-opera Greek gods got up to in their spare time.

Not that they liked Greek stuff so much as to overlook the Greeks' misdemeanors. The **Corinthians** found this out to their disadvantage when they joined an alliance against Rome. In 146 BC, Corinth was captured and wiped off the face of the earth; those of its inhabitants not massacred were sold into slavery. It was an event whose brutality shocked the entire Greek world – and many Romans as well – and it effectively broke the independent Greek spirit.

Yet some of the noblest Romans of them all were philhellenes. They learned Greek and spoke it in their villas and palaces, filling both with the works of the Greek imagination. The **Emperor Hadrian** was such a confirmed Greek fan that he was disparaged by his more austere country-men as "a little Greek" and he went so far as to rule the Roman Empire from Athens for several periods running into years at a time.

Finally, the Romans did the Greeks two big favors. They gave them peace, both among themselves and by protecting them from the threat of the barbarians. And they created the kind of stability that the Greeks could never have achieved, allowing time and space for Greek ideas and culture to diffuse throughout the civilized world.

BYZANTIUM

(330 AD-1453)

The writing was already on the wall for the Roman Empire in the 3rd century AD. In 251 the **Goths** broke through Rome's Danube front and went on to ravage Greece. They were finally expelled and the northern defenses repaired, but civilized life had taken a hit from which it never really recovered. In 285, **Emperor Diocletian** first divided the empire into a western and an eastern half, a process that became irrevocable in 395. Greece belonged to the eastern half, ruled from **Constantinople**, the New Rome founded by **Constantine the Great** in 330.

When the Western Roman Empire was finally extinguished by the barbarians in 476, the **Eastern Roman Empire**, which we can soon begin to call the **Byzantine Empire**, became the only game in town. It was a Christian empire, ironically, which carried the learning of the pagan Greeks safely down the stream of time.

No appraisal of modern Greece can be useful without some understanding of the power of the Byzantine ideal in the Greek mind. If you go to Greece and look only at Greek temples or theaters, and think only of Socrates and Euripides, you'll miss the most important influence of the last fifteen hundred years. Not that Byzantium is any longer counted among the powers of the earth: it finally went the way of all empires when Constantinople fell to the Turks on Tuesday, May 29, 1453 – a date that lives in infamy in the Greek consciousness. The last emperor, **Constantine XI**, last in a line stretching from Caesar Augustus, via Constantine the Great, took communion at the Church of the Holy Wisdom (**Hagia Sophia**) then went out to die defending the walls to the last.

Byzantium lives on in the churches and rituals of the **Greek Orthodox Church**. Whenever you see an old, black-garbed lady walking alongside the iconostasis in an Orthodox church, kissing the icons, the spirit of the Christian empire that survived for a thousand years, protected by God, is alive – as it is in the great monasteries that held in trust the sacred flame of Hellenism through centuries of Turkish occupation. The dream of reconquering Constantinople – still called simply The City – and recreating the Byzantine Empire has fired Greek imagination and politics into recent times, and probably does so to this day.

Greece was actually something of a backwater during the empire. **Emperor Justinian** even closed Plato's Academy in Athens. It absorbed the Byzantine way of life and thinking deep into its own culture, although constantly threatened and occasionally ravaged by Arab raiders, and not even the terrible blows inflicted during the empire's declining years by Catholic Christians from the west and Moslem Turks from the east would cause Greece's commitment to Byzantine Orthodoxy to waver.

Byzantium did Europe three big services. It civilized and Christianized the Slavs; it served as a bulwark, even if a crumbling one, against Turkish penetration at a time when the Ottomans were on the rampage; and it kept alive the learning of the ancient Greeks and Romans, which would help to fuel the Renaissance. A good day's work for anyone.

THE "TERRIBLE" TURKS

(1400-1922)

Don't talk to the Greeks about the Turks (the feeling is mutual). Don't ask for a Turkish coffee or a piece of Turkish delight or a Turkish carpet. Don't take a Turkish bath. Don't say how much you admired the minarets at Hagia Sophia in Istanbul. Don't say "Istanbul." And don't say you think it is a pity that almost every vestige of 500 years of Turkish rule has been erased from the Greek landscape. Not if you want to stay friends with the Greeks, that is.

Got that straight?

OK. The Ottoman Turks had conquered all of Greece by the 15th century. The "dead hand of the Turk" lay heavily on the land for nearly five centuries. Nothing worthwhile happened or was built. Oppression was the daily diet. In 1821, the **War of Liberation** broke out. Part of Greece won its freedom. The rest followed over the next century. The lights came on again. End of story.

The truth is about a million times more complex, and the whole Balkan area is still living with the legacy and consequences of the Ottoman years. Greeks look back on that time as a collective bad memory.

FREEDOM & INDEPENDENCE

(1821-1974)

With the exception of Britain's Lord Byron, who intervened with some particularly deadly poems and died of a fever in the process, the Greek rebels took on the Ottoman Empire alone from 1821 to 1825 when Britain and Russia, and later France, joined in. In 1827, the allies' combined fleet sank the Turkish fleet at the **Battle of Navarino**. A treaty signed at Adrianople (Edirne) in 1829 established a Greek state.

Greece then shopped around Europe for a king, and finally found one in an underemployed Bavarian prince who in 1832 became **King Otho I** of Greece. He lasted until 1862 before being overthrown. A Danish prince then stepped into his shoes as **King George I**.

At first, independent Greece consisted of only the Peloponnese, part of Thessaly, and a few islands. It was a long way short of being the Greece of today, but other bits and pieces followed over the next hundred or so years. They never did get Constantinople back and an invasion of mainland Turkey in 1919 turned into a disaster and was driven into the Aegean in 1922. This ended in an agreement between Greece and Turkey to swap minority populations. Some 1.5 million Greeks left Turkey and came to Greece as refugees.

On October 28, 1940, Greece earned a new public holiday, called "Ohi" ("No") Day, when the government said, guess what, to an ultimatum from Mussolini's Italy. The Italian army marched straight in, then ran straight back out again pursued by the Greeks.

Hitler sent panzers and stormtroopers to help the Italians. The Greeks were quickly beaten, and the British who had come to their aid were bundled off the peninsula. Crete was captured by German paratroopers who suffered heavy losses in taking the island. Four years of Nazi occupation was hard on Greece. More than half of the country's Jewish population was liquidated. When liberation finally came it was followed by a four-year civil war between Communists and Nationalists. With American and British help, the Nationalists won.

Civilian government was overthrown by a **military coup** in 1967 and a bunch of boneheaded and brutal army officers, **the Colonels**, took over. King Constantine II launched a counter-coup that failed and he went into exile. As such popularity as the Colonels' regime enjoyed faded away – propelled by a bloody tank assault on demonstrating students at Athens Polytechnic – the military regime engineered a coup in 1974 against President Makarios of Cyprus with the aim of forcibly uniting Cyprus with Greece. Turkey invaded Cyprus and still occupies more than a third of the island. The Greek junta collapsed.

DEMOCRACY RETURNS
(1974-Present Day)

With democracy's return, Greece has made some progress, joining the European Economic Community (now called the European Union) in 1981. It has even managed to have socialist administrations without provoking a military coup. But relations with Turkey teeter on the brink of armed conflict and the **Cyprus** problem remains unresolved. The socialist PASOK government of George Papandreou in the 1980s exasperated both NATO and the European Union and often seemed to prefer anti-American rhetoric to serious government.

As the new millennium approaches, Greece has the chance to play its full part in building the united Europe whose essence is the democratic system that the ancient Greeks bequeathed to the world. Whether it will follow its Socratic head and seize the chance, or yield once more to the mystic impulses of its Byzantine soul, remains to be seen.

5. PLANNING YOUR TRIP

Planning Your Trip

WHEN TO GO - CLIMATE & WEATHER

Spring is generally cool and sunny, with some rain likely in March and into April, and fields are carpeted with flowers. **Summer** is long and gets progressively hotter, drier, and dustier from May all the way to the middle of October. **Autumn** in what's left of October and November is characterised by some wild and wonderful rainstorms accompanied by thunder and lightning. **Winter** may be cold and rainy too, but often isn't rainy enough to restore water reservoirs and underground aquifers.

The best time to go is from **March to May**, or at the latest June. It isn't too hot yet and there are not yet too many tourists, although the numbers grow throughout this time. Best of all, the landcape in many places is still green and covered with wild flowers.

July and August are the dog days. Too hot, too many people, and too much pressure on the Greeks' usually sunny dispositions. In September, October, and into November things get progressively quieter. The landscape can be sun-blasted, stark, and dusty until the rain comes.

GETTING TO GREECE

Athens, as the capital and main city of Greece, is the single most important point of arrival for visitors to Greece. **Piraeus** is included in this description because, although a separate area administratively, the port of Athens is to all intents and purposes part of the city, just as it was in ancient times. The main air, sea, and land transportation links converge on this hub. This does not necessarily mean that it is always the best gateway to Greece, only that the chances are that this is where you will come in.

For details on arriving and returning home from Athens, consult Chapter 7, *Athens*, Arrivals & Departures section.

CUSTOMS & ENTRANCE REQUIREMENTS
Arriving

You are allowed to bring into Greece duty-free items for personal use only, as cameras (two still; one video), golf clubs, a radio or tape-player, portable computer, etc. Only if you are carrying more than is needed for personal use will you have to pay duty.

Officially you are supposed to declare everything in this line, but do you think the Greek Customs wants to hear from everyone who is carrying a camera, or a beat-up old six-string guitar? More importantly, you need to declare currency amounts above $1,000, especially if you want to take it out again. There is no such restriction on traveler's checks.

If you are arriving in Greece from outside the European Union (EU), you are allowed to bring in 200 cigarettes, 50 cigars, 250 grams of tobacco, 1 liter of liqor and 2 liters of wine. If you are coming from another EU country, the limits are higher, but the guidelines for "personal use" mean that in practice they are only about 50 percent higher.

Illegal narcotics are of course banned substances, and the penalties for possession, and especially trafficking, can be high. Bizarrely, however, the painkiller codeine, which is comonly used in pill form in other countries, is a banned substance in Greece.

Departing

During your flight home you will be given a Customs form to complete. You are supposed to declare the total value of all the items you acquired that were gifts or purchases, even from duty-free shops, and that are in your possession. Only one form is required per family.

As a United States resident, you are allowed to bring in duty-free no more than one liter of liquor, no matter what type, and no more than 200 cigarettes or 100 cigars (not Cuban ones). Though baked goods and cured cheeses are allowed, other fresh fruit is forbidden. All plants, cuttings, and seeds must be declared. If you are carrying more than $10,000 in currency of any kind, that too must be declared.

You are allowed a total exemption of $400 worth of items. If you exceed this amount you will have to pay 10 pecent duty on the next $1,000 worth of goods. After you pass the $1,400 plateau, each item you bring in is assessed whatever duty the regulations say apply to that particular type of item.

Duty can be paid by cash, check, and, in some locations, credit cards. Traveler's checks can be used if the checks do not total more than $50 more than your assessed duty.

For more information, contact the **US Customs Service**, *Box 7407, Washington DC 20044. Tel. (202) 927-6724.* Their booklet *Know Before You Go* spells out the details.

GETTING TO & AROUND THE ISLANDS

Bookings for **international** ferries can be made by many travel agents in the US, Europe, and in Greece itself, and at the ferry companies' ticket offices or agents in the ports of departure and arrival, including offices at intermediate points on the route. Bookings for **domestic** ferries can be made by many travel agents in Greece, particularly those at the ports of arrival and departure, and at the ferry companies' ticket offices or agents in those ports, and offices at intermediate points on the route. Passengers traveling exclusively between Greek ports – with no international point of departure or arrival – can do so only with Greek ferry companies.

Because there are many different ferry companies, serving different islands, from different places, at different times, on different routes, with different prices, and with timetables that change more often than the models at a Paris fashion show, no attempt has been made to give a comprehensive picture of the ferry schedules – which in any case would be out-of-date before the ink was dry. The **Greek Tourist Organization** in Athens does a heroic job of keeping track, and issues an update every week in summer, but even they can't say for dead-certain sure what the situation on the water will be.

Instead, the information provided in this book has been simplified while still enabling you to get around easily. The first rule is to make your booking at a travel agent, especially if you are transporting a car or want a cabin. The second first rule is to do it as far in advance as possible, especially for July and August. Otherwise, get your ticket from the one of the ferry companies' agents at the port of departure. In the *Arrivals & Departures* section for each island you will find the available routes and a local contact telephone number, the number of sailings in summer, duration of the crossing, and the price of a basic second class one-way ticket without accommodation for a foot passenger (if you can afford such a ticket you can always get to the island); if you have more money you can start thinking about cars, cabins, first class, and dining at the captain's table.

The point of origin or final destination of long-distance ferries is given, without listing all the intermediate stops, but the next important stop on the route is always given.

WHERE TO FIND MORE INFORMATION ABOUT GREECE & THE GREEK ISLANDS
United States
• **Greek National Tourist Organization**, *645 Fifth Avenue, 5th Floor, New York, NY 10022. Tel. (212) 421-5777; Fax (212) 826-6940*
• **Greek National Tourist Organization**, *611 West 6th Street, Suite 2198, Los Angeles, CA 90017. Tel. (213) 626-6696; Fax (213) 489-9744*
• **Greek National Tourist Organization**, *168 North Michigan Avenue, 4th Floor, Chicago, IL 60601. Tel. (312) 782-1084; Fax (312) 782-1091*

Canada

· **Greek National Tourist Organization**, *1300 Bay Street, Toronto, ON M5R 3K8. Tel. (416) 968-2220; Fax (416) 968-6533*
· **Greek National Tourist Organization**, *1233 Rue de la Montagne, Suite 101, Montreal, QC H3G 1Z2. Tel. (514) 871-1535; Fax (514) 871-1498*

Great Britain

· **Greek National Tourist Organization**, *4 Conduit Street, London W1R D0J. Tel. 0171/734-5997; Fax 0171/287-1369*

Australia

· **Greek National Tourist Organization**, *51-57 Pitt Street, Sydney, NSW 2000. Tel. 02/241-1663; Fax 02/235-2174*

Greece

· **Greek Tourist Organization**, *Odos Amerikis 2, 10564 Athens. Tel. 01/322-3111; Fax 02/322-2841*

6. BASIC INFORMATION

Basic Information

BUSINESS HOURS

Opening hours can vary widely, and at peak times in tourist areas shops and other services are almost always open longer than the posted minimum – some seem rarely to close at all. You can generally rely on them being open on Monday, Wednesday,and Saturday from 8:30 am to 2:30 pm, and on Tuesday, Thursday, and Friday from 5 pm to 8:30 pm. Typical tourist-zone times, along with times for supermarkets, would be 8 am to 10 pm, but don't count on this if you have an important purchase in mind. In winter, opening hours are 8 am to 1 pm and 2:30 pm to 5:30 pm Monday, Tuesday, Thursday, and Friday; 8 am to 1 pm on Wednesday and Saturday.

Government offices are usually open Monday to Friday from 8 am to 3 pm. Go early if you have important business to transact.

COST OF LIVING & TRAVEL

Greece is no longer the universally cheap paradise for foreign tourists that it once was. A combination of European Union membership, growing standards of living and the demand for better, and in some places the simple law of supply and demand have gradually brought average prices up closer to the level of Western Europe. Still, the law of supply and demand cuts both ways, and out of season in out-of-the-way places (assuming everything isn't closed) the picture is more favorable.

Even so, it is hard to see how you could do things on less than $50 (£33) a day per person if you want to eat, sleep in be-it-ever-so-modest a hotel and move around by boat and bus. As you add comfort requirements to your accommodation and quality to your taverna, take in some nightlife, and hire a car for short periods, your outlays will go up accordingly, with $100 (£66) a day per person being a far-from-extravagant figure in busier locations at peak times.

TYPICAL COSTS

A double room at a class C hotel on one of the popular islands will cost you in the region of $50 (£33) a day. Dinner for two, with wine, at a modest taverna in the same place would be about $40 (£26). Tourist-class ferry fares from Piraeus to a distant island, such as Rhodes, run to about $35 (£24) and to a relatively nearby one, such as Mykonos, to about $15 (£10).

ELECTRICITY

The electricity supply is 220 volts AC, 50 cycles, with two-pin (round) plugs. Adapters and transformers for connecting appliances with different specifications are on sale in shops and may be available from bigger hotels, whose rooms also generally have a 110-volt outlet for shavers.

HEALTH CONCERNS

There are no specific health concerns about traveling in Greece, beyond the relatively minor ones that the geeral disruption caused by travel and exposure to new foods – Greek food has a high olive oil content – may lead to stomach upsets until you get used to it. The same applies for alcoholic drinks: there is a natural tendency to overindulge in wine during long langurous evenings in tavernas. However, tap water is safe, although in some places bottled mineral water may taste better, and standards of food hygiene generally range from adequate to excellent.

Heatstroke can be a risk, especially in Athens in summer, when the added problem of smog makes things seem worse. It makes sense to wear a hat, and limit exposure to direct sunlight, especially if you are engaged in a strenuous hiking or climbing activity at the same time. Until you adjust to the high temperatures it may make sense to stick to shaded places as much as possible. Conversely, the decks of ferries can be chilly places, particularly when the meltemi wind is blowing, so dress warmly and find shelter from the wind in such circumstances.

Medical facilities in Greece are generally good, but the smaller the island you are on, the less likely there is to be the ability to respond to serious or rare problems. This might be a factor to take into account when renting mopeds, which are notoriously unsafe contraptions. In any case it is essential to ensure that your insurance policy covers you throughout your stay, and that you carry adequate health insurance documentation.

LANGUAGE GUIDE

The stress in Greek words is usually on the last-but-one vowel. Below is a handy guide to get you through many common travel situations:

ENGLISH–GREEK
Common Expressions
good morning – *kalimera*
good afternoon – *kalispera*
good night – *kalinihta*
hello – *yia sou*
goodbye – *herete*
please – *parakalo*
thank you – *efharisto*
yes – *ne*
no – *ohi*
how much? – *poso kani?*
how are you? (singular) – *ti kanis?*
how are you? (plural) – *ti kanis?*
very well – *poli kala*

pleased to meet you – *hero poli*
sorry/excuse me – *signomi*
where is? – *pou ine?*
I don't understand – *den katalaveno*

Basic Vocabulary

airport – *aerodromio*
America – *Ameriki*
American (m) – *Amerikanos*
American (f) – *Amerikanida*
automobile – *aftokinito*
avenue – *leoforos*
bank – *trapeza*
bathroom – *banio*
beach – *plaz*
beer – *bira*
breakfast – *proino*
bus – *leoforio*
bus station – *stathmos leoforion*
bus stop – *stasis*
cafe – *kafenio*
car ferry – *feribot*
dinner – *vradino*
Englishman – *Anglos*
Englishwoman – *Anglida*
gasoline – *venzini*
Greece – *Ellada*
Greek language – *Ellinika*
Greek (m) – *Ellinas*
Greek (f) – *Ellinida*
hotel – *xenodohio*
kilometer – *hiliometro*
kiosk – *periptero*
left – *aristera*

lunch – *mesimeriano*
market – *agora*
museum – *moussio*
okay – *endaksi*
passport – *diavatirio*
pharmacy – *farmakio*
police – *astinomia*
post office – *tahidromio*
postage stamp – *grammatosimo*
right – *deksia*
sea – *thalassa*
station – *stathmos*
street – *odos*
temple – *naos*
taxi – *taksi*
ticket – *isitirio*
today – *simera*
toilet – *toualeta*
tomorrow – *avrio*
traditional restaurant – *taverna*
train – *treno*
yesterday – *hthes*

Numbers

one – *ena*
two – *dio*
three – *tria*
four – *tessera*
five – *pende*
six – *eksi*
seven – *epta*
eight – *okto*
nine – *enea*
ten – *deka*

Days of the Week

Monday – *Deftera*
Tuesday – *Triti*
Wednesday – *Tetarti*
Thursday – *Pempti*
Friday – *Paraskevi*
Saturday – *Savato*
Sunday – *Kiriaki*

MONEY & BANKING

The unit of currency is the **drachmai** (Dr), called in English the **drachma**, or "drachs" for the trendy plural shorthand. Notes are in denominations of Drs 50, Drs 100, Drs 500, Drs 1,000 and Drs 5,000; coins in Drs 100, Drs 20, Drs 10, Drs 5, Drs 2 and Dr 1. The drachma is divided in 100 **lepta**, but the lepto (singular) is obsolete.

International credit and charge cards are widely accepted. Travelers checks – ideally dollars and German marks, although other hard currencies are usually acceptable – can be exchanged for Drs at banks, post offices, bureaux de change, and hotels, and can be used to settle bills in bigger hotels and some restaurants and shops, although a combination of commission charges (maximum 4 percent) and low rates can make this ruinous.

EXCHANGE RATES

$1 = ± Drs 250
£1 = ± Drs 375

Automated teller machines (ATMs) are widely available and accessible also by many credit cards and charge cards, as well as bank cards linked to one of the international systems such as Plus and Cirrus. Eurocheques are accepted with a supporting Eurocheque card, which also accesses many of the ATMs.

Most hard currencies are accepted at banks, and most major currencies at bigger hotels. Commissions and/or poor exchange rates usually mean that bureaux de change take a bigger cut than banks, but if the banks are closed you may have no alternative. Most banks are open Monday to Thursday from 8 am to 2 pm and on Friday from 8 am to 1 pm, while some banks in the main towns and resorts provide an afternoon service from 3:30 pm to 6:30 pm and on Saturday from 8 am to noon.

One way to beat exchange-rate blues is to use your credit card or charge card wherever possible – watch out for surcharges for accepting them. Rates used by the card companies are always close to the "real" currency cross rates. While waiting for your statement your own currency may appreciate against the drachma, in which case you gain, or depreciate, in which case you lose. There is no point saving on exchange rates and commission only to shell out ten times as much in interest charges to the card company because you didn't pay off the outstanding balance at once.

POST OFFICE

Most post offices are open Monday to Friday from 7:30 am to 2:30 pm. Bigger offices often stay open later and also open on Saturday and on Sunday morning. As well as selling stamps and delivering letters, the Post Office also provides airmail, express, registered, courier, package, poste-restante, fax and other services.

PUBLIC HOLIDAYS

• **New Year** – January 1
• **Epiphany** – January 6
• **Lent Monday** (Greek Orthodox) – variable
• **Greek National Day** – March 25
• **Good Friday** (Greek Orthodox) – variable
• **Easter Saturday** (Greek Orthodox) – variable
• **Easter Sunday** (Greek Orthodox) – variable
• **Easter Monday** (Greek Orthodox) – variable
• **Labor Day** – May 1
• **Pentecost Monday** (Greek Orthodox) – variable

- **Assumption of Our Lady** – August 15
- **Greek National Day** (Ohi Day) – October 28
- **Christmas Day** – December 25
- **Boxing Day** – December 26

SHOPPING

Clothing sizes are not the same throughout Europe. Below is a comparison chart showing sizes in the US, UK, and Greece.

Men's Suits

US	UK	Greece
36	36	46
38	38	48
40	40	50
42	42	52
44	44	54
46	46	56
48	48	58

Men's Shirts

US	UK	Greece
12	12	30/31
12.5	12.5	32
13	13	33
13.5	13.5	34/35
14	14	36
14.5	14.5	37
15	15	38
15.5	15.5	39/40
16	16	41
16.5	16.5	42
17	17	43

Men's Shoes

US	UK	Greece
5	4	37
5.5	4.5	38
6	5	38
6.5	5.5	39
7	6	39
7.5	6.5	40
8	7	41
8.5	7.5	42
9	8	42
9.5	8.5	43
10	9	43
10.5	9.5	44
11	10	44
11.5	10.5	45
12	11	46

Women's Suits/Dresses

US	UK	Greece
6	8	36
8	10	38
10	12	40
12	14	42
14	16	44
16	18	46
18	20	48
20	22	50
22	24	52

Women's Shoes

US	UK	Greece
5.5	4	37
6	4.5	38

Women's Shoes (continued)

US	UK	Greece
6.5	5	38
7	5.5	39
7.5	6	39
8	6.5	40
8.5	7	41
9	7.5	42
9.5	8	42
10	8.5	43
10.5	9	43
11	9.5	44
11.5	10	45
12	11	46

STAYING OUT OF TROUBLE

In Greece that is simple enough to do, so long as you go easy on the ouzo, retsina, and raki. In villages and remote areas it would be astonishing if you run into trouble with local people, unless you deliberately go out of your way to offend them by your attitude, dress, and behavior, or, in the case of men, if you go in unwelcome hot pursuit of local girls. Remembering that you are a guest – even if a paying one! – will help you to avoid such provocations.

In parts of resort areas where bars and discos are thick on the ground, the usual laid-back aspect can occasionally jump a few gears to a sudden frenzy brought on by too much drink and too much sun. Your fellow tourists will be the usual cause of this, however, so steer clear of any loud and aggressive "lager louts" you encounter. If a violent incident does break out near you, or involving you, try not to be around when the police arrive – unless you are the clear victim – as otherwise reasonable officers have a low threshold of tolerance for this kind of thing.

Drugs are the big no no. The Greek authorities don't like them and don't distinguish between possession and dealing. If you are caught with so much as a joint on you, your stay in Greece can be extended by a minimum of seven years as a guest of the state; you won't like the quarters.

Crime in general in Greece is low and violent offenses like muggings are not something you need worry much about – just enough to be sensible. Naturally in big cities and raucous resort areas at night you have to be a bit more on your guard, as such incidents do sometimes occur. Purse-snatching and theft from automobiles or hotel rooms can happen in Greece just as they can happen anywhere else.

Illegal possession of antiquities, or attempting to export them without official permission, is an offense.

Police

If you need the police in a hurry, call the tourist police (*Tel. 171*) to reach an English-speaking officer. Or call the police emergency number, *Tel. 100*. Otherwise, call the local main police station, whose numbers are listed in the Practical Information section I've provided for each island or locality.

TAXIS

Walk, drive, hitch, ride a donkey, crawl even ... anything rather than step into one of these mobile rip-off machines, where you'll most likely spend the entire trip arguing with the driver about meters, kilometers, fare and unfair. If you do find an honest Costas Hacknikarigos, cherish him for the national treasure he is.

It's a depressing thought that you'll have to argue with taxi drivers all over Greece. The equation is simple: $x = y$ squared, where x represents your reluctance to argue and y equals the fare. The best I can say about about Greek taxi drivers is that they are no worse than Chinese ones, and unlike Prague's they probably won't shoot you if you refuse to pay an obviously extortionate amount.

Still, you'll be left with some special entries in your diary: "Fought a stiff rearguard action on Corfu between the airport and the hotel and saved Drs 10,000;" "Explained the meaning of the term 'taximeter' to a driver in Athens, then introduced him to the operation of the device. He professed himself deeply moved by the march of science since Pythagoras's day."

That kind of thing. Fortunately there is a plus side: if the driver is honest, or can at least be put on the straight and narrow, there are no friendlier ones anywhere; and in normal circumstances they are far cheaper than a taxi in Western Europe would be.

Outlying resorts and bigger villages generally have at least one taxi, which can be called from a local taverna, or whose driver can probably be traced by asking at the village kafenion (cafe).

TELEVISION, RADIO, & THE PRESS

Greek television stations frequently feature English-language movies and series (mostly American and British) with their original soundtrack and Greek subtitles. Many hotels have satellite television, with stations including CNN International, BBC World Service Television, and BSkyB.

The Voice of America and BBC World Service Radio can also be picked up.

In addition, *USA Today* and the *International Herald Tribune* can be found in bigger news vendors in the main towns, and many British newspapers are widely available. *Time, Newsweek, US News & World Report* and *The Economist* are also on sale, as are many other US and British magazines.

TELEPHONE, TELEX, & FAX

The country code for Greece is *30*. When calling a Greek number from outside Greece, dial 30 for Greece, followed by the local area code minus its initial 0, followed by the subscriber number; when phoning a Greek number long distance from inside Greece, dial the whole area code, followed by the subscriber number; when phoning a Greek number locally, dial only the subscriber number.

When calling abroad from Greece, dial *00* before the country code for the country you are calling. Some country codes:
• **US & Canada**, *Tel. 1*
• **Great Britain**, *Tel. 44*

- **Australia**, *Tel.* *61*
- **New Zealand**, *Tel.* *64*
- **Ireland**, *Tel.* *353*
- **South Africa**, *Tel.* *27*

In the past it used to be important to know where the local **Greek Telecommunications Organization (OTE)** telephone office was, particularly for making international calls. Nowadays with international direct dialing (IDD) and telephone cards you can make international calls from most street telephones. Should you need to use OTE for making or receiving calls, or for telexes, faxes, or telegrams, and paying by cash, credit card, or collect, most towns and islands have at least one office.

If you are making a local telephone call, try to use an analog telephone (one with a real dial rather than a keypad), as all local calls using such phones cost Drs 11.5 no matter what their duration. Local calls from digital telephones cost Drs 11.5 per three minutes. A 100-unit telephone card *(telekarta)* costs Drs 1,500. Calls to the US and Canada at peak time are Drs 45 per minute.

Telephone cards, available from OTE offices and many street kiosks, cost Drs 1,500 for 100 units; Drs 6,500 for 500 units; and Drs 11,500 for 1,000 units. While the higher-unit cards are more economical in normal circumstances, simply having more units available may encourage you to make longer calls than necessary, and if something goes wrong with a higher-unit card it's a bigger loss.

The low-rate times for making calls within Greece are Monday to Friday from 10 pm to 9 am, and weekends from 3 pm on Saturday to 9 am on Monday. International low-rate times to North and South America are daily from 11 pm to 8 am; to Europe, the Middle East and Africa daily from 10 pm to 6 am; and to Australasia and Asia daily from 8 pm to 5 am.

Some useful telephone numbers:
- **Domestic Information**, *Tel.* *131*
- **International Information** (English-speaking operator), *Tel.* *161*
- **MCI CallUSA**, *Tel.* *00800-1211*
- **AT&T Direct**, *Tel.* *00800-1311*
- **Sprint Express**, *Tel.* *0800-1411*

TIME

Greece time is Greenwich Mean Time (GMT) plus 2 hours. The country is seven hours ahead of US Eastern Standard Time, eight hours ahead of Central Standard Time, nine hours ahead of Mountain Standard Time and ten hours ahead of Pacific Standard Time. It is one hour ahead of Western Europe, two hours ahead of Britain and Ireland, and eight hours behind Sydney, Australia.

TIPPING

Service charge is included in restaurants and tavernas to save you the trouble of having to work out how big a tip to give. Isn't that nice? Not if the service is lousy. It rarely is, unless you equate slow with lousy. In any case most people round up the amount for good service. You'll find that hairdressers, porters, taxi drivers, etc., like tips as much as anywhere but they don't necessarily expect them. If you think you've been scalped by your taxi driver don't add insult to financial injury by giving a tip.

WEIGHTS & MEASURES

Length	Metric	Multiply By
inch	millimeter	25.40
inch	centimetes	2.54
feet	meter	0.30
yard	meter	0.91
mile	kilometer	1.61

Area	Metric	Multiply By
square inch	square centimeter	6.45
square feet	square meter	0.09
square yard	square meter	0.84
acre	hectare	0.40

Volume	Metric	Multiply By
cubic inch	cubic centimeter	16.39
cubic feet	cubic meter	0.03
cubic yard	cubic meter	0.76

Capacity	Metric	Multiply By
fluid ounce	liter	0.03
pint (US)	liter	0.47
pint (UK)	liter	0.57
gallon (US)	liter	3.79
gallon (UK)	liter	4.55

Weight	Metric	Multiply By
ounce	gram	23.35
pound	kilogram	0.45
ton	tonne	1.02

7. FOOD & DRINK

Food & Drink

Greeks are rarely happier than when piling convivialy into the heaped up contents of as many food platters as will set a table groaning satisfyingly, almost but not quite collapsing. Read the description near the end of Book One of *The Iliad*, where Achilles and his buddies prepare and eat a magnificent feast. No vegetarians among those well-greaved Achaeans. You can almost hear Homer smacking his lips and see him checking his sundial in anticipation of dinner, as his loving recipe for slaughtering, flaying, spitting, roasting and consuming animals sacrificed to Apollo unfolds.

Nothing much has changed today, except that the throat-slitting and flaying are usually, though not always, done out of eyeshot of sensitive souls from places where meat grows inside freezer cabinets, ready prepared for the traditional microwave oven.

One of the delights of a Greek holiday, and one which seems to linger in everyone's memory long after those of ancient stones, wild disco nights, and hot beach days have faded, is dining in a waterside taverna as the scented warmth of a long Mediterranean evening rises up all round. The courses come slow and easy: simple, tasty food, and the waiter always has a story to tell when he arrives. Wine flows like the Kastallian Spring. At the end, long about midnight, the waiter tells you to pay tomorrow because he is too tired to count now. And tomorrow you're there first thing, to show that honesty is its own reward.

Don't, for God's sake, lock yourself up in a package-tour hotel restaurant, no matter what its star rating, eating international food for which "bland" would be a too charitable description. Get out and follow your nose wherever it leads you. Greeks love their food too much to forget how to make it properly. You can load the dice in your favor by going where the locals go – and I've pointed out plenty of these places for you in the destination chapters – even if they go there precisely because they think you won't. The Greek tradition of hospitality runs deep, and so long as you don't behave objectionably on their ground you'll soon find yourself part of the family.

The best tavernas are invariably places where you troop into the kitchen on arrival, and choose your own dishes by pointing at whatever is bubbling on the hob or warming in the oven that takes your fancy, while the cooks look on with all the satisfaction of artists at a private showing. Greeks, as you will discover, are past masters at celebrating summer around a table.

EATERIES

There is a vast range of eating establishments in Greece, which is both the cause and effect of a strong tradition of dining out among the population. While international eateries – Chinese, Italian, Indian – are becoming more common in big cities and popular resorts, the over-whelming majority sell Greek food.

Restaurants

Eating in a restaurant – an **estiatorion** – usually means better standards of service, more refined surroundings, and more carefully prepared food than the more popular tavernas. They also usually have better-trained waiters who can filet a fish before your very eyes and know that there is more to wine than splashing it into a glass. For this, they charge more.

Tavernas

The **taverna** is the great popular eating place in Greece, and where you are most likely to do your dining. They are not as fancy as restaurants, generally speaking, yet fancier than snackbars, and it is in tavernas that most Greeks eat out. You'll find that they vary a lot in look and quality, and it's not always easy to tell by the look of a place how good the food is. Particularly in busy tourist zones, where there are usually huge numbers of them, the owners know that rustic looking decor is a surefire tourist draw and beyond that they often don't care. It is equally true that good looking places can have excellent food, as indeed can ugly looking places.

Your best guide if you want to taste the genuine flavor of Greek food is to see where the locals go, and go with them. That doesn't mean that locally popular tavernas are always good and tourist-oriented ones are always bad, only that the probabilities usually work out that way.

Ouzeris

Originally an **ouzeri** was a place where people, men mostly, went to drink ouzo accompanied by **mezes** (snacks or appetizers). Some ouzeris are still like that. Others have developed into taverna-style eateries with limited menus, and often with a notably traditional character.

Snackbars

In cities and bigger resorts, fast-food outlets selling burgers, pizzas, and chicken wings are by now well established. Old-style snackbars are still popular, however, particularly for lunch breaks and other meals taken on the run. Grilled lamb in pita bread (**giros**) and grilled lamb on wooden skewers (**souvlaki**) are favorites, as are toasted cheese or ham sandwiches (**tostis**).

Dairy Shops

Selling milk, yogurt, ice cream and other dairy products, along with tea, coffee, and a range of snacks, a **galaktopoleion** is a popular place for breakfast and a quick lunch.

FOOD GLOSSARY

There is usually a lot of olive oil in Greek food, which can present problems to digestions not used to such rich fare. Go easy on this at first or, better still, drink lots of retsina – a Greek wine that has been flavored in pine resin barrels – which has a neutralizing effect on olive oil; the oil in turn has a neutralizing effect on the retsina, so there you have a perfect symbiotic relationship.

The following is only a sampling of the wide range of options to be found on menus, or on stoves, across Greece. Many of the dishes will sound familiar to you, as some are found throughout Southern Europe and the Middle East.

Starters (Orektika)

Dolmadakia – stuffed vine leaves, served hot or cold, usually with a lemon sauce

Hummus – chickpea paste with olive oil and garlic

Spanakopita – spinach pie

Tahini – a sesame seed paste with olive oil

Taramasolata – fish roe (eggs) mixed with olive oil

Tiropita – cheese pie

Tzatziki – chopped cucumber in yogurt with lashings of garlic (you might call this the kiss of death!)

Olives – black or green, often served with chopped raw garlic

Soup (Soupes)

Avgolemono – egg and lemon soup

Magiritsa – tripe soup with rice

Psarosoupa – fish soup

Soupa Horta – vegetable soup

Fish (Psaria)

Astakos – lobster

Barbounia – red mullet

Garides – scampi

Gouvetsi – shrimp stew
Kalamarakia – squid
Kisifias – swordfish
Ktapodi – octopus
Lithrinia – sea bass
Sinagrida – bream
Streidia – oysters

Meat

Arni - lamb
Giouvestsi – lamb with pasta
Katskia – goat's meat
Keftedes – grilled meatballs
Kirino – pork
Kotopoulo – chicken
Loukanika – sausages
Moussaka – oven-baked eggplant, minced meat, and potato, with a cheese
    sauce (you can also get vegetarian moussaka in some places)
Stifado – stewed meat
Vothino – beef

Vegetables (Horta)

Angouraki – cucumber
Anginara – artichoke
Avocanto – avocado
Bisellia – peas
Domata salata – tomato salad
Domates – tomatoes
Ekies – olives
Fasoulakia – beans
Grimidia – onions
Kolokithakia – courgettes
Marouli – lettuce
Mavromatika – black-eyed beans

Melizanes – aubergines
Patates – potatoes
Salata – salad
Skordos – garlic
Spinazi – spinach

Desserts (Glika)
Baklava - a pastry of honey and nuts
Loukoumades – fritters with syrup or honey
Rizogalo – rice pudding

Fruit (Frouta)
Banana – banana (surprisingly enough)
Fraoules – strawberries
Frapa – grapefruit
Kerasia – cherries
Lemoni – lemon
Milo – apple
Peroni – melon
Portokali – orange
Rodakina – peaches
Stafilia – grapes

Dairy Products
Avga – eggs
Feta – goat's cheese
Gala – milk
Pagoto – ice cream
Tiri – cheese
Voultiro – butter
Yiaourti – yogurt

Other

Alati – salt
Ladi – oil
Makaronia – macaroni
Meli – honey
Pilafi – rice pilaf
Piperi – pepper
Psomi – bread
Rizi – rice
Spageto – spaghetti
Xidi – vinegar
Zachari – sugar

DRINK GLOSSARY

Ouzo is the national drink: a strong, clear liqueur distilled from grape residue and flavored with aniseed, it turns cloudy when watrer is added, as it usually is. Greek brandy has a more workaday taste than French brandy, which if nothing else at least means that you don't have to go through the sniffing and warming up favored by the French before tossing off your glass. Pilsener-style beers are widely available.

Wine falls into two categories: what you might call ordinary wine, and **retsina**, the latter being stored in barrels line with pine resin which flavors the wine. You'll either love retsina, hat it until you acquire the taste for it and then love it, or just hate it full stop. Ordinary wine varies considerably in quality, with those from Halkidiki, Crete, and Rhodes having the best reputations, although that doesn't mean that all wines from these places are good. If you get to know and trust a taverna in the place where you are staying, you may find that their village wine of the house is both good value and good tasting.

Coffee is either Turkish coffee (which you had better call Greek coffee), strong and served either as sweet (glyko), medium (metrio), or with sugar (sketo); or Nescafe, which actually refers to any brand of instant coffee, served with or without milk.

Drinks

Bira - beer
Krasi aspro – white wine
Krasi kokkinelli – rosé wine
Krasi mavro – red wine
Nero – water
Portokalada – orange juice

THE COFFEE SHOP

*The coffee shop – **kafeneion** – is an all-male preserve, and all the women's rights rhetoric in the universe isn't about to change all that. It's a smoky, noisy den, alive with vigorous discussion on the vital issues of the moment – soccer, mostly, with politics thrown in for variation. In between times the denizens drink strong Turkish (sorry, Greek) coffee, play tavli (backgammon), at breakneck speed, and worry over their worry beads. The older men love the kafeneion.*

8. ATHENS

Athens

Athens – and here I vastly understate the case – isn't the most handsome capital in the world. It's not much of an exagerration to say that a visitor should hit the city on the run, catch the Acropolis and the National Archaeological Museum, grab a bite to eat in Plaka, and hightail it out of town before sundown. It's true that when you get to know Athens better and start to feel the pulse of the city, unexpected attractions reveal themselves in many seemingly unpromising areas. For a visitor on a tight time schedule, though, the fast-food approach to downtown greatly simplifies the problems of getting to grips with Athens.

As the local tourism authorities never tire of pointing out, Athens is the city where Western culture and democracy got their start, and today's Athenians are the heirs of Pericles, Aristophanes, Socrates, and their pals. Let's not get into any arguments over dead white European males, and accept this assertion (which is more than just a marketing slogan) as far as it goes. In the almost fifteen hundred years since the Emperor Justinian closed the renowned schools of pagan philosophy in favor of Christian education, Athens has been a hick provincial Byzantine town, a backwater under the Ottoman Turks, and the focus of waves of mass refugee migrations since the anti-Turkish wars of the 19th and 20th centuries. It doesn't have much of a history other than its classical one, so you can't blame it for accentuating the positive.

The positive is marvelous indeed, even although the passing centuries have taken their toll of the city's classical legacy. The **Parthenon**, for example, that shining symbol crowning the Acropolis, has been quite thoroughly blown up in its time. Anyway, the best surviving bits and pieces of the past are featured in this chapter (*Seeing the Sights*, below), so there is no need to go over them all here. The point is that aside from its ancient history, Athens can be a tough sell.

Large tracts of the city, particularly outside the center, are a kind of urban desert, little more than a bolted-together conglomeration of apartment blocks, shops, tavernas, snackbars and workshops, and mostly with traffic that verges on the frantic from dawn to midnight. If you walk, you will find that there are some marvelous local tavernas, that the shopkeepers are friendly, and that an occasional architectural curiosity or park presents itself for inspection. Mostly, though, the interest quotient is low and the surroundings unattractive. In most European cities I would always advise visitors to get off the beaten track of the main tourist zones, and explore the unfashionable areas, hoping for what serendipity might throw in your path. In too much of sprawling Athens, however, serendipity is out to lunch.

Still, you could easily spend a week in Athens without having cause to be bored. Take the time to see the major sights like the **Acropolis**, the **Agora**, and the **National Archaeological Museum** at a pace they deserve – a day each wouldn't be excessive; wander around the taverna-and-shops enclave of **Plaka** (and simply ignore anyone who tells you it's too touristy), the flea market in **Monastiraki**, and Cyclades-style **Anafiotika** below the Acropolis; if you've seen enough of them, move on to **Exarhia**, **Omonia**, and **Koukaki**; get your greens in the **National Garden** and **Areos Park**; climb the **Filopapou** and **Likavitos Hills** for the fresh air and the view; catch the bus or trolley at Plateia Syntagma; if you feel the need to go upmarket, start out around **Kolonaki** then head out to **Kifissia**; above all, eat, drink, and be merry.

Use the extensive bus and trolley network to get around easily, and then do your walking once you've arrived in the target zone. Don't be afraid to take taxis despite what you may hear or read to the contrary (and I join in the chorus of warnings; see Chapter 6, *Basic Information* section on Taxis) – so long as you make the ground rules on meters and fares clear to the driver at the outset, you'll find them to be inexpensive by European standards.

When, probably sooner rather than later, you arrive at saturation point with Athens, you'll find that one of the best things about the city is how easy it is to get away from it. A 20-minute metro ride to Piraeus, or a bus to Rafina, puts you on the dockside where ferries are lined up like streetcars at the depot, ready, willing, and usually able to take you anywhere in the sparkling Aegean that your heart desires.

ARRIVALS & DEPARTURES
BY AIR

Athens' **Ellinikon International Airport** lies east of the city at the Saronic Gulf resort of **Glyfada** (every year a new batch of package-tourists learns the noisily imparted lesson that Glyfada is not the ideal place for a restful break). There are two terminals, **East** and **West**. The former handles all airlines other than Olympic Airways, and the latter is Olympic's personal fiefdom. If you are arriving on a foreign carrier and switching to Olympic for an onward flight, or vice versa for a departing flight, you can take the interterminal shuttle bus that operates hourly from 8:30 am to 8:30 pm. Both terminals have currency exchange offices.

Getting To & From The Airport

If you arrived on an Olympic flight, you can take the hourly **Olympic Airways shuttle bus** from outside the terminal to Plateia Syntagma in Athens' city center. The blue-and-white public bus lines A1, A2, and A3 also serve the airport every 20 minutes or so; tickets cost Drs 75 (75 drachmas) and can be bought from the airport newsstand before boarding and validated onboard. These buses fill up quickly and are not ideal if you have a lot of luggage to maneuver. Depending on traffic conditions, journey time to Plateia Syntagma is around 30 to 40 minutes.

Taxis are usually plentiful at the airport, although you will certainly have to queue for one at peak times. Count on at least Drs 1,500 to downtown, plus Drs 100 for items of luggage over 10 kilograms. Make sure that the driver has the meter switched on.

Charter Flights

There are any number of **charter flights** from London, Paris, Amsterdam, Berlin – in fact all over northern Europe – to Athens and many of the Greek islands, from April through October. You book a charter flight from a travel agent in Europe, with the return set for between one and six weeks after departure. This will cost in the region of $200-$300, depending on where you fly from and when, and will be far cheaper than an unrestricted return flight to Athens, and probably though not necessarily cheaper than an APEX fare.

BY BOAT

You can't actually arrive in Athens by boat, but you can do the next worst thing: arrive in **Piraeus** by boat. In fact, Piraeus is much worse if you're leaving rather than arriving. On the way in you just want to get off the boat, most likely at the Great Harbor (which is not too great, really, only big). Two **railway stations** – one for northern Greece, and one for the south – lie at the western and eastern end respectively of Akti Kondili, the quayside road that parallels the north end of the harbor. Beside the southbound station is the **metro station** for Athens: **Monastiraki** and **Omonia** are the two main downtown stations in the capital.

If you go by **taxi**, count on at least Drs 1,500 to downtown, plus Drs 100 for items of luggage over 10 kilograms. Make sure that the driver has the meter switched on. The **green bus** line 040 runs every 15 minutes from Piraeus's Plateia Themistokleou to Plateia Syntagma in Athens.

You might also arrive at the port of **Rafina**, a 90-minute bus ride east of Athens, an altogether more civilized place than Piraeus, not for its looks but because it hosts far fewer ferry operators. The **orange bus** for Athens runs from in front of the harbor building to Odos Mavromateon close to the Areos Park and the **Viktoris Metro Station** in north-central Athens.

BY BUS

Long distance buses from other points in Europe arrive in Athens at either **Terminal A**, *Odos Kifissou 100, Tel. 01/512-4910*, in the western suburbs, or at **Terminal B**, *Odos Liossion 26, Tel. 01/831-7153*, in the northern suburbs.

BY TRAIN

There are two main railway stations in Athens, **Stathmos Larissis**, *Tel. 01/524-0646*, for passengers arriving from the north, and **Stathmos Peloponnisou**, *Tel. 01/513-4601*, for those coming from the south. It doesn't make too much difference on the way in, as both stations lie just 200 meters from each other off Odos Theodorou Diligiani northwest of the city center.

Trolleybus 1 runs from Stathmos Larissis along Odos Panepistimiou to Plateia Syntagma; bus 057 runs from Stathmos Peloponnisou along Odos Panepistimiou. A taxi from either station to Plateia Syntagma, or to Plaka, where many visitors choose to stay, should cost about Drs 750. The closest metro stations to the railways stations are **Viktoris** and **Omonia**.

ORIENTATION

The most important square, more or less smack dab in the middle of the city, is **Plateia Syntagma** (Constitution Square). Not much more than a big traffic island, it has a tourist office, banks, and exchange offices, with the **Parliament Building** as a target-marker and the adjacent **National Park** as an emergency oxygen supply. From Syntagma, **Odos Ermou**, a main shopping artery, runs to down-at-heel **Monastiraki** and the **flea market** around the metro station there. South of Odos Ermou lies **Plaka**, the atmospheric old Ottoman part of the city, only just saved from "developers" in the Sixties and Seventies and now a conservation area filled with taverns, bars, hotels, and craft shops – some good, some not so good.

The ancient **Acropolis** crowned by the **Parthenon** lies generally southwest of Plaka. Between Plaka and the Acropolis, amid the steeply rising streets that lead up to the historic monument, is **Anafiotika**, a beautiful warren of narrow alleys and pastel-hued cottages, the homes of migrants from the Cyclades Islands who brought the pre-tourist era graces of Anafi to the capital. Beneath the Acropolis lies the ancient **Agora**, while beyond it to the west are the equally historic hills of the **Areopagus** and the **Pnyx**, with the big **Filopapu Hill** park adjoining to the south.

Continuing southwards in this direction, you enter **Koukaki**. This is a district that hasn't much in it from the visitor's point of view in terms of "sights," yet is a tranquil and attractive place where Athenian life goes on undistracted by the need to pander to tourists and unswamped by traffic and pollution. It is close enough to the main tourist areas to be handy for them, yet far enough away to be unaffected.

Returning to Plateia Syntagma and going south along **Odos Amalias** brings you to the **Arch of Hadrian** and the entrance to the ancient Roman section of the city around the **Olympieion Temple**. Going northwest from Syntagma on **Odos Stadiou** leads to Athens' second most important square, also a major traffic intersection, **Plateia Omonia**. Nearby is the **National Theater**, while off to the north on **Odos Patission** is the **National Archaeological Museum** and its collection of superb treasures from ancient Greece.

GETTING AROUND TOWN

Putting the concepts "getting around" and "Athens" together in the same space will seem like a contradiction in terms to anyone who has actually tried to do the thing. Yet Athenians *do* get to work and tourists *do* get to visit the Acropolis, and although neither comes through the experience totally unscathed, the system still works after a fashion.

The fact is that Athens is big, crowded, polluted, and chaotic. When the city government announced the expansion of the tiny metro system and added that there would be disruption to the normal flow of traffic while construction work proceeded, Athenians shrugged and said, "So what else is new?"

Athenians are, however, a big part of the problem. If they drove with the philosophical self-control one might expect of the heirs of Plato and

Socrates life on the street would undoubtedly flow a lot smoother. Instead, they act like Cretan mountain-men surrounded by Turks, determined to sell their lives dearly and take no prisoners. In their hands, the horn becomes a weapon, a combined communicator-phaser, warning off all enemies while blasting open the path ahead.

By Bus & Trolleybus

City buses have hard seats and trolleybuses have soft seats. Otherwise there is little to choose between them in degree of discomfort, and as you will probably never actually get a seat the difference is academic. In compensation, there are lots of them, they are ridiculously cheap, and they go all over the place. Perhaps the most useful are **trolleybus lines 4 and 5**, which run very 10 minutes past Plateia Syntagma and Plateia Omonia to the National Archaeological Museum on Odos Patission; the **green bus 040** which runs every 15 minutes from Plateia Syntagma to Piraeus (but try to avoid rush-hour if you're heading for a ferry and are carrying luggage); and the modern, comfortable **blue-and-white express bus lines A and B** which run every 20 minutes to the airport.

Route lists and timetables are available from the **EOT office** at Plateia Syntagma, and information can also be obtained by telephoning 171.

You must have your ticket before you board the bus. Each ticket costs Drs 75 and you buy them in books from most newsstands; it's worthwhile buying at least 10 at a time to save the nuisance of constantly replacing them. The ticket is good for one journey anywhere on the route net and must be validated by inserting it into the orange machine on board. Inspectors occasionally check tickets and issue fines to anyone without a valid one.

By Car

It's a jungle out there and the indigenous *carnivores* are unforgiving with innocent intruders into their domain. If you are prone to masochistic tendencies, by all means drive in Athens: you'll get all the action you can handle. Timid folks with cars should creep into the city at 3 am, stash the vehicle in a car park and forget about it for the duration. Undecideds and in-betweens should drive straight in during the day: you'll find out fast enough if you can stand the heat or should leave the kitchen to the local cooks.

If you must drive, be prepared to wade in up to your armpits. It's mostly not that dangerous on the street, because congestion means that traffic usually moves slowly, although if a tiny space presents itself, everyone will stomp on the gas to fill it. Drive defensively, not offensively, for the sake of vulnerable and seemingly suicidal pedestrians and moped riders all around you, and try to pretend that the resultant chorus of blaring horns from offense-minded drivers is the *Ode To Joy*.

The biggest argument against sightseeing by car is that you won't see many sights that way. Only if you have medical grounds for not walking should you resort to four wheels, and in this case you are better off doing a deal with a taxi driver or booking a sightseeing city tour – neither of which options are recommended in normal circumstances. Athens' most interesting quarters and historic sights are all walking experiences. Where you have to go a distance between sights – for example from Plateia Syntagma to the National Archaeological Museum, use public transport.

Car rental is available from major international groups such as:
• **Avis**, *Tel. Leoforos Amalias 48. Tel. 01/322-4951*
• **Budget**, *Tel. Leoforos Syngrou 8. Tel. 01/921-4771*
• **Europcar**, *Tel. Leoforos Syngrou 4. Tel. 01/921-5789*
• **Hertz**, *Tel. Leoforos Syngrou 12. Tel. 01/922-0102*

Some good Athens-based car rental companies are:
• **Avance**, *Tel. Leoforos Syngrou 22. Tel. 01/924-0564*
• **Avanti**, *Tel. Leoforos Syngrou 50. Tel. 01/923-3919*
• **Retca**, *Tel. Odos Kalisperi 20. Tel. 01/922-4998*
• **Swift**, *Tel. Odos Nikis 21. Tel. 01/324-7855*

By Foot

It depends where you are going. You'll have to visit the main historic sites – the Acropolis, the Agora, the Olympieion, Keramikos, and the Pnyx and Areopagus Hills – on foot, for which may the ancient town planners be praised. The same applies to the upmarket shopping area around Plateia Syntagma, and the nearby National Garden, Parliament and Presidential Palace zone. Plaka, Monastiraki, and perhaps Koukaki are also best seen on foot. For everywhere else you are looking at using public transport, at least to get to the place where you want to be.

Walking in Athens in the withering heat of summer, swathed in the noxious fumes of the *nefa* that hangs over the city like a pall, is not a pleasant experience. It can even prove fatal – in the exceptionally hot and smoggy summer of 1987 an estimated 2,000 elderly people died of heat- and pollution-related illnesses, and "normal" summers take a lesser yet still worrying toll.

You have to be alert for traffic at all times, even on the sidewalk! While it would be clearly suicidal to try crossing Odos Amalias just after the traffic has been greenlighted, even narrow sidestreets can be dangerous, as cars are often parked on the sidewalk, forcing you onto the street, where drivers *will not stop* for pedestrians but expect you to keep out of their way somehow, no matter how limited the space. When you hear the sound of motorbikes coming up behind you on the sidewalk, don't suddenly jump to one side: either keep straight ahead or move smoothly to the side – riders are less inclined to crash into your back, if only because they might get hurt as well.

Be especially cautious at pedestrian crossings, with or without the "green walking figure" or "red standing figure" signals. The former are worse than useless as all drivers ignore them; while at the latter, traffic can often still turn right or left across your path, and drivers *will not stop* to give pedestrians priority.

By Metro

The present single-route metro system is a fairly undistinguished affair for a major capital. Yet it is clean, fast, and frequent (trains every 15 minutes on average). It runs from Kifissia in the north to Piraeus in the south, mostly above ground, stopping at downtown points such as Omonia and Monastiraki on the way. The same Drs 75 ticket that you use on the bus/trolleybus net is good for the metro, validated before entry.

A second metro line is currently being constructed. A word of warning: watch out for pickpockets at busy stations and on crowded trains.

By Motorbike, Moped, & Scooter

If you've got the nerve for it, and chrome-plated lungs as well, moped, motorbike, or scooter is a good way to get around quickly, weaving through the traffic jams with the greatest of ease. Why, you can even join other riders on the sidewalk! Try **Motorent**, *Odos Falirou 5, Tel. 01/923-4939; and Odos Kariatidon 11, Tel. 01/921-6331.*

If anyone tries to interest you in a health-threatening recreational substance known on the street as "a bicycle," just say no.

By Taxi

Taxis are colored yellow. You can hail one in the street with ease except during rush-hour when they are far harder to come by. Your problems are often only beginning once you get inside, however. Athens taxi drivers have cleaned up their act – or more accurately had it cleaned up for them by the city authorities – in recent years, a piece of news that is bound to excite your sympathy for anyone who had to deal with them in their pre-clean days.

Make sure the meter is on: don't move an inch with a cab that doesn't have its meter on and whose driver dismisses your request that he switch it on with an airy "No problem." The journey is sure to end in financial tears for one of you. Some drivers are not above dickering with the meter – switching it from fare rate "1" to the higher-rate "2," which should be used only between midnight and 5 am and for out-of-town trips. For long distances, such as Athens to the airport and Athens to Piraeus, or in the reverse direction, ask for an estimate of the fare: it invariably turns out to be more but at least you'll have established a ballpark figure.

You might find that there are other passengers already in a cab, all going to more or less the same place (somewhere in Athens), or that the driver picks up other passengers on the way. There's not much you can do about this other than sit back and enjoy the conversation, unless the driver tries to charge you the full fare for what should have been a short trip and instead amounted to a minitour of Attica.

In spite of all this, don't be afraid to use taxis. The fact is that they are ridiculously cheap compared to most European capitals (think of the smooth professionals in Amsterdam or Munich who will relieve you, perfectly legally, of five times as much for a similar journey).

Taxi fares are Drs 200 from flag fall, Drs 58 per kilometer thereafter within the city limits, and Drs 113 in the periphery and from midnight to 5 am. There is a Drs 300 surcharge from the airport (either terminal) and Drs 160 from Piraeus or the railway station. Items of baggage weighing more than 10 kilograms cost Drs 55 each. Waiting time is Drs 2,000 per hour. Telephone booking costs Drs 300 and telephone booking for a specified time costs Drs 500.

If you need to call a cab, here are some numbers of radio-controlled outfits:

- **Athina 1**, *Tel. 01/921-7942*
- **Aëtos**, *Tel. 01/801-9000*
- **Enotitia**, *Tel. 01/645-9000*
- **Hermis**, *Tel. 01/411-5200*
- **Express**, *Tel. 01/993-4812*
- **Glyfada**, *Tel. 01/894-6858*
- **Ikaros**, *Tel. 01/513-2316*
- **Kifissia**, *Tel. 01/801-8820*
- **Parthenon**, *Tel. 01/581-4711*
- **Piraeus 1**, *Tel. 01/418-2333*

WHERE TO STAY

While there may be reasons for taking a hotel in other parts of Athens (and in particular if you want top-of-the-range accommodation you will have to do so), still the best all-round location has to be **Plaka**. Why? It has the ambience, restaurants, relative freedom from traffic and is close to the main historical points of interest in the city. It also has late-night noise and too many souvenir shops, so you have to decide what factors are the most important. If you want to be where the action is, skip the following intermediate alphabetical area listings and zoom straight in on Plaka.

ATHENS LODGINGS FINDS & FAVORITES

In descending order of price, these are hotels that stand out in Athens as temples to good taste, good value, and good facilities, all of which should add up to good memories for those who lodge within.

• ***Grande Bretagne****, Plateia Syntagma. Tel. 01/331-4444, Fax 01/ 322-8034. Rates: Drs 75,000 to Drs 125,000. A taste of tradition, luxury and charm.*

• ***Pentelikon****, Odos Deligianni 66. Tel. 01/808-0311, Fax 01/801-0314. Rates: Drs 53,500 to Drs 88,000. Fashionable, elegant and refined.*

• ***Athenian Inn****, Odos Haritos 22. Tel. 01/723-8097, Fax 01/724-2268. Rates Drs 15,400 to Drs 22,000. Characterful small place in a quiet area.*

• ***Acropolis House****, Odos Kodrou 6-8. Tel. 01/322-2344, Fax 01/ 324-4143. Rates: Drs 11,300 to Drs 17,000. Friendly staff in a fine old Plaka house.*

• ***Achilleas****, Odos Lekka 21. Tel. 01/322-5826, Fax 01/324-1092. Rates: Drs 11,300 to Drs 13,900. Excellent price-quality ratio.*

Kifissia

The chic northern suburb, 13 kilometers from downtown, is a mass of elegant villas surrounded by gardens. The streets are lined with trees as well as gold in these parts and the air is easier on the lungs. Upmarket shopping, eating and drinking are all within easy reach. What isn't within easy reach is the city center, not by car, bus, or taxi anway. The quickest way there is by the metro system, whose northern terminus is in Kifissia.

PENTELIKON, Od*os Deligianni 66. Tel. 01/808-0311, Fax 01/801-0314. Rates (with tax): Drs 53,500 single; Drs 64,000 double; Drs 88,000 suite. Breakfast Drs 3,200. 44 rooms and suites. All credit cards.*

Amidst the villa-laden streets of Kifissia is the yellow-painted, neo-classical villa-style Pentelikon, built in 1923. You are meant to feel a sense of laidback luxury in your own country villa here, and you can be assured of personal attention from the staff to that end, as there are no fewer than a hundred of them for the 44 rooms. The rooms themselves are all individually styled with antique furnishings, and some have small balconies. Its Empire-decor bar is an attraction all by itself, with a satisfyingly large collection of bottles glowing like icons in the romantically low lamplight, and the Vardi's Restaurant is noted across Athens for its high-end French cuisine. Outside in the garden is a swimming pool.

Kolonaki

Lying between the two green areas of the National Garden and Likavitos Hill, Kolonaki is a good place for anyone who wants to be in a more refined area of the city, while still being close enough to the center not to feel left out. Hotels here are generally a cut above the average, yet one of the city's most charming hotels in more than just the cost and production-values sense is here: the Athenian Inn.

ATHENS HILTON, *Leoforos Vasilissis Sofias 46. Tel. 01/725-0201 and 0301, Fax 01/725-3110. Rates (with tax): Drs 116,200 single and double; Drs 149,0000 suite. Breakfast Drs 5,000. 453 rooms. All credit cards.*

The Athens Hilton is a big hotel, though not Athens's biggest. It has been occupying the same spot as a city landmark since 1963 and shows no signs of budging. Each of the 453 rooms has a private balcony: half of them give a view of the Acropolis, and the other half look towards the mountains. Air conditioned throughout, each room has telephone, satellite television and in-house movie channels, and minibar. There's a non-smoking floor (but you're allowed to not smoke on any floor). You can relax in the 15- by 24-meter swimming pool, the sauna and health club, and at the in-hotel hairdressers, eat and drink in two bars and three restaurants, spend any money you have left in the shopping arcade, park your car in the private garage, and shuttle backwards and forwards to the airport and the nearby city center in the hotel shuttlebus.

SAINT GEORGE LYCABETTUS, *Odos Kleomenous 2. Tel. 01/729-0711, Fax 01/724-7610. Rates (with tax): Drs 50,200 single; Drs 57,600 double; Drs 60,300 suite. Breakfast Drs 2,800. 150 rooms and suites. All credit cards.*

There seem to be endless permutations on how to transliterate the Greek letters of the big hill northeast of Plateia Syntagma. The city map of Athens spells it three different ways in its four references. For the purposes of this book, however, the Saint George Lycabettus Hotel is overlooked by, and partly named after, the Likavitos Hill. OK? Its proximity to the wooded lower slopes of the hill adds a few fresh-air scents and an occasional cooling breeze to the facilities – both experiences being welcome rarities in the depths of an Athenian summer – and the view of the hill from the roof garden gives you the feeling of being in the countryside.

There is a swimming pool, hairdressing salon, and a grillroom restaurant. The plushly fitted rooms have telephone, satellite television, and minibar.

ATHENIAN INN, *Odos Haritos 22. Tel. 01/723-8097, Fax 01/724-2268. Rates (with tax): Drs 15,400 single; Drs 22,000 double. Breakfast Drs included. 28 rooms. All credit cards.*

One of Athens's gems, whose praises were sung by no less a Greece booster than the writer Lawrence Durrell, and although that was several decades ago, the Inn retains an intrinsic Greekness in its cozy hospitality, look, and facilities that is absent from many of the efficient but cold modern hotels. There are relatively few rooms here and those are often booked by regulars or via grapevine recommendations, so give yourself plenty of time in advance. The hotel is on a quiet street in this smart area, the rooms are big, air conditioned, and some have balconies.

Koukaki

This might be one of the most underrated parts of Athens, a relatively quiet residential neighborhood, close enough to the Acropolis and Plaka to be convenient, and far enough away to be spared the worst aspects of wall-to-wall tourism. However, Koukaki is not only positive because of others' negatives. It has its own sense of what being Athenian today is about.

DIVANI PALACE ACROPOLIS, *Odos Parthenonos 19-25. Tel. 01/922-2945, Fax 01/921-4993. Rates (with tax): Drs 58,000 single; Drs 67,000 double; suite Drs 90,000. Breakfast Drs 3,800. 253 rooms and suites. All credit cards.*

Located on the edge of Koukaki in a quiet sidestreet close to the Acropolis, the Divani Palace has a big and airy foyer, and a roof garden complete with swimming pool and café terrace that has a view up to the ancient site. Rooms, though not overly big, are functional, modern, comfortable, air conditioned and equipped with satellite television, radio console, telephone and minibar. In the hotel basement can be seen part of Athens's Themistoclean Wall, dating from 479 BC – whether or not a hotel basement is the right place for an ancient monument is a moot point, yet there it is.

ROYAL OLYMPIC, *Odos Diakou 28-32. Tel. 01/924-8848, Fax 01/923-3317. Rates (with tax): Drs 30,000 single; Drs 40,000 double; Drs 80,000 suite. Breakfast included. 298 rooms and suites. All credit cards.*

Situated close enough to the Temple of Olympian Zeus (the Olympieion) that the god might take for part of his premises, the Royal Olympic offers good value. It is not a bad choice for someone coming by car from Piraeus who doesn't want to get immersed in the genuine city-center traffic chaos a little further along the road, and who appreciates the convenience of a hotel garage.

In this case the rooftop breakfast terrace has a great view of the Olympieion and well beyond it to Likavitos Hill. There's lots of green around the hotel, whose air conditioned rooms are elegantly furnished and have telephone, satellite television, and minibar. Other facilities include a ballroom, swimming pool, fitness center, sauna, hairdressing salon, lobby bar and rustic restaurant.

AUSTRIA, *Odos Mousson 7. Tel. 01/923-5151, Fax 01/924-7350. Rates (with tax): Drs 14,500 single; Drs 19,800 double. Breakfast included. 37 rooms. All credit cards.*

Austria might seem a strange name for a hotel in Athens, except that the owner is Austrian, so that explains it. The hotel is nothing fancy architecturally but is modern, comfortable, and well-equipped, and occupies a good location at the foot of Filopappou Hill and within easy walking distance of the Acropolis (although not within such easy walking distance of Plaka as the hotel makes out – at least *I* couldn't walk it in five minutes).

ART GALLERY HOTEL, *Odos Erechthiou 5. Tel. 01/923-8376, Fax 01/ 923-3025. Rates (with tax): Drs 11,000 single; Drs 13,200 double. Breakfast included. 22 rooms. No credit cards.*

You might pay a touch more to stay at this place than the facilities really justify. If you've even a drop of bohemian blood in your veins you'll think the little extra you pay is worth it. Owner Ioannis Assimakopoulos is an architect and as well as the extra zing that gives to the interior decor, he has made of his hotel a miniature art gallery, with some of the paintings on the walls having been produced by former residents of the house from its pre-hotel days. The hotel is a labor of love for Ioannis and it shows. Rooms are comfortable, with balconies and awnings. There is even a suite, which will set you back up to Drs 17,200.

TONY'S, *Odos Zaharitsa 26. Tel. 01/923-6370, Fax 01/923-5761. Rates (with tax): Drs 9,000 single; Drs 10,400 double; Drs 16,500 studio. Breakfast included. 26 rooms and studios. Visa, MasterCard.*

Models on assignment in Athens often book studio apartments at Tony's and reward him for his hospitality with signed photographs which he pins up at reception. As far as the facilities go, the rooms are comfortable, and the studios equipped with kitchen and fridge. Tony's is on a fairly quiet street close to the Areopagus and Acropolis, and is a lively, popular place.

Plaka

This is the place for anyone who wants to be at the center of the Athenian action in terms of local color and good restaurants, while within easy walking distance of the city's main tourist attractions and the central Plateia Syntagma. On the downside, the area can get noisy, though not so much with traffic as with late-night carousers, and the fact that you mostly have to walk may not appeal to some. There is a wide spread of accommodation, which includes some good Greek upper-range hotels, although the emphasis is on mid-range to budget choices and excludes the top international chains.

ELECTRA PALACE, *Odos Nikodimou 18. Tel. 01/324-1401, Fax 01/ 324-1875. Rates (with tax): Drs 28,600 single; Drs 35,000 double. Breakfast Drs 3,500. 106 rooms and suites. All credit cards.*

The Electra Palace combines a good Plaka location with top-notch facilities that include a rooftop swimming pool from where you can look at the Acropolis while floating on your back sipping a cocktail – and what would Socrates have made of that? The rooms are air conditioned, elegantly furnished and fully equipped. There is a private parking garage for anyone brave enough to drive a car in Athens (or more likely to sneak it into the city during the wee small hours and stash it in the garage for the duration), a restaurant and a bar, even a conference chamber and banqueting room.

ADRIAN, *Odos Adrianou 74. Tel. 01/322-1553, Fax 01/325-0461. Rates (with tax): Drs 16,200 single; Drs 21,600 double. Breakfast included. 22 rooms. American Express, Visa, MasterCard.*

Close enough to Hadrian's Library for guests to be able to read the books (if there were any), the Adrian's modern looks are not exactly in keeping with those of Plaka in general, but are likely to be reassuring to tourists who like their comforts guaranteed. The rooms are indeed bright, modern, and comfortable, though not in the luxury class, and all have private facilities, balcony, minibar, telephone, television and air conditioning. Breakfast is served on the rooftop terrace with a fine view of the Acropolis.

ACROPOLIS HOUSE, *Odos Kodrou 6-8. Tel. 01/322-2344, Fax 01/ 324-4143. Rates (with tax): Drs 11,250 single; Drs 17,000 double. Breakfast included. 19 rooms. Visa (by arrangement only).*

Room rates here may vary considerably, depending on what facilities the room has or doesn't have (more for air conditioning; less for no ensuite bathroom). The Acropolis House is one of the best bets in Plaka, and is spread across two characterful buildings: a 120-year-old "old" building, and a 60-year-old "new" building next door. High-ceilinged rooms, an eclectic mix of furnishings, and a cheery, helpful owner in Panos, complement its tranquil location on the edge of Plaka. Services include a fridge on each floor, a book-swap zone, and free use of the washing machine after four days. Biggest drawback, particularly for those on the fourth floor, is the lack of an elevator.

ATHOS, *Odos Patrou 3. Tel. 01/322-1977, Fax 01/321-0548. Rates (with tax): Drs 13,000 single; Drs 17,000 double. Breakfast included. 18 rooms. No credit cards.*

The Athos is the kind of marble-rich hotel that looks as if it would accept all major credit cards, yet it doesn't accept any. That is in spite of its modern, marble-rich façade, and rooms that are brightly furnished and come equipped with air conditioning, private bathroom, telephone, television and minibar. Toss in a restaurnt, lobby bar, room service, a laundry, dry-cleaning and ironing service, and you have a hotel that would grace any credit card bill, and more particularly your stay in Plaka should you prefer modern comforts to downhome charm.

ADONIS, *Odos Kodrou 3. Tel. 01/324-9737, Fax 323-1602. Rates (with tax): Drs 13,000 single; Drs 16,000 double. Breakfast included. 26 rooms. No credit cards.*

An elevator, balconies, and a roof terrace where breakfast is served and which has a superb view of the Acropolis are the most notable of the Adonis's attractions. The rooms, though clean and adequately equipped, are nothing special – bathrooms are of the soggy toilet paper variety, as the showers have no curtains and the shower-heads spray water in all directions. That said, the Adonis is well located, has a helpful enough though scarcely enthusiastic staff and is in general an acceptable place.

PLAKA, *Odos Kapnikareas 7 (corner of Odos Mitropoleos). Tel. 0/322-2096, Fax 01/322-2412. Rates (with tax): Drs 15,500 single; Drs 19,200 double. Breakfast included. 67 rooms. American Express, Visa, MasterCard.*

At least it's easy to remember the name of this hotel, located on the edge of Plaka and convenient for the Monastiraki metro station. The brightly modern, air conditioned rooms have telephone and television, and minibar on request. A bar, restaurant, and rooftop garden round off the facilities at this highly popular lodging.

NEFELI, *Odos Iperidou 16. Tel. 01/322-8044, Fax 322-8045. Rates (with tax): Drs 12,000 single; Drs 15,000 double. Breakfast included. 18 rooms. No credit cards.*

A brightly lit lobby provides an introduction to the warm welcome you'll get at this modernized, family-run hotel. The rooms are small and without balcony but all are clean, and the fixtures and fittings are nicely chosen, if nothing fancy. All rooms have bathrooms in the room and include a shower. Breakfast is served in the big, bright entrance hall.

AVA, *Odos Lysikratou 9. Tel. 01/323-6618, Fax 01/323-1061. Rates (with tax): Drs 9,500 single; Drs 13,500 double; Drs 14,500 studio. Breakfast included. 17 rooms and studios. American Express, Visa, MasterCard.*

At first glance the Ava seems a gloomy looking place, and a second glance tends to confirm the original impression. Not much in the way of sprucing up has been done here probably since Pericles was a boy. Thinking positively, however, it is clean enough, the staff are friendly and you'll be shaving a few thousand drachs off the price of similar accommodation elsewhere in Plaka.

JOHN'S PLACE, *Odos Patrou 5. Tel. 01/322-9719; no fax. Rates (with tax): Drs 6,000 single; Drs 7,000 double. No breakfast. 14 rooms. No credit cards.*

John's is a guesthouse rather than a hotel, for whatever the difference is worth. In fact, for travelers on a tight budget it's probably worth a lot, although don't forget you'll also have to stump up for an off-premises breakfast. However, the rooms are very modestly priced (including in some a third bed for no extra charge) and if they are very modestly equipped too, they are still clean and quite comfortable. Bathrooms with bathtubs and toilets with shower are outside in the hall.

Plateia Omonia

Why anyone wants to stay in the Omonia Square area is slightly beyond me, although I suppose it does have a kind of bustle – I wouldn't go nearly so far as to call it charm. However, searching for some other pluses, it is fairly central, close to the two railway stations, the National Archaeological Museum and the National Theater, and there are lots of shops, buses, and Athenians hereabouts. Anyway, there are hotels here, so some people must find a reason to stay.

TITANIA, *Leoforos Panepistimiou 52. Tel. 01:330-0111, Fax 01/330-0700. Rates (with tax): Drs 19,900 single; Drs 24,900 double. Breakfast Drs 2,300. 398 rooms. All credit cards.*

A completely refurbished hotel that has changed dramatically for the better and is located beside the university complex, virtually on Plateia Omonia and very convenient for the metro station and for the bus and trolleybus network that focuses on the square. There is an elegant restaurant serving both Greek and international cuisine, a coffee shop, piano bar and cocktail lounge, as well as parking garage and a rooftop terrace with a panoramic view. Babysitting is available and there is a parking garage in adjacent Odos Fidiou.

PALMYRA, *Odos Marnis 42. Tel. 01/524-5412, Fax 01/524-5412. Rates (with tax): Drs 15,400 single; Drs 17,600 double. Breakfast included. 90 rooms. Visa, MasterCard.*

One of the best moderately priced hotels in the area – indeed one that offers an excellent quality-price ratio taking the city as a whole. It lies between Plateia Omonia and the railway stations, and is modern inside and out, which makes a contrast in terms of freshness compared to some of the more characterful buildings in the city whose rooms favor the dingy side of life. They all have private bath and telephone, and although they lack a television, there is a television lounge. The bar is also kind of freash and pleasant.

Plateia Syntagma

The good thing about Plateia Syntagma is that it's central; the bad thing about it is, well, that it's central, because in Athens being in the center means noise, crowds, and air pollution. Not everyone minds these downside factors, as they apply to city centers the world over, and the upside of being where the action is presumably compensates.

GRANDE BRETAGNE, *Plateia Syntagma. Tel. 01/331-4444, Fax 322-8034; US and Canada toll-free Tel. 800-325-3589; United Kingdom toll-free Tel. 0800-353535; Australia toll-free 1800-073535; New Zealand toll-free Tel. 0800-443535; Ireland toll-free Tel. 1800-535353. Rates (with tax): Drs 75,000 single; Drs 84,000 double; Drs 125,000. Breakfast Drs 3,600. 364 rooms (including 23 suites). All credit cards.*

If you want to rub shoulders with royalty, statespersons, rock stars and common-or-garden millionaires, as well as less exalted folks, this is the place to do it, and all things considered it won't cost you too much for the privilege (if privilege it be). Members of the Kennedy, Rockefeller, and Rothschild clans as well as Indira Gandhi and Winston Churchill are among the august ones who have laid their heads to rest here, though not all at the same time. The Grande Bretagne dates from 1862 and used to be the Greek royal guesthouse, taking up its present role as a hotel in 1872, yet palatial it remains. Among its luxuries are marble floors and walls, chandeliers, magnificent tapestries and fine paintings, Georgian, Victorian and Edwardian furnishings, antiques, and candelabras with real beeswax candles that you can light in them. Who could ask for more?

Well, some people ask for a sports and health center and a swimming pool, but there the Grande Bretagne can't accommodate you. Try instead the hotel's Winter Garden with its colorful glass roof, the belle époque ballroom, the gourmet GB Corner Restaurant and the long, darkly wood-paneled GB Bar. Guest rooms and suites all have air conditioning, satellite television, music center, telephone, minibar, and marble bathtubs. There is 24-hour room service. You'll also get good views of the Acropolis from some rooms. The Grande Bretagne is an ITT Sheraton Luxury Collection hotel and was fully refurbished in 1991.

N.J.V. MERIDIEN, *Plateia Syntagma (corner of Odos Vasiliou Georgiou and Odos Stadiou). Tel. 01/325-5301, Fax 01/323-5856; US and Canada toll-free Tel. 800-543-4300; United Kingdom Tel. 0171/439-1244. Rates (with tax): Drs 80,000 single; Drs 90,000 double; Drs 150,000 suite. Breakfast Drs 3,900. 183 rooms and suites. All credit cards.*

Almost as well situated as the Grande Bretagne, the Meridien lacks the cachet of its historic neighbor but compensates with lower prices and the French style of its owners which guarantees that the in-hotel cuisine is formidable. In addition to a rooftop-terrace restaurant with a view of the Acropolis, there is the Marco Polo Restaurant, a graceful, hall-of-mirrors dining room specializing in Mediterranean cuisine, including Greek dishes; Café Columbus, a dazzlingly bright atrium crêperie; and the moody, leather-upholstered Explorer's Lounge. You'll have gathered that the resident theme is exploration, and if you explore the rooms you'll find them modern and tastefully decorated. Facilities include air conditioning and soundproofing, satellite television and in-house video, minibar, telephone, all-marble bathrooms that also have telephones, and balconies. Other services include 24-hour room service, laundry and valet, and babysitting.

ACHILLEAS, *Odos Lekka 21. Tel. 322-5826, Fax 01/324-1092. Rates (with tax): Drs 11,300 single; Drs 13,900 double. Breakfast included. 34 rooms. American Express, Visa.*

Just off the north end of Plaka and west of Plateia Syntagma, the Achilleas is a good, moderately priced choice for someone who wants to be central but doesn't fancy being in Plaka. It has a high standard of comfort for its price range, having been completely renovated and modernized in 1995. All rooms are tastefully decorated and have air conditioning, telephone, and television (some big rooms have twin double beds). A rooftop garden terrace offers a good view of the city center and to the Acropolis.

WHERE TO EAT

Dining out in Athens has a quality of excitement attached to it that is matched in few other big cities. One reason is that eating is the big pastime here, the highlight of the day. Sure, there are cultural and nightlife options too. But do you think any Athenian will pass up the chance of a good meal just to go to the opera? Not a chance.

Another reason is that eating out is a genuine pleasure, even in the simplest of neighborhood tavernas. As for choice, if you don't trip over at least a dozen restaurants within three minues of leaving your hotel, you're lodging in the wrong area. Wise up and check out.

To be sure, that choice mostly comprises Greek restaurants. In an area like Plaka, they stand in great lines, often with little obvious difference in price and quality between them. Yet Athens and the Athenians are still close to the village and island roots of Greek cuisine, and the most satisfying of culinary experiences in the city is to join the locals in their favorite taverna, and pile in alongside them.

ATHENS DINING FINDS & FAVORITES

In descending order of price, these are eateries that stand out as temples of good food, and which should leave a pleasant aftertaste in the memory of anyone who dines within.

• **Fourtouna**, *Odos Anapiron Polemou 22. Tel. 01/722-1282. Drs 6,500 to Drs 9,000. Deeply satisfying seafood.*

• **Eden**, *Odos Lissiou 12. Tel. 01/324-8858. Drs 4,000 to Drs 8,000. Stylish vegetarian restaurant.*

• **Epistrofi Stin Ithaki**, *Odos Em Benaki 45b, Exarhia. Tel. 01382-7523. Drs 4,000 to Drs 7,000. Stylish good food and personal service.*

• **Ouzeri Kouklis**, *Odos Tripodon 14. Tel. 01/324-7605. Drs 2,500 to Drs 4,000. Charming traditional eatery.*

• **O Platanos**, *Odos Diogenou 4. Tel. 01/322-0666. Drs 2,500 to Drs 4,000. Equally charming traditional eatery.*

Kolonaki

FOURTOUNA, *Odos Anapiron Polemou 22. Tel. 01/722-1282. Drs 6,500 to Drs 9,000. No credit cards. Seafood.*

Located at the foot of Likavitos Hill on the fringe of well-heeled Kolonaki, and famed throughout the city, Fourtouna is a godsend to the seafood lover in Athens whose standards are ocean deep yet whose pockets are shallow. You can think what you like of the boat-shaped buffet from which you select your very own denizens of the deep; what's lying on the deck is what counts, fresh off the boat from Piraeus. A fish m*eze* (appetizer) with ouzo or wine makes an ideal meal here

RODIA, *Odos Aristippou 44. Tel. 01/722-9883. Drs 5,000 to Drs 8,000. No credit cards. Traditional.*

You can get high after eating at Rodia – by taking the funicular at the end of the street up Likavitos Hill. On second thought, the dining here is enough of a high all by itself, not excluding the prices and the altitude of the noses of the clientele. Still, credit where no credit cards are due: Rodia does the business on the plate, with Greek dishes that are well above average in taste and refinement, and the ambience is warm and cozy. The chef is a black belt at oregano, and the herb appears in numerous dishes.

Koukaki

STROFI, *Odos Robertou Galli 25. Tel. 01/219-4130. Drs 3,500 to Drs 5,500. Visa, MasterCard. Greek chic.*

From the rooftop tables at this elegant restaurant you have a fine view of the Acropolis, looking up over the ruins of the Odeion of Herodes Atticus. The theatrical connection is appropriate as owner Vassilios Manologlou is a former head chef from the restaurant of the Athens National Opera, and there is more than a little theater in his presentation. On the walls are pictures of celebrity guests, including Rudolf Nureyev, Leonard Bernstein, Mikis Theodorakis, Nana Mouskouri, members of the Bolshoi Ballet, and that noted tightrope-walker Mikhail Gorbachev. Lamb dishes are the house specialty, but the extensive menu should have something for everyone.

Mets

MYRTIA, *Odos Trivonianou 32-34. Tel. 01/924-7175. Drs 10,000 to Drs 15,000. American Express, Diners Club, Visa, MasterCard. Downhome chic.*

Well, yes, downhome in the sense of how it looks and how it acts. How many traditional Greek village tavernas will set you back up to Drs 15,000 for a meal? Not many. Yet Myrtia, located near the Olympic Stadium, is nothing if not popular with in-crowd Athenians: enough that you may be advised to make reservations at especially busy times such as Friday and Saturday evening. Quality rules here, and if you can see past the pretensions and fake rusticity, the intrinsic good taste of the cooking shines through.

Plaka

Plaka stands out as a uniquely welcoming and attractive district. Here you can eat and drink to your heart's content, at a taverna's outdoor terrace or in a warm and smoky bouzouki bar; experiencing traditional Greek food or its more modern and fancier incarnations. Atmosphere and taste are all but guaranteed; the prices are mostly what the French would call "democratic;" and at many eateries you will dine shoulder-to-shoulder with Athenians who admire all those characteristics quite as much as, if not more than, you do.

MILTONS, *Odos Adrianou 91. Tel. 01/324-9129. Drs 7,000 to Drs 15,000. American Express, Diners Club, Visa, MasterCard. Modern.*

Greek cuisine meets international at Miltons, a different kind of Plaka dining experience. This translates into higher prices, yet the food and the service is far more refined than the Plaka norm. A particular specialty is red snapper flambéed in ouzo, and expertly topped, tailed, and fileted at your table. Shrimps flambéed in brandy are equally memorable. The light and airy terrace is separated from the street bustle by glass partitions and plants.

EDEN, *Odos Lissiou 12. Tel. 01/324-8858. Drs 4,000 to Drs 8,000. American Express, Diners Club, Visa. Vegetarian.*

Take all the Greek dishes you've come to know and love, remove the meat, and serve them up in a sober, arty ambience, and you have the basic ingredients of this garden of Eden. There is one more, however: the intrinsic good taste of meals prepared with thought and care rather than the "pile-em-high" approach of most tavernas. Eden is more popular with young professionals than with beads-and-sandals vegetarians. Its non-smoking section makes it a pearl beyond price in Athens. You shouldn't find it hard to locate Eden, as there are rather more signs in Plaka pointing out the way than there are for the Acropolis.

DAPHNE'S, *Odos Lyssikratou 4. Tel. 01/322-7971. Drs 4,000 to Drs 7,000. American Express, Diners Club, Visa, MasterCard. Greek chic.*

"Thank you for a lovely evening," wrote an apparently satisfied customer called Hillary Rodham Clinton on March 29, 1996. Of course it might have been the Hillary Rodham Clinton from the London Borough of Tooting, and even if it wasn't can you really trust the culinary views of a woman whose husband's highest edible delight is the great American hamburger? Yes, you can, and thanks for the tip, Hillary. The walls here are covered in murals that took the artist two years to create. Your meal will probably arrive quicker.

BYZANTINO, *Odos Kydathinaion 18. Tel. 01/322-7368. Drs 3,000 to Drs 6,000. American Express, Diners Club, Visa, MasterCard. Traditional.*
A bit more upmarket than the "average" Plaka taverna, although not so far up that it has lost its local flavor, Byzantino (or Vizantino as the name is also written) adds some fish specialties to the usual moussaka and grilled meats. The street terrace lies maybe too much in the flood of passersby; inside is better though not exactly tranquil either. A point-and-eat kind of place that changes its standard taverna menu by maybe one dish a day.
BAKALIARAKIA, *Odos Kydathinaion 41. Tel. 01/322-5084. Drs 3,000 to Drs 5,000. No credit cards. Traditional.*
This popular family-owned taverna in a basement on one of the Plaka's main streets dates from 1865, a time so remote in Athens' history that the capital was then little more than a hick provincial town – and no doubt a lot prettier than it is today. Bakaliarakia is very popular with locals and has an uncanny ability to fill up in the twinkling of an eye just after 8 pm: one second all the tables are free; the next they're all occupied. The dishes are individually prepared (usually fried), not already simmering in big pots. Try the dry white house wine for a real treat.
XYONOS, *Odos Angelou Geronta 4. Tel. 01/322-1065. Drs Drs 3,000 to Drs 5,000. No credit cards. Traditional.*
You can't get much more traditional than a taverna that's never felt the need to change its chairs or tables since it opened in 1935, and wouldn't recognize a credit card if one turned up in the *giouvetsi*. Xyonos is just such a place. It's kind of murky inside and has the feel of an eatery that has served one plate too many in its time. Don't let that fool you though: its lamb specialties in particular are a byword in Athens and beyond. This the old-style Plaka at its best. The house retsina is excellent.
THESPIS, *Odos Thespidos 18. Tel. 01/323-8242. Drs 2,500 to Drs 4,500. No credit cards. Traditional.*
A rambling taverna that spreads through several white-painted houses and terraces on different levels among the trees and narrow alleyways directly below the Acropolis cliff. Its colorful location coupled with a none-too inspired menu, make Thespis seem more suited to an alfresco tourist-trail lunch than to serious evening dining. In this more limited role

it fits the bill perfectly. If you don't mind having more groovy felines around than an episode of *Top Cat,* then you'll probably love this place. **OUZERI KOUKLIS,** *Odos Tripodon 14. Tel. 01/324-7605. Drs 2,500 to Drs 4,000. No credit cards. Traditional.*

Also known as To Gerani, there can be few more traditional tavernas in Athens than this one, where a fixed number of menu choices are prepared each day and you select which ones you want in the kitchen or let the waiter bring them to your table on a tray for your perusal instead. There can also be fewer concessions made to tourists, and there is no English menu. It's unlikely you'll be disappointed though, as the food has that undefinable magic ingredient called taste. Sit outside on the porch terrace and flambé your own sausages in ouzo.

O PLATANOS, *Odos Diogenou 4. Tel. 01/322-0666. Drs 2,500 to Drs 4,000. No credit cards. Traditional.*

You have to walk a short way from the bright lights of the main Plaka restaurant district, along a string of narrow alleyways off Odos Adrianou, before you come to Platanos. You'll find it in a tiny, tree-fringed square and you'll recognize it easily enough by the stream of local people heading there to dine simply and cheaply on no-frills Greek food. The atmosphere in this usually crowded taverna is noisy, warm, and friendly, although the service is a bit distracted at times. Choose your dishes from among the mass of pots in the kitchen and wash them down with the house retsina, which may well be the best in Athens.

Plateia Omonia

EPISTROFI STIN ITHAKI, *Odos Em Benaki 45b, Exarhia. Tel. 01382-7523. Drs 4,000 to Drs 7,000. Visa, MasterCard. Greek gourmet.*

In describing this ouzeri as "gourmet Greek," I'm merely reaching for a way to do justice to the meze specialties and other courses here. It has nothing to do with fat pocketbooks and Michelin stars – just look at the price range. Located in the Exarhia district to the east of Platei Omonia, Epistrofi aims to bring some of the legendary spirit of Ithaca, the homeland that Odysseus loved as much as life itself, to the busy streets of Athens. Note that this is a spiritual question (as is all good food), not a marketing device for Ithacan cuisine. Owners Georgios Vrailas and Giannis Mavroulakis genuinely make you feel a share in the age-old Hellenic civilization as you eat their fine food, washed down by superb wine from the barrel, in their simply decorated yet warmly atmospheric gem.

DAFNI, *Odos Ioulianou 65. Tel. 01/829-3914. Drs 3,000 to Drs 6,000. Visa, MasterCard. Traditional.*

Dafni is a traditional, rustic taverna lying between the National Archaeological Museum and Areos Park. On summer days you eat outside in a garden, under trellises, watched over by retsina barrels, and the food is as rustic and traditional – and as tasty – as the surroundings. Choose your dishes from the kitchen.

Plateia Syntagma

GB CORNER, *Hotel Grande Bretagne, Plateia Syntagma. Tel. 01/323-0251. Drs 5,000 to Drs 9,000. All credit cards. International.*

This place might sound like a corner café; in fact it's the restaurant of the Hotel Grande Bretagne, and a fancy spot in which to spot the business and political élite of Athens. Sounds boring? Well, it's more dull than boring. Takes itself too seriously by half, with its leather upholstery and lordly attitudes. You'll get good food, though, and can mix various international dishes with Greek ones – though ideally not on the same plate.

APOTSOS, *Leoforos Panepistimiou 10. Tel. 01/363-7046. Drs 3,000 to Drs 6,000. No credit cards. Traditional.*

One of the great Athens dining exeriences, more for the ambience than the food, although the meze in this fin de siècle ouzeri was a favorite of the late Jackie Kennedy Onassis and her husband Aristotle Onassis. It is still a haunt of celebs, politicos, arty types and assorted scribblers – legends in their own lunchtimes – while even some ordinary people manage to squeeze in amid the ruckus of the chattering classes. The visual style of Athens's belle époque (augmented, sad to say, by fluorescent striplighting) is what grabs you on entering and you eat surrounded by turn-of-the-century advertising slogans. Diners sit on village kafenion-style chairs at tiny tables; be careful with the ten ouzo and raki varieities on the menu if you don't want to slide off the former and under the latter. Apotsos is a daytime option only, open only from 11 am to 5 pm.

KENTRIKON, *Odos Kolokotroni 3 or Odos Voulis 7. Tel. 01/323-2482. Drs 3,000 to Drs 6,000. American Express, Diners Club, Visa, MasterCard.* Greek/international.

A big, brightly lit place that is not so easy to spot as it is inside a small arcaded square. The air conditioning is welcome on a hot day. Because this is more of a business area than a tourist one, luchtime tends to be busier and more animated than the evenings – well, it couldn't help but be, because Kentrikon is closed in the evening and on weekends. Dishes in this restaurant are not *so* much different from those of a good Plaka taverna, although they are generally prepared with greater care and less olive oil; the main difference is in the polished service and a clientele mostly composed of Athens professionals.

INTERNATIONAL CUISINE

If you feel the need to try something other than Greek food, you will find that Athens is not one of the world's great multiethnic metropolises. Still, there is a choice even if it is not a great one.

The following are a few suggestions in and near the city that are worth your while:

Chinese

• **Chai Long**, *Odos Mnisikleous 7b, Plaka. Tel. 01/331-4323*
• **Chang's House**, *Odos Doiranis 15, Kalithea. Tel. 01/959-5179*
• **China**, *Odos Efroniou 72, Ilissia. Tel. 01/723-3200*
• **Dim Sum**, *Odos Andrianeiou 46, Neo Psichico. Tel. 01/687-3327*
• **Far East** (serves also Japanese and Korean dishes), *Odos Stadiou 7, Syntagma. Tel. 01/323-4996*
• **Golden Dragon**, *Leoforos Syngrou 122, Koukaki. Tel. 01/923-2316*
• **Kowloon**, *Odos Kyprou, Glyfada. Tel. 01/894-4528*

French

• **Aubrevoir**, *Odos Xenokratous 51, Kolonaki. Tel. 01/722-9106*
• **Blue Pine**, *Odos Tsaldari 37, Kifissia. Tel. 01/807-7745*
• **Calvados**, *Odos Alkmanous 5, Ilissia. Tel. 01/722-6291*
• **Prunier**, *Odos Ipsilandou, Kolonaki. Tel. 01/722-7379*
• **Le Saint-Germain**, *Odos Chrstoforou Nezer 19, Glyfada. Tel. 01/894-4439*

Indian

• **Curry Palace**, *Leforos Possidonos 38b, Kalamaki. Tel. 01/983-8889*
• **Maharajah**, *Odos Notara 122 Piraeus. Tel. 01/429-4161*

Italian

• **Al Convento**, *Odos Anapiron Polemou 4-6, Kolonaki. Tel. 01/723-9163*
• **Barolo**, *Odos Adrianou 3, Thissio. Tel. 01/321-2512*
• **Casa di Pasta**, *Odos Gortinias 11, Kifissia. Tel. 01/623-3361*
• **Mona Lisa**, *Odos Loukianou 36, Kolonaki. Tel. 01/721-0385*
• **Sale e Pepe**, *Odos Aristipou 34, Kolonaki. Tel. 01/723-4102*

Japanese

• **Kiku**, *Odos Dimokritou 12, Kolonaki. Tel. 01/364-7033*
• **Kyoto**, *Odos Garivaldi 5, Koukaki. Tel. 01/924-1406*
• **Mitsiko**, *Odos Kidathineon 27, Plaka. Tel. 01/322-0980*

Lebanese

• **O Kipos tis Edem**, *Odos Ghini 19, Halandri. Tel. 01/685-3580*
• **Lahmantzoun**, *Akti Moutsopoulou 9, Piraeus. Tel. 01/413-5654*

Spanish

• **Comilon**, *Odos Varnali 26, Halandri. Tel. 01/682-6849*
• **Ispanika Gonia**, *Odos Theagenous 22, Pangrati. Tel. 01/723-1393*
• **Sevilla**, *Odos Theognidos 11-13, Agios Sostis. Tel. 01/923-3941*

Tex-Mex

• **American Classic**, *Odos Vasileos Pavlou 85, Kastela. Tel. 01/413-2953*

- **Blue Velvet**, *Odos Ermou 116, Thission. Tel. 01/323-9047*
- **Buffalo Bill's**, *Odos Kyprou 13, Glyfada. Tel. 01/894-3128*
- **Chilis**, *Odos Panagouli 6, Glyfada. Tel. 01/894-7281*
- **Dos Hermanos**, *Odos Kyriazi 24, Kfissia. Tel. 01/808-0020*
- **Rio Grande**, *Odos Loukianou 40, Kolonaki. Tel. 01/721-2642*

Vietnamese
- **Vietnam**, *Odos Achilloes 91, Amphithea. Tel. 01/981-8029*

SEEING THE SIGHTS
History, History, & Yet More History

Tourists have been coming to gawp at Athens's classical sites since at least the 5th century BC. If some of the victors of the Peloponnesian War had had their way, there would be no such sites left for us to gawp at, nor even a souvlaki stall, as they wanted defeated Athens erased from the face of the earth. Fortunately, the victors-in-chief, the otherwise dour and hard-handed Spartans, wouldn't allow this on the grounds that Athens had done all Greeks a big favor by its valiant resistance to the earlier Persian invasions.

So let's hear it for those fabulous Spartans, folks...

ATHENS SIGHTS FINDS & FAVORITES

- *The Parthenon. Even in ruins the ancient Temple of Athena Parthenos is quite possibly the most beautiful building on the planet.*
- *National Archaeological Museum. You'll come face to face here with the astonishing wealth of the finest surviving works of ancient Greece.*
- *National Garden. Amidst Athens' notorious smog, this big green park in the middle of the city is literally a breath of fresh air.*
- *Evzones. The fantastically uniformed soldiers who perform some weird and wonderful military maneuvers in front of the Parliament building.*
- *Anafiotika. Cyclades Islands village-style district lying beneath the Acropolis, on the edge of Plaka.*

Acropolis

You don't have to start your tour program with the Acropolis, *Tel. 01/ 321-0185; open Monday to Friday 8 am to 6:30 pm (4:30 pm in winter), Saturday and Sunday 8:30 am to 6:30 pm (4:30 pm in winter); admission Drs 2,000, students Drs 1,000, free on Sunday.* It may even be an idea to tease yourself for a few days with the sight of those ghostly columns and pediments floating in the hazy, nefos-suffused Athenian air, atop their rocky pinnacle. As you move through Athens, they have a tendency to appear at unexpected moments, from behind a vista of concrete apartment blocks, or through the windows of a passing bus that has very nearly run over your toes, or when you throw open your hotel room window in the morning. The temples have waited almost 2,500 years for your visit: they can afford to wait a few hours longer.

When you finally bestir yourself to go there, *don't* take a tour-bus to the entrance-gate, nor a taxi, nor a public bus. Walk through **Plaka** in the restful early morning, before the street-terrace taverna cacophony gets under way, and climb up through any of the streets leading to the pastel-shaded cottages of **Anafiotika**, nestled under the northern face of the Acropolis. Breathe in the freshening air and the atmosphere as you go, then walk along the tree-lined pathway to the entrance at the western end of the hill.

The Acropolis – the "City on the Rock" – is where human habitation in Athens began during the Neolithic period. Jutting 90 meters above its surroundings, the rocky hill was easily defensible, and as the ancient city grew and the population spread out from this protected core, the Acropolis became instead a religious center dominated by the cult of the city's protectress, the goddess Athena. What you see now are the remains of temples that date mostly from the age of Pericles, who controlled the city's affairs during the Golden Age of Athens between 461 and 429 BC.

You enter the Acropolis proper along the route of the ancient Panathenaic Procession, through a massive ceremonial gateway, the **Propylaea**, dating from 438-432 BC. The entrance is overlooked on the right by the beautiful little **Temple of Athena Nike**, 427-424 BC, and on the left by the ugly **Tower of Agrippa**, a monumental 2nd-century BC plinth which in 27 BC was kitted out with a now lost statue of Marcus Agrippa, the commander who won all the Roman Emperor Augustus's battles for him.

Once through the Propylaea, in ancient times you would have been confronted by a 9-meter-high bronze statue of **Athena Promachos**, sculpted by Phidias in about 458 BC. This was Athens's way of thanking the goddess for her help in seeing off the Persian invasion of 480 BC (ignoring the fact that the Persians had razed the city to the ground). It was said that Athenian sailors rounding Cape Sounion could see the sun glinting on the tip of the goddess's spear. Nowadays, you are confronted by a jumble of rubble that archaeologists say was the base of the statue, and sailors rounding Cape Sounion see only apartment blocks and smog.

Next up, dead ahead, is the **Parthenon**, an undistinguished heap of mouldering old stones, barely worth a second glance. (Just kidding.) This is, of course, the star of the show. Some would argue that all architectural endeavor since this emblematic building was raised between 447 and 432 BC has been a waste of effort, as the great temple commissioned by Pericles represents ultimate perfection and can never be surpassed, although it has been much imitated down the millennia.

The bare-bones facts are that the Parthenon was designed by Iktinos, put together by Callicrates, embellished by Phidias, and constructed in Pentelic marble. Those who see it as the greatest monument to the democratic spirit would do well to remember that it was paid for by money extorted from contributors to the Athenian protection racket we call the Delian League. Yet it is certainly the greatest monument to *something*, and inconvenient details can be overlooked in favor of its sheer beauty, even in ruins, and the miracle that it has survived at all the almost 25 turbulent centuries that separate us from its builders.

There are no straight lines in the Parthenon: if extended in space, all its subtly curved axes would meet at a point beyond the building itself. It is eight closely spaced Doric columns in width and 17 columns in length, marking another break from the more traditional, smaller, and squarer style of Greek temple. The Parthenon cost 470 talents of silver (a talent weighed just under 26 kilograms) at a time when the state's annual budget, excluding payments from the Delian League, amounted to some 400 talents.

Sculpture played a big part in the Parthenon's marble hymn to the eternal glory of Athens: both pediments had elaborately conceived sculpture groups featuring Zeus and Athena; there were 92 sculpted metopes; and a 160-meter frieze depicting the annual Panathenaic Procession ran around the outer wall of the cella. Some sculptures remain on the Parthenon, some are in the Acropolis Museum, and others are on display in various foreign museums (see sidebar below, *Lord of the Marbles*).

In the Parthenon's inner sanctum stood a 12-meter-high, chryselephantine (gold-and-ivory) statue of **Athena Parthenos**, sculpted by Phidias, which cost more than the temple itself and required some 40 talents of pure gold in its construction, according to the historian Thucydides. Homer's "Athena of the flashing eyes" had its most awesome representation here, as the huge eyes were made of gemstones. The statue was apparently destroyed by fire after being removed to Constantinople in 400 AD.

Since tourists are not allowed inside the Parthenon, the only thing you can do is walk around the outside, thinking whatever thoughts you find appropriate to the occasion, and more likely than not trying to avoid bumping into about 3,000 other people doing likewise.

Follow that, as Phidias probably didn't say. The **Erechtheion** does a good job of following the Parthenon's class act. Built in fits and starts during the long Peloponnesian War and probably completed in 395 BC, the little temple facing the Parthenon, and dedicated to Erechtheus, Athena, and Poseidon, is an oddly shaped building graced by the six famous **Caryatids**. These sculpted maidens doing duty as columns supporting a little porch are not actually the six famous caryatids, but copies – 25 years of Athens's acid rain having done more damage than 2,500 years of rough-and-tumble history. The originals are now kept behind glass in the Acropolis Museum (except for one which is in the British Museum).

Between the Erechtheion and the Pantheon you might be able to make out faint traces of an earlier **Temple of Athena**, destroyed by the Persians in 480 BC, and the **Altar of Zeus**. Continuing to the eastern end of the Parthenon, there are more substantial signs of the **Temple of Rome and Augustus**, a *tholos* (circular temple) dedicated to the boorish new masters of the world in 27 BC. It probably spoiled the entire Acropolis in its time (but everyone likely assured Augustus that it was exactly what the place needed).

Beside this enigmatic ruin is the **Acropolis Museum**, *Tel. 01/323-6665; open Monday 11 am to 6:30 pm (4:30 pm in winter), Tuesday to Sunday 8:30 am to 6:30 pm (4:30 pm in winter); admission included in the price of the Acropolis ticket.* The museum is filled with alarming sculptures of people with parts missing, suggesting that ancient Athens was populated by amputees. You can thank the Persians for this impression, as they were the ones who smashed up the Acropolis's archaic statues.

The Athenians later buried the bits and pieces, and much later still delighted archaeologists dug them up. In one sculpture group an enraged Athena, with bristling aegis (shield), gets ready to sock it to a wimpy giant, in a tolerable impersonation of Miss Piggy zapping Kermit. A more elegant *kore* (female figure) still shows traces of paint, reminding us that in ancient times the entire Acropolis was colored like a garish fairground attraction.

From the Acropolis's southern ramparts you get a fine view over another group of ancient monuments built into the Acropolis hillside: the **Theater of Dionysos**, dating from around 330 BC, and the **Odeion of Herodes Atticus**, a theater that opened in 174 AD and still hosts performances of ancient Greek plays today, although there was a 1,500-year intermission between times. *Odos Dionissiou Areopagitou. Tel. 01/322-4625. Open daily 9 am to 2:30 pm. Admission Drs 500, students Drs 300.* Between them lie the ruins of the 2nd-century BC **Stoa of Eumenes II**, and other odds and ends such as the fragmentary **Asklepieion** (420-300 BC).

LORD OF THE MARBLES

The British **Lord Elgin** occupies a distinguished place in the Greek pantheon of historical rogues. To understand why, you must visit the **British Museum** in London, whose star attraction is the **Elgin Marbles** – sculptures from the Parthenon removed by him when he was Britain's ambassador to the Ottoman Sublime Porte in Constantinople at the start of the 19th century.

Greece was then an unwilling part of the Ottoman empire, or "under the dead hand of the Turk" as the Greeks would have it. Elgin sought and received permission from the Ottoman authorities, who could care less about some bits and pieces of old Greek rubble, to ship them to England for safekeeping.

In so doing, the good lord may have saved the marbles from the attentions of genuine looters, or destruction in the Greek War of Liberation, and certainly from the effects of Athens's noxious 20th-century atmosphere. He bankrupted himself in the course of what he clearly thought was a noble endeavor. Whatever the rights and wrongs of the case, the Greeks want their marbles back and the British Museum is hanging on to them, arguing that it acquired them perfectly legally. Possession, of course, is nine-tenths of the law.

In a minor footnote to this cultural tug-of-war, anyone who plays chess using one of those no-nonsense, straight-up chess sets with carved wooden pieces, holds a bit of the Parthenon in their hands, in a manner of speaking, each time they make a knight move. The piece's head is modeled on the horse's head removed from the Parthenon's east pediment by Elgin.

If you don't believe me, check.

Getting Down to the Agora

There was nothing an ancient Athenian liked better after a hard day's sacrificing up on the Acropolis than to wander down into the Agora and chew the fat with his buddies. The Agora was the combined marketplace, business center, and center of government. Athenians then, as now, lived life outdoors as much as possible, and the Agora was where they hung out. *Odos Adrianou (north side), Odos Polignotou (east side), Plateia Theseio (west side). Tel. 01/321-0185. Open Tuesday to Sunday 8:30 am to 3 pm. Admission Drs 1,200, students Drs 600.*

Once inside the the archaeological park, you may be struck by two thoughts: that the Agora is a mightily confusing jumble of old stones, and that the many trees make a great shady place for a picnic. Both are accurate. Still, plans incised in bronze at various spots help you to make sense of the place. Remember that a thousand years of classical history (not to mention 500 years of Ottoman history that has been surgically removed) passed through here, time enough for things to change radically.

The north entrance on Odos Adrianou gives you a fine view of the Athens-Piraeus metro line that neatly bisects some of the Agora's historic ruins, leaving outside the boundary the **Stoa Poikile** (Painted Stoa), dating from about 450 BC and currently under excavation, where the Phoenician-Cypriot Zeno of Kition expounded his Stoic philosophy. Also on the wrong side of the tracks are the remains of the late 6th-century BC **Royal Stoa**, the office of the Archon, and a Roman-era basilica and colonnade.

Turn right past the hard-to-identify 5th-century BC **Altar and Temple of Ares**, a place that ancient Athenian pooches couldn't have liked much, as they were the principal performers in sacrifices to the war god here. Beyond this is what's left of the **Temple of Apollo Patroös**, and the nearby **Stoa of Zeus Eleutherios**, dating from around 430 BC, one of many places where Socrates yanked the chains of his fellow citizens so effectively that they sentenced him to death.

Keep climbing in this direction until you arrive at the **Hephaesteion** (also known as the **Theseion**), from the 440s BC, and said to be the best-preserved temple in the whole of Greece because its roof is mostly intact. Tourists are not allowed inside, however, and from the outside it doesn't look much different from temples whose roofs are mostly not intact, yet it is undoubtedly impressive.

From here you wander south then east back down into the Agora, to a cluster of government buildings dating from the 5th century BC – the **Boulouterion**, or city hall; the **Metroön**, where government archives were housed; and the **Tholos**, a circular hall where the council executives conducted city business. Facing these is a long, low plinth, the **Monument of the Eponymous Heroes**, which held statues representing the tribes of Attica and was also used as a public noticeboard. Beside this stands a replica of a headless, armless and legless **Statue of Hadrian** (how could they tell?).

The center of the Agora is dominated by the **Odeon of Agrippa**, a theater dating originally from 15 BC and rebuilt as a gymnasium 400 years later. It still has some massive statues of Tritons lining the entrance. Behind that are the remains of the long 2nd-century BC **Middle Stoa**.

Along the east end of the site is the **Stoa of Attalos**, which dates from 1956. That's no mistake: the original stoa, paid for by King Attalos II of Pergamum and built between 159 and 138 BC, was rebuilt in the 1950s with money donated by American stoa enthusiasts. It's interesting to see, yet somehow it takes away the magic of imagining what such a building would really have looked like – apparently much like a pre-concrete-and-glass-era bank or insurance company office. Inside, however, is the **Agora Museum**, *Tel. 01/321-0185; open Tuesday to Sunday 8:30 am to 3 pm; admission included in the price of the Agora ticket.* There are many finds from excavations here, including a little pottery beaker of the kind that Socrates used (perhaps the very one) to drink his fatal draught of hemlock.

A little way east of the main Agora site is the **Roman Agora**, on Odos Pelopida near Monastiraki metro station. One half of it, containing the 2nd-century AD **Library of Hadrian**, is closed due to ongoing excavations: if you put your nose through the railings, though, you get a good view of the book niches. The other half contains most notably the 2nd-century BC **Tower of the Winds**, *Tel. 01/324-5220; open Tuesday to Sunday 8:30 am to 3 pm; admission Drs 500, students Drs 300.* – in Greek, the Horologion of Andronicus Kyrrhestes). This is a charming, marble octagonal building that was a combined waterclock, sundial, and weathervane (and possibly planetarium). Each face has a relief representation of the wind that blew from that direction (see sidebar, *Of Time and Tides*, below). In the Ottoman period it was used as a fraternity house by the local Whirling Dervishes.

OF TIME & TIDES

The Tower of the Winds in the Roman Agora is a fascinating piece of ancient high tech. Although the sundial lines inscribed on the octagonal structure can still be seen, the weathervane and the mechanisms of its clepsydra (waterclock) are long since lost. Yet the basic principle of the clepsydra is known, as it was based on waterclocks designed by the inventor Ctesibios, who lived in Alexandria around 270 BC.

Water was siphoned at a constant rate from an elevated bronze cistern into another, smaller cistern in which was a hollow metal ball. As water flowed into the small cistern the ball slowly floated upwards. The ball was connected by a chain-and-pulley sytem to a disk inscribed with hour (and possibly constellation) signs which turned as the ball rose and so recorded the passing of time.

The revolving bronze Triton on the rooftop held a wand that pointed to the prevailing wind, identified by one of the eight relief panels depicting the particular wind blowing from each of the cardinal points. The sundial was the low-tech end of this multitasking sytem, while the domed ceiling may have been decorated with zodiacal signs, making the Tower the city planetarium as well.

The Roman City

Starting with Sulla's sack of Athens in 86 BC, the rotten Romans were always strutting around, "borrowing" pieces of Athenian sculpture or other movable assets, then "forgetting" to bring them back. Nero was just one of many such slick-haired, light-fingered Italian cads. There wasn't much the Athenians could safely do about it, other than make rude gestures when the Romans' backs were turned.

The philhellene Emperor Hadrian (ruled 117-138 AD), who was disdained by old-fashioned Romans as a "little Greek," set out to make amends. Among the results of his efforts were the **Arch of Hadrian**, which stands at the corner of Odos Amalias and Odos Andrea Singrou, marking the boundary of the "city of Theseus" and the "city of Hadrian."

Behind the arch can be seen the 15 surviving Corinthian columns of the 104 that once embellished the giant **Temple of Olympian Zeus** (or Olympieion), *Tel 01/922-6330, Leoforos Vasilissis Olgas; open Tuesday to Sunday 8:30 am to 3 pm; admission Drs 500, students Drs 300.* The temple was finished by Hadrian in about 130 AD, having been started no less than 645 years earlier by Peisistratus. One of the columns has been left lying where it fell during an earthquake, broken into neat salami-slices that make it easy to appreciate the effort that must have gone into making it.

Around the temple are bits and pieces of other ancient buildings, including a Roman-era bath house, and perhaps most interesting of all, the remains of the **Hippades** and **Diomeian Gates** in the **Themistoclean Wall**, dating from 479 BC, along with adjacent sections of the wall. It is interesting to compare these sections with the description in Thucydides' *History of the Peloponnesian War,* in which he tells of the wall's rapid construction in the aftermath of the Persian invasion, using any materials that came to hand, while Themistocles maneuvered to keep the unenthusiastic Spartans in the dark until its completion.

Dead Center

A little to the west of the Theseio metro station is the entrance to **Kerameikos**, *Odos Ermou 148, Tel. 01/346-3552; open Tuesday to Sunday 8:30 am to 3 pm; admission Drs 500, students Drs 300.* This is the cemetery of ancient Athens. The site includes two of the most important gates in the **Themistoclean Wall**: the **Dipylon Gate** and the **Sacred Gate**, with the cemetery lying outside the walls. Along either side of the **Street of the Tombs** are many funerary monuments with sculptures, reliefs, and inscriptions.

Among them is a copy of the **Stele of Hegeso**, a sculptured relief showing a deceased woman, identified in the inscription as Hegeso Proxeno, taking a jewel from a box held by a servant girl – a moving image of the simple, fleeting joys of life, whose poignancy still touches us across the centuries (the original is in the National Archaeological Museum). The on-site **Oberlaender Museum** has more of the same for people who prefer necromancing the stones indoors. Admission is included in the price of the Kerameikos ticket.

More than a kilometer further out, off Odos Alexandreas, is the location of **Plato's Academy**. Sadly, there is almost nothing to see, and little real point in trying, as the former groves of academe are swamped by modern buildings.

Homes of the Muses

Museums, actually, but don't you find that "Homes of the Muses" sounds more interesting?

If you only visit one museum in Athens, it should be the **National Archaeological Museum**, *Odos Patission 44. Tel. 01/821-7717; open Monday 12:30 to 7 pm, Tuesday to Friday 8 am to 7 pm, Saturday and Sunday 8:30 am to 3 pm (winter closing times from Monday to Friday is 5 pm); admission Drs 2,000, students Drs 1,000.* There are more than 50 exhibition rooms here, each of which merits close attention. Even if you devote only a minimal five minutes to each room you are still looking at four hours to get around.

For anyone who loves the history of ancient Greece, having studied it from afar, the most amazing thing about this museum may be the fact that so many images seen only in book and magazine illustrations really exist. There they are, behind glass, or standing right out in the open. The gold **Mycenaean royal death mask** that early archaeologist/explorer Heinrich Schliemann thought was "the face of Agamemnon" stares at you with sightless eyes from a time three centuries before the Trojan War; the **boy jockey** urges his bronze steed onwards in an endless race against competitors long since turned to dust; and **Poseidon** (or is it Zeus?) shows off the superhuman reproductive gear that gets so much exercise in Greek mythology.

Among many other highlights are the **Flying Fish Fresco** from Milos; the gravely dignified **Sounion Kouros**; a miniature of **Athena Parthenos** that was probably an ancient tourist souvenir and shows the general lines of Phidias's lost colossal statue of the goddess from the Parthenon; an amusing sculpture of an untypically, if understandably coy Aphrodite about to take her sandal to a satyr with wandering hands; the spellbindingly beautiful Minoan-era **Thira Frescoes**, including those of two boys boxing, and a fleet of ships at sea, from the island whose destruction in a volcanic eruption in 1470 BC may have given rise to the Atlantis legend; and the **Antikythera Computer**, a complex mechanical device that seems to have used to compute planetary movements.

Of pottery in all shapes and sizes, bronze and marble sculpture, funerary monuments, jewelry, household and personal objects, inscriptions, children's toys, and other objects from all over the ancient Greek world (and including a section on ancient Egypt), there is a more than elegant sufficiency.

Until recently housed in a wing of the National Archaeological Museum, the **Numismatic Museum** was at the time of going to press in the process of moving to the restored mansion of Heinrich Schliemann, former headquarters of the Archaeological Society, at *Leoforos Panepistimiou 22; opening times at the new location will probably (not definitely) be Tuesday to Sunday 8:30 am to 3 pm, and admission Drs 400.* The museum's collection of around 300,000 Greek coins dating from ancient to modern times includes many of the famed "owls of Laurion" – 5th-century BC Athenian silver drachmas stamped with the owl symbol of Athena and made with silver from the mines at Laurion (modern Lavrio) near Cape Sounion.

Before or after visiting the museum you might want to run your eyes over the three neo-classical building complexes on Leoforos Panepistimiou between the museum and Plateia Omonia. These are the **Athens University** from 1838-1864; the **Academy of Athens** from 1859-1887; and the **National Library** from 1887-1902. The Academy gives some kind of idea of what a classical Greek temple complex might have looked like – if you ignore the parked autos, that is.

Other Museums

• **National Gallery and Alexandros Soutsos Museum**, *Leoforos Vasileos Konstantinou 50. Tel. 01/723-5937. Open Tuesday to Saturday 9 am to 3 pm, Sunday 10 am to 2 pm. Admission Drs 500.* A modern museum that focuses its collection on recent but not contemporary Greek painters, although visiting exhibitions frequently bring a wider range to its walls. Four works by El Greco are its highlights.

• **Byzantine Museum**, *Leoforos Vasilissis Sofias 22. Tel. 01/721-1027. Open Tuesday to Saturday 9 am to 3 pm, Sunday 9 am to 2 pm. Admission Drs 500.* Athens is not a great center of Byzantine religious and cultural history, having been a backwater during this era. The museum, housed in the Villia Ilissia dating from 1848, compensates for this sad fact with Greece's finest collection of Byzantine sculptures, mosaics and frescoes, icons, ecclesiastical vessels and vestments and church furniture and ornamentation.

• **Museum of Cycladic and Ancient Greek Art**, *Odos Neofytou Douka 4. Tel. 01/722-8321. Open Monday to Friday 10 am to 4 pm, Saturday 10 am to 3 pm. Admission Drs 400, students Drs 200.* Anyone whose interest has been piqued by the Cycladic exhibits at the National Archaeological Museum, or who didn't get much beyond the bars in Mykonos, can steep themselves in 5,000 years of island culture here.

• **Athens City Museum**, *Odos Paparigopolou 7. Tel. 01/323-0168. Open Monday, Wednesday, Friday and Saturday 9 am to 1:30 pm. Admission Drs 400.* Housed in the palace of independent Greece's first king, Otho I, it mostly features objects and images from the small city that was 19th-century Athens.

• **Greek Folk Art Museum**, *Odos Kydathineon 17. Tel. 01/322-9031. Open Tuesday to Sunday 10 am to 2 pm. Admission Drs 500, students Drs 300.* Features examples of embroidery, ceramics, metalwork, paintings and other traditional crafts from all over Greece, as well as puppet theater.

• **Athens Traditional and Folk Art Center**, *Odos Hatzimihali 6. Tel. 01/324-3987. Open Tuesday and Thursday 9 am to 9 pm; Wednesday, Friday and Saturday 9 am to 1 pm and 5 to 9 pm; Sunday 9 am to 1 pm. Admission free.* Houses a similar, though smaller, range of exhibits to the Folk Art Museum (above), focusing on Athens.

• **Benaki Museum**, *Odos Koumbari 1 (corner of Leoforos Vasilissis Sofias). Tel. 01/362-6266. Open Monday to Saturday 9 am to 3 pm. Admission Drs 500.*

One of few places in Athens where Ottoman-era artifacts are on display, along with classic and modern Greek artworks, and Byzantine and Coptic religious art.

• **Greek Popular Musical Instruments Museum**, *Odos Diogenous 1-3. Tel. 01/325-0198. Open Tuesday and Thursday to Sunday 10 am to 2 pm, Wednesday noon to 7 pm. Admission Drs 400.* Displays folk music instruments from the last 300 years or so, and offers a chance to play some of them.

• **Historical and Ethnological Museum**, *Odos Stadiou 113. Tel. 01/323-7617. Open Tuesday to Sunday 9 am to 1:30 pm. Admission Drs 500, students Drs 200.* Focuses on traditional Greek costumes.

• **Ilias Lalaounis Jewelry Museum**, *Odos Kallisperi 12. Tel. 01/922-1044. Open Monday and Wednesday 9 am to 9 pm; Thursday, Friday and Saturday 9 am to 3 pm; Sunday 10 am to 31 pm. Admission Drs 800.* An eclectic private collection features the work of its founder and examples of jewelry from ancint times.

• **Natural History Museum**, *Odos Levidou 13, Kifissia. Tel. 01/808-6405. Open Tuesday to Thursday, Saturday and Sunday 9 am to 2 pm. Admission Drs 500.* Its collection focuses on the flora and fauna of Greece and how it has changed (mostly for the worse) through time.

• **Theatrical Museum**, *Odos Academias 50. Tel. 01/363-8275. Open Monday to Friday 9 am to 3 pm, Sunday 10 am to 1 pm. Admission Drs 300.* In the city where theater began, this collecton offers an insight into the art's more recent form.

• **War Museum**, *Odos Rizari 2. Tel. 01/729-0543. Open Tuesday to Sunday 9 am to 2 pm. Admission free.* Greek weapons and engines of war down the centuries.

• **Jewish Museum**, *Leoforos Amalias 36. Tel. 01/322-5582. Open Sunday to Friday 9 am to 1 pm. Admission free.* Greece's Jewish history dates from classical times, and using everyday objects, religious works and documents, the museum outlines their history. That history very nearly came to an end during the Nazi occupation of World War II, when all but 10,000 of Greece's prewar population of almost 80,000 Jews were exterminated.

Plaka

Lying between Plateia Syntagma and the Acropolis, **Plaka** is an attraction all by itself. Not so many years ago this old district, whose Ottoman-era graces have not succumbed entirely to the city's love-affair with concrete – although it was a close call at one time – was seedy and rundown. It has raised itself up by its own collective bootstraps, and now, much restored, has become the city's most popular tourist district. Athenians like it every bit as much as tourists, perhaps because its warren of narrow streets, many of them pedestrian-only, lined with small shops, tavernas and homey hotels, conjure up an image of ancient Athens that is light years away from the apartment-block wasteland that fills the Attic plain.

Plaka is touristy, with lots of tavernas and souvenir shops, some of which come close to being either twee or tacky, and others of which go the whole way. Yet there are many excellent tavernas, some interesting craft shops, and bags of atmosphere. Joining Athenians on their summer-evening volta through Plaka's pedestrians-only streets, when the colored lamp are lit, the taverna terraces are full, and bonhomie flows as vigorously as retsina in the restaurants, adds another dimension to the city from the familiar one of choking auto pollution amidst the mad whirl of Athens's traffic.

Other Areas of Interest

Adjoining Plaka to the south, clustered in the lee of the Acropolis, is **Anafiotika**. You could esily believe here that a particularly beneficent southeast wind (a *Euros* to give it the mythological name) lifted a hilly Cycladic Islands village entire into the air and set it down gently on the alien soil of Athens. Reality has more to do with economic opportunity that brought craftsmen from Anafi island to work on King Otho's palace in the 1830s. They brought their island sensibility with them and built it into their new quarters. Anafiotika really is a place apart. A stroll through its tranquil, narrow alleys and amidst its brightly painted cottages, where it seems that the wine-dark sea lies just around the next corner, is the perfect anecdote to one gulp too many of Athens's corrosive air.

Adjoining Plaka to the west is the bustling and atmospheric but also rundown and slightly seedy **Monastiraki** district, whose main claim to fame is its flea market, which fills the streets around the metro station with bargain basement goods of often dubious quality. Pickpockets work the crowds here, so keep a tight grip on your removables.

The **Koukaki** district lying generally south of Filopapou Hill is one of the underrated parts of the city, despite its lack of conventional "sights." It compensates for this by being a calm and attractive residential area that seems more genuinely Athenian than tourist-oriented areas such as Plaka. Its traffic and pollution levels are also way below those around Plateia Syntagma and Plateia Omonia. Having said that, the lack of anything to see is Koukaki's main drawback and it is perhaps best used as a place to be in Athens and to get away from it at the same time.

North Athens is where the groves of suburbia lie, and no suburb is more elegant than **Kifissia**. You can even take a horsedrawn carriage tour around its 19th-century villas and their gardens from the main square. This is also a place for upmarket shopping and dining, although there are few sights, as such, other than the **Natural History Museum** (see under *Other Museums*, above).

Green Athens

The **National Garden**, *open from sunrise to sunset*, facing Plateia Syntagma between Odos Amalias and Odos Irodou Atikou is a national treasure quite as valuable as the Parthenon – or so it will seem on a sweltering summer's day, when the big park's shady tangle of trees and bushes, its oxygenated air, and even its overpopulated duck pond add up to a blessed place of escape.

The only possible criticism of the National Garden is that the undergrowth gets a bit too tangled along quiet pathways that may conceal the kind of urban dangers familiar in all big cities. It makes sense to stick to the busier places, particularly at sunset (which is in no way to say that this is a dangerous place; only that you should exercise due caution). Adjoining the National Garden to the south are the more ornamental **Zappeion Gardens**, surrounding the Zappeion Hall.

I wonder if Saint Paul had as much trouble staying on his feet on the smoothly worn and slippery surface of the **Areopagus Hill** as most modern visitors have. This 115-meter-high rocky outcrop off the western edge of the Acropolis is where the ancient Council of the Areopagus met to conduct important legal trials, and where Saint Paul delivered his "Sermon to an Unknown God" in 51 AD, converting the Athenian citizen Dionysos, who became the first Bishop of Athens and was sanctified as Dionysos the Areopagite.

Further west is wooded **Filopapou Hill**, surmounted by a monument to the 2nd-century Roman consul Caius Julius Antiochus Philopapos. Descending the north slope takes you past the Byzantine **Agios Dimitrios Church**, which is followed by an ascent of the 109-meter-high **Pnyx Hill**, seat of the ancient Athenian Assembly and therefore the original home of democracy. Beyond this is the **Hill of the Nymphs**, crowned by a 19th-century observatory.

The most prominent hill of all in the city is **Likavitos Hill**, northeast of Plateia Syntagma, and said to be a rock intended for the Acropolis that was dropped by Athena. The hill is now a park and its summit, with the **Church of Agios Georgios** can be reached by a funicular from Odos Ploutarchou. Also on the hill is the modern **Likavitos Theater**, *Tel. 01/322-1459*, where open-air music, theater, and dance performances are given in summer.

The **Areos Park** lies north of Leoforos Alexandras, beyond the National Archaeological Museum, and makes a welcome break from a busy area that has little to recommend it other than the museum. Look out for the broad avenue lined with statues of heroes from Greece's War of National Liberation in the 1820s.

Parliament

Not the debating chamber itself, where as in all such places more heat than light is generated – and Athens is hot enough already. No, it's the fantastically uniformed soldiers, the *evzones,* who parade up and down outside **Parliament** in front of the **Tomb of the Unknown Soldier**, *Plateia Syntagma (east side); the Changing of the Guard ceremony takes place daily at*

6 pm. Like slow-motion windup toys, the *evzones* are the main attraction here. With their tasseled hats, skirts, tights and pom-pom shoes you might think that any enemy meeting them on the battlefield would die laughing; close up you see that they are very big fellows indeed and undoubtedly know exactly what to do with their rifles and polished bayonets.

What they mostly do, of course, is stamp around, stand motionless for long periods of time, and star in a million tourist photos and videos. The Parliament building dates from 1842 and was originally a royal palace, being converted to its present role in 1934. *Evzones* also strut their stuff outside the nearby **Presidential Palace**, on the other side of the National Garden, on Odos Irodou Atikou.

Byzantine Churches

Although not noted for its Byzantine history, Athens does have a few churches from this era worth visiting. Their icons and iconostaseis, gloomy interiors and glowing lamps, and votive offerings left by the faithful are reminders that although many foreign visitors to Greece focus on classical antiquity for their sightseeing, the thousand-year Byzantine period had a much more profound and recent impact on Greek culture and the Greek character.

Among churches worth going out of your way for are the small 12th-century **Agios Eleftherios** in Plateia Mitropoleos, beside the big 19th-century Orthodox Cathedral; 11th-century **Karnikarea**, Odos Ermou; 11th-century **Agias Dinamis**, beneath an arcade on Odos Mitropoleos; the late 10th-century **Agioi Apostoloi tou Solaki** in the Agora, beside the rebuilt Stoa of Attalos; 14th-century **Metamorfosis** in Monastiraki across the square from the metro station; 12th-century **Agios Ioannis stin Kolona**, Odos Euripidou; 12th-century **Agia Triada** and 11th-century **Agios Nikodemos** on Odos Filellinon; **Agios Nikolaos Rangavas** in the Anafiotika district; and 11th-century **Agioi Theodoroi** at Plateia Klafthmonos.

Although opening times vary, you can usually find them open in the morning and on Sunday. Dress should be respectful of religious sensibilities.

NIGHTLIFE & ENTERTAINMENT
CULTURAL OFFERINGS

Athens lacks the depth of major cultural facilities common in other European capitals. On the other hand it does have top-fight cultural venues, and it can reach for a 1,800-year-old theater whenever it wants to put on something that little bit special. So eat your heart out London and Paris (and don't even bother getting out of bed Amsterdam and Brussels).

Dance

If you would like to see some genuine Greek folk dances, and in a romantic setting, you can do no better than spend an evening at the **Dora Stratou Dance Theater**, *Filopapou Hill (tickets from Odos Scholiou 8, Plaka, Tel. 01/924-4395 and 01/921-4650)*. The open-air theater has at least one performance each evening in summer, and sometimes two, of genuine folk dances in costume from all over Greece, accompanied by traditional music.

Modern dance performances are occasionally given at the **Megaron Athens Concert Hall**, *Leoforos Vasilissis Sofias, Tel. 01/729-0391*.

Festivals

The **Athens Festival** dates back temporally to 1955. In spirit, however, it reaches back to the city's glory days, a fact exemplified by its use of the Odeion of Herodes Atticus, dating from the 160s AD, for performances of classic plays by Sophocles, Aristophanes, Euripides, and Aeschylus. You'll also get classical music, opera, ballet, rock, jazz, blues and many other performances.

The central box office is at *Odos Stadiou 4, Tel. 01/322-1459*. Ticket prices vary depending on who is paying to see what, and generally run from Drs 1,500 to Drs 2,500 for students, and from Drs 2,500 to Drs 10,000, and sometimes more, for responsible members of society. Most events are held at one of these locations:

- **Odeion of Herodes Atticus**, *Odos Dionissiou Areopagitou. Tel. 01/323-2771 (box office)*.
- **Likavitos Theater**, *Likavitos Hill. Tel. 01/722-7209*.

Film

Watching Bruce Willis blow away the bad guys in Greek would seriously diminish the experience – imagine not being able to understand those wry quips! Don't worry: in Athens it is the Greeks who have trouble understanding them, as movies are shown in their original language (usually Hollywoodese), with Greek subtitles. All city center cinemas are modern, comfortable, and equipped with Dolby stereo sound systems (some have digital sound). They also have a maddening popcorn-and-cola break right in the middle of the movie, in mid-quip often enough.

All the big Hollywood fims turn up here sooner or later, usually several months after their US release. Screening times vary, but there are normally three each evening between about 5 and 11 pm. Admission is around Drs 1,800. For a full listing of the programs of the 70 or so cinemas in the city, look in *Athens News,* the *Hellenic Times,* and *Scope Weekly.* The following are some of the more centrally located cinemas:

• **Aavora**, *Odos Ipokratous 180. Tel. 01/642-3271*
• **Apollon**, *Odos Stadiou 19. Tel. 01/323-6811*
• **Astor**, *Odos Stadiou 28. Tel. 01/323-1297*
• **Asty**, *Odos Korai 4. Tel. 01/322-1925*
• **Attikon**, *Odos Stadiou 19. Tel. 01/322-8821*
• **Elly**, *Odos Akadimias 64. Tel. 01/363-2789*
• **Embassy**, *Odos Patriarhou Ioakim 5. Tel. 01/722-0903*
• **Ideal**, *Odos Panepistimiou 46. Tel. 01/382-6720*
• **Opera Assos Odeon**, *Odos Akadamias 57. Tel. 01/362-2683*
• **Titania**, *Corner of Odos Panepistimiou & Odos Themistokleous. Tel. 01/362-2683*

Opera

The **Athens Opera** is the main performer at the **Greek National Opera House**, *Odos Akadimias 59-61, Tel. 01/361-2461.* Ticket prices range from Drs 2,000 to Drs 10,000. Performances are also held at the **Megaron Athens Concert Hall**, *Leoforos Vasilissis Sofias (next to the US Embassy), Tel. 01/728-2333.*

Private Galleries

In these galleries you can also look, and even make loudly disparaging comparisons with Phidias, if you so chose, after only the briefest of friskings to confirm the presence of your AmEx Platinum Card. Galleries have a tendency to come and go, and opening times to vary, so you should check ahead before visiting.

- **Aenaon Gallery**, *Odos Antersen 18, Katehaki. Tel. 01/677-5086*
- **Aigokeros Gallery**, *Odos Aristodimou 4, Kolonaki. Tel. 01/722-3897*
- **Anemos Gallery**, *Odos Kiriazis 36, Kifissia. Tel. 01/808-2027*
- **Argo Gallery**, *Odos Merlin 8, Kolonaki. Tel. 01/362-2662*
- **Athens Gallery**, *Odos Pandrossou 14, Plaka. Tel. 01/324-6942*
- **Bosch Gallery**, *Odos Kifissias 6-8, Paradisos Amarousiou. Tel. 01/682-4244*
- **Chrisothemis Gallery**, *Odos 25 Martiou 20, Halandri. Tel. 01/681-1418*
- **Galerie Artio**, *Odos Dinokratous 57. Tel. 01/723-0455*
- **Gallery Skoufa**, *Odos Skoufa 4, Kolonaki. Tel. 01/360-3541*
- **Iliana Tounda Gallery**, *Odos Armatolon 48. Tel. 01/643-9466*
- **Jean Bernier Gallery**, *Odos Marasli 51. Tel. 01/723-5657*
- **Rebekka Kamchi gallery**, *Odos Sofokleous 23. Tel. 01/321-0448*
- **Thema Gallery**, *Odos Patriarhou Ioakim 53. Tel. 01/723-7483*
- **Titanium Gallery**, *Leoforos Vasileos Konstandinou 44. Tel. 01/721-1865*
- **Zoymbolaki Gallery**, *Plateia Kolonaki 20. Tel. 01/360-8278*
- **Zygos Gallery**, *Leoforos Vasilissis Sofias 65. Tel. 01/722-9272*

Son-Et-Lumière

If you don't fancy seeing a *son-et-lumière,* you can always go and see a sound-and-light show instead. It's on **Filoupapou Hill**, facing the Acropolis entrance, beyond the Areopagus Hill, and it shows and tells of the ups, downs, then part-way ups again of the Parthenon from Pericles' day to our own. It's not what you might call a rigorous examination of the historical and archaeological record, but it is illuminating in its way.

The daily English performance is at 9 pm between April and October. Tickets are Drs 1,500 for adults, Drs 750 for students. *Tel. 01/322-1459 or 01/922-6210.*

Symphony

Ticket prices range from Drs 2,000 to Drs 12,000; but look out for the Sunday performances of the **Athens State Orchestra**, where tickets go for a knockdown Drs 1,000 to Drs 1,500. The main concert venue is the **Megaron Athens Concert Hall**, *Leoforos Vasilissis Sofias (next to the US Embassy), Tel. 01/728-2333.*

Theater

Most theater performances in Athens are in Greek, naturally enough. Not all are, however, and you will catch regular English-language plays at:
- **Hellenic American Union (Theater Auditorium)**, *Odos Massalias 22, Kolonaki. Tel. 01/360-7495 or 01/362-9886.* As well as cultural programs and movies, you can learn to speak Greek here.
- **American College of Greece (Pierce College Auditorium)**, *Odos Gravias 6. Tel. 01/600-9800 or 01/748-6580*

NIGHTLIFE

Much of Athens's nightlife consists of waving knives and forks over something substantial on a plate atop a table at a taverna's street terrace, while drinking in the atmosphere of a jug of retsina. Not all of it, you'll be glad (or sorry) to hear. And there are plenty of places to let your hair down as well.

Discos

- **Divina**, *Odos Argiropoulou 2. Tel. 01/801-5884*

Rock Cafes

- **Anaglyfo**, *Odos Harakopou 93, Kalithea. Tel. 01/957-1103*
- **Berlin**, *Odos Iraklidon, Thissio. Tel. 01/342-0488*
- **Crow's Nest**, *Odos Filadelpheos 4, Kifissia. Tel. 01/801-0301*
- **Deka**, *Odos Arditou 10, Mets. Tel. 01/924-3660*
- **Green Door Café**, *Odos Kallidromiou 52, Exarhia. Tel. 01/383-9159*
- **Memphis Booze**, *Odos Vendiri 7, Kolonaki. Tel. 01/722-4104*
- **Nick's Place**, *Odos Spefsipou 26-28, Kolonaki. Tel. 01/724-1235*

• **Octana**, *Odos Methonis 46, Exarhia. Tel. 01/383-6244*
• **Ostria**, *Odos Ekonomou 6, Exarhia. Tel. 01/330-0907*
• **Stadio**, *Odos Markou Mousourou 1, Mets. Tel. 01/923-5818*

Bouzouki & Traditional Music

There are lots of places where you can hear bouzouki music, some of it good, some of it bad, and most of it indifferent. Aficionados of the form rate the following addresses highly:
• **Bistrot**, *Odos Harokopou 131, Kalithea. Tel. 01/951-1709*
• **Labirides**, *Odos Deliyanni 4, Kalithea. Tel. 01/922-7710*

Rembetika

There is a strong revival in this melancholy music, brought by Greek refugees from Turkey in the 1920s, and as distinctive in its way as the American Blues.
• **Aperito**, *Odos Dimokritou 25, Kolonaki. Tel. 01/363-3954*
• **Boemissa**, *Odos Solomou 19, Exarhia. Tel. 01/384-3836*
• **Ble Parathira**, *Odos Mitilinis 28. Tel. 01/862-6702*
• **Kastro**, *Odos Veikou 2, Galatsi. Tel. 01/293-0873*
• **Ladadika**, *Odos Filellinon 5. Tel. 01/331-4291*
• **Rembetika Istoria**, *Odos Ippokratous 181, Exarhia. Tel. 01/642-4937*
• **Steki**, *Odos Kalypsous, Kalithea. Tel. 01/952-4515*

Blues

If *rembetika* doesn't seem like your scene, and you think that if you want to hear melancholy music it might as well be the homegrown variety, these suitably noisy, dark, and smoky venues should fill the bill.
• **Blues**, *Odos Panormou 20, Ambelokipi. Tel. 01/643-3372*
• **Rhythm 'n' Blues**, *Odos Tositsa 11, Exarhia. Tel. 01/822-8870*

Jazz

Athens has a vigorous jazz scene, considering that the music is scarcely associated with Greece.
• **Epoca Jazz Club**, *Odos Sinopis 6, Ambelokipi. Tel. 01/748-6231*

• **Half Note Club**, *Odos Trivonianou 17, Mets. Tel. 01/921-3310*
• **French Quarter**, *Odos Mavromichalli 78, Exarhia. Tel. 01/645-0758*
• **Jazz Club 1920**, *Odos Ploutarchou 10. Tel. 01/721-0533*
• **Peninda Eksi (56)**, *Odos Ploutarchou 56. Tel. 01/723-1424*
• **Tsakalof Jazz Bar**, *Odos Tsakalof 10, Kolonaki. Tel. 01/360-5889*

Strip Joints

If you're in Athens and you have a sudden urge to view the undraped female form, you'll find plenty of exhibits at the National Archaeological Museum, and the process there will be highly educational too. Here endeth the sermon...

By the way, if you happn to find yourself accidentally in one of these places, and an incredibly beautiful woman falls head over heels in love with you at first sight, conditional only on you buying her the drink of her choice, and you fall for it, I've got some choice real estate in Florida's swamplands for you to consider buying.

• **Babes**, *Odos Michalakopoulou 23, Ilissia. Tel. 01/724-8294*
• **Diamonds and Pearls**, *Odos Posidonos 35, Kalamaki. Tel. 01/984-7164*
• **Sirocco**, *Leoforos Andreas Syngrou 225. Tel. 01/942-4986*

Gay Bars

Can you spot the similarity in the first five addresses below? Enough said? The Makrigiani district lies directly south of the Acropolis, across Odos Dionissiou Areopagitou, bordering the Koukaki district.

• **City**, *Odos Korizi 4, Makrigiani. Tel. 01/924-0740*
• **E...Kai**, *Odos Iossif Ron Rogon 12, Makrigiani. Tel. 01/922-1742*
• **Granazi**, *Odos Lembessi 20, Makrigiani. Tel. 01/325-3979*
• **Endechomeno**, *Odos Lembessi 8, Makrigiani. Tel. 01/923-0264*
• **Lamda**, *Odos Lembessi 15. Tel. 01/922-4202*
• **Mi-Ar**, *Odos Mochonission 28. Tel. 01/865-8872*
• **Odyssea**, *Odos Ermou 116, Monastiraki. Tel. 01/325-1671*
• **Test Me**, *Odos Pipinou 64. Tel. 01/822-6029*

If you're looking for a lesbian bar, go to **Mexico**, *Leoforos Thisseos 249, Kalithea. Tel. 01/951-0075.*

Bowling

Can bowling really be considered as nightlife? If you do it at night, I suppose.

• **Bowling Center Glyfada**, *Odos Dousmani 3, Glyfada. Tel. 01/894-0103*
• **Bowling Center Kifissia**, *Odos Kolokotroni 1, Kifissia. Tel. 01/808-4662*
• **Bowling Center Pireas**, *Odos Profitis Ilias, Kastela. Tel. 01/412-7077*
• **GBS**, *Odos Patission 382. Tel. 01/228-2543*
• **Sporting Club**, *Odos Babi Anninou 7. Tel. 01/223-0056*

PRACTICAL INFORMATION

Banks & Currency Exchange

All Greek banks are authorized to transact foreign exchange business so there is no shortage of outlets in Athens, although the bigger city center branches are better equipped to handle this than small neighborhood offices. Most banks in Athens are open Monday through Thursday from 8 am to 2 pm and Friday from 8 am to 1:30 pm. Centrally located bank branches are:

• **National Bank of Greece**, *Odos Karageorgi Servias 2. Tel. 01/321-0411*
• **Commercial Bank**, *Odos Sophokleous 11. Tel. 01/321-0911*
• **Ionian Bank**, *Leoforos Panepistimiou 45. Tel. 01/322-5501*
• **Bank of Greece**, *Leoforos Panepistimiou 21. Tel. 01/320-1111*
• **Credit Bank**, *Odos Stadiou 40. Tel. 01/325-5111*

At busy places such as Plateia Syntagma, there are ATMs that can be accessed by major credit and charge cards, as well as by Eurocheque cards and cards linked to the Cirrus, Plus, and other international networks. Separate wall-mounted machines at such places exchange bills of major foreign currencies for drachmas.

There are several bank bureaux de change offices in the Arrivals Hall at Athens International Airport; their rates vary slightly so it may be worth comparing if you are exchanging big amounts. At many street bureaux de change you can be faced with poor exchange rates and high transaction fees (the latter can be particularly ruinous if you make lots of small transactions). You should *always* ask what the rates and fees are in advance of any transaction, and keep a pocket calculator handy to work out the bottom line (while bearing in mind that these bureaux are open when the banks are not). The bigger hotels will also exchange the major foreign currencies and traveler's checks, but at poorer rates than the banks. For fair dealing in non-bank exchange transactions, your best bets (both of them near Plateia Syntagma) are:

- **American Express**, *Odos Ermou 2. Tel. 01/324-4975*
- **Thomas Cook**, *Odos Karageorgi Servias 4. Tel. 01/322-0005*

Several foreign banks are located in Athens, and these can be more convenient, particularly for their own customers, when handling transfers of funds from home. Look for:

- **Bank of America**, *Leoforos Panepistimiou 39. Tel. 01/325-1901*
- **Bank of Nova Scotia**, *Leoforos Panepistimiou 37. Tel. 01/324-3891*
- **Barclays Bank**, *Odos Voukourestiou 15. Tel. 01/364-4311*
- **Chase Manhattan Bank**, *Odos Korai 3. Tel. 01/323-7711*
- **Citibank**, *Odos Othonos 8. Tel. 01/322-7471*
- **National Westminster Bank**, *Odos Merarchias 7, Piraeus. Tel. 01/411-7415*
- **Royal Bank of Scotland**, *Odos Akti Miaouli 61. Tel. 01/452-7483*

For money transfers go to **Western Union**, *Odos Menekratous 11, Tel. 01/927-1010.*

Bookstores

You can expect to pay 30 to 60 percent more for US- and UK-published books than you would at home. For good selections of English language books, and staff who speak some English, try the following bookshops:

- **Compendium**, *Odos Nikis 28. Tel. 01/322-1248*
- **Pantelides**, *Odos Amerikis 11. Tel. 01/362-3673*
- **Eleftheroudakis**, *Odos Nikis 4. Tel. 0/322-9388; Leoforos Panepistimiou 17. Tel;. 01/331-4180*
- **The Booknest**, *Leoforos Panepistimiou 25-29. Tel. 01/323-9703*

Crime & Safety

By no stretch of the imagination can Athens be described as a violent or dangerous city. Visitors who come from places that can be so described are likely to love the freedom from such fears and the easygoing nature of streetlife in the city.

However, Athens is still a big city and suffers to an extent from big-city problems found all over the world. Mostly petty, drug-related crime is on the increase. Your first priority is to be aware of your surroundings at all times, though not to the point of paranoia. Watch out particularly for the pickpocket conventions at busy metro stations and on crowded buses, or when joining the crush to board ferries at Piraeus. Withdrawing cash from an ATM at night may also be a time for watching your back.

If you are tempted to commit crime, be aware that possession of illegal drugs is a serious offense in Greece and is so treated by the courts; the same, though on different grounds, applies to illegal possession of antiquities. Oddly enough, possession of **codeine**, a common painkiller, is illegal in Greece. Although the police generally have better things to do with their time than mount codeine busts, arrests do occur for possession of large amounts.

See *Emergencies*, below, for police telephone numbers.

Cultural Institutes

- **American Library**, *Odos Massalias 22. Tel. 01/363-7740*
- **American School of Clssical Studies**, *Odos Souidias 61. Tel. 01/723-6313*
- **British Council**, *Plateia Kolonaki xx. Tel. 01/363-3211*
- **Goethe Institue**, *Odos Omirou 14-16. Tel. 01/360-8111*
- **Hellenic American Union**, *Odos Massalias 22, Kolonaki. Tel. 01/360-7495 or 01/362-9886*

Embassies & Consulates

- **United States** *Leoforos Vasilissis Sofias 91. Tel. 01/721-2951*
- **Great Britain** *Odos Ploutarchou 1. Tel. 01/723-6211*
- **Canada** *Odos Ioannou Gennadiou 4. Tel. 01/725-4011*
- **Australia** *Odos Dimitriou Soutsou 37. Tel. 01/644-7303*

• **New Zealand** *Odos Semitelou 9. Tel. 01/771-0112*
• **Ireland** *Leoforos Vasileos Konstantinou 7. 01/723-2771*
• **South Africa** *Leoforos Kifissias 60. Tel. 01/680-6645*

For visa and residence permit extensions, go to the **Aliens Bureau**, *Leoforos Alexandras 173, Tel. 01/770-5711.*

Emergencies
• **Police**, *Tel. 100* (city); *Tel. 109* (suburban)
• **Tourist Police**, *Tel. 171*
• **Fire**, *Tel. 199*
• **Ambulance**, *Tel. 166*
• **Medical**: Lifeline, *Tel. 175;* First Aid, *Tel. 150;* Doctors on Call (2 pm to 7 am), *Tel. 105* (Athens-Piraeus), *Tel. 101* (outside the metro area); Hospital Referrals, *Tel. 106;* Poison/Overdose Treatment, *Tel. 01/779-3777;* SOS Médécins, *Tel. 01/331-0310* (24-hour medical service).
• **Pharmacies**, *Tel. 107.* The duty-list for out-of-hours pharmacies changes daily: current addresses and opening times are listed daily in the *Athens News.*
• **Auto Breakdown**, *Tel. 104*
• **Lost & Found**, *Tel. 01/642-1616*

Lost & Found
You stand a reasonable chance of getting back something that you've lost. For items lost on public transport, including taxis, call *01/770-5711.* Otherwise, try the tourist police on *171.*

Maps
The **EOT** (Greek tourist board) **information offices** have free maps of the city, and your hotel reception may have copies of the free map produced by the Minion Shopping Mall, which is adequate for the central zone.

Places of Worship

- **Anglican** – *Saint Paul's Church, Odos Filellinon 27. Tel. 01/721-4906.*
- **Baptist** – *Athens Baptist Bible Church, Odos Dipla 14. Tel. 01/806-2825.*
- **Catholic** – *Saint Denis's Cathedral, Leoforos Panepistimiou 24. Tel. 01/362-3603.*
- **Greek Orthodox** – *Metropolis, Odos Mitropoleos. Tel. 01/322-1308.*
- **Jehovah's Witnesses** – *Leoforos Kifissias 77. Tel. 01/682-7315.*
- **Jewish** – *Beth Shalom Synagogue, Odos Melidoni 8. Tel. 01/325-2823.*
- **Muslim** – *Athens Mosque, Caravel Hotel, Leoforos Vassiliou Alexandrou 2. Tel. 01/729-0721.*
- **Pentecostal** – *United Pentecostal Church International, Odos Poulion 4-6. Tel. 01/645-3304.*

Post Office

The main downtown post office is at *Plateia Syntagma. Tel. 01/323-7573; open Monday through Saturday from 7:30 am to 8:30 pm and Sunday from 7:30 am to 1:30 pm.* Take bulky packages and parcels weighing more than 1 kilogram to the post office at *Odos Stadiou 4. Tel. 01/322-8940; open Monday through Saturday from 8:30 am to 3:30 pm.*

Don't seal parcels, as they will probably have to be opened for inspection, in case you're trying to smuggle the Parthenon out of the country in pieces.

Press & Broadcast Media

There are plenty of local newspapers on sale in Athens, but they're all Greek to me (sorry: I just had to say that once, and now it's done). The *International Herald Tribune, Wall Street Journal,* and *USA Today* are widely available from newsstands, as are the main British daily newspapers. The same goes for *Time, Newsweek, Business Week, The Economist,* and other weekly news and business magazines.

The English language *Athens News* is published daily (except Monday) and often available free at hotels and is a good source of Greek and international news summaries, plus cultural and other Athens information. There is also the weekly *Hellenic Times,* the monthly *Athenian,* which is strong on cultural topics, and the free monthly *Athens Today,* which has lots of information about hotels, restaurants, nightlife, etc.

Depending on your hotel, you may have the possibility of watching CNN International, BBC World Service Television, MTV, Eurosport, FilmNet and the soap-laden Sky network. Greek stations often show English-language (mostly American) movies with Greek subtitles. Program information for the main stations can be found in the *Athens News.*

Metropolitan Radio Athens broadcasts brief cultural listings, and news and weather summaries in English on 98.4 FM. The daily cultural listings are at 7:30 am and 8:30 pm; news and weather summaries are at 8:30 and 9:30 am, and 12:30, 4:30 and 7:30 pm.

Telephone

The country code for Greece is *30;* the area code for Athens (including Piraeus and the suburbs) is *01.* When phoning an Athens number from outside Greece, dial *30* for the country, followed by only the *1* of the area code, followed by the subscriber number; when phoning an Athens number from inside Greece, but outside Athens (including Piraeus and the suburbs), dial the whole area code, *01,* followed by the subscriber number; when phoning an Athens number from inside Athens (including Piraeus and the suburbs), dial only the subscriber number.

In the past it used to be important to know where the OTE telephone office was, particularly for making international calls. Nowadays with international direct dialling and a telephone card *(telekarta)* you can make international calls from most street telephones. Should you need to use OTE for making or receiving calls, or for telexes, faxes, or telegrams, and paying by cash, credit card, or collect, the main downtown offices are at *Odos Stadiou 15* (beside Plateia Syntagma) and *Plateia Omonia (both open Monday through Friday from 7 am to midnight and on weekends from 8 am to midnight);* and *Odos Patission 85 (open 24 hours a day).*

Tourist Information

The **Greek Tourist Office** (**EOT**) national headquarters address is *Odos Amerikis 2. Tel. 01/322-3111, Fax 01/323-6684.*

EOT also has information booths at:

- **Plateia Syntagma**, *Odos Karageorgi Servias 2. Tel. 01/322-2545;* and *Odos Ermou 1. Tel. 01/322-1459*
- **Athens International Airport**, *Arrivals Hall, East Terminal. Tel. 01/969-4500*
- **Piraeus**, *Zea Marina. Tel. 413-5716*

9. ISLANDS OF THE SARONIC GULF

Islands of the Saronic Gulf

The islands of **Aegina**, **Poros**, **Hydra**, and **Spetses** are layed out like stepping stones down through the **Saronic Gulf** from Athens. All are within range of a daytrip from the capital, although the farthest, Spetses, stretches the timetable a bit to do it. Despite being so close to the big city and being mostly overrun with Greek and foreign tourists come summer, they are still genuine Greek islands. You have to get to them by boat, for one thing, and once there the traditional magic of being on a Greek island asserts itself.

SALAMIS (SALAMINA)

There is little incentive to visit Salamis although it is indeed a Saronic Gulf Island, lying at the very head of that noble body of water. Salamis had its fifteen minutes of fame in 480 BC, when the grand fleet of Persia's King Xerxes was trashed by the inferior navy of the Greek coalition in the narrow Skaramangas Straits between the island and the mainland. It is really only a suburb of Athens now, bathed in polluted water and air from the big city and the smokestack industries along the Attic coast. You can get there by car ferry every half-hour from **Perama**, west of Piraeus.

On the coast facing the mainland, there is little to see other than dormitory suburbs, but in the south and southwest there are rugged hills

---

SARONIC ISLANDS FINDS & FAVORITES

• **Temple of Aphaia**. One of the most remarkable surviving ancient temples in Greece, though it is dedicated to an obscure goddess (see Aegina).

• **Eginitiko Arkhontiko**. A strikingly handsome, historic mansion that has been converted into a hotel, and retains both the charm and the splendor of Aegina's brief 19th-century reign as the capital of Greece – and all at a very reasonable price (see Aegina).

• **Trireme**. An all-sailing, all-rowing replica of the wooden galleys with three banks of oars that gave the ancient Greeks command of the seas is moored at the Greek Naval Academy in Poros town (see Poros).

• **Hydra town**. Thanks to its legacy of stonebuilt, early 19th-century mansions, and a scenic location around a steep-sided bay, this is one of the most charming of all Greek towns (see Hydra).

---

and some good beaches, the only problem with them being the suspect quality of the seawater. Near **Ambelakia** on the east coast is a stone mound identified as the **Memorial to the Fallen** from the Battle of Salamis.

The south coast is the most scenic and interesting part of the island. In 1997, archaeologists found a clay pot bearing the name of the Athenian dramatist Euripides in a cave near **Peristeria**, and believe this to be the cave where the reclusive playwright, who was born in the year the Battle of Salamis was fought, wrote masterpieces like *The Trojan Women*. The cave will be opened to the public when excavations are complete.

AEGINA (EGINA)

It is **Aegina's** fortune and its misfortune that it lies so close to Athens: a mere 21 kilometers offshore from Piraeus. It is too easily reachable via a regular stream of car ferries and hydrofoils. On weekends, public holidays, and throughout July and August the Athenian madhouse transports itself there en masse, their numbers boosted in summer by package tourists. At other times the island can be a remarkably tranquil place, just far enough away from Athens to be a different world entirely.

In ancient times, Aegina also suffered from its situation under the frowning gaze of Athens – Aristotle commented that the island spoiled the view from Piraeus (nowadays, the reverse is true). The Aeginetans introduced money to Europe in the 7th century BC, minting beautiful silver coins stamped with a tortoise emblem; they had a powerful fleet and a maritime trading network that reached as far as the Black Sea and Spain; and their **Temple of Aphaia** was one of the finest cult complexes in the world.

Athens didn't much like any of this and in 457 BC moved to take out its rival, defeating Aegina's navy and forcing the island's capitulation. Those famous philosophers, paragons of democracy, and lovers of beauty ethnically cleansed Aegina, expelling its people and replacing them with famous philosophers, paragons of democracy, and lovers of beauty – with Athenians in fact. The Spartans let the Aeginetans return after Athens lost the Peloponnesian War.

That's about it history-wise for more than 2,200 years, when Aegina was the capital of liberated Greece between 1826 and 1828. Would you blame the locals for wishing they could attach sails to their island and float away to someplace with nicer neighbors? Nowadays, Aegina is famed for its pistachio nuts, which are said to be the best in Greece and can be bought by the metric ton in little kiosks around the island. Aegina is hilly, scenically beautiful, and has never given up entirely its rural ways, a fact that makes exploring the interior a restful experience.

ARRIVALS & DEPARTURES
By Sea

There is a wide range of car ferry, passenger-only boat, and hydrofoil connections from **Piraeus's Great Harbor** to Aegina. You can count on one car ferry every hour at peak times, some of which serve only Aegina, while some continue southwards to other islands of the Saronic group. Most car ferries call at either **Aegina town** or **Souvala**, and some at both; others sail to Agia Marina. They leave from berths at Akti Posidonos and Akti Miaoulou. Tickets cost Drs 1,200 one-way to Aegina town and Souvala, and Drs 1,300 to Agia Marina. Journey time to Aegina town is about an hour and a half.

Hydrofoils operated by CERES Flying Dolphins sail hourly to Aegina from a berth beside the Harbor Building at Plateia Karaiskaki in **Piraeus's Great Harbor**, to Aegina town, Agia Marina, and Souvala (this is an exception to the rule that jetfoils always leave from Piraeus's Zea Marina). Tickets cost Drs 1,870 one-way to Aegina town and Agia Marina, and Drs 1,760 to Souvala for the 30-minute crossings.

ORIENTATION

At 83 square kilometers, Aegina is the biggest of the Saronic Gulf Islands and lies 21 kilometers south of Piraeus. Its permanent population numbers around 12,000. Roughly triangular in shape, the island is some 35 kilometers long and 28 kilometers across its waist. The main town is **Aegina town** on the northwest coast, while the villages of **Souvala** on the north coast, **Agia Marina** and **Portes** on the east coast, and **Perdika** on the south coast, are resorts.

The important **Temple of Aphaia** overlooks Agia Marina, while the south is dominated by 532-meter **Mount Oros**. Offshore to the west are the islets of **Angistiri** and **Moni**.

GETTING AROUND THE ISLAND
By Bus & Taxi

There are buses every 45 minutes from Aegina town to Agia Marina, passing the Temple of Aphaia on the way; hourly buses from Aegina town via Souvala to Vagia and from Aegina town via Marathonas to Perdika; and buses every two hours from Agia Marina to Portes. The bus station in Aegina town is outside the ferry terminal, on Leoforos Kazantzaki.

By Moped & Bicycle

There are numerous rental firms in Aegina town and the resorts, with rates for mopeds ranging from Drs 3,000 to Drs 5,000, and bicycles around Drs 1,000. Bicycles are a good way to see the island and to get away from the crowds at the coast. Go carefully on mopeds because walls and hedges line many of the narrow island roads, and the first you may know of oncoming traffic is when you run into it.

WHERE TO STAY

EGINITIKO ARKHONTIKO, *Odos Aeakou 1, Aegina town. Tel. 0297/ 24968, Fax 0297/24968. Rates (with tax): Drs 8,800 single; Drs 13,200 double. Breakfast Drs 1,200. 12 rooms. Diners Club, Visa.*

Built in 1820 and fully renovated in 1988, this handsome traditional mansion lies in the heart of Aegina town, some 100 meters from the ferry terminal. From 1827-29 this was the meeting place of the first Greek government, and later the house where Nikos Kazantzakis worked on his novel *Alexis Zorba*. The mansion has two interior courtyards, and each of the guest rooms is furnished differently, while retaining the style of a country mansion. There is no air conditioning but ceiling-mounted fans instead, and the ceilings themselves have restored Venetian frescoes. There is a bar and television room on the first floor, and a roof garden where breakfast is served in summer. Early reservation is recommended.

DANAE, *Leoforos Kazantzaki 43, Aegina town. Tel. 0297/22424, Fax 0297/26509. Rates (with tax): Drs 9,200 single; Drs 12,300 double. Breakfast included. 52 rooms. No credit cards.*

Located about a kilometer from the ferry terminal, in a tree-lined avenue overlooking the sea, the Danae is a modern, two-story, balcony-lined hotel with a small swimming pool out front, and easy parking. The rooms are sparely but modernly decorated and equipped and each has a private bathroom, balcony, and telephone. Other hotel facilities include a restaurant and bar. This is good value.

BROWN, *Toti Hatzi Paralia 3, Aegina town. Tel. 0297/22271, Fax 0297/23586. Rates (with tax): Drs 8,200 single; Drs 11,200 double. Breakfast included. 25 rooms. No credit cards.*

On the waterfront at the south end of the harbor, the Brown is an elegant old building that has been refurbished with a touch of modern class, and with an additional accommodation section added. Some rooms overlook the courtyard garden and all have telephone and private bathroom. There is easy parking.

EPHI, *Odos Paleas Choras 6, Souvala. Tel. 0297/52214, Fax 0297/53065. Rates (with tax): Drs 7,000 single; Drs 11,000 double. Breakfast Drs 1,200. 32 rooms. No credit cards.*

If you find that Aegina town is too busy, try Souvala on the north coast: it is quieter though not exactly quiet. This hotel doesn't have much in the way of architectural character, having been built in the 1970s, but it is a friendly place and its owner makes his guests welcome. Each of the modernly furnished rooms has a balcony, telephone and private bath-room, half of them have seaviews, and a few have air conditioning. There is indoor and outdoor dining, a bar, television room, and free parking.

WHERE TO EAT

BOSTITSANOS, *Fish Market, Aegina town. Tel. 0297/23995. Drs 4,000 to Drs 6,000. American Express, Visa. Seafood/traditional.*

Built in 1829, when Aegina town was the capital of Greece, Bostitsanos has welcomed such notables as General de Gaulle and Olaf Palme in its time, and was a fixture on the jetset scene. The restaurant specializes in seafood from the Saronic Gulf. You choose your own fish and the price depends on its weight. Barbounie and dourado are favorites here, but you can have other fish also, as well as grilled octopus and squid, prawns, baked lobster, fried and grilled mussels, crab, etc. There are also meat dishes, with roast suckling lamb being a popular choice. A fine selection of French and Greek wines complements the dishes, but you could do worse than opt for the excellent house retsina.

BABBYZ, *Paralia, Aegina town. Tel. 0297/23594. Drs 3,000 to Drs 5,000. No credit cards. Seafood/traditional.*

On the seafront south of the port, Babbyz specializes in seafood. Various prawn dishes are a particular favorite with the local clientele here.

TO MARIDAKI, *Odos Dimokratias, Aegina town. Tel. 0297/24014. Drs 2,500 to Drs 4,500. No credit cards. Seafood.*

Plenty of seafood choices on the menu, either as part of a multi-dish *meze* meal or as individual dishes. All are served with a touch of French style both in the cooking and the decor.

VATSOULIA, *Odos Agii Assomati, Aegina town. Tel. 0297/22711. Drs 2,500 to Drs 4,000. No credit cards. Traditional.*

Unlike many of the restaurants in Aegina town this one does not specialize in seafood, but has a wide range of other dishes on the menu, including rabbit and barbecued chicken.

SEEING THE SIGHTS

Most ferries and the hydrofoils from Piraeus serve **Aegina town** on the island's northwest coast. This is a surprisingly graceful place, a condition it owes to its brief reign as Greece's capital in the 1820s when a bunch of neo-classical mansions, now decked out in faded pastel shades, were built on the seafront to house the government in style. Look for the pretty, whitewashed little **Church of Agios Nikolaos** at the harbor, along whose southern stretch is the floating fruit and vegetable market, with produce changing hands over the sternposts of *caïques* (long, narrow boats) tied up to the quay.

At the north end of the harbor are the scant remains of a 6th century BC **Temple of Apollo** and the **Acropolis of Aegina**, with part of one Doric column still on its feet to identify the site, Tel. *0297/22248; the archeological zone is open Tuesday to Sunday 8:30 am to 4 pm; admission Drs 500 (the museum is closed temporarily, with no reopening date announced)*. There is an **on-site museum** featuring a small but interesting collection of finds from around Aegina, including pottery and terracotta figurines from the Bronze Age through Mycenaean times to the Classical era, an inscription referring to the goddess Aphaia, fragments of sculpture from the Temple of Aphaia depicting scenes from the Siege of Troy, and a sculpture of a sphinx.

In front of this site, and lying mostly just below the surface of the sea, are the remains of the moles of Aegina's ancient **naval harbor**, where the island's 60 trireme warships were based.

Some 8 kilometers east of Aegina town, on the road to the seaside resort of Agia Marina, are the ruins of **Palaiochora**, open daily 8:30 am to 6 pm; *admission free*, the island's main town in Byzantine times, when the population had abandoned the coastal settlements in fear of raiding corsairs, and which is now abandoned in its turn. This is a kind of church graveyard, or more accurately a graveyard of churches. At one time in the town's history there were apparently 365 churches, one for each day of the year. Now there are the remains of 28, some with icons and frescoes to be seen.

Aegina's main claim to fame – apart from pistachio nuts – is the **Temple of Aphaia**, a couple of kilometers uphill from Agia Marina amidst pine forests, Tel. 0297/32398; *open Monday to Friday 8:15 am to 5 pm, Saturday and Sunday 8:30 am to 3 pm; admission Drs 800, students Drs 400.*. The temple is a remarkable survival, partly because of its dedication to the otherwise obscure and little-worshipped deity Aphaia, a fertility goddess and protectress of women, and not least because it owed nothing to those too-clever-by-half Athenians across the water.

Dating from the end of the 6th century BC and the beginning of the 5th, this is the best-preserved temple from the Archaic period in Greece. It was decorated with sculptures depicting scenes from the Siege of Troy, most of which are now in Munich. Partly reconstructed and with 24 of its original 32 columns in place, including those which grace a unique top deck in the interior, and with traces of its red-painted stucco wall covering still visible, the temple and its complex of associated buildings form an evocative ruin with a fine view over the Saronic Gulf – you can easily see the Athenians coming.

An even better view can be had from the 532-meter summit of Mount Oros in the south-central region of Aegina. In summer the crowds tend to stick to the coast and it is pleasant to stroll or cycle in the agricultural interior.

Among the island's main resorts are **Agia Marina** on the east coast, an overbuilt package tourism destination with almost zero charm. **Souvala** on the north coast is prettier, with a nice sweep of taverna-lined harborfront. The southwest coast resort of **Perdika** is an attractive fishing village with a fine beach – en route to Perdikas from Aegina town you pass through the village of **Marathonas**, which has good beaches lying on either side along the bay, and tree-shaded waterside tavernas.

NIGHTLIFE & ENTERTAINMENT

As the main beach resort, **Agia Marina** is where the noisiest discos are. Aegina town is more sedate, with a seat at a taverna's outdoor terrace enough for most tastes.

SHOPPING

On Aegina it has to be **pistachio nuts**: there are several kiosks selling them across the street from the ferry terminal. Buy fresh produce from the caïques of the floating market along the Paralia south of the terminal.

EXCURSIONS & DAY TRIPS

In summer, six caïques and several car ferries daily make the 20-minute crossing from Aegina town to the small offshore island of **Angistiri**, which has a population of 500 and an area of 17 square kilometers. Angistiri has started to become a full-fledged tourist destination in recent years thanks to its fine beaches, but hasn't quite got there yet. Explore the fishing village of **Skala**, where the caïques dock, and among whose neighboring stretches of sand is a fully unclothed nudist beach. A minibus runs four times daily from Skala to the pretty inland village of **Limenaria**.

If Angistiri isn't small enough for you, there are around 12 caïque sailings from Perdika on Aegina to the even smaller islet of **Moni**, a 10-minute crossing.

PRACTICAL INFORMATION

- **Banks** – The **National Bank of Greece** has a branch in Aegina town on the Paralia at the corner of Odos Pileos, open Monday through Thursday from 8 am to 2 pm, and to 1:30 pm on Friday.
- **Doctors** – **Aegina Hospital** is at Odos Nosokomiou, Aegina town, *Tel. 0297/22222.*
- **Police** – The central police station is at *Odos Leonardou Lada, Aegina town, Tel. 0297/22100.* The tourist police are at the same location, *Tel. 0297/23243.*
- **Port Authority** – *Tel. 0297/22328*
- **Post Office** – The main post office is at *Plateia Ethnegersias, Aegina town,* open Monday through Friday from 7:30 am to 2 pm.
- **Telephone** – The area code for Aegina is *0297.* The Greek Telecommunication Organization (OTE) office is at Odos Aiakou, *Tel. 0297/22499.*
- **Tourist Information** – There is no Greek Tourist Organization (EOT) office on Aegina. Maps of the island and descriptive booklets can be bought from news vendors and souvenir shops.

POROS

With **Poros** you get two islands for the price of one, which is just as well really, as otherwise there isn't much to the place. That said, plenty of people like their Greek islands to come with little or nothing, and a significant number like there to be as much of little or nothing as possible. Poros town occupies most of the small island of **Sfalria** facing the Peloponnese coast no more than a 360-meter stone-skip across the water. The bigger island is called **Kalavreia** and the two are separated by a narrow canal.

ARRIVALS & DEPARTURES

By Sea

There are two car ferries a day from **Piraeus's Great Harbor** to Poros, sailing via **Aegina**, and continuing to **Hydra** and **Spetses**. They leave from berths at Akti Posidonos and Akti Miaoulou. Tickets cost Drs 1,690 one-way from Piraeus, journey time 3 hours.

Hydrofoils operated by CERES Flying Dolphins sail to Poros twice daily on weekdays, and every 2 hours on average on weekends from Piraeus's **Zea Marina**. About half of the services are via **Aegina**. Tickets cost Drs 3,380 one-way for the 1-hour direct journey.

The nearest mainland port is **Galatas**, with a ferry making the 360-meter crossing every 20 minutes at peak times; the fare is Drs 80. If you're strapped for cash, you could probably swim across.

ORIENTATION

There's not much in the way of orientation needed for Poros. With an area of 23 square kilometers and a permanent population of 5,000, it lies 45 kilometers south of Piraeus, and 360 meters off the Peloponnese coast at the northeastern tip of the Argolid Peninsula. Green and hilly, the island consists of **Poros town** and a few adjacent beaches, and not much in the interior apart from 390-meter **Mount Vigla** in the middle.

GETTING AROUND THE ISLAND

By Bus & Moped

One bus runs every 20 minutes along the south coast from **Neorion Beach** in the west to **Zoödochos Pigi Monastery** in the east. You can hire mopeds and bicycles at several locations near the ferry quais.

WHERE TO STAY

NEON AEGLI, *Askeli Beach . Tel. 0298/22372, Fax 0298/24345. Rates (with tax): Drs 12,000 single; Drs 16,000 double. Breakfast included. 74 rooms. Visa, MasterCard.*

Shaded by trees along the shore at Askeli Beach, the Neon Aegli is a biggish hotel with little in the way of architectural style but plenty of facilities. The modern, efficiently comfortable rooms all have a balcony with seaview, air conditioning, telephone, television and private bathroom, and minibar on request. There a small private beach with a beach bar, and the hotel also has a restaurant, cafeteria, bar with live music in the evening, and private parking.

GEORGIA MELLOU RESIDENCE, *Odos Kolokotronis 10. Tel. 0298/22309. Rates (with tax): Drs 6,000 double. Breakfast Drs 1,000. 6 rooms. No credit cards.*

These rooms to let in the center of Poros town, near the church, have balconies looking out on the port. The rooms are basic but clean, with shared bathroom, and a refrigerator in the corridor.

WHERE TO EAT

EPTA ADELFIA, *Tombazi Plateia Iroon. Tel. 0298/22446. Drs 3,000 to Drs 6,000. No credit cards. Traditional taverna.*

Otherwise known as the Seven Brothers, this is one of the stalwart old Poros tavernas, and one that has kept its standards high even although it has become a fixture on the tourist circuit. Expect to pay a little, but not much, more than in other places of similar quality. Epta Adelfia has, however, retained the traditional Poros style, while many of the town's tavernas have gone chic without quite being able to translate that into taste on the plate.

O PANTELIS, *Plateia Iroon. Tel. 0298/22581. Drs 2,500 to Drs 5,000. No credit cards. Traditional taverna.*

On a typical summer evening, tables at this taverna's tiny outdoor terrace are worth their weight in the currency of your choice – although if you do get one, you'll find that the tab isn't excessive in drachmas considering the quality of the food, the friendly service, and the atmospheric dining experience. Go easy with the excellent retsina here: they've got plenty of it in those big barrels and it's devilish good stuff.

SEEING THE SIGHTS

Poros town is busy in summer – overrun in fact – which detracts from its charming aspect of red pantiled roofs atop graceful houses, shops and tavernas, anchored along the narrow strait separating Poros from the mainland. The setting is a notably scenic one. Still, Henry Miller's remark that sailing through the Straits of Poros was "a joy too deep almost to be remembered," like the passage out of the womb, seems a trifle overstated today, when the brief joy of the ferry crossing is only too easily forgotten.

Maybe the most interesting spectacle on Poros is a ship, although if your opinion of Greek nautical prowess has suffered from exposure to Greek ferries, you might find this hard to believe. The ship in question belongs to the Greek Naval Academy headquartered in Poros town, and she is in fact a **trireme**, a replica of the triple-banked galleys that swept those pesky Persians right out of the water at the Battle of Salamis in 480 BC. When she is not photogenically rounding Cape Sounion, or engaged on other such special photo-ops for the Greek Navy, the trireme can be seen moored north of the ferry terminal at Poros town.

The island is wooded and hilly, topping out on the 360-meter summit of **Mount Vigla** north of Poros town, and is a pleasant enough place for walking and cycling. Its beaches aren't much to write home about, though. The scant remains of the 6th-century BC **Temple of Poseidon** in the center of the island wouldn't be worth a pitcher of warm ouzo if it wasn't for their connection with the Athenian orator Demosthenes, who committed suicide here in 322 BC. You can easily walk the two kilometers up from Poros town through wooded scenery.

If you're stuck for something to do after communing with the shade of Demosthenes, the other big excitement on Poros is the **Monastery of Zoödochos Pigi**, *open daily dawn to dusk, admission free,* in a little green-fringed valley close to the sea on the south shore of Kalavreia. The monastery church has a fine gilt iconostasis.

PRACTICAL INFORMATION

• **Banks** – The **National Bank of Greece** is at *Odos Agiou Nikolaou 68,* open Monday through Thursday from 8 am to 2 pm, and to 1:30 pm on Friday.
• **Doctors** – **Poros Health Center**, *Tel. 0298/22222.*
• **Police** – The police station is *on Odos Agiou Nikolaou, Tel. 0298/22256.*

The tourist police are at the same location, *Tel. 0298/22462.*

• **Port Authority** – *Tel. 0298/22274*

• **Post Office** – The post office is *on Plateia Karamanou,* open Monday through Friday from 7:30 am to 2 pm.

• **Telephone** The area code for Poros is *0298.* The Greek Telecommunication Organization (OTE) office is at *Odos Kalomiri 30, Tel. 0298/ 22275.*

• **Tourist Information** There is no Greek Tourist Organization (EOT) office on Poros.

HYDRA (YDRA)

It wasn't until the 17th and 18th centuries that history caught up with sleepy **Hydra,** when it became a base for wealthy merchants, sea captains, pirates and smugglers, all growing fat on profits from trade between the Ottoman Empire and Europe, and who left a legacy of beautiful mansions. In the 19th century, the descendants of those hard-headed gentlemen got a rush of patriotic blood to their heads. Hydriot admirals and sailors played a vital part in the Greek struggle for independence from Turkey that broke out in 1821, and the island provided more than half the warships in the rebel fleet. This effort drained Hydra's energies and it slumbered on in faded style from then until tourism woke it up with a jolt in the Sixties and Seventies.

If you want to discover Hydra you're going to have to get up off your ass and walk, or get up on your ass and ride. Donkeys and Shanks's pony are the main forms of transport on this little island, where cars and mopeds are effectively banned. The absence of mopeds, those tiny two-stroke horrors which have turned the entire Mediterranean basin into an acoustic torture chamber, is a joy not easily expressed in words. Suddenly, you can experience all kinds of new audio sensations: the silken rustle of wavelets on the shore, birds trilling in the treetops, insects humming amidst the flowers, goat-bells tinkling in the hills.

So, your ears will be in good shape and your lungs will feel the benefit of all that fresh air. Hydra, however, is far from being an island of blessed calm. In summer, hordes from Athens and Europe descend on it like

Visigoths on a well-earned break. Pity the poor monks and nuns, whose monasteries were established here when this was a barren place, devoid of interest and unwelcome guests. Now there is wealth in abundance and the religious folks are the main points of interest for beach-surfeited visitors (many of whom probably can't tell one end of a crucifix from another, and think that icons date from way back in time to the origins of the Macintosh operating system).

Hydra town used to be one of the main rendezvous of the "beautiful people," and their hangers-on. Nowadays, the really beautiful people have moved away to places where the paparazzi need longer lenses to reach them. Still, some fairly beautiful people, and others who could easily become beautiful given time, flock here and parade themselves in all the expensive places. The spectacle can be quite distracting – for about five minutes.

ARRIVALS & DEPARTURES
By Sea

There are regular car ferries from Piraeus's **Great Harbor** to Hydra, most of them sailing via the islands of **Aegina** and **Poros**, and continuing to **Spetses**. At peak periods, there are two sailings daily, joined by a third on Saturday and Sunday. They leave from berths at Akti Posidonos and Akti Miaoulou. Tickets cost Drs 1,800 one-way from Piraeus, Drs 850 from Poros; journey time from Piraeus is around 4 hours and from Poros 1 1/2 hours.

Hydrofoils operated by CERES Flying Dolphins sail hourly to Hydra from Piraeus's **Zea Marina**. Tickets cost Drs 3,960 one-way for the 100-minute direct journey.

The nearest mainland port with connections to and from Hydra is **Ermione**, with six hydrofoils daily at peak periods; the fare is Drs 1,720 one-way for the 20-minute crossing.

ORIENTATION

With an area of 50 square kilometers and a permanent population of 3,000, Hydra is 63 kilometers south of Piraeus. Long and thin, its rocky and mostly barren landscape stretches 49 kilometers from east to west, and 12 kilometers at the widest part of the north-south axis. It lies 7 kilometers offshore from the Argolid Peninsula in the Peloponnese.

The main settlement is **Hydra town**, roughly in the center of the north coast, and there are a few outlying villages: **Mandraki** lies on the coast north of Hydra town, **Vlihos** and **Molos** on the coast south of Hydra town, and **Episkopi** overlooking the south coast. The interior is dotted with monasteries, some of them in ruins.

GETTING AROUND THE ISLAND
By Caïque & Water Taxi

Caïques run regularly from the harbor in Hydra town to beaches – such as they are – up and down the coast. The trips take from 15 to 20 minutes and cost Drs 360 per person one-way. Water taxis can be hired to do the same trips, they can cost ten times as much, and get there ten times as fast.

WHERE TO STAY

MIRANDA, *Odos Miaouli 32, Hydra town. Tel. 0298/52230, Fax 0298/53510. Rates (with tax): Drs 14,000 single; Drs 17,000 double. Breakfast included. 14 rooms. American Express, Visa.*

It's none too cheap here, but you get what you pay for, including a room that houses art exhibitions. Built in 1810 as a wealthy sea captain's pied-à-terre, the Miranda began its hotel career in 1962 and in 1990 was totally restored to point up its antique character. It is now a national monument recognized by the Ministry of Culture and is a classic of old Hydra architecture. The ceilings of the big guest rooms are decorated with paintings by Venetian and Florentine artists, and the furnishings include antiques dating from the 18th and 19th centuries. You enter through a walled courtyard.

MISTRAL, *Aegina town. Tel. 0298/52509, Fax 0298/53469. Rates (with tax): Drs 13,400 single; Drs 16,200 double. Breakfast included. 20 rooms. American Express, Visa.*

Located high up in the town, yet still only 150 meters from the port, over which it has a fine view, the Mistral is another of Hydra's old stonebuilt mansions that have been converted to hotels and entirely restored. Furnished in traditional style, each room has a radio, telephone, and private bathroom. Breakfast and drinks are served in the flower-bedecked garden terrace. In some of the rooms you can have air conditioning on request.

ANGELIKA, *Odos Miaouli 42, Hydra town. Tel. 0298/53202, Fax 0298/ 53698. Rates (with tax): Drs 11,000 single; Drs 13,500 double. Breakfast included. 15 rooms. No credit cards.*

Located some 250 meters from the ferry terminal, the Angelika takes pride in its family ownership and warm welcome, and transmits the message to guests. It's a friendly place, where the rooms are plain but comfortable and all of them have a private bathroom.

SOPHIA, *corner of Odos Miaouli and the waterfront, Hydra town. Tel. 0298/52313 Rates (with tax): Drs 6,000 single; Drs 7,000 double. Breakfast not included. 5 rooms. No credit cards.*

You'll have to book early to get into this popular little place. The rooms are clean, but simply furnished and with shared bathrooms. However, the Sophia's reasonable rates and location at the heart of the Paralia compensate for this. The major drawback of the location is that there are some noisy bars and tavernas in the area.

WHERE TO EAT

TO STEKI, *Odos Miaouli. Tel. 0298/53517. Drs 3,500 to Drs 7,000. No credit cards. Meze.*

The seafood meze is excellent here, and the cavalcade of little dishes adds up surprisingly quickly to a filling meal, so it can pay to be conservative with the number of meze dishes you order. If you dine outdoors, take the time to at least look into the indoor dining room, to see its fine wall-paintings of local scenes.

BARBA DIMAS, *Odos Tombazi. Tel. 0298/53166. Drs 2,500 to Drs 6,000. No credit cards. Traditional.*

With only six tables, Barba Dimas can make dining, or trying to dine there more of a frustration than anything. Except that it is rightly judged by locals to be one of their finest eateries. No menu, just take a chance on the cook's inspiration for the evening. You're not likely to be disappointed.

DOUSKOS, *Odos Rafaelias ??. Tel. 0298/xxxx. Drs 2,500 to Drs 5,000. No credit cards. Traditional.*

Not being on the fashionable waterfront, this taverna is more popular with local people than with tourists, and in a place as touristy as Hydra that is really no bad thing. Still, the old folks who congregate on the tree-shaded terrace here will make you welcome, and the food is good.

LULU'S, *Odos Miaouli. Tel. 0298/52018. Drs 2,500 to Drs 4,000. No credit cards. Traditional.*

Among the good food at a good good price on the menu in this taverna, which is among the oldest on Hydra, the moussaka is not to be missed.

SEEING THE SIGHTS

The big attraction – you can even say the only attraction – on Hydra is **Hydra town**. It clusters on the rocky hillsides that form a natural theater around the harbor, and is a strikingly handsome place, with many stonebuilt *arkhontiko* mansions dating from the 18th and 19th centuries standing on the narrow quayside along the harbor and the narrow streets uphill. There are **windmills** and bits of windmills on the rocky hills either side of the harbor, and parts of the walls and other strongpoints of the 19th-century fortifications.

Mansions that once belonged to Hydriot heroes of the War of Independence are dotted all around the town, as well as mansions that belonged to the less heroic. Most are private dwellings, hotels, or restaurants, but that doesn't make them any less interesting. One that can be visited is the **Arkhontiko of Admiral Iakobos Tombasis**, *Tel. (0298) 52291; open daily July and August, 10 am to 8 pm; admission free,* which stands above the west side of the harbor and now belongs to Athens Polytechnic's Art School. It hosts exhibitions in July and August.

Closer inspection shows some of those quaint stone buildings to be far-from-quaint little art galleries, with prices every bit as soild as the stonework. For Hydra is an Artist's Haven. Creative sensibilities from many nations breath deep the invigorating air and soak up the heady potions that spur artistic endeavor – which is to say the café terraces and bars are usually full. There are a lot of people wearing what look like black pajamas, and more males with ponytails than you'd find on a Kentucky stud farm.

Just behind the waterfront is the **Monastery of Panagia**, *ppen daily, admission Drs 100 (donation)*, dating from the 17th and 18th centuries, whose virtues haven't proved enduring even though it uses stone recycled from the Temple of Poseidon on nearby Poros island; it now houses local government offices. You can wander around the courtyard here. The monastery church has some notable icons.

Apart from the monastery on Hydra town's waterfront, there are others which form a wide semicircle in the hills south of town, overlooked by 590-meter Mount Eros. They are **Agia Efpraxias**, **Profitis Ilias**, **Agias Matronis**, **Agias Triadas**, and **Agios Nikolaos**, while **Zourvas Monastery** breaks the circle by occupying a position in the northeast. You can hike to them along tracks through the rough, scenic countryside. Dress for both men and women should be respectable: no beachwear, shorts, miniskirts, or bare arms.

Beaches of any kind are in short supply on Hydra, and sand beaches are entirely absent. Pebble beaches are the best that's on offer. You can walk to **Mandraki beach**, about two kilometers north of Hydra town, and **Kamini beach**, about one kilometer south, as well as others a little more distant. An alternative is to go by frequent caïque service from the harbor at Hydra town or, if money is no object, by water taxi.

NIGHTLIFE & ENTERTAINMENT

The in place for a waterfont-terrace drink in Hydra town is the **Pirate Bar**, near the clock tower, *Tel. 0297/52711*; it has nothing Greek about it but the cocktails are pretty good. A consistently good disco is **Disco Heaven**, uphill from the west end of the harbor, *Tel. 0297/52716*; if the climb takes too much out of you for dancing, you can always just admire the great view of the harbor instead.

SHOPPING

As a self-proclaimed, self-important, and self-satisfied "artist's resort," Hydra town has enough art galleries and designer boutiques to constitute an obstacle to shipping.

PRACTICAL INFORMATION

• **Banks** – The **National Bank of Greece** is on *the Paralia, near Odos Miaouli,* open Monday through Thursday from 8 am to 2 pm, and to 1:30 pm on Friday.

• **Doctors** – **Hydra Medical Center** is on *Odos Votsi. Tel. 0298/53150.*

• **Police** – The police station is at *Odos Votsi 9, Tel. 0298/32205.* The tourist police are at the same location, *Tel. 0298/52205.*

• **Port Authority** – *Tel. 0298/52279*

• **Post Office** – The post office is off *Odos Ikonomou,* open Monday through Friday from 7:30 am to 2 pm.

• **Telephone** – The area code for Hydra is *0298.* The Greek Telecommunication Organization (OTE) office is on *Odos Votsi, Tel. 0298/52262.*

• **Tourist Information** – There is no Greek Tourist Organization (EOT) office on Hydra.

SPETSES

Lying at the entrance to the Argolic Gulf, just around the corner of the Argolid Peninsula from the Saronic Gulf, **Spetses** is the furthest of these islands from Piraeus that is still just about doable as a day trip. It has become a popular tourist destination, and suffers the usual invasion in July and August and on weekends from April to October. At other times, and away from the few tourist beaches, it is a calm, green fertile island, partly reforested with Aleppo pines, the trees that earned Spetses the name Pityoussa (Pine Tree Island) in ancient times.

Spetses joined the other Argo-Saronic islands in making a notable contribution to Greece's struggle for independence from Ottoman rule in the 1820s, providing ships, men, and a remarkable woman: **Captain Laskarina Bouboulina**, a naval commander who defeated a Turkish squadron (Tailhook Society members please take note).

Offshore from Spetses is the islet of **Spetsopoula**, owned by the Niarchos family, commercial rivals of the Onassis clan.

ARRIVALS & DEPARTURES
By Sea

There is one ferry a day from Piraeus's **Great Harbor** to Spetses, sailing via **Aegina**, **Poros** and **Hydra**. It leaves from a berth at *Akti Posidonos*. Tickets cost Drs 2,400 one-way from Piraeus, journey time 4 1/2 hours.

Hydrofoils and fast catamarans operated by CERES Flying Dolphins sail up to seven times a day to Spetses from Piraeus's **Zea Marina**, some of the services being via **Aegina**, **Poros** and **Hydra**. Tickets cost Drs 4,675 one-way for the 1{3/4}-hour direct journey.

The nearest mainland port is **Kosta**, with three ferry services a day making the 20-minute crossing, which costs Drs 250.

ORIENTATION

With an area of 22 square kilometers and a permanent population of 4,000, Spetses lies 86 straight-line kilometers south of Piraeus (the sea route is about half as long again), and 3 kilometers off the Peloponnese coast at the southwestern tip of the Argolid Peninsula. It is roughly oval shaped, 9 kilometers long and 6 kilometers wide. **Spetses town** on the coast facing the mainland is the main settlement, and there are a few coastal hamlets dotted around the island near the beaches.

Water is scarce on Spetses, as almost every drop has to be shipped over from the mainland. Taking a shower can be a slow and none too wet experience.

GETTING AROUND THE ISLAND
By Bus & Boat

Cars are banned on Spetses. From **Spetses town** one bus runs every hour between 7 am and 10 pm along the north coast from the harbor to **Ligoneri**, a village with beaches either side; it gets very crowded. Another bus runs hourly between 10 am and 4 pm from the municipal beach along the south coast, through **Agia Marina** to **Agii Anargiri**; it gets very crowded too.

Water taxis – high-powered, high-priced speedboats – run like bats out of hell from Spetses town harbor, the **Dapia**, where the ferries and hydrofoils dock, to the beaches and back again to pick up more passengers willing and able to shell out up to Drs 8,000 to circumnavigate the island. Caïques take longer to get to the beaches, but cost only Drs 1,000.

By Moped, Bicyle, & Carriage

Although cars are a no-no, the distinctive charms of the moped are given free rein; you can rent them just about everywhere for around Drs 3,000 a day. Bicycles can also be rented at several locations near the ferry quais, while horsedrawn carriages, available for rent on the Paralia, make for a slower but more romantic way of getting around.

WHERE TO STAY

POSIDONION, *Dapia. Tel. 0298/72006, Fax 0298/72208. Rates (with tax): Drs 16,000 single; Drs 19,000 double. Breakfast Drs 2,000. 55 rooms. American Express, Diners Club, Visa, MasterCard.*

A rather special place, the Posidonion dates from 1911 and has retained much of the style of the belle époque, when it was *the* place where the well-heeled chose to stay in Spetses, and still is. It has high, decorated ceilings and lots of mirrors, and two grand pianos in the public spaces. The rooms are big. There is a garden terrace facing the sea.

SARONIKOS, *Dapia. Tel. 0298/73741. Rates (with tax): Drs 8,000 double. Breakfast included. 20 rooms. No credit cards.*

Just off Plateia Dapia beside the harbor, the Saronikos is a good low-cost option for Spetses town. The rooms have old furniture not special enough to be considered antique, and bathrooms are shared. It is clean and friendly, with a good position, and some rooms overlooking the water.

WHERE TO EAT

THE BAKERY, *Odos Botassi. Drs 3,000 to Drs 6,000. Visa, MasterCard. Fashionable.*

Anywhere else this than Spetses, this place would make a pleasant change from an unrelenting diet of traditional tavernas. In Spetses, however, the challenge is finding a traditional eatery at all. That said, The Bakery has a wide range of international dishes on the menu and a nice relaxing atmosphere to go aong with the cooking. It even does have some good traditional dishes.

STELIOS, *Paralia. Tel. 0298/73748. Drs 2,500 to Drs 5,000. No credit cards. Traditional.*

For dining at the waterfront in a no-frills Greek eatery, there is no better choice in Spetses than Stelios.

SEEING THE SIGHTS

Although they straggle attractively along a scenically situated harbor, **Spetses town's** whitewashed building do not possess as much character as Hydra's stonebuilt ones. **Spetses Museum**, *located in the Hatziyianni Mexis Mansion off Odos Evangelistrias, open Tuesday to Sunday 9 am to 3 pm, admission free*, includes examples of local arts and crafts, and relics of Spetses' contribution to the War of Independence from Turkish rule in the 1820s, most notably a casket containing the mortal remains of the fiery female naval commander Laskarina Bouboulina.

The **Old Port**, now scarcely in use, lies south of the municipal beach and is a more attractive place and with less tourist clutter than the new one. The nuns at the nearby **Convent of Agios Nikolaos** will be happy to sell you pots of their excellent homemade yogurt so long as you dress respectably. North of town is the **Anargiros and Koryalenios School**, now no longer in use, where the writer John Fowles taught in the early 1950s, and which later appeared in his Spetses-inspired novel *The Magus*.

The **Bekiri sea caves** near the beach at Agii Anargiri on the west coast are worth getting up from the beach for, but not making a special trip to get there. Get away from the tourist crush by hiking into the **pine forests** of the interior (take water with you if you want to come hiking out again).

PRACTICAL INFORMATION

• **Banks** – The **National Bank of Greece** is at *Plateia Dapia,* beside the harbor, open Monday through Thursday from 8 am to 2 pm, and to 1:30 pm on Friday.

• **Doctors** – The **Spetses Rural Clinic** is at *Odos Evangelistrias, Tel. 0298/ 72472.*

• **Police** – The police station is on *Odos Botassi, Tel. 0298/73100.*

• **Port Authority** – *Tel. 0298/72245*

• **Post Office** – The post office is on *Plateia Karamanou,* open Monday through Friday from 7:30 am to 2 pm.

• **Telephone** – The area code for Spetses is *0298.* The Greek Telecommunication Organization (OTE) office is on *Odos Santou,* near the Star Hotel, *Tel. 0298/72399.*

• **Tourist Information** – There is no Greek Tourist Organization (EOT) office on Spetses.

10. CRETE

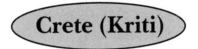

Crete (Kriti)

There is an island called Crete
In the midst of the wine-dark sea.
Homer – The Odyssey

Crete is the biggest Greek island, and lies at the southern boundary of the Aegean Sea, not quite midway between mainland Greece and the North African coastline of Egypt. This island is of prime importance in European history because it gave the continent its first civilization, the **Minoan**, whose dazzling culture, based on palace complexes at **Knossos** and other excavated sites, was already up and running by 2800 BC. Crete is one of few places in Greece where the classical heritage takes second place to a culture of far greater antiquity.

Nothing like the Minoans' impact on Crete has been seen since. The Greco-Romans and Byzantines left an imprint, of course, but it is not too harsh a judgment to say that the island was a cultural backwater throughout their 2,000-year tenure. They were followed by the Venetians, whose determined effort to hold out against the encroaching Ottoman empire is indicated by fortresses of great strength all over the island – each one of which surrendered or was overrun by the Turks in the end. In spite of

CRETE FINDS & FAVORITES

• *National Archaeological Museum. The wonders of the ancient Minoans uncovered by archaeologists are on display here, in what is one of the world's most important historical collections (see Heraklion).*

• *Knossos. The great palace complex of the Minoans flourished from 1900 BC to 1400 BC, before it was destroyed. Now it has been partially and beautifully reconstructed, giving visitors a unique insight into a vanished civilization (see Heraklion).*

• *Rethimno and Hania. Although far from being unscathed by Crete's tourist boom, the old centers of these two towns retain enough of their original Venetian and Ottoman graces to make them among the most handsome towns in Greece (see Western Crete).*

• *Samaria Gorge. A deep fissure, 14 kilometers long, in the Lefka Mountains of western Crete, traversing which has become an essential rite-of-passage for fit and healthy nature lovers on the island (see Western Crete).*

• *Lassithi Plateau. Some 5,000 windmills spin their canvas blades on this fertile plateau at an altitude of 900 meters, and overlooked by the great mass of Mount Dikti (see Eastern Crete).*

• *Kato Zakros. Walk softly in this unspoiled little village in a still-unspoiled corner of the east coast, where Minoan remains mark the site of one of their important harbors (see Eastern Crete).*

a series of bloody rebellions in the 19th century, it wasn't until 1912 that Crete was incorporated into the modern Greek state.

In May 1941, Crete was invaded from the air by the élite German Parachute Division, which suffered such heavy losses in its hard-fought victory over the island's British, Australian, New Zealander and Greek defenders that Hitler never used it offensively again. Crete endured four years of Nazi occupation characterized by increasingly strong and effective Greek resistance, and increasingly ferocious German reprisals.

Tourism has developed at breakneck pace on this island, and in many places has overwhelmed not only the natural world, but also the natural

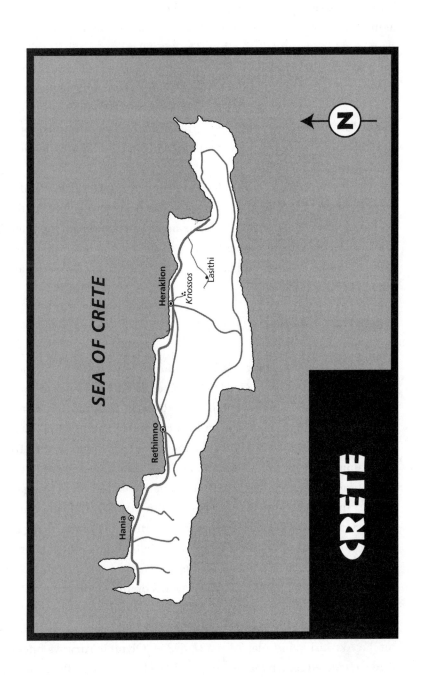

hospitality that was once the pride of the Cretans. This is most notable along the coast, of course, and in particular in the boilerhouse months from mid-June to mid-September. The coastal strip can still beguile, but the real Crete lies elsewhere. On a morning when the sun comes up with the breakfast tray, it is not easy to be sniffy about beaches, but you should be strong, leave the toasting bodies behind, and take the road into the **Lefka, Idi**, or **Dikti** mountains. By turning your back on the beach you will find another Crete, far removed in spirit from the heavily developed coastal resorts.

Crete's mountains are quickly reached from Heraklion and the coastal resorts. There are few good access roads, however, and once there the going can get "adventurous." The mountains dominate the island's interior. Their cool air is a benediction in summer, as you pass through pretty mountain villages and take the opportunity to get closer to nature along hiking trails.

ARRIVALS & DEPARTURES
By Air

Crete's **Nikos Kazantzakis International Airport** is five kilometers east of Heraklion, *Tel. 081/245644*. **Olympic Airways** operates seven scheduled return flights on Tuesday, Wednesday, Saturday, and Sunday; and six on Monday, Thursday and Friday, to Heraklion from Athens, flying time 45 minutes. In addition, there are four flights a week from Thessalonika, flying time 1 hour 50 minutes; four a week from Rhodes, flying time 45 minutes; two a week in summer from Mykonos, flying time 1 hour; three a week in summer from Thira (Santorini), flying time 40 minutes; and one a week in summer from Larnaka in Cyprus, flying time 1 hour 10 minutes. For current departure flight times and ticket prices, contact Olympic in Heraklion at: *Plateia Eleftherias, Tel. 081/229191; Reservations, Tel. 081/244802*. Travel agents on the island can also book onward flights.

In the west of the island, **Hania Airport** is 14 kilometers east of Hania, on the Akrotiri Peninsula, *Tel. 0821/63264*. **Olympic Airways** operates three scheduled return flights a day to Hania from Athens, flying time 45 minutes; and two a week from Thessalonika, flying time 1 hour 45 minutes. Contact Olympic in Hania at: *Odos Stratigou Tzanakaki 88, Tel. 0821/40268; Reservations, Tel. 0821/57701.* In the east of the island, **Sitia Airport** is six kilometers west of Sitia, *Tel. 0843/24666.* **Olympic Airways** operates a minimum of two scheduled return flights a week to Sitia from Athens, flying time 1 hour 25 minutes; and one a week from Karpathos, via Kasos, flying time 1 hour. Contact Olympic in Sitia at: *Odos Eleftheriou Venizelou 56, Tel. 0843/22270.*

There are any number of charter flights from all over northern Europe to Crete's three airports, from April through October. You book a charter flight from a travel agent in Europe, with the return set for between one and six weeks after departure. This will cost in the region of $200 to $300, depending on where you fly from and when, and will be far cheaper than an unrestricted return flight to Athens, and probably cheaper than a Super-Apex fare. Crete can also be a starting point for touring the Aegean islands, as you avoid Athens and Piraeus and there are reasonable ferry connections.

By Sea

In the high season there is one international car ferry connection a week from Heraklion to **Haifa** in Israel, via Limassol in Cyprus. Journey time to Limassol is 22 hours, to Haifa 42 hours. *Tel. 081/244912.* Heraklion is also a stopover on the once-a-week high-season service from **Ancona** in Italy to **Kusadasi** on the west coast of Turkey, opposite Samos. Journey time to Ancona is 59 hours, to Kusadasi 14 hours. *The international ferry can be reached at Tel. 081/244912.*

Domestic car ferry connections from Piraeus's **Great Harbor**, *Tel. 081/229646,* offer plenty of choice, covering the northern Crete ports of, from west to east, Kasteli, Souda (for Hania), Rethimno, Heraklion, Agios Nikolaos, and Sitia. In most cases there are good frequencies in summer. Heraklion gets the lion's share, with two direct sailings daily at peak times. Journey time is 13 1/2 hours; one-way deck tickets cost Drs 6,450. Other ferries make the journey to and from **Piraeus** via various of the Cyclades Islands, including **Amorgos, Andros, Ios, Milos, Mykonos, Naxos, Paros,**

Thira (Santorini), **Siros**, and **Tinos**. These connections vary in fequency from one a week to four a week, and the routes also vary. *For these islands, the car ferry number is 081/244912.*

An irregular car ferry service, *Tel. 0822/22024*, connects **Piraeus** with Kasteli on Crete, sailing via various ports on the east Peloponnese coast, and the islands of **Kythira** and **Antikythira**. Nominally, in summer, there are two sailings a week. Tickets cost Drs 5,170 one-way for the 9-hour journey to Piraeus. Three times a week in summer there is a car ferry between **Thessalonika** and Heraklion, *Tel. 081/229646*. Journey time is approximately 22 hours; one-way deck tickets cost Drs 10,750.

Heraklion and the east coast ports of Agios Nikolaos and Sitia have connections to several of the Dodecanese Islands, including **Rhodes** and **Karpathos**. There are two sailings a week, *Tel. 081/226297*. Journey time to Rhodes is 11 hours; one-way deck tickets cost Drs 6,300.

ORIENTATION

With an area of 8,260 square kilometers and a coastline of 1,050 kilometers, Crete is some 260 kilometers from east to west, 60 kilometers from north to south in the center, and supports a permanent population of 550,000. It is big enough to be divided into four of the Greek administrative districts called prefectures: **Heraklion** (Iraklio), **Rethimno**, **Lasithi**, and **Hania**. You could easily spend the summer exploring Crete and still not get anywhere near to seeing all of it. If you are including it in a tour of Greece and its islands, the chances are you will have to be content with no more than a glimpse of its many charms.

The north coast is the easiest part to travel in, and is far more heavily developed than the south coast, which is more rugged and less accessible. That has not stopped development of resort areas in the south also.

Climate-wise you may be surprised at how strong the wind can blow here, especially on the south coast, at the top of the tourist season. Spring and fall are still the best times to visit, because they are quieter and cooler, with spring being the best of the two thanks to the burgeoning spring flowers that light up the landcape. As a bonus, Cretans' natural courtesy hasn't yet been frayed into irascibility by the summer turmoil.

GETTING AROUND THE ISLAND

By Bus

With its strategic position in the middle of the north coast, **Heraklion** is the focal point of Crete's extensive bus network. There are two main bus terminals in the city:

• **Terminal A**, *Odos Makariou. Tel. 081/245017.* Eastbound: Agios Nikolaos, every 45 minutes on average, 1 1/2 hours; Ierapetra, six daily, 2 1/ 2 hours; Sitia, four daily, 3 1/2 hours; Lassithi, two daily, 2 hours. Westbound: Rethimno and Hania, every 30 minutes on average, 1 1/ 2 hours and 2 1/2 hours.

• **Terminal B**, *Hania Gate. Tel. 081/255965.* Phaistos, eight daily, 2 hours; Agia Galini, eight daily 2 1/2 hours; Matala, six daily, 2 hours.

Bus line 1 runs from two to four times an hour between Hania Gate, Plateia Eleftherias, and Heraklion Airport, journey time 20 minutes.

There are also romantically ramshackle village buses running between villages not served by a regular bus route (which means most villages) and the nearest big town: Heraklion, Rethimno, Hania, Kastelli, Agios Nikolaos, Sitia, and Ierapetra. They usually run from the village to the town in the early morning and return again in the early evening. By their nature these "services" are unpredictable at best and are often used, though not during the summer, for transporting schoolkids.

By Boat

The southwest coast has a regular ferry service – regular in summer at any rate – connecting the towns of **Paleohora**, **Sougia**, **Agia Roumeli**, **Loutro**, **Hora Sfakion**, and the offshore islet of **Gavdos**. You'll need to use the boat to get away from Agia Roumeli at the southern end of the Samaria Gorge, and of course to reach Gavdos. Otherwise it is more of a convenience than a necessity in an area where roads are poor are buses few and far between.

By Car

Car is by far the best way to see the island. You may miss a little local color by not taking the bus, but at the busiest time of the year that usually means not fighting with mobs of fellow tourists, and an occasional exasperated Cretan, for a place. There are masses of rental firms in all the resorts, and it pays to shop around. If you prefer to stick to the tried-and-tested, try:

• **Alamo**, *Heraklion Airport. Tel. 081/245619*
• **Avis**, *Odos 25 Avgoustou 40, Heraklion. Tel. 081/229402*
• **Budget**, *Heraklion Airport. Tel. 081/243918*
• **European**, *Heraklion Airport. Tel. 081/224090; Odos Idomeneou 21, Heraklion. Tel. 081/246710; Odos Kothri 26, Ierapetra. Tel. 0842/22167; Odos Akti Koundourou 23, Agios Nikolaos. Tel. 0841/25704*
• **Europcar**, *Heraklion Airport. Tel. 081/244022; Odos 25 Avgoustou 38, Heraklion. Tel. 081/289497; Hania Airport. Tel. 0821/63553; Odos Sofokleou Venizelou 70, Rethimno. Tel. 0831/54440; Odos Akti Koundourou 31, Agios Nikolaos. Tel. 0841/24343*
• **Hertz**, *Heraklion Airport. Tel. 081/229702*

By Taxi

Be careful with taxis in Crete: this is a big island, and your hotel might easily be a long way from the nearest airport or ferry terminal, particularly if you arrive in Heraklion and have a destination in the east or west. This can work if you have lots of money, or if three or four fare-paying passengers share the cost.

Otherwise, the usual strictures about taxi use in Greece apply: make sure that the meter is on and set for the correct tarrif, or agree on a ballpark figure with the driver before getting in.

HERAKLION (IRAKLIO)

Like most Greek cities, **Heraklion** is missing a little in the looks department, but again like most Greek cities it has historic monuments and other points of interest that, along with the natural exuberance of its 100,000 residents, go some way towards compensating for the kind of determined ugliness that is modern Greek architecture's "gift" to the world. It also has a fine seafront location.

Heraklion was founded by the Saracens in 824 AD as a pirate base and was known by them as Handax, a name that has come down to us as Candia. In 961, the Emperor Nikephorus Phocas captured it for Byzantium and the Byzantines held it until Venice took over in 1210. Most of the city's finest monuments, including the walls and the harbor fortress, date from the Venetian period.

The Ottoman Turks finally captured Heraklion in 1669 after 21 years of trying. (Fifteen years into this mother of all sieges, and with the Turks still firmly established on the wrong side of the walls, the Ottoman commander, Hussein Pasha, was called to Constantinople to receive a signal honor from the Sultan: he was publicly garroted.) The Turks seem to have been so exhausted by their efforts that they went to sleep for a couple of hundred years.

Only a few kilometers outside of town is one of the most moving, memorable, and controversial sites anywhere on the planet: **Knossos**, the palace center of the enigmatic, beauty-loving Minoan civilization that was flourishing 1,500 years before the Parthenon was set upon the Acropolis in Athens.

ORIENTATION

Plateia Venizelou is Heraklion's main square, more or less smack dab in the middle of the old city, with **Plateia Kallergon** and the **El Greco Park** adjoining it to the north. If you walk east, south, or west of here you'll evenually bump into the **Venetian Walls** that separate the old town from the new. Go north instead and you'll quickly reach the sea, and the frowning **Venetian Fortress** that dominates the harbor. At the eastern, inner section of the walls is **Plateia Eleftherias**, Heraklion's other big square and another important landmark, beside which stands the Greek National Tourist Office (EOT), and adjacent to that the **Archaeological Museum**, which falls into the absolutely-must-see-no-matter-what category.

Beyond the walls things get fuzzy, and you will do better to pass through the outer city by bus or taxi rather than on foot, especially if you are heading for **Knossos**, five kilometers south of the city center.

WHERE TO STAY

ASTORIA, *Plateia Eleftherias 11. Tel. 081/229002, Fax 081/229078. Rates (with tax): Drs 23,500 single; Drs 27,000 double. Breakfast Drs 3,000. 141 rooms. American Express, Diners Club, Visa, MasterCard.*

Fully renovated in 1994, this Sixties-era hotel occupies one of the best, or at least one of the most convenient downtown locations in Heraklion: across Plateia Eleftherias from the Archaeological Museum, and close to the main eastern gate in the city walls. Considering that this is a category A place, rates here are very reasonable. For your money you get a mainly business-orientated hotel, yet one with facilities for tourists, including an all-important swiming pool. The air conditioned rooms are fully equipped to the standard expected of such a prestige establishment.

LATO, *Odos Epimenidou 15. Tel. 081/228103, Fax 081/240350. Rates (with tax): Drs 13,000 single; Drs 18,000 double. Breakfast Drs included. 50 rooms. American Express, Diners Club, Visa, MasterCard.*

Rooms with a view of the harbor are a main attraction at this good-quality, good-value hotel, which offers some characteristics of a seaside hotel without falling into the resort category. The airy marble reception area leads to modernly furnished, air conditioned rooms with private facilities, minibar and satellite television. The absence of a swimming pool may be seen as a disadvantage by some.

APOLLON, *Odos Minoos 63. Tel. 081/250025, Fax 081/250047. Rates (with tax): Drs 7,000 single; Drs 10,000 double. Breakfast Drs 1,000. 50 rooms. Visa, MasterCard.*

A good midlevel choice with a satisfactory price-quality ratio, although the hotel itself is scarcely distinguished in its architecture. It is in the rooms, however, that the benefits show through. Pine furnishings, bright walls and blue-painted doors give a Cycladic feel to the interiors, which are well cared for and with a few nice extra touches, like fresh flowers. All rooms have a balcony, ad the hotel has a bar, restaurant and television lounge.

REA, *Odos Kalimeraki 4. Tel. 081/223638. Rates (with tax): Drs 7,000 double. Breakfast Drs 850. 16 rooms. No credit cards.*

A good budget place not far from Plateia Venizelou, and with a warm welcome, the only problem being that the area can be quite noisy. The rooms are clean and bright, although some have shared bathrooms.

LENA, *Odos Lahana 10. Tel. 081/223280. Rates (with tax): Drs 5,000 single; Drs 6,500 double. Breakfast Drs 1,000. 15 rooms. Visa.*

Close to the harbor, off Odos Vironos, the Lena is another good budget deal, with better-looking rooms than is the norm for this price range, although you may have to share a bathroom.

WHERE TO EAT

TA PSARIA, *Odos 25 Avgostou. Drs xx. No credit cards. Seafood.*

With a big outdoor terrace near the harbor, Ta Psaria is as close as you can get to the source of its consistently excellent seafood dishes. The swordfish steak is particuarly good here.

ANTIGONIS, *Odos Knossou 38. Drs 2,500 to Drs 4,500. No credit cards. Traditional.*

Because it is not in a tourist-frequented zone – except insofar as it is on the road to Knossos, just beyond the the Venetian walls – Antigonis escapes the temptation to compromise its authentic Cretan dishes. This, and its good prices, makes it popular with local people.

IPPOCAMPOS OUZERI, *Odos Mitsotaki 3. Drs 3,000 to Drs 5,000. No credit cards. Traditional/meze.*

A meze specialist on the seafront overlooking the harbor, this place has a good welcome and an atmospheric location to go along with the food. The fish dishes are always good.

SEEING THE SIGHTS

Starting in Plateia Eleftherias beside the main east gate in the **Venetian Walls**, you might pause to imagine, if you can, the idea of flying rats. During the 17th-century siege of the city, the Ottoman Turks apparently catapulted rats over the walls in an effort to ignite bubonic plague – the Black Death – among the defenders. Nice folks. Head north a couple of blocks to the **National Tourist Office**, *Odos Xanthoudidou 1,* and pick up some of their brochures and stuff.

You are now faced with a critical choice. Opposite you is the **Archaeological Museum**, *Odos Xanthoudidou, Tel. 081/226092; open Monday 12:30 to 7 pm, Tuesday to Sunday 8 am to 7 pm; admission Drs 1,500, students Drs 750, free on Sunday.* The museum is filled with marvelous finds from Crete's ancient Minoan sites, such as Knossos. The question is: should you visit Knossos first and fill your mind with visions of this beautiful culture under a clear blue sky, and then fill in the myriad details at the museum; or take the reverse approach. In either case, don't underestimate this place: it is one of the most memorable sights in all of Greece. You should devote at least half a day to the museum, and preferably longer.

In this 20-gallery treasure trove is kept the world's best collection of Minoan artefacts: gold, metalwork, glorious frescoes from the Minoan palaces, pottery, stone carvings, painted sarcophagi, and any number of everyday objects. In addition there is a scale-model reconstruction of the palace at Knossos. Among the many marvels, look out in particular for: golden jewelry and ornaments; the **Phaistos Disk**, dating from around 1700 BC, with its still undeciphered writing in Linear A; the **Snake Goddess**, a statuette in faïence of a bare-breasted woman, perhaps a priestess, brandishing two snakes above her head; the **Bull's Head Rhyton**, a gold-chased black stone libation vase in the shape of a bull's head; superb Minoan frescoes, including the famed **Dolphins**, the **Bull-Leapers**, and **la Parisienne**, the latter a woman so elegantly dressed and coiffed, so perfectly primped and primed, that she might have stepped straight out of the Champs-Elysées; and the **Kamares Vases**, pottery with beautiful, multicolored motifs found in the Kamares Cave on Mount Idi.

From here you can backtrack to Plateia Eleftherias and turn right along Odos Dedalou, to Plateia Venizelou. Here you can marvel at the marble **Morosini Fountain**, built in 1628, or more likely marvel at how other people can marvel at it, because as fountains go this one isn't exactly a showstopper. It's pretty enough, though, with a petal-shaped pool and four sculpted lions on the central plinth. Opposite is the reconstructed Venetian-style **San Marco Basilica**, the original of which dated from the 13th century, and in its modern incarnation is a cultural center. Beside it is the reconstructed 17th-century **Venetian Loggia** (the original got zapped by the Luftwaffe during World War II), a noblemen's club that now functions as City Hall. Also in this area, along Odos Agiou Titou, is the 15th-century Byzantine **Church of Agios Titos**, converted by the Turks to a mosque, destroyed in 1856, and reconverted to a church in 1922, after Crete's union with Greece. The head of Saint Titus occupies a gilt reliquary in the church.

Take a break in the cool green quarters of the **El Greco Park** adjacent to Plateia Kallergon, or at the **Delimarco Fountain**, dating from 1666, then head north along Odos 25 Avgoustou to the harbor. The **Old Port** is almost a closed circle of quay lined with fishing boats. At the tip of its western arm stands the **Rocca al Mare**, *Tel. 081/246211; open Tuesday to Sunday 8:30 am to 3 pm; admission Drs 500.* Don't let the romantic Italian fool you; this is another one of those down-and-dirty fortresses that Venice, the Most Serene Republic, scattered around the Aegean and Ionian Seas, the better to keep the clamps on their unwilling Greek subjects, and in mostly fruitless efforts to hold the Turks at bay.

If you're into battlements and cannon ports, you'll love this place; if you're a normal, sensitive human being, admire the colorful fishing boats instead. It's also known as the **Koules Fortress**, and has the mandatory Lion of Saint Mark symbol at the entrance. The vaulted chambers along the harbor are the **Arsenal** and **Shipyard**, where Venetian galleons were built and fitted out.

Turn west on the seafront Odos Sophocles Venizelou, to the **Crete Historical and Ethnographic Museum**, *housed in the 19th-century Kailokairinos Mansion near the Xenia Hotel, Odos Lysimachou Kalokairinou 7, Tel. 081/288825; open Monday to Friday 9 am to 5 pm, Saturday 9 am to 3 pm; admission Drs 1,000.* Though not so spectacular as the Archaeological Museum, this one gives a wider insight into the island, giving space to its Byzantine religious heritage, traditional crafts and folklore, a painting by El Greco, the epic Battle of Crete in 1941, a room devoted to the life and work of local author Nikos Kazantzakis, and, in a rare nod to Crete's Ottoman period, sculpted Turkish gravestones.

South of here, just off the old city center, is the **Byzantine Museum**, *Plateia Agias Ekaterinis, Tel. 081/242111; open Monday to Saturday 9 am to 2 pm; admission Drs 500.* Formerly the Church of Agia Ekaterini, this contains a collection of icons, including six by the 16th-century Cretan master Mikhaïl Damaskinos, who was a teacher of El Greco. In the same area is the 18th-century **Agios Minas Cathedral**, which has Orthodox church chants every Sunday at 5 pm. Beside it is the small **Agios Minas Church**.

Other City Sights

• **Bembo Fountain**, *Plateia Komarou (south end of Odos 1866).* Dates from 1588.

• **Tomb of Nikos Kazantzakis**, *Marengo Bastion on the south side of the Venetian Walls.* The simple last resting place of one of Crete's most loved sons, the author of *Alexis Zorba.* "I hope for nothing. I fear nothing. I am free," reads the inscription.

Knossos

If there was only one reason for visiting Crete, **Knossos** would be it. The ancient palace which the star-crossed British archaeologist Sir Arthur Evans discovered in 1900 and promptly named the Palace of King Minos, quoting Homer as his historical source, conjures up that sense of empathy with the past which so many visitors to ancient places seek, and which so few places supply in reality. This is no mystifying jumble of rubble, but an apparently living world. In some parts of the palace it seems as if the Minoans left just before you got there, instead of 3,300 years ago. *Tel. 081/ 231940. Open Daily 8 am to 9 pm. Admission Drs 1,500, students Drs 750, free on Sunday. Take the number 2 bus from Plateia Venizelou. If you drive, avoid the nearby, paid-for private parking areas if possible, and park at the free public car park.*

An original palace was built on the site around 1900 BC and destroyed by an earthquake two centuries later. Rebuilt in grander style, it became the religious and administrative center of a maritime empire, a thalassocracy, that extended through the Cyclades Islands to mainland

Greece, and traded with the Egyptians and other countries of the Levant. The brilliant court life here came to an abrupt end about the middle of the 14th century BC, in a cataclysmic event that has been linked to the volcanic eruption on the island of **Thira** (Santorini) 105 kilometers north of Crete. Mycenaean invaders seem to have moved in to pick up the pieces, and the palace was destroyed by fire around 1400 BC.

Modern archaeologists decry Evans's partial reconstruction as being more flight of fancy than rigorous science, yet most non-specialists would surely thank him, as the result is a marvelous evocation of the Minoan world. There are the dazzling replica frescoes of elegant women and men, and scenes of dolphins and flowers (the originals are in the Archaeological Museum in Heraklion), restored red-black-and-gold painted columns, some 1,200 rooms, including the official state rooms and apartments of the Minoan rulers, drainage systems, and light wells for illuminating the deepest recesses.

The inescapable impression is of a culture fascinated by life and light and color, of a people who had transcended their origins and created something that was new and bright in the world. Being human, they also had a fascination with death, and the bull-leaping ritual depicted in their frescoes must often have led to the deaths of the leapers – a human sacrifice to the gods represented by the bulls.

Among the many points of interest to see are the **Procession Fresco**, fragments of which line a long corridor adjacent to the west entrance; the so-called **Theater** beside the north entrance; the **King's Megaron** and **Queen's Megaron** near the east entrance; and, around the **Central Courtyard**, the elegantly simple **Throne Room** on the western side, the **Water Chamber** and **Grand Staircase** on the east side, and the **Priest-King Fresco** on the south side. Every so often you will come upon the double-ax emblem of the Minoan kings, and there are plenty of restored bull's horn sculptures on top of the walls.

The site extends over some 22,000 square meters, filled with the palace, the houses of officials and priests, storerooms, meeting rooms, courtyards, homes of servants, and a cemetery. It's not such a big place, although at midday under a blistering sun it can seem all too big. Try to

WE'RE TALKING BULL HERE

The Minoans had a fascination for bulls that makes the Spanish seem like sheep farmers. If their frescoes are anything to go by, leaping acrobatically over the horns of a fired-up bull was their equivalent of bareback rodeo riding. Occasionally, this fascination went over the top in other ways. Take the mythological tale of the **Minotaur**.

King Minos was supposed to sacrifice a bull to Poseidon, but didn't. Poseidon didn't take no bull from nobody, so he arranged for Minos's wife, Queen Pasiphae, to fall in love with a bull. Pasiphae, to make things more interesting for the bull, got Daedalus to make her a hollow wooden cow-thing, in which she hid and ... well, a wild night was had by all, and Pasiphae later gave birth to a monster called the Minotaur, with the head of a bull and the body of a man.

Minos had Daedalus build a labyrinth to hold the Minotaur, which was supplied with Athenian youths to eat. The brave Athenian prince Theseus arrived on the scene, and fell in love with Minos's daughter Ariadne, who gave him a ball of thread which Theseus used to retrace his steps from the labyrinth after slaying the Minotaur.

Theseus and Ariadne sailed away and lived happily ever after – for a couple of weeks, until Theseus got bored with her and dumped her on the island of Dia, north of Crete.

Is the tale of the labyrinth an elaborate metaphor for the intricate layout of the palace at Knossos and the Minoans' fascination with bulls? Or is it total you-know-what?

get here early, before the sun and the tour-group crowds become too much of a hassle, and the magic drains out of the experience.

PRACTICAL INFORMATION

- **Banks & Currency Exchange** – Most banks are open Monday through Friday from 8 am to 2 pm (1:30 pm on Friday). A few operate an extended tourist service in summer from 5 to 7 pm on weekdays and

8 am to 2 pm on weekends. American Express is represented by Adamis Tours, *Odos 25 Avgoustou 23, Heraklion*. *Tel. 081/246202, Fax 081/224717.* Thomas Cook is at *Odos 25 Avgoustou 27, Heraklion*. *Tel. 081/224323, Fax 081/246186.*

• **Doctors – Heraklion General Hospital**, *Odos Venizelou*. *Tel. 081/239502.* For an ambulance, call *166*.

• **Police** – The central police station of heraklion is in *Plateia Venizelou*. *Tel. 081/283190.* The tourist police are at the same location. *Tel. 081/284589 and 282677.* In emergencies, call *100*.

• **Port Authority** – *Tel. 081/244912*

• **Post Office** – The main post office in Heraklon is at *Plateia Daskalo Yiannis,* open Monday through Friday from 8 am to 8 pm.

• **Telephone** – The area code for Heraklion is *081.* The main office of the Greek Telecommunications Organization (OTE) is at *Odos Minoutavrou 10, near El Greco Park.*

• **Tourist Information** – The Greek Tourist Organization (EOT) office in Heraklion is at *Odos Xanthoudidou 1, Tel. 081/228203.* The office is opposite the Archaeological Museum.

CENTRAL CRETE

This area more or less coincides with that of Heraklion Prefecture, although from a visitor's point of view, natural boundaries are more important than political ones. It extends from the edge of Heraklion, and across Crete's highest mountain, 2,456-meter **Mount Idi**, to the south coast.

WHERE TO STAY

FRANGISKOS, *Matala. Tel. 0892/42380. Rates (with tax): Drs 6,000 single; Drs 11,000 double. Breakfast included. 36 rooms. No credit cards.*

Among the best of the bunch in Matala, and less than a hundred meters from the beach. The rooms are a good standard for the price, and the hotel taverna is quite reasonable too.

SELENA, *Agia Galini. Tel. 0832/91273. Rates (with tax): Drs 6,000 single; Drs 8,000 double. Breakfast included. 8 rooms. No credit cards.*

Has a good position in terms of its view of the sea and easy access to the harborside. This involves a certain penalty in decibels from the bars and tavernas roundabout. Still, the welcome here is good and the rooms are simply but comfortably furnished in modern style.

MANOS, *Agia Galini. Tel. 0832/91394. Rates (with tax): Drs 6,000 double. Breakfast included. 10 rooms. No credit cards.*

Close to the bus station in Agia Galini, this good-value but otherwise undistinguished hotel (undistinguished is now, sad to say, a characteristic of once distinguished Agia Galini) has the advantage of convenience. The owners have at least tried, and the rooms are spotlessly clean, with modern furniture, and greenery-draped balconies.

DIMITRI, *Matala. Tel. 0892/23726, Fax 0892/42740. Rates (with tax): Drs 3,000 single; Drs 5,000 double. Breakfast Drs 800. 10 rooms. No credit cards.*

Although some way back from the beach (which is anyway an overrated attraction), Dimitri's compensates by being traveler-friendly in a way that budget travelers appreciate: the rooms are cool and comfortable, with balcony, and the owner doesn't skimp attention in making sure his guests have an enjoyable stay.

WHERE TO EAT

CORALI, *Plateia, Matala. Drs 3,000 to Drs 5,000. No credit cards. Traditional/grill.*

A resonable choice in Matala, mainly because it is back from the sea, its prices are OK, and it isn't pretending to be something it isn't.

ARISTON, *Agia Galini. Drs 2,500 to Drs 4,000. No credit cards. Traditional.*

One of the few places in Agia Galini whose soul hasn't been taken over by the devil of mass tourism that prowls here by night. It doesn't seem to care overmuch what it looks like, and local families appreciate it.

SEEING THE SIGHTS
Minoan Ruins

Some 15 kilometers south of Heraklion, around the village of **Arhanes**, is a cluster of Minoan sites. Excavations in the village have uncovered a summer palace, while at Fourni Hill one kilometer northwest of Arhanes are vaulted tombs dating from 2500 BC onwards, and at Anemospilia south of the village, on **Mount Giouhtas**, is a Minoan religious sanctuary. The sites are fragmentary only, but if you have been intrigued by visiting Knossos you might find them interesting.

While we're on the subject of Minoan sites in central Crete, we might as well cover all the big ones. At **Amnissos**, five kilometers east of Heraklion, and **Nirou Hani**, five kilometers further to the east, are remnants of the harbors where the Minoans based their ships. More substantial ruins can be seen at **Tilissos**, *Tel. 081/831241; open daily 8:30 am to 3 pm; admission Drs 600, students Drs 300.* The site is four kilometers southwest of Heraklion, where, set among the trees in this hilly landscape, are the remains of one of the biggest Minoan towns.

At **Phaistos** (Festos), *Tel. 0892/91315, open daily 8 am to 7 pm; admission Drs 1,200, students Drs 600,* a few kilometers inland from the south coast resort of Matala, on the verdant breast of the Messara Plain, lies the second most important Minoan palace after Knossos. Covering 9,000 square meters, its main difference with Knossos is that it was relatively unornamented with frescoes. It has also not been partially reconstructed, so it falls more easily into the jumble-of-stones category that archaeologists love.

Finally, between Phaistos and the dusty big village of Timbaki (better known to old Crete hands as Timbuktu), lies **Agias Trias**, *Tel. 0892/ 91360; open daily 8:30 am to 3 pm; admission Drs 500, students Drs 250.* This site has the remains of what seems to have been the summer palace of the rulers of Phaistos.

Roman Ruins

Just so the Romans don't feel left out of this archaeological beanfeast, you can visit **Gortis**, 15 kilometers up the Heraklion road from Phaistos, where the ruins of the Roman capital of Crete, **Gortyn**, are to be seen (*Tel. 0892/31144; open Tuesday to Sunday 8:30 am to 3 pm; admission Drs 800, students Drs 400*). Why the usually streetsmart Romans chose to locate their capital in this remote spot rather than at one of the natural harbors on the north coast, is anybody's guess. Maybe the golf was better. Anyway you can clamber over what's left of the Governor's Palace, the Temple of Apollo, the Odeon, the Nymphaeum, and other imperial bits and pieces. Look out for the stone tablets in archaic Doric at the Odeon, displaying the **Code of Gortyn**, a statement of the rights of man dating from 450 BC that was given a favorable notice by Plato. Also at Gortyn is the ruined 6th-century, three-aisled **Basilica of Agios Titos**, dedicated to Saint Titus, who in the 1st century was converted by Saint Paul and went on to found Crete's first Christian community.

Caves & Museums

On the southern slopes of Mount Idi, a 4-hour trek into the mountains north of **Kamares**, lies the **Kamares Cave**, which was sacred to the Minoans, possibly as a shrine to the goddess Eileithyia. The Kamares Vases on display at Heraklion's Archaeological Museum were found here. On the Nida Plateau, still higher up this side of the mountain yet more easily reached from Anogia in the direction of Heraklion, is the **Ideon Cave**. Although this one also has Minoan associations, its fame stems from Greek mythology as the place where Zeus was raised.

You've probably had about enough ancient history for now, but there's one last piece of history, this time more recent, to seek out before we hit the beach: the **Nikos Kazantzakis Museum**, *Myrtia village, 22 kilometers southeast of Heraklion, Tel. 081/741689; open Monday, Wednesday, Saturday, Sunday 9 am to 1 pm and 6 to 8 pm; Tuesday, Friday 6 pm to 8 pm; closed Thursday; admission Drs 500.* Mementoes of the great Cretan writer are on display in his partly reconstructed family home, including photographs, a film of his life, and other memorabilia.

Other Sights

• **Vathipetro**, *19 kilometers south of Heraklion.* Ruins of a Minoan country villa, including wine-press, olive-press, weaving rooms, and potter's kiln.

• **Komos**, *along the coast from Matala.* Remains of the Minoan port of Phaistos.

• **Vrondissi Monastery**, *in the southern foothills of Mount Idi, near Zaros.* Has a carved fountain dating from the 15th-century, and a magnificent view.

• **Varsamonerou Monastery**, *in the southern foothills of Mount Idi, near Vorizia.* The Church of Agios Phanourios at this abandoned monastery has superb Byzantine frescoes from the 15th century.

SPORTS & RECREATION
Beaches

Now for the beaches. Not so long ago, **Agia Galini** on the south coast could be compared with the Saint Tropez of the Fifties. Just as Saint Tropez ain't what it used to be, neither is Agia Galini. The once pretty little fishing village where you thought yourself in Greek heaven with a clean, simple room over a donkey stable, and where the solitary bamboo beach-disco got washed away every year by the winter storms, has made its mint from tourism and suffered the consequences. The harbor area still retains a few percentage points of its original charm and there are plenty of rooms to rent in the houses, apartments, hotels and villas that jostle for space on the steep hillside above the sea.

Time was when **Matala** was a fixture on the hippie trail almost on a par with Marrakesh. The little fishing village south of Timbuktu ... sorry, Timbaki, has a good beach bordered by caves overlooking the sea, where in the Sixties and Seventies those exotic birds-of-passage used to roost. They got up to all kinds of unsavory activities here: making love, smoking non-carcinogenic substances, dreaming of an end to war, and creating a world shortage of retsina. You'll be relieved to hear that that's all over now. Matala has achieved its destiny as a concrete-and-tarmac beach resort with all the intrinsic charm of a Big Mac.

Away from the resorts in the Agia Galini-Matala area, the south coast is wonderfully scenic, though not always easily reached other than on foot or by jeep. You could do worse than base yourself at **Pitsidia**, a pretty village a few kilometers inland from Matala, and explore from there. It's a harsh fact, though, that most of the once picturesque fishing villages hereabouts have been well and truly spoiled. Those that haven't, like **Tsoutsouros** and **Lendas**, had less charm to lose in the first place.

As for the north coast, I can think of nothing good to say about most of the resorts on either side of Heraklion. They're anonymous assemblages of hotels and restaurants. People who like this sort of thing will undoubtedly like this sort of thing.

WESTERN CRETE

Based on the handsome north coast harbor towns and resorts of **Rethimno** and **Hania**, western Crete is mostly relatively less developed than the central or eastern parts of the island. These two places provide part of an answer to the question (better whisper it): What good did the Turks do during their more than two centuries' occupation of Crete?

In the middle there is the giant bulk of the **Lefka Ori** (White Mountains), through which slices the jagged slash of the **Samaria Gorge**. In the far west are some of the best beaches and most isolated places on the island.

You'll find hotels and restaurant selections below for the two main towns in this part of Crete, Rethimno and Hania.

ARRIVALS & DEPARTURES

You can approach the west two ways by road. One, from Heraklion, is the scenic but tame coast road westwards through Rethimno to Hania; the other starts at Agia Galini and winds spectacularly through the mountain villages to Rethimno, or via Hora Sfakion on the south coast northwards along the eastward flank of the Lefka Mountains to Hania.

GETTING AROUND
By Bus

From Rethimno: Heraklion, every 30 minutes on average, 1 1/2 hours; Hania, every 30 minutes on average, 1 hour; Agia Galini, four daily, 2 hours.

From Hania: Samaria Gorge, four daily, 1 hour; Kastelli, hourly on average, 30 minutes; Paleohora, four daily, 1 1/2 hours; Hora Sfakion, four daily, 1 1/2 hours.

WHERE TO STAY

BYZANTINE, *Odos Vosporou 26-28, Rethimno. Tel. 0831/55609, Fax 0831/52315. Rates (with tax): Drs 4,000 single; Drs 7,000 double. Breakfast included. 14 rooms. No credit cards.*

The name is entirely appropriate, as the Byzantine actually dates from Crete's Byzantine period and is located in the Old Town. Despite its venerable age, the building has been thoroughly renovated and all its rooms have private bathroom. This is a beautifully characterful place in the most characterful part of town, and you'll be paying a very reasonable price for that as much as for the facilities.

ZANIA, *Odos Pavlou Vlastou 3, Rethimno. Tel. 0831/28169. Rates (with tax): Drs 7,000 double. Breakfast included. 5 rooms. No credit cards.*

The owner's French is better than her English, and she'll be happy to show you just how *joli* her 19th-century, Ottoman-era mansion turned hotel is. The guest rooms are big and well furnshed, but you'll have to share the bathroom and shower.

DOMA, *Odos Eleftheriou Venizelou 124, Hania. Tel. 0821/51772, Fax 0821/41578. Rates (with tax): Drs 13,000 single; Drs 18,000 double; Drs 41,000 suite. Breakfast included. 25 rooms (including three suites). American Express, Diners Club, Visa, MasterCard.*

Built in 1900, the beautiful Doma was first the Austrian then the British consulate in Crete before, in 1972, being transformed into a hotel. And what a hotel. This is one of the most distinguished buildings in town, with a colonnaded porch and wrought-iron balconies. The rooms all have private bathrooms and the hotel has a fine seaview – as well as a collection of hats and other headgear from around the world.

AMFORA, *Defteri Parodos Theotokopoulou 20, Hania. Tel. 0821/93224, Fax 0821/93226. Rates (with tax): Drs 13,000 single; Drs 17,000 double. Breakfast included. 21 rooms. Visa, MasterCard.*

This Venetian-era building is built around a courtyard in the Old Town, not far from the Maritime Museum, and antique furnishings from the period add to the sense of realism in the hotel's excellent presentation. The rooms boast a few facilities that the Venetian didn't have, however, including private bathrooms, and some even have their own kitchen area. You get a fine view of the harbor from the roof garden.

WHERE TO EAT

AKROGIALI, *Akti Papanikolaou 19, Hania. Drs 4,000 to Drs 8,000. Credit cards. Seafood.*

Occupies a seaside location west of the harbor, and specializes in fish fresh off the boat. You will notice that there are at least as many locals in evidence as there are tourists, and although the style is a long way from chic, the ambience and the food are good.

RIZES, *Odos Koraka 21, Hania. Drs 2,500 to Drs 5,000. No credit cards. Traditional.*

An inexpensive taverna close to Plateia 1866 where the clientele are mostly local people, you choose your dishes by pointing to them, and the wine flows from the barrel in an impressive stream.

ZIZI'S, *Platanes. Drs 3,000 to Drs 5,000. No credit cards. Traditional/ seafood.*

Never mind the French-sounding name, Zizi's is as dyed-in-the-wool Cretan as they come. Located five kilometers east of town, at the seaside village of Platanes on the the old coast road to Heraklion, it attracts locals from all around, who would probably prefer that it remains an insider's tip.

ALANA, *Odos Salaminos 11, Rethimno. Drs 3,500 to Drs 7,000. No credit cards. Traditional/seafood.*

On the road from the harbor to the southern end of the Fortezza, Alana is just far enough from the harbor's tourist-charged hype to seem as if it occupies a different world. The plant-bedecked ambience around an old Venetian fountain complements local dishes at a fair price.

SEEING THE SIGHTS
Rethimno

Some 72 kilometers west of Heraklion and with a population of around 20,000, **Rethimno** is a picturesque place, well supplied with Venetian and Ottoman architecture in the Old Town clustered around its tiny harbor and along the municipal beach to the east. Almost everywhere in Crete the locals have been zealous in excising anything that looks even vaguely Turkish, but in Rethimno you'll find typically Ottoman-style wooden balconies, and even minarets. Outside of the Old Town, it's a different story: unprepossessing suburbs and hotels crowding into whatever space there is.

Start your exploration at the National Tourist Office (EOT), *Odos Eleftheriou Venizelou*, on the waterfront facing the **Municipal Beach**. This is a very inviting beach, but don't swim here when the red warning flags are flying, and be cautious at all other times, as the currents are life-threatening. From here walk westwards along the Paralia, to the curving, rocky breakwater at the eastern end of the **Old Port**. Facing you across the narow inlet is a small **Venetian lighthouse**. Pick your way though the massed tables of the harborside café terraces outside the old Venetian and Turkish waterfront houses, and out at the western end (if you get here early in the morning, before the maddening crowds arrive for breakast, you'll find the harbor is a magicaly tranquil, light-dappled place).

This brings you to the **Historical and Folk Art Museum**, *Odos Mesologiou 28, Tel. 0831/23667; open Monday to Saturday 9 am to 1 pm and 7 to 9 pm; admission Drs 300*. The museums displays local costumes, rugs, household and work objects.

Keep going through the narrow streets into the short, fat peninsula at whose tip stands the 16th-century **Venetian Fortress**, also known as the **Fortezza**, *Odos Melisinou, Tel. 0831/29975; open Tuesday to Sunday 8:30 am to 3 pm; admission Drs 500*. Its stout walls run more than 1,200 meters along Plaeokastro Hill, and do a fair job of dominating Rethimno and its sea approaches, as well as providing a memorable view. Yet in 1645, in what was by then a familiar experience for the Venetians, they proved to be a paper tiger when the Turks came at them in earnest. The mosque inside the walls, although accompanied by an Orthodox chapel, tells its own story of Venetian surrender.

Just in front of the Fortezza is the **Archaeological Museum**, *Odos Melisinou, Tel. 0831/29975; open Tuesday to Sunday 8:30 am to 3 pm; admission Drs 500*, with a not-wildly-exciting collection of sculptures, dishes, glassware, and other objects dating from the Minoan to the Byzantine period, and a modest collection of Roman coins.

Other Sights in Rethimno

• **Rimondi Fountain**, *Odos Thessalonikis.* Dates from 1629. Water spouts from sculpted lion's mouths.
• **Municipal Garden**, *West of the old town, off Odos Pavlou Kountouriotou.* Its trees and plants make a welcome, green place of escape from the summer sun, and the venue of Rethimno's annual wine festival (see "Festivals," below).
• **Kara Pasha Mosque**, *Odos Arkadiou and Odos Viktoros Ougos*
• **Nerantzes Mosque**, *Odos Manouil Vernadou, near Plateia Titou Petichaki*
• **Veli Pasha Mosque**, *Odos Dimokratias*

Near Rethimno

Make your first stop the **Monastery of Arkadi**, in the hills about 25 kilometers southeast of Rethimno, *open daily from dawn to dusk; admission free.* The monastery is a symbol of the fierce resistance Cretans have always put up against would-be conquerors. In 1866, during the struggle for liberation from Turkey, the Abbot Gabriel, rather than surrender, ignited a powder magazine in the abbey, blowing up himself and a thousand defenders and refugees, as well as masses of Turkish troops who were on the point of beaking in. The monastery's ornate Venetian façade has been partially restored.

A westward loop from Rethimno leads through some wonderful countryside and coastal scenery, and takes in several interesting sites at the same time. Most of this can be done by bus in summer, but car is of course easier and quicker. Go west along the coast road until **Georgioupoli**, where you can either divert southwards for seven kilometers to **Lake Kournos**, Crete's only freshwater lake, or continue on the country road that turns southwards at **Vrisses** then winds scenically through the eastern foothills of the **Lefka Mountains**.

It finally hits the south coast at **Hora Sfakion**, an all-but rockbound village with a small fishing harbor and some houses in traditional Cretan village style alongside modern developments. From here you can take a ferry to the barely inhabited offshore islet of **Gavdos**, or even hop westwards by passenger or car ferry along the coast to **Paleohora**.

More likely, you will turn eastwards instead along the south coast, passing through some pretty little hill villages. At **Patsianos**, a southern loop touches the shore at **Frangokastello**, a ruined Crusader-style castle with turreted battlements (*permanent access; admission free*). What were the Venetians trying to protect in 1371 when they built it? Maybe the excellent beaches in the area, because there doesn't seem to be much else of value. Anyway, there it is, 12 kilometers east of Hora Sfakion, looking thoroughly like the alien invader it is. Cretan legend tells that the ghosts of a heroic band of freedom fighters wiped out here by the Turks in 1821 appear on the shore at dawn each year on May 17.

Some 20 kilometers eastwards is the increasingly busy south coast resort of **Plakias**, which nevertheless make a reasonable base for exploring this part of the coast, and 12 kilometers beyond that is the first of the two **Monasteries of Preveli**, this one abandoned. Continue on the road for a few kilometers more until you arrive at the second, overlooking the sea. The monastery church, *open daily 9 am to 7 pm; admission free,* has some fine icons. Dress respectfully. Below it, the palm tree-lined **beach** is superb and except at the busiest times of the year retains its tranquil charm.

You need to retrace your steps a little way until you reach the road at **Assomatos** that winds northwards through the hills to back to Rethimno, perhaps with an eastwards diversion at **Koxari to Spili**, one of the prettiest mountain villages in the area. Look out for Crete's rare imperial eagles around here. Back on the road north, you pass through **Armeni**, near which a Minoan cemetery has been uncovered.

Hania

Like Rethimno, **Hania** has been shaped historically by the hand of Venetians and Turks as well as Greeks, and it is an attraction all by itself. Especially the Old Town, and especially out of the high tourist season, when you have a better chance of absorbing the atmosphere. The Venetian dominance began in 1252, and lasted until the Turks captured the city in 1645 after a 55-day siege. This town of some 65,000 people was, from 1898 until 1971, the capital of Crete, and stands on the site of ancient Kydonia, dating back to Minoan times. Unfortunately, Hania suffered the enthusiastic attentions of the Luftwaffe during World War II, and the town was heavily damaged by bombing. Still, much that is original remains, and the rebuilding at least aimed at the original spirit.

Having picked up information from the National Tourist Office (EOT), O*dos Kriari 40, at the corner of Plateia 1866,* the best place to begin a tour of Hania is inside the **Venetian Walls**, at that easily recognizable landmark, thanks to its multiple white domes, the **Janissaries Mosque** at the **Outer Harbor**. From here you should walk along the narrow paralia, with its massed waterside taverna terraces, graceful streetlamps, and quays strangely devoid of boats, to the western tip of the harbor.

Here stands the **Maritime Museum**, *Odos Angelou, Tel. 0821/26437; open Tuesday to Sunday 10 am to 4 pm; admission Drs 500,* whose two floors combine civil, military, and marine biology sections to give a good idea of Hania's and Crete's naval history. It includes navigation instruments, ship models, nautical maps, and paintings dating back to the 1821 revolution. Across the harbor mouth is the **Venetian Lighthouse** at the end of the breakwater.

From here you can follow the course of the Venetian Walls to the arrowhead-shaped **Shiavi Bastion**, which was clearly designed to skewer any outfit unwise enough to try storming it, but which, in typical Venetian style, failed to do any such thing against the Turks in 1645. Beyond this is the **Archaeological Museum**, *Odos Halidon 21, Tel. 0821/24418; open Monday to Friday 8:30 am to 3 pm; admission Drs 500,* in the former 16th-century Venetian Basilica of San Franciscus which later did duty under the Turks as a mosque. You'll find Minoan pottery, sarcophagi and children's toys, and Roman mosaics, coins, and statues among the exibits. The fountain in the courtyard is Turkish.

Cross Odos Halidon, past the **Orthodox Cathedral** opposite, and keep on towards the Walls. Off Odos Tsouderon is the **Old Market**, *closed Sunday,* a covered market in the style of a Turkish bazaar, dating from the 19th century.

Other Sights in Hania

· **Historical Museum and Archives**, *Odos Sfakianaki 20. Tel. 0821/22606. Open Monday to Friday 10 am to 4 pm. Admission Drs 400.* The most interesting part of this museum's collection of documents, books, and records is the archive of some 3,000 old photographs and postcards of the island.

· **Folklore Museum**, *Odos Halidon 46b. Tel. 0821/23273. Open Monday to Friday 10 am to 4 pm. Admission Drs 400.* When the Cretans weren't fiercely resisting foreign invaders, they had time for folk arts and crafts, as this museum shows with its collection of antique household objects, work tools, clothing and woven cloth.

· **Municipal Park**, *Odos Tzanakaki.* A shaded refuge with a small zoo in the middle.

Near Hania

If you arrived in Hania by boat, and if you want to leave again by boat, that means coming to and going from the harbor town of **Souda**, six kilometers eastwards across the neck of the **Akrotiri Peninsula**, on the southern shore of **Souda Bay**, and connected by regular bus with Hania. The Souda-Akrotiri area hosts major NATO and Greek naval and air bases. NATO operations have slowed since the end of the Cold War, but as Greece and Turkey rattle sabers in each other's faces the tempo of Greek military activity here has picked up. Be careful of who and what you photograph.

Notable exceptions to this stricture in the scenic Akrotiri Peninsula are 17th-century **Agia Triada Monastery** near Koumares, and 16th-century **Gouvernetou Monastery** at the northern tip, overlooking the sea. *Both can be visited free by the respectfully dressed.* Greek history watchers might also like to visit the hilltop grave at **Profitis Ilias**, six kilometers northeast of Hania, of local hero Eleftherios Venezelos (1864-1935). He was Prime Minister of Greece from 1910-20 and again from 1928-32, during the first of which periods in office he "liberated" vast areas in Thrace, the Aegean, and Anatolia from Turkey, only to watch his successor promptly lose it all again.

Traveling westwards from Hania takes you into one of the least developed and most beautiful parts of Crete. You might not believe this if you arrive in July and August, but remember that during those months all bets on tranquility are off. In spring and fall it's a different story. The **Gulf of Hania** is lined with seaside resorts. One of them, **Maleme**, is where the élite German Parachute Division landed during the Battle of Crete in 1941.

You may even have first set foot in Crete at **Kastelli** (or **Kissamos** as it is also called), if you came on the seemingly endless ferry trek from Piraeus down the eastern Peloponnese coast, via Kythira and Antikythira. Your trek hasn't ended when the ferry finally docks either, as the terminal is a kilometer or so west of Kastelli.

On the west coast, 14 airline kilometers from Kastelli, and about twice as far as the road goes, is **Falassarna**, a small village with one of the biggest beaches on the island. I won't go so far as to say it's a deserted beach, at least not always, but it is a good one. Archaeologists are still excavating the Roman-era town and port here.

The cliff-lined west coast is wild and scenic, with a few pretty resorts worth stopping at on the way, like **Sfinari**, on the way southwards to the **Monastery of Chrissoskalitissa** (Monastery of the Golden Step), so-called because one of its entrance steps is supposedly made of gold. If you continue south on the rough road to the coast opposite the islet of **Elafonissi**, you've a real treat in store – you can get there without paying for a ferry, aboard Shanks's pony! You can, in fact, walk the short distance there over sand and through shallow water. Not that there's much to do when you get there.

A wide backtracking semicircle eastwards through **Elos** and **Strovles** leads eventually to the pretty resort village and ferry terminal of **Paleohora**, which has some excellent beaches and a ruined Venetian fort, and from where you can jump the local ferry going eastwards to **Sougia**, **Agia Roumeli**, **Loutro**, and **Hora Sfakion**, then southwards, to the island of **Gavdos**. This island, with an area of 35 square kilometers and a permanent population of about 50, is, according to legend, the island of Calypso, the nymph goddess who gave Odysseus such a hard time in *The*

Odyssey by lavishing gifts on him, sleeping with him every night, and promising to make him immortal (well, Odysseus thought this was having a hard time). The ferry arrives at the truly tiny port of **Karave**, from where you can hike four kilometers southwards to the southernmost point in Europe at **Cape Tripiti**. Meanwhile, back in Hania, intrepid explorers are taking the first bus south to the Lefka Mountains at the village of **Xiloskalo**, from where they will make a 6-hour trek through the **Samaria Gorge National Park**, *Hania Forest Service, Tel. 0821/22287; open May through October (at other times there is a risk of flash floods), starting between 6:30 am and 3 pm; admission (in season) Drs 1,000*. This is the deepest gorge in Europe, and has become a rite of passage for fit and healthy tourists. If you plan to be among them – and traversing the narrow, jagged slash through the mountains is a memorable experience – be advised that you won't be alone. At peak times in July and August, the gorge can seem like Times Square or Picadilly Circus on a busy Saturday afternoon; and the going gets a little rough, though not impossibly so.

You start the descent along a steep pathway, and the view down into the wooded valley, with mountains rising in green, rocky waves all around, is spectacular. As you arrive at the valley floor, through which a small stream flows in summer, the cliff walls close in on either side and tower above you. If you are lucky you might spot the shy, Cretan mountain goat or an imperial eagle, but most of these rare creatures have decamped to quieter places. The ruined village of **Samaria** marks roughly the halfway point. Time your trek right and you'll emerge from the gorge as lunch is being served at one of the tavernas in the busy, landlocked village of **Agia Roumeli**, from where five boats a day sail between 9:30 am and 6 pm, with a sixth at 7:15 pm on Sunday, to Hora Sfakion, to be met at the harbor by buses for Hania.

PRACTICAL INFORMATION

• **Banks & Currency Exchange** – **Commercial Bank of Greece**, *Plateia Avgoustou Stratiotou, Rethimno*; **National Bank of Greece**, *Odos Dimokratias 2, Hania*. Most banks are open Monday through Friday from 8 am to 2 pm (1:30 pm on Friday). A few operate an extended tourist service in summer from 5 to 7 pm on weekdays and 8 am to 2 pm on weekends. **Thomas Cook Rethimno**: *Odos Paleologou 3. Tel. 0831/51923, Fax 0831/54561.* **Thomas Cook Hania**: *Plateia Syntrivani. Tel. 0821/88770, Fax 0821/71543.*

• **Doctors** – **Rethimno Hospital**, *Odos Trantalidou. Tel. 0831/27814.* **Hania Hospital**, *Odos Kapodistriou. Tel. 0821/43811.*

• **Police** – Rethimno: *Plateia Iroon. Tel. 0831/25247;* Tourist Police, *Odos Iroon Polythechniou. Tel. 0831/28156.* Hania: *Odos Karaiskaki 44. Tel. 0821/45876;* Tourist Police: *Odos Karaiskaki 44. Tel. 0821/71111.*

• **Port Authority** – Rethimno: *Tel. 0831/22276.* Hania: *Tel. 0821/43052.*

• **Post Office** – The main post office in Rethimno is at *Odos Moatsu 19.* In Hania, the main post office is at *Odos Tzanakaki 3.* Both are open Monday through Friday from 7:30 am to 8 pm

• **Telephone** – The area code for Rethimno is *0831;* for Hania *0821.* The Greek Telecommunications Organization (OTE) office in Rethimno is at *Odos Pavlou Kountouriotou 28.* OTE Hania is at *Odos Tzanakaki 5.*

• **Tourist Information** – Greek Tourist Organization (EOT) office in Rethimno: *Odos Eleftheriou Venizelou. Tel. 0831/9148.* Hania: *Odos Kriari 40. Tel. 0821/22943.*

EASTERN CRETE

Although it shares some defining characteristics with the west of the island – ports, a mountain range, a tendency for tourism development to thin out at the edges, and in the **Lassithi Plateau** a landscape as distinctive in its way as the Samaria Gorge – the east is no mirror image of the west. For one thing, Minoan sites are thicker on the ground here, and the ports of **Agios Nikolaos** and **Sitia** lack the Venetian and Ottoman hearts of Rethimno and Hania.

Agios Nikolaos is in fact one of the wildest resorts in the whole Mediterranean, lacking only an easily accessible beach of outstanding quality to match the best (or the worst, if you prefer) of such places. Also unlike the west, it is easier to make a circuit here by road from Heraklion, touching the entire coast and venturing into **Mount Dikti** from all angles, before returning to Heraklion from the south.

GETTING AROUND

By Bus

From Agios Nikolaos: Heraklion, every 45 minutes on average, 1 1/2 hours; Elounda, one every hour, 20 minutes; Kritsa, hourly on average, 30 minutes; Sitia, five daily, 1 1/2 hours.

From Sitia: Paleokastro and Vaï, four daily, 45 minutes; Ierapetra, 5 daily, 1 1/2 hours; Kato Zakros, two daily, 1 hour.

WHERE TO STAY

CORAL, *Akti Koundourou. Tel. 0841/28363, Fax 0841/28754. Rates (with tax): Drs 10,000 single; Drs 16,500 double. Breakfast Drs 1,500. 170 rooms. Visa, MasterCard.*

Although a big resort hotel on the beach north of Agios Nikolaos, the Coral offers a good price-to-quality ratio. Its fairly standard resort hotel-style rooms have private bathroom and balcony, and the hotel itself has a restaurant and swimming pool.

DU LAC, *Odos 28 Oktovriou 17, Agios Nikolaos. Tel. 0841/22711. Rates (with tax): Drs 4,000 single; Drs 6,000 double. Breakfast Drs 900. 33 rooms. No credit cards.*

Without much in the way of looks, the Du Lac is on the south shore of Lake Voulismeni and has reasonable rooms with balcony and a view of the lake. You can have breakfast on the terrace overlooking the lake. Easy parking may be an added attraction here.

WHERE TO EAT

FAROS, *Odos Akti Pagaloun, Agios Nikolaos. Drs 4,000 to Drs 6,000. No credit cards. Traditional.*

A seaside taverna that has a touch more class than the average in Agios Nikolaos, and is generally less expensive than those around the lake.

ITANOS, *Odos Kipros, Agios Nikolaos. Drs 3,000 to Ds 5,000. No credit cards. Traditional/grill.*

Charcoal-grilled food is a specialty at this big, popular taverna close to the bus station.

SEEING THE SIGHTS

The best I can say about the package-tour resorts east of Heraklion is that you can get past them quickly enough on the coast road. Unless you're in urgent need of a comfort station, the first worthwhile stop is **Malia** – no longer the village itself, sad to say, only the ancient Minoan palace complex three kilometers beyond it on the coastal plain, Tel. 0897/31597; *open Tuesday to Sunday 8:30 am to 3 pm; admission Drs 800.* The ruins here are smaller than those at Knossos, and don't have its reconstruction or frescoes, so they ought to be less impressive. Yet you might easily find them more evocative, because they're usually quieter and the scale of the roofless and mostly wall-less rooms and chambers is more human.

If you're driving or otherwise touring, before Malia, at the coastal village of **Stalida**, turn inland southwards through **Mohos** on the wonderfully scenic road climbing towards 1,485-meter **Mount Dikti**, via the 900-meter-high **Lassithi Plateau**, one of the most remarkable landscapes on Crete. There is a constellation of pretty farming villages around the plateau, the most convenient of which – and of course the busiest in summer – is **Tzermiado**. What makes Lassithi special is not so much its scenic location or its fertile farmland and burgeoning orchards, impressive as these are: it's the 5,000 slender windmills with canvas sails scattered across the plateau that sets the seal on its beauty, giving it an other-wordly, ethereal, and timeless aspect. Close up, the windmills look less romantic, more like small oil-derricks wrapped with rags.

Keep twisting and turning along this sideroute, through **Agios Georgios**, until you come to **Psihro**, higher up than Tzermiado and with a superb view over the plateau. A few hundred meters outside Psihro you can visit the **Dikteon Cave**, *Tel. 0844/31316; open Monday to Friday 8 am to 7 pm, Saturday and Sunday 8:30 am to 3 pm; admission Drs 900.* In Greek mythology, this is the place where Rhea hid to give birth to Zeus because her husband Chronos, having been warned that one of his children would replace him as top god, ate each kid god as soon as it was born. Other than this fact, and some stalagmites and stalactites, it's a place that only a speleologist could love.

Back on the coast road again, you should aim to reach the western arm of the **Gulf of Mirambellou** at **Elounda**, on a marvelously rocky stretch of coast sheltered by the **Spinalonga Peninsula**. Elounda is still a fairly calm and charming little harbor town, a status that probably won't last, as unfettered tourist development devours the charm of Crete's favored children faster than Chronos swallowed up the infant gods of Olympus.

A regular shuttle-service of excursion boats leaves from the harbor at Elounda, and from even prettier **Plaka** a few kilometers up the coast, for tiny **Spinalonga Island**, off the tip of the peninsula. Until as recently as the 1950s this was a quarantine station for lepers, and it is a somber experience to tour their humble, crumbling dwellings, and see the charnel house at the church where there bones were jumbled together. *Tuesday to Sunday 8:30 am to 3 pm. Admission Drs 500.*

Such roads as there are on this part of the coast lead to **Agios Nikolaos**, the main town and resort on the Gulf of Mirambellou, and indeed in the whole of eastern Crete. Agios Nikolaos is one of those places that arouses mixed emotions. The town is built around a harbor that leads via a narrow channel to a roughly circular inlet, called **Lake Voulismeni**, around whose yacht-infested circumference are piled hotels, bars, tavernas, and discos. Whatever Agios Nikolaos once was, it is no longer, as the young and chic from all over western Europe pour in every summer and turn the place into a riot of high-intensity carousing. Yet something Cretan remains at the heart of Agios Nikolaos, which the ravening hordes can't quite take away.

If you're staying in Agios Nikolaos by choice and by design, you probably won't be interested, but there are a couple of reasonably good museums in town. The **Archaeological Museum**, *Odos Konstantinou Paleologou 74, Tel. 0841/24943; open Tuesday to Sunday 8:30 am to 3 pm; admission Drs 500,* has finds from several Minoan, Dorian and Roman sites in the area, although the best of them are in Heraklion's Archaeological Museum. The **Folk Art Museum** is in the same building as the tourist office, *Odos Koundourou 22, Tel. 0841/22357; open Sunday to Friday 10 am to 1:30 pm and 6 to 9:30 pm; admission Drs 300.* Agios Nikolaos's beaches are no good: you'll have to go out of town to sleep off the excesses of the night before on a halfway decent stretch of sand.

About 10 kilometers inland from Agios Nikolaos in the hills to the west is **Kritsa**, a village that is popular as a time-out for tourists from the coastal resorts and that has developed arts and crafts industries to accommodate them. On the way there you pass the Byzantine **Church of Panagia Kera**, *Tel. 0841/51525; open Monday to Saturday 9 am to 3 pm, Sunday 9 am to 2 pm; admission Drs 400,* whose interior is filled with magnificent frescoes from the 14th and 15th centuries. North of Kritsa are the ruins of the major Dorian town of **Lato**, *open Tuesday to Sunday 8:30 am to 3 pm; admission Drs 300,* founded in the 7th century BC, and spread over two hillsides, with temples, theaters, and other buildings.

Around the south coast of the Gulf of Mirambellou there are some white sand beaches hidden in various rocky places, and generally more or less unoccupied. About 14 kilometers out of Agios Nikolaos, along a hillside overlookng the water, is **Gournia**, a Minoan settlement from the 15th century BC, *Tel. 0842/94604; open Tuesday to Sunday 8:30 am to 3 pm; admission Drs 600.* Gournia lacks the spectacular aspect of Knossos yet in compensation gives you a better idea of how ordinary Minoans' houses were laid out, as opposed to the palaces of the high and mighty.

Sitia, 60 kilometers further along the Gulf of Mirambellou, is Crete's easternmost ferry port, and makes a good base for exploring this end of the island. It is a handsome enough place, and although it has itself neither the good looks nor frenetic lifestyle of Agios Nikolaos, it occupies a more naturally attractive setting around a hill-lined harbor. Besides, the beaches are better. There is a fairly uninteresting **Venetian Fort** overlooking the harbor, and a fairly interesting **Archaeological Museum**, *Odos Piscokefalou 3, Tel. 0843/23917; open Tuesday to Sunday 8:30 am to 3 pm; admission Drs 500.* Some of the better finds in the museum include ivory sculptures from a cluster of Minoan sites on the east coast.

One of those sites is **Kato Zakros**, in the middle of the east coast, *Tel. 0843/93323; open Tuesday to Sunday 8 am to 2:30 pm; admission Drs 600.* The village also happens to be a delicately attractive and fairly quiet small resort. This is the kind of place that can be killed stone-dead in a minute with a touch of the developer's tragic wand. The Minoans built a palace and other installations here at what was an important trading harbor for them. Inland from Kato Zakros, there is the dramatically named 8-kilometer-long **Valley of the Dead** – a valley where the Minoans interred their dead, if you must ask.

Northwards up the coast, in the **Sideros Peninsula**, you shouldn't miss the lovely, palm-tree-lined beach at **Vaï**. Sad to relate, neither will any of your fellow tourists in this part of Crete, so a lonely ramble is not to be expected – yet the scene is still notable and more like a South Seas Island poster than a real place. Other, less famous beaches in the area have fewer pilgrims worshiping at the shrine of the golden sands.

Most people doing this stretch of Crete end up finally at **Ierapetra** on the south coast, then wonder why they bothered, and move on. It has one of those Venetian forts which, if you're like me, you'll start to think of as irritating carbuncles on the face of Crete. Why couldn't the Venetians just have stayed home, paddling their gondolas? In compensation, and to end on an upbeat note, the coastline all around here is scenic, and as you head back to central Crete you'll find it is worthwhile diverting away from the main road to visit some of the small seaside villages that hang at the end of their side roads, like pendants from a necklace.

PRACTICAL INFORMATION

- **Banks & Currency Exchange** – **Commercial Bank of Greece**, *Odos Roussou Koundourou, Agios Nikolaos*. **National Bank of Greece**, *Plateia Venizelou, Sitia*.
- **Doctors** – **Agios Nikolaos Hospital**, *Odos Paleologou. Tel. 0841/25221.*
- **Police** Agios Nikolaos: *Odos Kontogianni. Tel. 0841/22321;* Tourist Police, *Odos Kontogianni. Tel. 0841/26900.* Sitia: *Odos Odos Mykonos 24. Tel. 0843/22266;* Tourist Police: *Odos Mykonos 24. Tel. 0843/ 34200.*
- **Port Authority** – Agios Nikolaos: *Tel. 0841/22312.* Sitia: *Tel. 0843/ 22310.*
- **Post Office** – The main post office in Agios Nikolaos is at *Odos 28 Oktovriou 9.* Open Monday through Friday from 7:30 am to 8 pm. In

Sitia, the main post office is at *Odos Ethnikis Antistaseis 2*. Open Monday through Friday from 7:30 am to 2 pm.

• **Telephone** – The area code for Agios Nikolaos is *0841*. The Greek Telecommunications Organization (OTE) office is at the corner of *Odos 25 Martiou and Odos Sfakianaki*. Sitia area code is *0843*. OTE: *Odos Kapetan Sifis 22*.

• **Tourist Information** – Greek Tourist Organization (EOT) office in Agios Nikolaos: *Odos S. Koundourou. Tel. 0841/22357*.

11. KYTHIRA

...while rounding Cape Malea, I was swept by the waves and the tide,
and by the North Wind, and driven off course beyond Kythira.
Homer –The Odyssey

Kythira is a geographical nuisance that nobody knows what to do with. It lies off the south Peloponnese coast, just about where the Ionian Sea, the Aegean Sea, and the Sea of Crete mix their waters. It used to be administered by the British as one of their Ionian Islands dependencies, so is often considered one of that group, although it is a long way off and has no direct connection to them. It is now administered from Piraeus, with which it has a slow and infrequent ferry connection via the Saronic Gulf, Argolic Gulf, and various ports on the east Peloponnese coast.

You are as likely to be greeted with "G'day" here as with *"Yia sou,"* as many of the island's inhabitants have made their fortune in Australia and brought it on home to Kythira. Having invested the fruits of their labors Down Under in land and houses back home, the Oz-Kythirans aren't exactly keen on sharing the rewards with tourists, at least not to the extent of having their island overrun with the kind of crass tourism development that has blighted many another Greek island.

"So much the better," I can almost hear you say. "How do we get there?" Patience, patience: all will be explained. It's not an easy place to get to, or away from, except by air; accommodation is thin on the ground and tends towards the expensive; there isn't much to see or do; and it takes a while to get used to seeing Greeks wearing Antipodean-style long shorts and knee-length woollen socks, though mercifully not bush hats with corks dangling on strings from the brim.

Back in ancient times, Hesiod, in his *Theogeny,* placed Aphrodite's foam-born birth at Kythira (see sidebar below) – a proposition Cypriots would take issue with, citing Homer as *their* authority. It was a Minoan-era trading station, and during the Peloponnesian War was captured by Athens in 424 BC and used as a naval base for raiding the Spartans' homeland. The island became known as Porphyris, meaning "Purple Isle," because it was a source of the murex shellfish from which purple die was extracted: in Roman times the color could only be used by the ruling elite, and so you hear of emperors being born or raised "to the purple."

The entire population was sold into slavery by the corsair Barbarossa in 1537. Kythira became part of the modern Greek state in 1864 when it was included in the package deal by which the British handed over the Ionian Islands to Greece. Apart from Aussies and Aphrodite, there isn't much to Kythira. It has a spare, hilly beauty, and loads of those increasingly rare and precious 20th-century resources: nothing, peace, and tranquility.

OF SONS & LOVERS

Hesiod's tale of Aphrodite's birth went something like this (sensitive souls are advised to fast-forward at this point): Cronus, one of the Titans who preceded the Gods, didn't much like his old man Uranus, the ruler of the sky, so he castrated him. Uranus's unhitched tackle fell into the sea off Kythira and a white foam arose from it which shaped itself into the goddess Aphrodite.

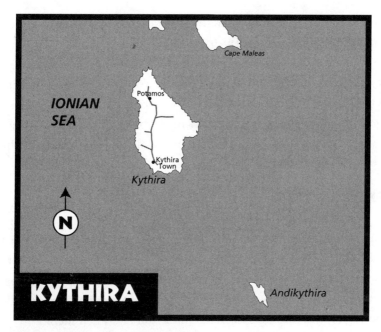

ARRIVALS & DEPARTURES

By Air

There are three **Olympic Airways** return flights from Athens every day in summer. Flying time is 50 minutes. **Kythira Airport** lies in the northeastern part of the island, about eight kilometers southeast of Potamos and 15 kilometers north of Kythira town. For current flight times and ticket prices, contact Olympic at *Odos Eleftheriou Venizelou 49, Potamos, Tel. 0735/33362.*

By Sea

An irregular car ferry service connects Piraeus's **Great Harbor** with Agia Pelagia on Kythira, sailing via various ports on the east Peloponnese, and continuing on from Kythira town, via **Antikythira**, to Kasteli on **Crete**. Nominally, in summer, there are two sailings a week. Tickets cost Drs 5,170 one-way for the 9-hour journey from Piraeus, and Drs 3,685 for the 4-hour trip from Crete.

Hydrofoils operated by Flying Dolphins sail to Agia Pelagia on Kythira from Piraeus's **Zea Marina**, via **Hydra** and **Spetses**, four times a week in summer, weather permitting: on Monday, Wednesday, Thursday and Saturday. Tickets cost Drs 9,315 one-way for the 5 1/4-hour journey.

The nearest mainland ports with direct car-ferry connections to and from Kythira are **Neapoli**, across the water from Agia Pelagia, and **Githio**, at the head of the Laconic Gulf, with one ferry a day in summer (feel free to say something laconic if you miss it). Tickets cost Drs 610 one-way for the 1-hour crossing from Neapoli, and Drs 1,460 for the 2 1/2-hour crossing from Githio.

ORIENTATION

Kythira lies off the entrance to the **Laconic Gulf**, and looks a bit like a misshapen cork falling from a bottle's neck towards Crete. It lies 182 airline kilometers south of Athens, and twice that distance in ferryboat kilometers from Piraeus. The Peloponnese is nearer, the mainland being only 14 kilometers away at the closest point. Crete lies 79 kilometers to the southeast, with the small island of Antikythira between them.

With an area of 278 square kilometers and a population of under 4,000, Kythira is a rocky and hilly place, reaching up to 506-meter **Mount Myrmingari** in the west, and is 29 kilometers long and 18 kilometers wide. The main settlement is **Kythira town** (aka Chora), above the south coast, with a few kilometers to the south the fishing village of **Kapsali**. Villages are sprinkled through the interior, and a few at the coast. In the north the main village is **Potamos**, and north of that is the island's main harbor, the charm-free port of **Agia Pelagia**.

GETTING AROUND THE ISLAND

By Bus & Taxi

If Kythira's bus service was any worse equipped it wouldn't exist. One bus running twice a day, once in the morning and once in the afternoon, makes the journey up and down the island's middle from **Agia Pelagia** in the north through **Potamos**, **Karvounades**, **Livadi**, and **Kythira town** (Chora) to **Kapsali** in the south, then back again. And that's it. End of story.

Taxis there are, but giving Greek taxi drivers a seller's market – more like a seller's monopoly – is only a cat's whisker away from legalizing mugging. If you have arms and legs to spare, be prepared to expend them. Fares from Kythira town to the airport can run up to Drs 4,000, and from Agia Pelagia to Kythira town up to Drs 5,000.

By Moped & Car

Mopeds can be picked up at several outlets beside the harbor at Agia Pelagia, Kythira town, and Kapsali. Try **Moto-Rent**, *Tel. 0735/31600*, beside the harbor at Kapsali for well-maintained bikes.

Rental autos are available in Kythira town from **Tserigo Rent**, *Tel. 0735/31030*, in the main street.

WHERE TO STAY

KYTHERIA, *Seafront, Agia Pelagia. Tel. 0735/33321, Fax 0735/33825. Rates (with tax): Drs 10,000 single; Drs 13,000 double. Breakfast included. 10 rooms. No credit cards.*

Conveniently situated beside the harbor in otherwise undistinguished Agia Pelagia, this is a comfortable hotel with traditional decor and style, operated by a friendly Australian-Greek couple. All rooms have private bath and some are air conditioned.

PORPHYRA, *Potamos. Tel. 0735/33329. Rates (with tax): Drs 11,000 double. Breakfast Drs 1,500. 8 rooms. No credit cards.*

A dazzlingly white-painted pension with tiled roofs and blue-painted doors and shutters, established in a rambling old mansion built in the traditional style. The Porphyra's rooms have telephone, private bath, television and refrigerator. You can escape from the sun in the shade of the big attached garden.

TA KYTHERA, *Manitohori. Tel. 0735/33329. Rates (with tax): Drs 10,000 double. Breakfast Drs 1,000. 7 rooms. No credit cards.*

This delightful pension in a refurbished villa dating from 1827 stands beside the main road north of Kythira town at the hamlet of Manitohori, with a fine view over the town and down to the sea at Kapsali. The rooms are decorated and equipped in simple village style, but each with private bathroom and refrigerator.

WHERE TO EAT

In and around Kythira town, **ZORBA'S** taverna on the main street, **MIRTOÖN** on the road to Kapsali, and **ARTEMA** and **ZERBAS** on the seafront at Kapsali, are all popular local eateries.

In Livadi, try taverna **TOXOTIS**, and in Agia Pelagia, taverna **FAROS**.

SEEING THE SIGHTS

There *are* sights on Kythira, though not many and not spectacular. It is the island as a whole that attracts, with its beautiful natural scenery, charming villages, and absence of hassle and hustle.

Kythira town is itself a sight, dominated by the stout walls and crumbled interior of its **Venetian Castle**, *open permanently; admission free,* dating from 1316, atop a steep-sided, rocky crag overlooking the town. The town is built in the Cycladic style, a cluster of whitewashed buildings looking like a pile of white bricks caught in the act of tumbling down the hillside on which it stands. There is a small **Archeological Museum**, uphill on the Livadi road, *open Tuesday to Friday 8:30 am to 2 pm, Sunday 9:30 am to 1 pm; admission free.*

The Venetian Castle also is a prominent landmark from **Kapsali**, Kythira town's port downhill from the capital. The village is calm and pretty. It is built around twin bays separated by a narrow peninsula, and has good though not extensive beaches. The headlands around the harbor are crowned with little whitewashed churches.

Palaiopolis on the east coast, at the northern corner of Agios Nikolaos Bay, is where the Minoans had their trading station, and **Palaiokastro** a little way inland is where stood the once famed and now vanished **Temple of Aphrodite**, described by Pausanias in the 2nd century BC as the most sacred temple in Greece. Christianity appropriated some of the pagan shrine's columns and other materials to build the **Church of Agios Cosmas** at Palaiopolis. The walls of the post office at nearby **Avlemonas** are decorated with seashells: in the harbor below, brightly-colored caïques bob on the crystal-clear water against a backdrop of ocher cliffs.

Milopotamos in the west is noted for the 12th-century frescoes in the gloomy cave that is the **Church of Agia Sophia**. Northwards, near Potamos, are the ruins of the Byzantine town of **Palaiochora**.

SPORTS & RECREATION
Beaches

There is an embarrassment of riches in terms of beaches on Kythira, most of them deserted and only a few offering tourist facilities. The best beaches are around **Diakofti**, sheltered by the offshore islet of Makronissi. Other good bets are those at **Platia Amos**, north of Agia Pelagia.

SHOPPING

Kythira's honey has a reputation as among the best in Greece, and it can be bought in glass and stone jars at shops around the island and at the **Sunday-morning market** in **Potamos**.

PRACTICAL INFORMATION

- **Banks** – The **National Bank of Greece** has branches in Kythira town and Potamos, both open Monday through Thursday from 8 am to 2 pm, and to 1:30 pm on Friday.
- **Doctors** – The island's **Medical Center** is *in Potamos, Tel. 0735/33325.*
- **Police** – The police station is in Kythira town, *Tel. 0735/31206.*
- **Port Authority** – Agia Pelagia, *Tel. 0735/33280;* Kapsali, *Tel. 0735/ 31222.*
- **Post Office** – There are post offices in Kythira town and Potamos, open Monday through Friday from 7:30 am to 2 pm.
- **Telephone** – The area code for Kythira is *0735.* The Greek Telecommunication Organization (OTE) office is in Kythira town. *Tel. 0735/ 31212.*
- **Tourist Information** – There is no Greek Tourist Organization (EOT) office on Kythira.

12. THE IONIAN ISLANDS

The Ionian Islands

You'll search in vain throughout the Aegean Sea for these islands, for they lie not in the Aegean, but way over to the west of mainland Greece, in the **Ionian Sea**. That's why they are called the **Ionian Islands**. Incidentally, they should not be confused (as if you would do such a thing!) with Ionia, which was the part of ancient Hellas on the west coast of present-day Turkey.

Altogether there are some 40 islands in the Ionian archipelago, stretching from off the Albanian coast in the north to the Peloponnese in the south, but some of them are no more than chunks of rock. The three biggies geographically and touristically are **Corfu**, **Kefallonia**, and **Zakynthos**; occupying a middle-sized position are **Ithaca** and **Lefkada**; while two of the more notable littlies are **Paxos** and **Meganissi**.

CORFU (KERKYRA)

Fertile Scheria is the home of the Phaecians,
A race descended from the Gods.
Homer – The Odyssey

The first thing to note about **Corfu** is that it isn't actually called Corfu, except by the 90 percent of its annual population who go there as tourists.

224 GREEK ISLANDS GUIDE

IONIAN FINDS & FAVORITES

•*Corfu Old Town*. A warren of narrow streets, shaded arcades, little squares, crumbling houses with shutters closed against the sun, and genuine Greek charm, even though most of it dates from the Venetian period (see Corfu).

•*The Sweet Red Wine of Antipaxos*. For a very small island, Antipaxos has a wonderful surprise in store on the oenology front (see Paxos).

•*Porto Katsiki*. A powerful contender for the best beach in Greece (see Lefkada).

•*Smuggler's Cove*. In the northwest corner of Zakynthos. This sight may be a bit touristy, with its foundered smuggler's boat half buried in the sand at the foot of steep seacliffs, but it is no less memorable for that (see Zakynthos).

Greeks call it Kerkyra, although their way of writing the word makes it look like Kepkypa. Keep Kerkyra in mind when you're asking for ferry tickets and you can't go wrong. (This is to save you having a similar experience to those travelers in northern Italy who never find Florence, but who have a marvelous time in some place called Firenze.)

The island looks a bit like a seahorse that has swum across the Ionian Sea from Italy and is about to fetch up on the Balkan shore, with its head almost touching Albania and its tail waving in the face of Epirus. Time was when the northeast coast of Corfu was one of the most unlikely – and for sure one of the warmest – frontiers of the Cold War. If you went for a swim from any of the small beaches near Kassiopi and strayed too far out, you could cross an invisible line in the water and find yourself an involuntary guest of the Socialist People's Republic of Albania.

Today, of course, you can see Albanians lined up ten deep on the other side of the 5-kilometer strait, wondering how they can get across, and Corfu is the genuine worker's paradise. Or is it? Well, it all depends on what you mean by paradise. Corfu has come a long way since the

ALBANIA

Kerkyra

Corfu
(Kerkyra)

GREECE

Paxos
Antipaxos

Lefkada

Lefkada

IONIAN
SEA

Ithaca

Ithaca

Argostoli
Kefalonia

N

Zakinthos

Zakynthos

IONIAN
SEA ISLANDS

Durrell brothers, authors both, rhapsodized about their idyl there in the 1930s, escaping from Depression-stricken England to a dream island in the sun, and a fair amount of the journey has been downhill. Most of that can be laid at the door of package tourism.

ARRIVALS & DEPARTURES
By Air

Corfu's **Ioannis Kapodistrias Airport**, *Tel. 0661/30180*, is three kilometers south of Corfu town, on the Kanoni Peninsula between Lake Halikiopolou and the sea. **Olympic Airways** operates four scheduled return flights a day at peak periods to Corfu from Athens, flying time 50 minutes, as well as three flights a week from Thessalonika, flying time 1 hour. For current departure flight times and ticket prices, contact Olympic in Corfu town at *Odos Kapodistriou 20, Tel. 0661/38694.* Travel agents on the island can also book onward flights.

There are any number of charter flights from London, Paris, Amsterdam, Berlin – in fact from all over northern Europe – to Corfu, from April through October. As Corfu is one of the logical starting points for a tour of Greece and the islands, you may find this a good option if you want to fly. You book a charter flight from a travel agent in Europe, with the return set for between one and six weeks after departure. This will cost in the region of $200 to $300, depending on where you fly from and when, and will be far cheaper than an unrestricted return flight to Athens, and probably cheaper than a Super-Apex fare. The disadvantage is that you have to get back to Corfu for your return flight, unless you got the ticket cheap enough to be able to toss the return away and get back by another route.

If you're not on a package tour and being picked up by a tour company bus or are renting a car, taxi is the only direct way to town or to your chosen resort. The fare to Corfu town is around Drs 1,500. Buses for Corfu town going along the coast road stop about 500 meters from the airport; most people can manage this even with luggage if taxi fare is a problem.

By Sea

International car ferries and car-carrying catamarans sail between **Ancona**, **Bari**, **Brindisi**, and **Venice** in Italy and Corfu town, some of them connecting with **Igoumenitsa**, on the mainland opposite, others to **Patras** on the west coast of the Peloponnese, and some of the latter going via **Paxos**, **Ithaca** and **Kefallonia**. At peak periods there are at least five vessels a day in each direction calling at Corfu town.

Bookings can be made by shipping agents in Corfu: **Hermes Travel Service**, *Odos Eleftheriou Venizelou 46, Tel. 0661/39747;* **Ilios Holidays Ltd.**, *Odos Xenofondos Stratigou 46, Tel. 0661/38089;* **Spyros Vergis Travel**, *Odos Ethnikis Antistaseos 2, Tel. 0661/25000.* International ferries arrive and depart from the New Port, west of the New Fortress.

The closest mainland ferry port is **Igoumenitsa**, and at peak periods there are car ferries (*Tel. 0661/32655*) every hour between there and Corfu town from 5:45 am to 10 pm. Journey time is 1 3/4 hours; one-way tickets cost Drs 1,100. In summer there is one car ferry a day between Gaios, the main settlement on **Paxos**, and Corfu (*Tel. 0661/32655*). Journey time is 3 1/4 hours; one-way tickets cost Drs 1,800. A passenger-only catamaran (Tel. 0661/32655) connects twice a day with **Paxos**. Journey time is 1 1/4 hours; this vessel also sails to and from **Preveza** and **Amfilohia** on the mainland southeast of Paxos, journey time 2 3/4 hours and 3 hours 50 minutes respectively; one-way tickets cost Drs 1,320, and Drs 2,420. Domestic ferries arrive at and depart from the Old Port, between the New Fortress and the Old Town.

By Bus (via Igoumenitsa)

There are three buses a day between **Athens** and Corfu town (four on Sunday), leaving from the bus station at *Odos Kifissiou 100, Tel. 01/512-9443.* Journey time is 11 hours; one-way tickets cost Drs 7,260, plus the ferry fare. Contact the Corfu town long-distance bus terminal for departure times, *Tel. 0661/32158.*

ORIENTATION

At 592 square kilometers, Corfu is the second biggest of the Ionian Islands, and the seventh biggest Greek island, and has a population of around 110,000. This last figure will seem laughable if you arrive in July or August, when you might guess at more like 110 million. The coastal resorts, once little more than fishing villages, are overrun with tourists in summer, yet that doesn't mean you have to be surrounded by bodies oozing suntan lotion. It's a big island, with rugged mountains in the north and south where there are plenty of places to escape the maddening crowds. You can even still find yourself a deserted beach, or anyway a beachette, especially if you are willing to expend some sweat in the search and scramble down rocky hillsides.

Corfu has something many other Greek islands might trade their Homeric heritage for: **water**. No less than 112 glorious, life-sustaining centimeters of the stuff droppeth as the gentle rain from heaven every year. That's three times more than Crete gets, and it accounts for Corfu's reputation as the Green Isle, and for the tidal wave of floral color that flows across the landscape come spring. Tourists usually take a dim view of rain. You'll be pleased to hear that Corfu's is pretty well-behaved, mostly working its magic during the winter months, apart from an occasional spectacular summer thunderstorm when it seems the entire Ionian Sea has been lifted into the sky then dropped on your head. You'll be grateful for every millimeter of it every time you step into the shower.

Corfu town, roughly in the middle of the east coast, facing the mainland, is the main town and port on Corfu. South of the town is a coastal strip lined with resorts, including **Benitses**. From Corfu town, a coastal road runs around most of the island. The northeastern stretch from **Pirgi** to **Kassiopi** is particularly rugged and scenic, as it winds through the foothills of 908-meter **Mount Pantokrator**.

The southern stretch from Corfu town to **Kavos** is particularly rugged and scenic too, although the road cheats by swerving from the east coast to the west then back to the east again. Finally, the western stretch from **Sidari**, through **Paleokastritsa** to **Agios Matheos** is also particularly rugged and scenic. In the middle, from Corfu town to **Pelekas** in the west, lies the fertile **Ropa Plain**, scenic but not particularly rugged. The south even has a Greek islands rarity: wetlands along the banks of **Lake Korission** and the **Messongi River**.

GETTING AROUND THE ISLAND
By Bus

There are two bus stations in Corfu town. **Long-distance buses**, colored green, run from the New Fort bus station on Odos Avramiou, west of the fort, to Paleokastritsa, Kassiopi, Kavos and other villages, and are operated by **KTEL**, *Tel. 0661/39985 or 0661/30627.* Tickets cost from Drs 350 to Drs 700.

In and around Corfu town, **urban buses**, *Tel. 0661/32158 or 0661/ 31595,* colored blue, operate from the bus station on Plateia San Rocco, but are more conveniently boarded at the Spianada. Tickets cost Drs 150. Line 2 buses run along the seafront to the **Kanoni Peninsula** every 30 minutes in summer, serving the hotels and restaurants there; you can pick this one up at the Esplanade. Lines 5 and 6 continue south and stop near the airport. Buses for **Athens** also leave from the urban station.

By Car

If you brought your own or a rented car with you, the only thing you need worry about is the standard of Greek driving and late-night drunk drivers in the resorts – which, after all, is enough to keep you fully supplied with driving worries throughout your stay. Holes in the roads are mostly more of an irritant, although you will occasionally encounter, but hope-fully not run into, a hole big enough to damage your car.

Among more than a hundred firms around the island, rental cars are available in Corfu town from:
- **Hertz**, *Odos Ethniki Lefkimis. Tel. 0661/38388*
- **Alamo**, *Odos Ethnikis Antistaseos 2. Tel. 0661/45315*
- **Europcar**, *Odos Eleftheriou Venizelou 32. Tel. 0661/46931*
- **Budget**, *Odos Xenofondos Stratigou 32. Tel. 0661/22062*

It's worth shopping around for good rates, bearing in mind that the cheapest cars and jeeps may be poorly maintained and lack vital fixtures and fittings, such as seatbelts that work. Some local firms give almost as good service as the international majors and are liable to charge less. Try:
- **Kosmos**, *Odos Eleftheriou Venizelou 4. Tel. 0661/40390*
- **Ionian Cars**, *Kassiopi. Tel. 0663/81317*

By Moped & Scooter

Mopeds, scooters, and off-road bikes, often in a more-or-less poorly maintained state, are widely available for rent throughout the island for from Drs 3,000 to Drs 4,000. A good local firm in Corfu town is **Mamola**, *Odos Xenofondos Stratigou 32, Tel. 0661/30797.*

By Taxi

The rule here, as everywhere else in Greece, is "don't go by taxi if you can possibly avoid it." The best that can be said about Corfiot taxi drivers is that they are no worse than taxi drivers anywhere else in Greece. With this ominous warning ringing in your ears, you can call a cab at *Tel. 0661/ 33811,* and *Tel. 0661/41333,* or pick one up in the street or at the stands – in Corfu town at Plateia San Rocco, Plateia Spilia, and at the Esplanade.

There are always taxis lurking around at the ferry terminal, the airport, and outside major hotels like the Hilton. Outlying resorts and bigger villages have taxis, which can be called from one of the above numbers or picked up in the street, or whose driver can probably be traced by asking at the village kafenion (cafe).

WHERE TO STAY

CORFU HILTON, *Odos Nafsikas, Kanoni. Tel. 0661/36540, Fax 0661/ 36551. Rates (with tax): Drs 40,000 single; Drs 55,000 double. 273 rooms. Breakfast Drs 5,000. American Express, Diners Club, Visa, MasterCard.*

It may not be very traditional, at least not traditional Greek, but the Corfu Hilton compensates by being a world apart on its big chunk of the Kanoni Peninsula south of Corfu town. It's 100 meters from the sea, but with its two swimming pools you might never need to see the sea. Air conditioned throughout, and with central heating too in case global warming turns out to be a bust, the Hilton has everything you need from a resort hotel, including an 18-hole golf course 25 minutes from the hotel. The rooms are spacious, furnished in deluxe style, and equipped with private bathroom with bath and shower, minibar, satellite television, in-hotel video channel, telephone, and hairdryer.

Other hotel facilities and services include two bars, two restaurants, 24-hour room service, two swimming pools, two tennis courts, bowling center, health club, jogging track, and a casino.

CAVALIERI, *Odos Kapodistriou 4. Tel. 0661/39041, Fax 0661/39283. Rates (with tax): Drs 23,000 single; Drs 31,000 double. 48 rooms. Breakfast Drs 2,000. American Express, Diners Club, Visa.*

The Cavalieri took its biggest hit during World War II, when it got itself bombed, so the antique-looking interior is more of a good makeup job than a reality. Still, it is a good makeup job, and the hotel is one of the handsomest places in Corfu town. The rooms tend more towards modern and functional rather than plush, but are air conditioned and have a minibar and television. The hotel has 24-hour room service.

NISSAKI BEACH, *Crouzeri, Nissaki. Tel. 0663/91232, Fax 0663/ 22079. Rates (with tax): Drs 16,000 single; Drs 30,000 double. 239 rooms. Breakfast included. American Express, Diners Club, Visa, MasterCard.*

It would be harder to imagine a bigger or better-equipped hotel than this one on the coast midway between Ipsos and Kassiopi, 25 kilometers north of Corfu town. The superb sports facilities alone constitute an invitation to stay: apart from the swimming pool, there is tennis, volleyball, basketball, and a fitness center. With its beachfront position and well-equipped, air conditioned rooms, this takes some beating as a resort experience. The hotel operates a free daily bus service to Corfu town.

BELLA VENEZIA, *Odos Zambeli 4. Tel. 0661/46500, Fax 0661/20708. Rates (with tax): Drs 15,000 single; Drs 20,200 double. 32 rooms. Breakfast Drs 1,600. Visa, MasterCard.*

This is one of the modest gems of Corfu, a hotel in a classic 19th-century building which was formerly occupied by the National Bank of Greece, and then by a girl's high school. Converted to a hotel in 1988, the Bella Venezia has made the transition in style. Its air conditioned rooms are furnished in the traditional way and each has private bathroom, television, and telephone. There is a snack bar below, and a garden terrace where breakfast is served. This a quiet location on the edge of the old town.

ARCADION, *Odos Kapodistriou 44. Tel. 0661/37670, Fax 0661/45087. Rates (with tax): Drs 11,900 single; Drs 14,900 double. 55 rooms. Breakfast Drs 1,700. No credit cards.*

You can't get much more in the center of things than with this hotel overlooking the Spianada and the Old Fortress, as well as being caught up in the evening volta and the nightlife associated with it. The rooms are plainly furnished, although each has a private bathroom, telephone, and balcony. The Arcadion's draw comes from a combination of its location, character, and price. It's good value for the money.

ASTRON, *Odos Donzelotou 15. Tel. 0661/39505, Fax 0661/39986. Rates (with tax): Drs 12,000 single; Drs 15,000 double. 33 rooms. Breakfast Drs 1,500. No credit cards.*

Overlooking the Old Port, the Astron is a neoclassical Corfu mansion that is looking a little the worse for its years, although the revolving doorway still works okay. Most of the comfortable rooms have a balcony with a view of the sea, and the hotel itself has a tennis court and private parking.

APRAOS BAY, *Apraos, Kassiopi. Tel. 0663/98204, Fax 0663/63686. Rates (with tax): Drs 11,000 single; Drs 14,000 double. Breakfast included. 16 rooms. No credit cards.*

Occupies a wooded location close to the beach at Apraos outside Kassiopi village on the northeast coast, and provides a more personal service than is common on this part of the coast. Its small number of rooms helps in that respect. A fairly new hotel, it offers comfortable rooms with private bathroom.

VILLA FUNDANA, *near Paleokastritsa. Tel. 0663/22532, Fax 0663/ 22453. Rates (with tax): Drs 13,000 double (up to five people). Breakfast Drs 1,300. 10 bungalows. No credit cards.*

Located in the hills above Paleokastritsa, the Villa Fundana is a country home with loads of character dating from the Venetian period in the 17th century, and set amidst gardens, olive groves and orchards. The self-contained bungalows that have been built around it make for a different kind of Corfu vacation experience, one more oriented towards country matters than the sea, and far removed in spirit from the great bed factories at the coast. Each is equipped in rustic style. Sports facilities here are good, and there is a swimming pool, a bar in the old olive-press room, and easy parking.

HERMES, *Odos Markora 14. Tel. 0661/39268, Fax 0661/58403. Rates (with tax): Drs 9,500; Drs 11,500. 33 rooms. Breakfast included. No credit cards.*

Located in a fairly busy street in a good position on the edge of the New Fortress and the Old City, the Hermes sends a message in its friendly welcome and reasonable rates, although it is one of those places that looks better architecturally than it really is comfort-wise. Most rooms have private bathroom. There is easy parking for guests.

ZEPHYROS, *Paleokastritsa. Tel. 0663/41211. Rates (with tax): Drs 7,500 single; Drs 11,000 double. Breakfast Drs 750. 16 rooms. No credit cards.*

Across the road from the municipal beach, this is a small and reasonably personal hotel in an area where bigger establishments are the norm. The rooms are big and clean though modestly furnished, and those at the front have balconies with a fine view of the harbor and the sea.

WHERE TO EAT

REX, *Odos Kapodistrias 66. Tel. 0661/27127. Drs 4,000 to Drs 9,000. American Express, Diners Club, Visa, MasterCard. Stylish.*

The Rex is something of an institution in Corfu town, taking the basic ingredients of the Greek kitchen upmarket in both style and presentation in its 19th-century mansion setting near the Liston building. You can get the traditional moussaka and souvlaki, all right, but if you prefer something a bit more adventurous, such as chicken in kumquat sauce, this may be the place for you.

VICEROY, *Kontokali. Tel. 0661/90830. Drs 4,000 to Drs 8,000. Visa, MasterCard. Indian.*

Although the chef at this restaurant on the road north of Corfu town between Kontokali and Gouvia is not Indian, there is no way of telling from the quality of the fare, which is well up to the standards of curry-fancying London, if not perhaps Bombay. Look for such specialties as prawn or chicken tikka masala, which are among many dishes on the menu cooked in the tandoor: the traditional Indian clay oven. Curry dishes are not over-spiced, which will suit those not quite up to the fiery taste of India.

SAN SOFIA, *Perama. Tel. 0661/21145. Drs 4,000 to Drs 8,000. American Express, Diners Club, Visa, MasterCard. Italian.*

One sure sign of San Sofia's quality is that it is perennially popular with the many Italian vacationers on Corfu, which after all was once part of the Venetian, not to mention the Roman, Empire. This is no pizza parlor, but look out for a wide range of seductive regional specialties, and a few surprise items like the spaghetti in black cuttlefish-ink sauce. The wine list eschews many internationally popular labels in favor of ones that are insider's tips in Italy. Piano music accompanies the meals most evenings. You'll find San Sofia at Perama, south of Corfu town, near the Alexandros Hotel.

TOULA'S, *Agni village. Drs 3,000 to Drs 7,000. No credit cards. Seafood/ traditional.*

This is surely one of the best-located and charming restaurants on Corfu: you eat right beside the sea in a village with only a handful of houses, on the northeast coast between Kaminaki and Kalami, north of Nissaki. The food matches the setting, being mostly seafood, including excellent prawns and lobster, as well as a wide range of Ionian Sea fish – the meze is the best way to sample this. There are also some meat dishes, however.

VENETIAN WELL, *Old Town. Tel. 0661/44761. Drs 3,500 to Drs 6,000. No credit cards. International.*

The menu here mixes Greek dishes with a kind of world music of international cuisine, and the thing is you never know what will be coming up from one day to the next, at least not until the day's offerings are chalked up on the menu board. The Venetian well in question dates from 1669 and the Venetian Well's outdoor tables cluster around it. Inside, there is an interesting wall mural showing people eating and apparently enjoying the experience, which if not wildly original is at least reassuring.

LUCCIOLA INN, *Sgombou village. Tel. 0661/99224. Drs 3,000 to Drs 6,000. No credit cards. Sophisticated regional Greek.*

Lucciola expands the range of Corfu eateries by featuring regional specialties from around Greece. And it does so in a venue that is strikingly memorable: a 19th-century country house converted to a restaurant, whose tree-shaded garden makes a restful and romantic place to dine on a fine summer evening. Sgombou is on the Paleokastritsa road in the hills above Corful town.

TAI PAN, *Odos Nafsikas, Kanoni. Tel. 0661/47775. Drs 3,000 to Drs 6,000. Visa, MasterCard. Chinese.*

More than just a change from wall-to-wall Greek tavernas, this Chinese restaurant set in a garden beside the Hilton Hotel is an experience in its own right, and delivers the kind of taste that might get them talking in Hong Kong. All the old favorites are here – shark's fin soup, sweet-and-sour prawns, duck in black bean sauce, etc. – along with some dishes from Thailand and Singapore

NAVTIKON, *Odos Theotoki 150. Tel. 0661/30009. Drs 3,000 to Drs 6,000. No credit cards. Traditional.*

You'll find Navtikon near the old harbor. This taverna dates from just after the war and a time when Corfu was a lot closer to its farming and fishing roots. Glad to say that Navtikon hasn't strayed much, if at all, from the traditions it has inherited, even although the clientele is at least 50 percent tourists. The afelia – pork cubes cooked in red wine and coriander – is especially good.

EUROPA, *Odos Xenofondos Stratigou 12. Tel. 0661/25323. Drs 3,000 to Drs 6,000. No credit cards. Traditional.*

A taverna that spreads its tables out on to the streets of the Old Town, with a view of the harbor and the sea. The view inside is equally memorable and the food is among the best of the traditional Greek tavernas in Corfu.

IANNIS, *Odos Iassonos ke Sosipatros, Anemomilos. Tel. 0661/33061. Drs 2,500 to Drs 4,000. No credit cards. Traditional.*

It can sometimes be difficult to choose between Greek tavernas, which mostly all look very inviting, kind of rustic, and friendly. The real test is in the eating, of course, and by the time you find out that it doesn't taste as good as it looks it is always too late. Have no such fears at Iannis, where the range of dishes that you can peruse bubbling away on the cookers in the kitchen is immense, and each one of them delivers. The octopus here is especially good.

SEEING THE SIGHTS
Corfu Town

If this should be your first acquaintance with a Greek town, don't draw too many conclusions from it. They don't all look this good. Corfu hasn't been Greek, politically speaking, for most of the last thousand years, and the 411-year Venetian domination (1386-1797) in particular left its architectural mark as has no other period, always excepting the tourist boom of recent decades. The British too left their legacy, and a cricket pitch on the Spianada (Esplanade) is used by local enthusiasts for the sport, their existence alone being enough to distinguish Corfiots from all other Greeks.

Start at the **Spianada**, one of the biggest open, green areas you'll see in many a Greek town, and particularly impressive in one with a population of just 32,000. Its tree-shaded, flower-bedecked acreage fits well with Corfu's image as the Green Isle, although the original reason for having an open space in front of the Old Fortress was to give Venetian gunners behind the walls a nice, clear field of fire for killing Turks while suffering little in the way of distraction from return fire. There may be streets running through it, and noisy traffic around it, but the Spianada itself is a restful, shaded place, dotted with Greek and colonial-era monuments, and the main setting for the evening *volta*.

Having given the Spianada a quick once-over, swerve to the east past the horse-drawn tourist carriages and the statue of the German soldier-of-fortune **Marshal Schulenburg**, who played a heroic part on the Venetian side during the Turkish siege of Corfu in 1716, cross the bridge over the sea-moat dug in the 16th century, and stroll into the **Palaio Frourio** (Old Fortress), dating from the 1550s, *Tel. 0661/48310; open Tuesday through Friday 8 am to 7 pm, weekend 8:30 am to 3 pm; admission.* You may as well leave your camera behind, as photography is not permitted within the fortress (in case the Turks get hold of some top-secret Venetian military information). The promontory was known as Korypho in medieval times, hence Corfu. This is Corfu's twin peaks, with both hills on the steep promontory extending eastwards from the Spianada having once been heavily fortified redoubts. Inside the walls, among the piled-up cliffs, there's a clocktower, lighthouse, a neo-classical style British church dating from 1830, and a sound-and-light show on summer evenings. From the walls you get a fine view over Corfu town and across the straits to the hills of mainland Greece and Albania.

Back on the other side of the moat again, in the northwest section of the Spianada is a **cricket ground**, a spiritual relic of the British colonial period that the locals have taken to heart: you can listen to the thwack! of leather on wood, argue about whether or not "No ball!" was the right decision by the umpire, and watch wickets tumble as the overs pass – if you see what I mean. Across from the Spianada, on Odos Eleftherias, is the **Liston**, a long, arcaded building whose design is modeled on the rue de Rivoli in Paris, and whose arches are now occupied by cafe tables. Built between 1807 and 1814, its name comes from the "list" of blue-blooded families who once owned the arcades.

Beyond the north end of the Spianada, you'll find the **Palace of Saint Michael and Saint George**, *Tel. 0661/30443; open Tuesday through Sunday 8:30 am to 3 pm; admission Drs 700.* This is another piece of Corfu's British heritage. Built between 1818 and 1823 in the neo-Classical Regency style as a frat house for members of the knightly order named for the two saints, it served also as a residence for the British governor, and became a Greek royal palace when the Ionian Islands were handed to Greece in 1864. Now a **museum**, it combines collections of Asian art – more than 10,000 pieces, including Chinese and Japanese porcelain – assembled by two Greek diplomats, with Orthodox religious art from local churches, and the restored State Rooms of the knights.

Now it's time to plunge into the warren of narrow streets, shaded arcades, little squares, crumbling houses with shutters closed against the sun, and genuine Greek charm of the **Old Town**. You're on your own here, directions-wise, as I never got anything but lost in this characterful maze. There are, however, a few landmarks that you might stumble over, such as the **Money Museum**. Start at the **Town Hall** in Odos Voulgareos, a *loggia*-style building which dates from 1663 and was formerly a theater and opera hall, built in white marble from Corfu's Mount Pantokrator.

In the Old Town proper is the **Church of Agios Spyridon**, *Odos Agiou Spyridonou; open daily from dawn to dusk; admission free.* This is the final resting place of Corfu's patron saint, Saint Spyridon, whose mummified body lies inside the church in a silver casket. He is allowed out four times a year on important feast days and carried in procession around town. Another big day in his calendar is his name day, December 12, when the Orthodox faithful converge on the church to kiss his feet which, mercifully, are enclosed in slippers.

See also the **Cathedral of Panagia Spiliotissa** (Our Lady of the Cave), *Odos Agia Theodora; open daily from dawn to dusk; admission free,* in which another silver casket is occupied by the remains of Saint Theodora (the cathedral is also known as **Agia Theodora Augusta**, as the lady in question was a 10th-century Byzantine empress).

Keep going north towards the Old Port and the main ferry terminal at the New Port to its west. Bristling between the two harbors is the imposing bulk of the Venetian **Neo Frourio** (New Fortress), dating from the 1580s, *Tel. 0661/27477; open daily 9 am to 9 pm; admission Drs 400.* It's now mostly used as a Greek navy base and only parts of its casements and galleries are open to the public. You might be interested to visit both of Corfu town's Venetian forts, although if you've already been to other islands you're probably suffering from Venetian fort indigestion. If so, withdraw without making an attempt on this one's walls, and backtrack to the southern end of the Spianada.

Beyond the Corfu Hotel is the **Archaeological Museum**, at the corner of Leoforos Dimokratias and Odos Vraila, *Odos Armeni Vraila 1, Tel. 0661/ 30680; open Tuesday through Sunday 8:30 am to 3 pm; admission Drs 800.* The centerpiece of the museum's collection is the superb Gorgon pediment from the early 6th century BC Temple of Artemis which stood in ancient Corcyra in the suburbs south of Corfu town. It depicts the Gorgon Medusa with Pegasus and Chrysaor, and other mythological creatures. There are many other bits of sculpture and other objects from all periods of Corfu's ancient history.

You can either keep walking south towards the airport, or board the line 2 coast-road bus from the Spianada for the short trip to the **Kanoni Peninsula**, on which the Corfu Hilton – and perhaps more importantly, the remnant of ancient **Corcyra** – stands. There's not much left above ground of the Greco-Roman city, **Paleopolis** as it is now called, for which fact the Goths of the 6th century would no doubt be proud to accept most of the blame, with the 14 centuries of decay since their raid doing the rest. At the neck of the peninsula, look out for the fragmentary remains of the 6th century BC **Temple of Artemis** near the crumbling **Villa of Mon Repos**, which dates from 1824 and was a summer residence of the Greek royal family (Britain's Prince Philip, husband of Queen Elizabeth II, was born there).

At the peninsula's southern tip, beyond the acropolis of Corcyra, you can jostle with the crowds at the overlook to snap a picture of the most-photographed scene in Corfu: two islets – **Vlacherna** with its brilliant-white monastery, reached across a short causeway; and beyond that, **Pondikonisi** (Mouse Island), whose monastery peeps out shyly at the world from behind a canopy of trees (and which is one of two Corfiot islets that are given the role of the Phaecian ship in *The Odyssey* that was turned to stone by a wrathful Poseidon for taking Odysseus back to Ithaca). There's also a 500-meter causeway across the bay to **Perama**.

Other Corfu Town Sights

- **Byzantine Museum**, *Odos Arseniou. Tel. 0661/38313. Open Tuesday through Sunday. Admission Drs 800.* Located in the church of Panagia Antivouniotissa, the museum mostly displays religious icons.
- **Maitland Memorial**, *Spianada. Open permanently. Admission free.* A memorial in colonnaded, neoclassical rotunda style, to Sir Thomas Maitland, the first British Lord High Commissioner – a fancy name for governor – of the Ionian Islands (1815-23).
- **Dionysios Solomos Museum**, *Address. Tel. 0661/30674. Open Monday through Friday 7 am to 9 pm. Admission free.* The house where the poet from Zakynthos, Dionysios Solomos, who wrote the words of the Greek national anthem, the *Hymn to Freedom,* lived fom 1828 until his death in 1857.

• **Agion Iasonos ke Sosipatros**, *Odos Iasonou ke Sosipatrou. Open daily from dawn to dusk. Admission free.* South of Cofu town, between the town and the suburb of Kanoni, the domed 11th-century Byzantine church is dedicated to the two early 1st-century martyrs who brought Christianity to Corfu. It contains some faded frescos.

Northern Corfu

Because of the shape of Corfu and the position of Corfu town in the middle, the island divides neatly into two halves for exploration purposes, using the capital as a natural base. Pursuing the earlier metaphor of Corfu being shaped like a seahorse, to go north is to get inside the head of the beast. The ideal way to do this is by hired car or motorbike, as this gives you the opportunity to branch off on any side route that takes your fancy and to pick up accommodation on the way without too much hassle; yet the main elements can also be done by bus.

Drive north on the coast road through **Kondokali**, an uninteresting resort built around a manmade beach, with the former leper-colony islet of **Lazaretto** offshore. Keep on to **Gouvia**, a resort with a shingle beach and enclosed in the arms of a wide bay. Near the beach are some curious arched structures which are the remains of the Venetian shipyard. The road which had been tending northwest to this point now swings north to Dassia, Ipsos, and Pirgi.

From this resort village, you can turn inland and start the long climb towards **Mount Pantokrator**, up through the pretty mountain villages **Spartilas** and **Strinilas**, with steadily expanding vistas opening up all around you. If you dare to take your eyes off the hairpin bends, that is. The final stretch is best done on foot, on a rough track past the 14th-century **Pantokrator Monastery**, *open daily*, to the summit. The view – all the way to Italy on a clear day, and easily across to the Greek mainland and Albania – and the cool, scented mountain air make the experience well worth the climb.

Meanwhile, back at the coast, you skirt the foothills of Mount Pantokrator on the marvelously scenic coast road and swing eastwards around the bay, through **Nissaki**, which tumbles down a wooded hillside to its little fishing port and shingle beach, to **Kalami**. Anyone who knows and loves the Greek island books of English author Lawrence Durrell will find Kalami a place of tragedy as much as a place of pilgrimage. The Corfu of the 1930s (when he lived in the village), that he describes, and by extension the Greece also, has gone for good. By itself this is not surprising (so has Dustbowl America); it's the tourist clutter that has replaced it that makes you wish you had either never read Durrell's book, *Prospero's Cell*, or had only read it and never seen the reality. Yet Kalami is not bad: it's even quite pretty, if you look at it through the eyes of the 1990s, and not of some vanished time that the locals themselves couldn't bring to an end fast enough.

With such reflections for cold comfort, push on to **Kassiopi**. A major resort town, bursting at the seams in summer, it has a castle and a fine fishing and tour-boat harbor. Kassiopi was more important still in ancient times, when the Emperor Nero is said to have played his trusty lyre in the Temple of Zeus (possibly located on the site of the 16th-century **Panagia Kassiopitra Church**); and during the Venetian period, when it was a naval base.

The north coast road continues through more resorts to **Sidari**, also reached by bus direct from Corfu town, and from whose harbor excursion boats leave for the offshore islands of **Erikoussa**, **Othoni**, and **Mathraki**, the last of which has beaches where loggerhead turtles nest. West of Sidari is a narrow rocky inlet, the **Canal d'Amour**, named I suppose by some francophone Corfiot PR person; anyone swimming here is said to be guaranteed to find the love of his or her life – although if you try it in anything other than a calm sea, getting smashed to pieces on the rocks seems more likely.

The main west coast resort, **Paleokastritsa**, is probably best done direct by bus or car from Corfu town, on a road that runs up over the island's hilly spine, 25 kilometers to the resort. You've got the full panoply of resortland here, in an incredibly beautiful setting on the intricately carved west coast. If all the hedonism hereabouts starts to get to you, join the crowds seeking spiritual solace at brightly painted, 18th-century **Panagia Paleokastritsas Monastery**, *open daily in summer 7 am to 1 pm and*

3 pm to 8 pm.; admission free, but the monks will look benignly on a donation.
The monastery occupies a rocky promontory at the resort. This location
is one of those where would-be interpreters of Homer's *Odyssey* place the
palace of King Alkinoos (see sidebar later in this chapter, *The Wanderer
Departs*).

One of the best views on an island that seems to have been built with
superb views in mind, is from the **Bella Vista** overlook near **Makrades**,
north of Paleokastritsa, looking down to where the popular resort nestles
at the foot of wooded hillsides around its network of bays. Near **Krini**
village in the same area is the stout-walled 13th-century **Angelokastro
Castle**, *open daily; admission free,* atop a steep, greenery-swathed crag. This
is the kind of castle whose defenders, having seen the attackers coming
from about a hundred miles off, probably laughed out loud and made
rude gestures at them when they got up close, knowing they hadn't a
prayer of ever getting inside.

Most of the hill villages in this area are worth a passing look, if only
to get a glimpse of what Corfu was all about in the days before tourism,
and the beaches along the wide sweep of **Agios Georgios Bay** are excellent
and relatively quiet.

Southern Corfu

The coastline immediately south of Corfu town is the least appealing
part of the island from an esthetic point of view, and part of the price the
emerald isle has paid for its tourism-generated wealth.

Resorts like **Benitses**, 12 kilometers to the south, are frequented by
raise-hell-all-night-sleep-all-day people who probably think Homer is
either a baseball term or something to do with watching TV on a Sunday
afternoon. Still, let's not get too sniffy: most of us like to raise a little hell
now and then; and there is no evidence that Homer could disco, far less
take his turn at a *karaoke* bar. The real downside is that hooligans and lager
louts muscle in on the scene too, and not all the fun is good and clean.

On the way to Benitses, beyond **Gastouri** village, is the **Achilleion
Palace**, *Tel. 0661/56210; open daily 9 am to 4 pm; admission Drs 800.* built
by one of those fruitcake 19th-century European bluebloods, the Empress

Elisabeth of Austria, who seems to have avoided the Electra and Oedipus complexes and run full tilt into an Achilles one instead. The sulky hero of *The Iliad* was her beau idéal, and she built this bijoux summer palace in his honor in 1891. It's a dazzlingly white, neoclassical, marble, wedding-cake extravaganza – or monstrosity – filled with statues of Homeric heroes, including one of the dying Achilles. In the evening, the Achilleion is transformed into a casino, and a scene from the James Bond movie *For Your Eyes Only* was shot here.

After busy **Moraïtika** and **Mesongi**, the main road runs into the middle of the long and narrow southern peninsula, with clusters of quieter beach resorts branching off from it on either side. **Agios Georgios** on the western shore is one such, interesting for nearby **Lake Korrission** as much as for its own tranquil virtues.

The hot Corfu scene has moved away in recent years from Benitses to **Kavos** in the far south of the island, popular with the kind of people who make Benitses seem like a sleep-all-night-sleep-all-day resort. You won't get much sleep here at night, but if you're the kind of person who likes what this once tranquil fishing village has become, you probably won't want any. More sensitive souls are advised to pass through Kavos in a rush, either by taking a boat excursion to **Paxos** and **Antipaxos** islands, or by continuing down to the island's tip at **Cape Asprokavos** and its ruined **Panagia Arkhoudilia Monastery**, from where you can see Paxos shimmering in the haze.

THE CORFU FESTIVAL

*The **Corfu Festival** takes place in September, and unfolds a program of music, opera, theater and dance. Check with the EOT office in Corfu town for current program details at Tel. 0661/37520, Fax 0661/30298.*

EXCURSIONS & DAY TRIPS

Excursion boats sail daily from Kassiopi and Kavos on Corfu to **Paxos** and its smaller neighbor, **Antipaxos**.

PRACTICAL INFORMATION

• **Banks & Currency Exchange** – Most banks are open Monday through Friday from 8 am to 2 pm (1:30 pm on Friday). A few in the resorts operate an extended tourist service in summer from 5 to 7 pm on weekdays and 8 am to 2 pm on weekends. American Express is represented by **Greek Skies**, *Leoforos Kapodistriou 20a, Corfu town, Tel. 0661/32469, Fax 0661/25888.* Thomas Cook has offices at *Odos Ethnikis Antistaseos 6, Tel. 0661/48174, Fax 0661/25348* and *Odos Kapodistriou 32, Tel. 0661/21077, Fax 0661/37547.* Hotels will exchange most convertible foreign currencies and traveler's checks, but at a poorer rate than the banks. German marks, British pounds, US dollars, French francs, and Italian lire are the currencies favored by owners of small hotels, tavernas and shops.

• **Bookstores** – You'll find the latest Clancy, King, Steel and such like among the limited range of mostly bestsellers at many news vendors and often in supermarkets and souvenir shops. In Corfu town, a wider and better selection can be found at **Xenglossos**, *Odos Markou 24, Tel. 0661/44044.*

• **Churches** – Services are held in English every Sunday at the **Holy Trinity Anglican Church**, *Odos Mavili 21, Corfu town, Tel. 0661/31467.* For Roman Catholic services in Greek, go to **Agios Frankiskos**, *Odos Paleologou, Corfu town.*

• **Consulate** – The **British Consulate** is at *Odos Menekratous 1, Corfu town. Tel. 0661/30055.* They might be willing to help other "friendly" nationals in a tight spot, if only with advice.

• **Doctors** – Your hotel should have a list of local English-speaking doctors. In an emergency, phone *166* for an ambulance. In less urgent cases, contact **Corfu General Hospital**, *Odos Polithroni Kostanda, Corfu town, Tel. 0661/45811.*

• **Maps** – These can be bought from most news vendors, souvenir shops and hotel shops for Drs 500.

• **News & Information** – Day-old British newspapers are widely available. The *International Herald Tribune, USA Today,* and the international editions of *Time* and *Newsweek* can be bought at the newsstand on

Leoforos Alexandras, and in the Hilton Hotel shop. The local English-language weekly *Corfu News* costs Drs 300 and is available at news-stands, in hotels, and in the tourist information office, while the daily *Athens News* is on sale for Drs 250. ERT1 radio (91.8 MHz) broadcasts a weather bulletin in English at 6:30 am, and news at 7:40 am; ERT2 (981 KHz) has news in English at 2.20 and 9.20 pm.

• **Police** – In emergencies call *100* for the municipal police; *109* for the rural police. The main police station is at *Odos Alexandras 17, Corfu town, Tel. 0661/39575.* The tourist police, for lost property, general assistance and reporting complaints against service providers, are at *Odos Zavitsianou 15, Corfu town, Tel. 0661/30265.*

• **Post Office** – The main post office is at *Leoforos Alexandras, Corfu town, Tel. 0661/25554.* It is open Monday through Friday from 7:30 am to 8 pm, Saturday 7:30 am to 2 pm, Sunday 9 am to 1:30 pm. Local post offices are open Monday through Friday from 7:30 am to 2 pm.

• **Telephone** – The area code for Corfu town and surroundings is *0661;* for Paleokastritsa *0663;* for Kavos *0662.* The main Greek Telecommunication Organization (OTE) office in Corfu town is at *Odos Mantzarou 9, Tel. 0661/34699.*

• **Tourist Office** – The Greek Tourist Organization (EOT) is at *Odos Zavitsianou 15, Corfu town, Tel. 0661/37520, Fax 0661/30298.* Corfu town's Tourist Information Office is at *Plateia Solomou. Tel. 0661/28509.*

PAXOS (PAXOI)

At just 25 square kilometers and with a 46-kilometer coastline, **Paxos** is the big baby of the Ionian Islands, and lies cradled in the Ionian Sea some 15 kilometers south of Corfu. The permanent population numbers under 3,000. If Paxos was further from Corfu, that number wouldn't vary much through the year, but it isn't, so it does. A constant stream of daytrippers from the bigger island looking for a break from Corfu's mad whirl, plus visitors from the mainland, drive the population figure up in summer. Don't despair, though: few of them stray far from the beach and you can always get away by going inland.

Oil is big business on Paxos. Before you go looking for Greeks wearing Stetsons, be advised that the oil in question is olive oil and has been since Minoan times at least. Paxos olive oil is widely considered to be the state-of-the-art in Greece. A bottle of local, cold-pressed virgin oil makes for a good souvenir.

Paxos has no airport, so you'll have to do without the charming sight and sound of charter jets landing every five minutes. It's tough at first, but you get used to it.

ARRIVALS & DEPARTURES
By Sea

Considering that it lies on the challenged side of small, Paxos is tolerably well served by boat. From mid-July to mid September there is a car ferry, *Tel. 0662/32269*, most days from **Brindisi** in Italy, via Paxos, to **Patras** on the Greek mainland. Journey time from Brindisi is 10 hours, to Patras 8 hours; one-way deck-passenger tickets cost Drs 13,200.

In summer there is one car ferry a day, *Tel. 0662/32256*, to Gaios, the main settlement on Paxos, from **Corfu**, journey time 3 1/4 hours; one-way tickets cost Drs 1,800. A passenger-only catamaran, Tel. 0662/32033, connects twice a day with **Corfu**, journey time 1 1/4 hours; this catamaran also sails to and from **Preveza** and **Amfilohia** on the mainland southeast of Paxos, journey time 1 hour 20 minutes and 2 hours 25 minutes respectively; one-way tickets cost Drs 3,300.

The closest mainland port is **Parga**, from where excursion boats sail daily in summer to Gaios. Excursion boats also sail daily from Kassiopi and Kavos on **Corfu** to Paxos and its smaller neighbor, Antipaxos.

ORIENTATION

Paxos is only 10 kilometers long and 4 kilometers across. **Gaios** is on the east coast, with the villages of **Longos** and **Lakka** on the coast in the northern part of the island, and several hamlets along the main road connecting these three places and scattered around the coast. It is a hilly, tree-covered place, without ever becoming mountainous, although the cliffs of the west coast tend towards the spectacular, and contrast with the gently sloping pebble beaches of the east coast. Many of the trees are olive trees, from which comes the renowned Paxos olive oil, and there are extensive vineyards also.

GETTING AROUND THE ISLAND
By Boat
There is a daily excursion by caïque from Gaios to the Sea Caves on the west coast, price Drs 1,000.

By Bus & Taxi
There is a bus every hour in summer from Gaios to Lakka, six of them traveling via Longos. A taxi or two can usually be found waiting for the ferry or in the main square in Gaios.

By Foot
Dust off those appendages at the end of your legs. Paxos is small enough to do on foot, and charming enough to make the voyage worthwhile. On a hot summer day (the only kind of summer day here) you have to expend a little sweat, but there are lots of olive trees to picnic under, and plenty of peace and quiet to keep you company on the way.

By Moped & Bicycle
Mopeds are quick, easy in the heat, and noisy. Bicycles are slower, harder in the heat, and quiet. The choice is yours. There are a several rental firms for both along the harborfront in Gaios, and at Lakka.

WHERE TO STAY
There are only a few hotels on Paxos. Private accommodation is quite readily available, and although the supply gets tight at peak tourist times, at other times in the season you will find local people offering rooms when the ferry docks. You can expect to pay up to about Drs 6,600 for a single and Drs 7,600 for a double with shower.

Antipaxos has no hotels and only a few private rooms to let.

PAXOS BEACH, *near Gaios. Tel. 0662/32211, Fax 0662/32166. Rates (with tax): Drs 20,400 single; Drs 29,800 double. Breakfast and dinner included. 42 rooms. No credit cards.*

A bungalow-style resort beside the sea a 15-minute walk south of Gaios, and surrounded by olive groves, it fits the laidback way of life on Paxos like a glove. With a little imagination your stone-built bungalow, simply but comfortably furnished in the style of a village house, becomes a genuine fisherman's cottage overlooking the sea. Facilities include a beach shop, bar, restaurant, dance floor, windsurfing store, children's play area, minigolf, tennis courts, and small-boat hire.

ILIOS, *Gaios. Tel. 0662/31808. Rates (with tax): Drs 6,000 double. No breakfast. 15 rooms. No credit cards.*

A very simple and basic hotel, but clean and comfortable enough, that offers a low-cost alternative to the Paxos Beach and to the private rooms for rent.

WHERE TO EAT

The **BLUE GROTTO** taverna on the waterfront in Gaios specializes in seafood and does it well, while **TAKA TAKA** complements it near the village's main square.

In Lakka, try the traditional **SOURIS** taverna; in Longos, the taverna vasi**LIS**, which specializes in seafood.

SEEING THE SIGHTS

You could easily imagine that ferries arriving at **Gaios** have to breath in to squeeze through the narrow channel leading to the village. The tree-covered islet of **Agios Nikolaos**, on which is a Venetian fortress, does an almost perfect job of stopping up the bay around which stand Gaios' elegant 19th-century Ionian-style mansions. It is backed up in this by **Panagia** islet a little further offshore, on which is a monastery of the same name.

Lakka at the north of the island, where the main water sports center is, can get relatively crowded in high summer. The village has a small but interesting **Aquarium**. Nearby **Longo** is quieter. The beaches at both places are nothing special, being only pebble, but both have tavernas and private accommodation. There are mineral springs around the village of **Otzia** south of Gaios.

White cliffs and sea caves at **Agios Apostoli** on the west coast are an attraction here, particularly the **Ipapanti Grotto** two kilometers around the coast from Lakka. Among the notable sights on this cliff-lined coast is a tall offshore rock called the **Ortholitho**.

NIGHTLIFE & ENTERTAINMENT

August 15, the feast of the **Assumption of Our Lady**, is celebrated with a procession to the Monastery of Panagia, followed by not-so-religious singing and dancing in the main square in Gaios.

Lakka and Longos are the unlikely venues of a **Classical Music Festival** in September.

SPORTS & RECREATION

The British **Greek Islands Sailing Club**, *Tel. 0662/31744*, runs a sailboat and windsurfing school at Lakka, and the waters of sheltered Lakka Bay are their playground. **Planos Travel** in Lakka can arrange accommodation in private homes around the village.

EXCURSIONS & DAY TRIPS

Unless you're staying for a while on Paxos, and would consider a trip to Corfu as a worthwhile excursion, you're probably already making your day trip or excursion by being on Paxos in the first place. One step further remains: to tiny **Antipaxos** (despite the name, Antipaxans holds no grudges against Paxans). The island lies just over two kilometers south of Paxos and is only four kilometers long. Its permanent population is about 200, most of whom live in a single village overlooking the sea, **Ormos Agrapidias**.

Excursion boats leave every hour in summer from Gaios to Antipaxos, which has a few private rooms to let and somple simple tavernas. Return tickets cost Drs 1,500. The big attraction – or more accurately the little attraction, considering the overall size of the place – is its white sand beach. This really is the idylic picture-book deserted Greek beach, and it says a lot about thirty-plus years of tourism "development" in Greece that you must come to such an out-of-the way place to find one.

Antipaxos has vineyards, from which come a rare and renowned **sweet red wine**, which is on sale in the village.

PRACTICAL INFORMATION

- **Banks & Currency Exchange** – The Paxos Beach Hotel in Gaios, travel agencies, and some stores and tavernas accept traveler's checks in payment. It is best to have an adequate supply of drachmas before arriving on Paxos.
- **Doctors** – There is a Medical Clinic in Gaios, *Tel. 0662/31466.*
- **Police** – The police station is in Gaios, *Tel. 0662/31222.*
- **Port Authority** – *Tel. 0662/31259.*
- **Post Office** – The post office is in Gaios, open Monday through Friday from 7:30 am to 2 pm.
- **Telephone** – The area code for Paxos and Antipaxos is *0662.* The Greek Telecommunications Organization (OTE) office is in Gaios, *Tel. 0662/xx.*
- **Tourist Information** – There is no Greek Tourist Organization (EOT) office on Paxos.

LEFKADA (LEFKAS)

Question: When is an island not an island?

Answer: When you can walk there without getting your feet wet.

By this simple definition, **Lefkada** has not been an island since a bridge spanning the narrow gap between it and the mainland was built. Yet insular it remains.

Thucydides records that during the Peloponnesian War, Lefkada, unlike the other Ionian Islands, was allied with Sparta. In 427 BC a Peloponnesian fleet was hauled over the isthmus at Leucas (Lefkada town) to avoid engaging a superior Athenian fleet, and in 426 BC a force of Athenian allies from Corfu, Kefallonia, and Zakynthus laid waste the island and came close to capturing the town. Naval operations again unfolded around Lefkada, in 31 BC, off what is now Aktion Airport on the mainland, when Octavian, the future Roman Emperor Augustus (or more accurately his military commander Agrippa), defeated Mark Antony and Cleopatra at the **Battle of Actium**.

The island is still mostly unspoiled by tourism. It's busily trying to remedy that unfortunate situation, however, and you can look forward to the level of spoliation increasing year after year until it reaches a satisfactory level.

ARRIVALS & DEPARTURES
By Air

There is no airport on Lefkada itself, but **Aktion Airport**, *Tel. 0685/ 22355*, is as good as, since it is just 25 kilometers away by road on the mainland near **Preveza**. **Olympic Airways** operates one return flight a day to Preveza from Athens, flying time 55 minutes. For current flight times and ticket prices, contact Olympic in Lefkada town at *Odos Dörpfeld 1, Tel. 0645/22430;* or in Preveza at *Odos Spiliadou 5. Tel. 0685/28674.* Travel agents on the island and in Preveza can also book onward flights.

Four buses a day take 30 minutes to make the trip between Lefkada town and the airport; tickets cost Drs 300.

By Bus

Four buses a day travel between **Athens'** bus terminal at *Odos Kifissiou 100, Tel. 01/513-3583* and Lefkada town. Journey time is 5 1/2 hours; one-way tickets cost Drs 5,900. Contact the Lefkada town bus terminal for departure times, *Tel. 0645/22364.*

By Sea

Ferries are less important to Lefkada than to the other Ionian Islands. In summer there are two ferries a day, *Tel. 0645/32222,* from Vasiliki in the south to Fiskardo on **Kefallonia**. Journey time is 1 hour; one-way tickets cost Drs 1,030.

Another ferry sails twice a day, *Tel. 0645/92528,* from Nidri, midway along the east coast, to Fiskardo on **Kefallonia**, and three times a day from

Nidri to the small island of **Meganissi** southeast of Lefkada. Journey time to Fiskardo is 1 1/4 hours, and to Meganissi 30 minutes; one-way ticket prices are Drs 1,085 and Drs 930 respectively.

ORIENTATION

At 303 square kilometers, Lefkada is the third biggest of the Ionian Islands and has 117 kilometers of coastline. The population numbers around 24,000, and while this figure heads skywards through July and August, the island is big enough that overcrowding never becomes a real problem, except in the northeast, and there are plenty of out-of-the-way places to get out of the way to. Lefkada is some 35 kilometers long and 12 kilometers across the middle. It is shaped something like a hooked finger pointing towards Kefallona and Ithaca.

Lefkada town, situated in the northeast, across the narrow strait from the mainland, is the "capital." Other important towns are the ferry ports of **Nidri** on the east coast and **Vasiliki** in the south. Coastal towns and villages are connected by a road that circles the island. The interior is mountainous, reaching up to 1,158-meter **Mount Elati** in the center, and is less well served by road. The wild and wonderful west coast has some spectacular clifftop vistas, and what is perhaps the best beach in Greece lies golden under the sun at **Porto Katsiki** in the southwest.

The small island of **Meganissi**, off the southeast coast and reachable from Nidri and by tour boats from the resorts, is worth a visit. To its north is **Skorpios** island, private fiefdom of the Onassis clan.

GETTING AROUND THE ISLAND
By Bus & Taxi

In summer, buses run every hour from the bus station in Lefkada town through the east coast resorts and the ferry port of **Nidri** to **Vlicho**, with four of them continuing to the ferry port of **Vasiliki** on the south coast, and two of these branching off also to the resorts of **Poros** and **Sivota**. Five buses a day travel via **Tsoukalades** in the north to **Agios Nikitas** on the northwest coast, while four take a parallel route further inland to reach the west coast and continue as far south as **Athani, Agios**

Petras and **Sivros**. Finally, five buses a day travel southwards to the inland hill village of **Karia**, noted for its handmade embroideries and lace. Buses are operated by **KTEL**, *Tel. 0645/22364.*

Taxis wait at the ferry terminals when boats are due, and outside major hotels, such as the Xenia in Lefkada town.

By Car

Rental autos are available from several local firms around the island. Try **Douvitsas**, *Odos Lefkatas 28. Tel. 0645/26528.* Jeeps are needed for some of the more scenic locations, such as the west coast beaches, and cost around Drs 20,000 a day.

By Moped & Scooter

Mopeds, scooters, off-road bikes, and mountain bikes are widely available for rent throughout the island. Moped rentals run to about Drs 4,000 a day; mountain bikes Drs 1,500.

WHERE TO STAY

APOLLON, *Seafront, Vasiliki. Tel. 0645/31122, Fax 0645/31122. Rates (with tax): Drs 11,000 single; Drs 14,000 double. Breakfast included. 34 rooms. Visa, MasterCard.*

The rooms in this hotel overlooking the main windsurfers' beach all have private bath and telephone. There's an in-hotel restaurant, a rooftop terrace, and easy parking.

LEFKAS, *Odos Panagou 2, Lefkada town. Tel. 0645/23916, Fax 0645/ 24579. Rates (with tax): Drs 11,000 single; Drs 14,000 double. Breakfast included. 93 rooms. No credit cards.*

This is a well-established and well-equipped hotel just 50 meters from the sea. The arcaded ground floor is surmounted by balconied rooms with a view of the water, and although the hotel isn't much to look at it deserves its reputation for quality. There are the usual accoutrements of a big hotel: private bathrooms, telephone, restaurant, bar, snackbar and television room. There is also a children's playground and a hotel minibus.

NIRICOS, *Agia Mavra, Lefkada town. Tel. 0645/24132, Fax 0645/ 23756. Rates (with tax): Drs 10,000 single; Drs 12,000 double. Breakfast included. 36 rooms. Visa, MasterCard.*

On the waterfront in the north of the town, on the corner of Odos Dörpfeld, facing the Venetian castle, the Niricos is a classy place, white painted and with long balconies, red tiled roof, and street cafe. The rooms are spacious, modernly furnished, with private bathroom and telephone, and have long balconies overlooking the water. There is private parking.

GORGONA, *Nidri. Tel. 0645/92268, Fax 0645/92268. Rates (with tax): Drs 7,000 single; Drs 9,000 double. Breakfast Drs 1,000. 16 rooms. No credit cards.*

Not far from the sea and and standing in the grounds of a well-tended garden, the Gorgona is a nice-looking and well-fitted modern hotel with an owner who makes his guests feel at home. There are potted plants and flowers all over. The rooms are spacious, bright, and have big pine beds and small pine tables, private bathroom, balcony overlooking the garden, and telephone. Other facilities include a television lounge, breakfast room, private parking, and refrigerators at the guests' disposal.

BYZANTION, *Odos Dörpfeld 4, Lefkada town. Tel. 0645/22629, Fax 0645/24055. Rates (with tax): Drs 6,000 single; Drs 9,000 double. Breakfast included. 16 rooms. No credit cards.*

There's a mixture of the old and the new at this hotel, which combines timbered ceilings with the most modern pine furnishings. It overlooks the sea and has a big balcony covered with geraniums.

WHERE TO EAT

ALEXANDER THE GREAT, *Vasiliki. Drs 3,000 to Drs 9,000. No credit cards. Seafood/traditional.*

One of a bunch of more-or-less equal tavernas on the waterfront at Vasiliki. Still, some of them are more equal than others, and the Alex is the best of the bunch. Go for the seafood here: the kalamari is especially good.

EVTYCHIA, *Odos Stratigou Mela, Lefkada town. Tel. 0645/23137. Drs 2,500 to Drs 5,000. No credit cards. Traditional.*

Popular with local people, despite its location on one of the most touristy streets, the Evtychia caters for diners indoors or at its outside terrace in a narrow sidestreet.

REGANTOS, *Odos Georgiou Messinis, Lefkada town. Tel. 0645/22855. Drs 3,000 to Drs 7,000. No credit cards. Seafood/traditional.*

On a street behind Odos Stratigou Mela, Regantos covers most of the options of Greek food, but has a soft spot for seafood. Be careful of the exact price of any fish you order if your budget is tight; otherwise just sit back and enjoy the friendly service and the big platefuls.

MIRAMARE, *Harborfront, Vasiliki. Tel. 0645/31138. Drs 2,500 to Drs 4,000. No credit cards. Traditional.*

Although it is near the fishing boat dock at the harbor, and its name means "Seaview," seafood is not the priority in this rustic taverna, where meat and vegetable dishes originating in Lefkada's farmland interior take pride of place.

SEEING THE SIGHTS

Unless you are coming up the coast by ferry from Kefallonia and Ithaca, you will probably start your exploration of Lefkada at the bridge and causeway that form a slender connection to the mainland near **Lefkada town**, in the northeast. This is an attractive place, retaining elements of its Venetian-era charm, and with a fine location looking across the narrow strait to the mainland hills of Akarnania. Its red roofs look romantic from a distance, like the pantiled roofs characteristic of the Mediterranean, and it is only close up that you see they are made of painted tin and corrugated iron.

Lefkada town is a bustling place, but low in accommodation possibilities and attraction sights, other than the local Italianate churches and monasteries, and whose nearest beach is five kilometers to the south.

An exception is the **Archaeological Museum**, *Odos Faneromenis 21, Tel. 0645/23678; open Tuesday to Sunday 9 am to 1 pm; admission Drs 500.* The museum houses finds from excavations around the island, including Mycenaean-era objects uncovered by German archaeologist Wilhelm Dörpfeld, an adopted local hero who advanced the theory that Lefkada, not Ithaca, was the Ithaca of Homer's *Odysseus*. Less controversial theories attend finds from Kaligoni south of Lefkada town, which is the site of the now mostly vanished Acropolis of ancient Leucas. The **Castle of Santa Maura**, *admission free*, founded in 1300, stands by the waterside.

On the east coast route down to the ferry ports at Nidri and Vasiliki, you pass through heavily touristed resorts until you arrive at even more heavily touristed **Nidri**, which is a major sailboat center thanks to the sheltered waters hereabouts. Offshore you can see, and sail around on tour boats, but not land on, the cypress-covered islets of **Madouri**, where one of Lefkada's two noted 19th-century poets, Aristotelis Valaoritis (the other is Angelos Sikelianos), lived; and **Skorpios**, privately owned by the Onassis family, and in whose little church Jackie Kennedy married Aristotle Onassis in 1968.

Inland a few kilometers, and uphill from Nidri is the village of **Neohori**, from where a truly magnificent view of the islet-studded coast can be had. Just south of Nidri, but reachable by land only around Vliho Bay, is **Cape Agia Kyriaki**. Beside the little church of the same name on the headland is the grave of Wilhelm Dörpfeld, who died in 1940.

The southeastern corner around **Poros**, **Mikros Gialos**, and **Sivota** has some fine beaches lying along sweeping bays. This area is quieter than Nidri, but is doing its best to catch up.

Vasiliki, on the south coast at the head of **Vasiliki Bay**, as well as being a quietly charming fishing village that is growing fast as a ferry terminal, has acquired a well-deserved reputation as one of Europe's premier **windsurfing** locations, thanks to the topography of the hill-lined bay which daily sees a steadily increasing offshore breeze combined with calm waters. An infrastructure of shops, rental outfits, and rooms-to-let has grown up to serve the tanned, mostly stubble-chinned practitioners of the sport.

The spectacular clifftop vistas and cliff-foot beaches of the all-but deserted west coast are a major resource for those yearning to breath free far from the huddled masses: only problem is getting there. Off-road bikers have the best chance, although some of them can be reached by caïques from Agios Nikitas and Vasiliki. Among the latter are the glorious golden sands at **Porto Katsiki**, among the best in the Mediterranean. Enjoy their beauty and isolation while you can: in Greece such natural wonders don't long survive the commercial exploitation they inevitably engender.

South of here, at the tip of the rugged **Lefkatas Peninsula**, in ancient times there stood a once famous and now vanished Temple of Apollo. This point, **Kavos tis Kiras**, is "Sappho's Leap," a 70-meter white cliff from which the poetess Sappho of Lesbos is said to have jumped to her death around 580 BC to end the heartbreak of her unrequited love for the boatman Phaon.

Getting away from the coast, the bus from Lefkada town to the inland village of **Karia** climbs up through a green, wooded landsape. The village's women are among the most faithful practitioners of the Lefkadan art of handmade embroidery. You can see them sitting in their doorways working on the complex designs, and you can buy their products in the village shops and in shops around the island.

NIGHTLIFE & ENTERTAINMENT

The **Lefkada Festival of Arts and Letters** takes place in August, and in the same month is the **Karia Festival**, in the village that is the center of Lefkada's traditional handmade embroidery and lace crafts.

SPORTS & RECREATION

Windsurfing fans gather in their hundreds at Vasiliki, where the wide waters of the bay are big enough for all and the conditions add up to some of the best in Europe. **Sailboating** is popular at Nidri, and increasingly at Sivota as well.

SHOPPING

Handmade embroidery and **lace**, mostly from the inland village of **Karia**, are specialties of Lefkada and widely available for sale.

EXCURSIONS & DAY TRIPS

Tour boats leave regularly from Nidri and nearby resorts to cruise round the islets of **Madouri**, **Sparti**, and the Onassis family's private island in the sun, **Skorpios**.

Ferries leave three times a day from Nidri for the small island of **Meganissi**, sailing to the port villages of Vathi and Spartohori (see *Arrivals & Departures* above). Tour boats also make the trip from the southeast-coast resorts. Just 23 square kilometers in area and with a population of 1,500, Meganissi is a magical little place, with pretty little villages, good beaches, and the **Papanikolis Sea Cave**, the second biggest such formation in Greece.

PRACTICAL INFORMATION

- **Banks & Currency Exchange** – The **National Bank of Greece** in Lefkada town is on *Odos Stratigou Mela*, open Monday through Thursday from 8 am to 2 pm, and to 1:30 pm on Friday. There are banks and bureaux de change in all the main resorts.
- **Doctors** – **Lefkada Hospital** is in Lefkada town at *Odos Valaoritis 24, Tel. 0645/22465.* Vasiliki has a Clinic, *Tel. 0645/31065.*
- **Maps** – A map of the island can be bought from most news vendors, souvenir shops, and hotel shops for Drs 500.
- **Police** – The main police station and tourist police office is in Lefkada town at *Odos Stratigou Mela 55, Tel. 0645/22100* and *0645/22346.* There are also offices in Nidri, *Tel. 0645/95207* and Vasiliki, *Tel. 0645/31012.*
- **Port Authority** – Nidri, *Tel. 0645/22322.*
- **Post Office** – The main post office is in Lefkada town at *Odos Stratigou Mela 183.* This and other village post offices are open Monday through Friday from 7:30 am to 2 pm.
- **Telephone** – The area code for Lefkada is *0645.* The Greek Telecommunication Organization (OTE) office in Lefkada town is on *Odos Patanerominis, Tel. 0645/22099.*
- **Tourist Information** – There is no Greek Tourist Organization (EOT) office on Lefkada. You can get some information, from the tourist police, travel agencies, and from hotels.

ITHACA (ITHAKI)

I am Odysseus, the son of Laertes ... My homeland is far-seen Ithaca, on
which rises the green-fringed slopes of Mount Neriton ... My country is rugged,
but its sons are courageous ... No other country can be so precious in a man's
eyes as his own, and that is how I feel about Ithaca.

Homer – The Odyssey

The island of Odysseus, **Ithaca** has benefited greatly from the favorable publicity penned 2,800 years ago by Homer. Rarely can a man have been so desperate to get home as Odysseus, with the possible exception of Steve Martin in *Planes, Trains, and Automobiles*.

You would think that there would be something special on Ithaca to indicate why he bothered. Not a bit of it – if you exclude its peace and tranquility, which might seem like a talisman to anyone who had spent ten years in combat and another ten being chased across the ocean by a highly irritable deity. Tranquility still has its charms, and one of the nice things about Ithaca is that there is just about nothing to do here (if you're a tourist, that is; the Ithacans themselves are busy enough).

Still, the island is a sight all by itself, with its hills bare of trees and masses of little bays at their feet, the ever-present sea and the fine views of Kefallonia in one direction and the mainland in the other. Yet Ithaca exists as much in the imagination as in reality; it is hard to accept that there is no palace (at least no sign of one has ever been found), no faithful Penelope or exasperated Telemachus, and the only people resembling riotous suitors are the amiable groups in the tavernas.

ARRIVALS & DEPARTURES

By Bus (via Astakos)

There are three buses a day between **Athens** and **Astakos** on the mainland, leaving from the bus station at *Odos Kifissiou 100, Tel. 01/512-9293*. Journey time is 5 hours; one-way tickets cost Drs 4,950.

By Sea

From mid-July to mid September there is a car ferry twice a week, *Tel. 0674/33120*, from **Brindisi** in Italy, via Piso Aetos on Ithaca, to **Patras** on the Greek mainland. Journey time is 13 1/2 hours from Brindisi, 4 hours to Patras; one-way deck passenger tickets cost Drs 13,200.

The closest mainland ferry port is **Astakos**. There is one car ferry a day, *Tel. 0674/32104*, from Monday to Friday, and two a day at weekends, with a 1 hour 50 minute transit time between there and Vathi (Ithaca town); one-way tickets cost Drs 1,640.

In summer, the short crossing from Ithaca to **Kefallonia** is made by two car ferries a day, *Tel. 0674/32104*, from Frikes in the north to Fiskardo; four a day from Piso Aetos in the south to Sami; two a day from Vathi to Sami; one a day from Vathi to Agia Efimia; and one a day from Vathi to Poros. Journey times are under 1 hour; one-way tickets cost Drs 1,060.

ORIENTATION

At 96 square kilometers, Ithaca lies 3.5 kilometers eastwards across the **Straits of Ithaca** from **Kefallonia**, and 28 kilometers west of the Greek mainland. Its permanent population numbers around 4,000. Shaped like an irregular hour-glass, with two bulges connected by a narrow strip of land, the island is some 23 kilometers long, eight kilometers across at the widest point and barely one kilometer wide at its slimline waist.

The main town, officially also called Ithaca and marked that way on many international maps, but known to locals as **Vathi**, lies east of the waist, tucked into a corner of the **Gulf of Molo**.

GETTING AROUND THE ISLAND
By Bus & Taxi

A bus runs three times a day in summer between the main square in Vathi and Kioni, stopping at the villages of Agros, Stavros, and Frikes on the way.

Taxis can usually be found waiting for the ferry or in the main square in Vathi, *Tel. 0674/33030*.

By Moped & Bicycle

Mopeds can be rented from several firms in Vathi, Kioni, and Frikes for around Drs 3,000 a day. Mountain bikes cost about a third of that, but cycling can be hard going on Ithaca's steep roads amid the summer heat.

WHERE TO STAY

With few hotels – and those relatively expensive – if you're traveling on a budget you will want to find rooms in private accommodation or at tavernas with a couple of rooms attached (these can be noisy places until quite late, if you're trying to get some sleep). Try any of the agencies around the main square in Vathi for bookings, or discuss with one of the local people who often wait for the ferries. Prices range from Drs 6,000 to Drs 8,000 for a double. If you prefer to arrange this in advance, and for July or August you should, contact **Polyctor Tours**, *Tel. 0674/33120, Fax 0674/33130.*

MENDOR, *Paralia, Vathi. Tel. 0674/32433, Fax 0674/32293. Rates (with tax): Drs 8,800 single; Drs 12,200 double. Breakfast Drs 1,000. 36 rooms. No credit cards.*

A family-owned hotel on the waterfront in Vathi, the Mendor is maybe a little expensive for what it is, but that's Ithaca, and in compensation the rooms are clean and comfortable, with private bathroom and telephone. The hotel has its own restaurant and a roof garden.

ODYSSEUS, *Paralia, Vathi. Tel. 0674/32381, Fax 0674/32239. Rates (with tax): Drs 12,100 double. Breakfast included. 9 rooms. No credit cards.*

Further round the harbor on the western side from the Mendor, the Odysseus is also smaller and more modern. There is a taverna out front overlooking the harbor, and all the rooms have private bathroom and telephone.

WHERE TO EAT

The **TREHANTIRI** taverna in the center of Vathi is a good place with reasonable prices, as are **KOTSILIORIS** behind the paralia, and **TO KSIAKI** and **GREGORY'S**, around the north end of the bay. Just outside town, on the road south to Perahori, try the open-air tables at taverna **TSIRIBIS**.

SEEING THE SIGHTS

In **Vathi**, the houses and other buildings hug the curving south shore of Vathi Bay, a natural harbor backed by steep hills and in which is the tiny islet of **Lazareto**, which has been "sculpted" into the form of a boat. The **Archeological Museum**, *open Monday through Friday 9:30 am to 2:30 pm; admission free,* may not have Odysseus's bow and arrows, but it does have an interesting collection of pottery dating from the 8th to the 6th century BC. Outside of town, a 4-kilometer uphill walk leads to the village of **Perakhori**, which has fine views over Vathi.

If you want to trace locations from the *Odyssey* here – or at any rate scenes that local lore says are locations from the story – walk three kilometers west of Vathi and into the hills above Dexia Bay to the **Cave of the Nymphs**, equated with the "beautiful twilit cave sacred to the Naiads," where Odysseus hid the "tripods and vases, the gold and woven robes" that the Phaecians had given him, while the bay itself might be the one "sacred to the ancient sea-god Phorcys" where the Phaecians put the sleeping Odysseus ashore, and the hills the "forested slopes of Neriton" (808-meter **Mount Niritos** further north has also been speculatively identified and named as this hill, although its slopes are now bare).

Some four kilometers south of Vathi, along a rough road, a rugged footpath leads off to another cave, this one identified as that of the swineherd **Eumaeus**, and another kilometer beyond the footpath is the **Spring of Perapighadi**, said to be the "deep, black" Fountain of Arethusa where Eumaeus watered his pigs, overlooked by a cliff that may or may not be the **Raven's Rock**. On a hill north of **Stavros** village in the northwest of the island is the site archaeologists speculate may have been the site of **Odysseus's palace**, with a small museum whose exhibits include pre-Mycenean tripods, *open Wednesday through Monday 10 am to 3 pm; admission free (but a donation is welcome).*

The small fishing villages and minor resorts of **Frikes** and **Kioni** in the northeast are both scenic spots, the latter being a preservation area, and there are rock and pebble beaches roundabout and tourist facilities in the villages themselves.

THE WANDERER DEPARTS

Homer would surely have looked favorably on a much later poet's vision of an aging Odysseus, his years of fighting and wandering on the wine-dark sea far behind him, contemplating old age and summoning his strength for one last encounter with destiny:

> *"Some work of noble note may yet be done,*
> *Not unbecoming men that strove with Gods.*
> *The lights begin to twinkle from the rocks:*
> *The long day wanes: the slow moon climbs: the deep*
> *Moans round with many voices. Come, my friends,*
> *'Tis not too late to seek a newer world,*
> *Push off, and sitting well in order, smite*
> *The sounding furrows: for my purpose holds*
> *To sail beyond the sunset, and the baths*
> *Of all the Western stars, until I die."*

Tennyson, Ulysses

PRACTICAL INFORMATION

- **Banks** – The **National Bank of Greece** has a branch in Vathi, between the harbor and the main square, open Monday through Thursday from 8 am to 2 pm, and to 1:30 pm on Friday.
- **Doctors** – **Ithaca General Hospital**, *Vathi, Tel. 0674/32222.*
- **Ferry Information** – *Tel. 0674/32145*
- **Police** – The main police station is in *Vathi, Tel. 0674/32205.*
- **Port Authority** – *Tel. 0674/32909*
- **Post Office** – The post office in Vathi is open Monday through Friday from 7:30 am to 2 pm.
- **Telephone** – The area code for Ithaca is *0674*. The Greek Telecommunication Organization (OTE) office is on the Paralia.
- **Tourist Information** – There is no Greek Tourist Organization (EOT) office on Ithaca.

ZAKYNTHOS (ZANTE)

Zante, fior' di Levante (Zante, flower of the Levant)
– Old Venetian Saying

The island of **Zakynthos** is the third biggest of the Ionian group, and the southernmost if you ignore some rocky bits and pieces that lie beyond. Zakynthos is semi-undiscovered, compared to Corfu anyway, just as it was 3,500 years ago when the island was colonized by settlers from Psophis in the Peloponnese, led by Zakynthos, the son of King Dardanos of Troy. They apparently called their settlement Psophis, and its location is the cause of much head-scratching among archaeologists. And that's about it, history-wise – if you exclude a traumatic visit by the Vandals in 474 AD – until a hot summer's day in 1953 when Zakynthos came close to emulating Atlantis.

An earthquake measuring 7.5 on the Richter Scale ripped through the island and knocked everything flat. The elegant, arcaded Venetian squares and towers of **Zakynthos town** (the Venetians occupied the island from 1489 to 1797, calling it Zante) were shaken to pieces. What the 'quake didn't destroy the subsequent fires did. Scenic beauty has taken an equally heavy hit along the coast since 1980 from modern package tourism and the straggling resorts that are its seemingly inevitable accompaniment.

Zakynthos looks as if it has been tilted from west to east. The west is a jumble of hills that reach up to the 758-meter summit of **Mount Vrachionas** and plunge steeply into the sea; the east is flatter and more fertile and contains most of the population, although even on this side the coast tends towards the hilly in places. Resortland is mostly in the southeast, around the **Gulf of Lagana** and down to the tip of the **Vassilikos Peninsula**, with another strip of resorts northwest of Zakynthos town.

In the north, beside Cape Skinari, are the **Kianou Caves**, famed because the water that flows through them is of a blue so translucently clear as to be almost preternatural. In this area also are a bunch of Orthodox monasteries, including notable **Anafonitrias Monastery**, where

Zakynthos's man in heaven, Saint Dionysios, spent his declining years. Not far away, at **Smuggler's Cove**, the remains of a boat which came to grief while on a smuggling mission lies half-buried in the sand beneath sheer cliffs.

Zakynthos attracts by its sheer verdant beauty – although Homer's "forest-clad Zakynthos" has given way to an olive-citrus-and-currant-tree-clad Zakynthos – rather than by anything Homeric that might or might not have happened here. The Venetians, who knew a thing or two about Greek islands, weren't overdoing things by calling this one "the Flower of the Levant." Take the time to get up off the beach and explore the scenic inland vistas of hills, farms, and villages. You won't regret it.

ARRIVALS & DEPARTURES
By Air

Zakynthos Airport, *Tel. 0695/28322*, is six kilometers south of Zakynthos town, in the southeast of the island between the capital and the resort of Laganas on Lagana Bay. **Olympic Airways** operates two return flights a day at peak periods to Zakynthos from Athens, flying time 55 minutes. For current departure times and ticket prices, contact Olympic in Zakynthos town at *Odos Alexandrou Roma 16, Tel. 0695/28611*. There are regular charter flights from all over northern Europe to Zakynthos. Travel agents on the island can book onward flights. Taxi fare to town is Drs 1,500.

By Bus (via Kilini)

There are three buses a day between **Athens** and Zakynthos town (four on Sunday), leaving from the bus station at *Odos Kifissiou 100, Tel. 01/512-9432*. Journey time is 7 hours; one-way tickets cost Drs 4,660, plus the ferry fare. Contact the Zakynthos town bus terminal for departure times, *Tel. 0695/22656*.

By Sea

From mid-July to mid September there is a car ferry, *Tel. 0662/32269*, every two days from Brindisi in Italy, via Paxos, to Patras on the Greek mainland. Journey time from Brindisi is 16 hours, to Patras 4 hours; one-way deck-passenger tickets cost Drs 13,200.

The closest mainland ferry port is Kilini, and in summer there are nine car ferries a day, *Tel. 0695/41500*, between there and Zakynthos town, but this number drops gradually to three a day in winter. Journey time is 1 1/2 hours; one-way tickets cost Drs 1,150. In summer there are two car ferries a day, *Tel. 0695/42417*, from Agios Nikolaos in the north of the island to Pessada on **Kefallonia**. Journey time is 1 1/4 hours; one-way tickets cost Drs 880.

ORIENTATION

Zakynthos is shaped like ... well, a genetically challenged lobster crawling along the Peloponnese coast springs to mind after a few too many ouzos. It is 402 square kilometers in area, 36 kilometers long, and 20 kilometers across at the widest point, and with a coastline of 123 kilometers. The Peloponnese coast is only 18 kilometers to the east, compared to Corfu some 160 kilometers away to the north, giving the island a greater affinity with the former rather than with the Ionian Islands as a whole. The population numbers around 36,000, a figure that soars in July and August.

Zakynthos town in the southeast faces the Peloponnese and the mainland ferry port at Kilini. All the good roads are in this area, leading to the nearby resorts, and into the olive and citrus plantations, and finally running into the hills along the spine of villages in the center of the island. Mean annual rainfall of 98 centimeters isn't so mean really – 17 centimeters less than Corfu gets – but still tropical rainforest compared with some Aegean islands. Citrus farmers don't complain about the 13 hours of sunshine every day in July and August, so why should you?

GETTING AROUND THE ISLAND
By Bus

The bus station in Zakynthos town is on *Odos Filita, one block behind the harbor, Tel. 0695/22656.* Buses run every hour or so in summer from here along the north coast to Alikes, and south to the Laganas resort area, but trying to board one at an intermediate stop can be difficult because they fill up quickly; and as few as one a day (or never) to most other villages. The Athens bus also arrives at and leaves from here.

By Car

Rental autos are available from around Drs 25,000 a day with unlimited kilometers for the smallest cars from several firms, among the best of which are:

• **Hertz**, *Odos Lombardou 38, Zakynthos town. Tel. 0695/45706.*
• **Europcar**, *Odos Lombardou 74, Zakynthos town. Tel. 0695/41541.*
• **European**, *Odos Foskolou 18, Zakynthos town. Tel. 0695/28458.*

Be wary of renting cheap cars and jeeps, which may be poorly maintained and lack vital fixtures and fittings, such as seatbelts.

By Moped & Scooter

Mopeds, scooters and off-road bikes are widely available for rent throughout the island. Good rental outlets in Zakynthos town are at *Leoforos Dimokratis 3,* and *Odos Ethnikis Antistasis 6.* There is plenty of choice at the resorts.

By Taxi

You can call a cab at *Tel. 0695/23628* or pick one up in the street and at the stands – in Zakynthos town at the ferry terminal and Plateia Solomou. Taxis wait at the ferry terminal when boats are due, at the airport, and outside major hotels. Outlying resorts and bigger villages have taxis, which can be called from one of the hotels.

WHERE TO STAY

ZANTE PARK, *Laganas. Tel. 0695/51948, Fax 0695/51949. Rates (with tax): Drs 36,000 single; Drs 40,000 double. 96 rooms. Breakfast Drs 2,000. American Express, Diners Club, Visa, MasterCard.*

A Best Western hotel, the Zante Park offers consistent quality and the vast range of services you would expect from a top-rated resort hotel. If you want to be in the middle of the highly developed resort culture along Laganas Bay, you might as well be in the best aspect of it. A low-rise hotel beside the beach and built around a long swimming pool, the Zante Park is fully air conditioned, and has a buffet breakfast, restaurant, cocktail bar, poolside snackbar, lounge, games room, fitness center, sauna, beauty salon, 24-hour room service, laundry/valeting service, babysitting service, nurse, and children's playground.

All rooms have private bathroom with bathtub and shower, minibar, television with satellite channels and in-house video, telephone, and balcony.

DIANA PALACE, *Plateia Agiou Markou. Tel. 0695/23070, Fax 0695/ 27949. Rates (with tax): Drs 21,150 single; Drs 25,380 double; Drs 33,500 suite. Breakfast Drs 2,000. 78 rooms. American Express, Diners Club, Visa, MasterCard.*

Zakynthos town's top-rated hotel dominates the approach to the lovely central square. Air conditioned throughout, and centrally heated too (although that seems superfluous), all its rooms are luxuriously appointed and equipped with a desk, minibar, television, and telephone, and of course private bathroom with bathtub and shower. In addition, there is a swimming pool, fitness center, room service, restaurant, cocktail bar, and private parking.

MATILDA, *Vassilikos. Tel. 0695/35430, Fax 0695/35429. Rates (with tax): Drs 19,250 single; Drs 25,300 double. 53 rooms. Breakfast Drs 1,500. Visa, MasterCard.*

This is a very attractive, modern resort hotel, 150 meters from the beach and built in a style that emulates, more or less, the traditional style of Ionian architecture, with red-tiled roofs and long balconies. The rooms are in low-rise groups alongside the two swimming pools and sundeck, and all have private facilities and telephone.

MEDITERRANEE, *Planos, Tsilivi. Tel. 0695/26101, Fax 0695/26101. Rates (with tax): Drs 13,200 single; Drs 19,800 double. Breakfast included. 46 rooms. Visa.*

Built in 1989, the Mediterranée has a sightly Moorish feel to its design and is set in an extensive garden 125 meters from the beach, with some of the rooms being in the main building and others scattered in separate units around the grounds. The air conditioned rooms are furnished in modern style, with private bathroom and telephone, and there is a modestly-sized, L-shaped outdoor swimming pool.

STRADA MARINA, *Odos Lombardou 14. Tel. 0695/42761, Fax 0695/ 28733. Rates (with tax): Drs 11,000 single; Drs 18,200 double. 112 rooms. Breakfast included. American Express, Diners Club, Visa, MasterCard.*

A chic hotel right on the waterfront. This a hotel that has grown amoeba-like as it keeps pace with Zakynthos's expanding popularity. There is a swimming pool on the roof, and a roof garden which, oddly enough, is also on the roof. The rooms are all luxuriously furnished, air conditioned, and have private bathroom, telephone and television.

PALATINO, *Odos Kolokotroni 10. Tel. 0695/27780, Fax 0695/45400. Rates (with tax): Drs 13,000 single; Drs 16,000 double. 30 rooms. Breakfast included. American Express, Diners Club, Visa, MasterCard.*

Located just north of Plateia Agiou Markou, the Palatino is a very smart, modern hotel, painted a rather fetching shade of pink on the outside, and opting for cool efficiency on the inside. The air conditioned rooms either overlook the sea or the hills, and in either case have a balcony. Furnishings are bright and modern, maybe not with bags of character, but certainly comfortable and with private bathroom and telephone. The cocktail bar and television lounge retain the same accent on modernity, with lots of black in the furnishings and decor.

LEVANTE, *Argassi. Tel. 0695/22833, Fax 23608. Rates (with tax): Drs 12,000 single; Drs 15,000 double. Breakfast Drs 1,200. 63 rooms. No credit cards.*

One of the more notable beachside hotels in this busy resort area on the coast south of Zakynthos town, because it has a traditional, pension style rather than being a standard resort hotel.

YRIA, *Odos Kapodistriou 4. Tel. 0695/44682, Fax 42894. Rates (with tax): Drs 14,000 double. 11 rooms. Breakfast Drs 1,500. No credit cards.*

A small and homely, family-owned hotel, but well-equipped also, the Yria was built in 1984 and fully renovated a few years back. The hotel has been thoughtfully furnished to be more pleasant than the average hotel style and the effect is enhanced by plants and flowers, although its streetfront is undistinguished. Its room are all air conditioned and have private bathroom, television and telephone.

PHOENIX, *Plateia Dionysiou Solomou 2. Tel. 0695/42419, Fax 0695/ 45083. Rates (with tax): Drs 8,500 single; Drs 12,000 double. 35 rooms. Breakfast included. No credit cards.*

Considering that this hotel occupies one of the best locations in Zakynthos town, overlooking the handsome main square, and is certainly convenient for the ferries, the Phoenix doesn't rise to the temptation of overcharging. Its rooms are plainly furnished but clean and comfortable.

MONTREAL, *Alikes. Tel. 0695/83421, Fax 0695/83341. Rates (with tax): Drs 6,600 single; Drs 11,000 double. 31 rooms. Breakfast included 1. No credit cards.*

Overlooking the sea at Alikes Bay, this modest hotel gets its unusual name (for Greece, that is) from the fact that its owner-brothers once lived in the Canadian city. They have brought some of its charm and their own brand of traditional Greek hospitality to their hotel. All rooms have private bathroom and telephone, and the hotel has watersports facilities on the beach.

IONION, *Odos Alexandrou Roma 18. Tel. 0695/22511, Fax 0695/ 23739. Rates (with tax): Drs 8,000 single; Drs 10,000 double. 29 rooms. Breakfast included. No credit cards.*

Well located in the center, on a street right at the heart of things and with its own parking. Its balconies are big enough, with a giant bougain-villea for decoration. This is a good, relatively low-cost option, as these things go in Zakynthos, with clean and comfortable rooms.

WHERE TO EAT

CROSS TAVERNA, *Skiza village, near Kambi. Drs 3,000 to Drs 6,000. No credit cards. Country traditional.*

Situated overlooking the sea near this clifftop village midway along the west coast, beside the white cross commemorating victims of the Greek Civil War that followed World War Two. It's a spectacular setting in a rugged area and is a good place to watch the sunset over a traditional moussaka and a carafe of the houe retsina.

PARTHENON TAVERNA, *Agia Marina, near Macherado. Drs 3,000-Drs 5,000. No credit cards. Country traditional.*

The country-style Greek food here is every bit as memorable as the superb view from its outdoor hilltop terrace overlooking the fertile eastern plain of Zakynthos.

ELLAS, *Odos Agiou Ioannou Logotheton 13, Zakynthos town. Tel. 0695/28622. Drs 2,500 to Drs 4,000. No credit cards. Traditional.*

If you want to slip away from the tourist-oriented eateries and join the locals at table, this is one of the best places to go. It's one of those typical, point-and-eat places that isn't much in the style department but knows how to cook Greek food. In the evening, tables are spread out in the adjacent garden and live Greek music entertains the diners.

LATAS, *Odos Tertseti, Zakynthos town. Tel. 0695/26178. Drs 2,500 to Drs 4,000. No credit cards. Seafood/traditional.*

There's live Greek music while you eat at this atmospheric taverna not far from the Venetian Kastro. Latas specializes in seafood, but has meat and vegetable dishes also.

TO ROLOI, *Odos Vasileos Konstantinou 11, Zakynthos town. Tel. 0695/23587. Drs 2,500 to Drs 4,000 . No credit cards. International.*

The name means The Clock in English, but it's a fair bet that you won't be watching the clock much here, as the idea is to linger over your meal, Greek-style, even although the menu includes popular dishes from other European countries – pizza, for example.

SEEING THE SIGHTS
Zakynthos Town

Squeezed between the sea and the steep hills on which the Venetian Castle stands, **Zakynthos town** is long and narrow – 2.5 kilometers by maybe 600 meters – and a bright, handsome place, despite having been rebuilt since the Big One in 1953 and expanded fast since 1980 to deal with the surge of tourists.

The Venetians took over the craggy hilltop where the populace had sheltered from raiding pirates for their fortress, and the townspeople gradually filtered downhill to live along the shore, a process encouraged by development of the harbor facilities first under British, and later Greek rule from 1815 onwards.

You won't easily get lost in Zakynthos town, whose population is around 12,000. On the other hand there's not an awesome amount to see and do: no great classical sites or exhibits in the museum. It's more a place for soaking up the atmosphere of a Greek island harbor town, which is at least more authentic than that of the resorts, eating out, and doing some shopping. Most of what action there is is centered on the two main squares at the north end of town, **Plateia Solomou** and **Plateia Agiou Markou**; the **harbor**; and the two main shopping and services streets, **Odos Alexandrou Roma** and **Odos Tertseti** in the center.

The town was rebuilt after the 1953 earthquake with at least some of the graces the Venetians had left behind. Especially around **Plateia Solomou**, with its arcaded Venetian-style buildings and tree-shaded gardens; and around smaller **Plateia Agiou Markou** (also known as the Platiaforos) whose cafes and tavernas spill tables, chairs, and parasols out into the square. Starting in Plateia Solomou, you can think poetical thoughts in front of the marble statue of **Dionysios Solomos** (see sidebar below), then visit the **Byzantine Museum**, *Plateia Solomou, Tel. 0695/ 22714; open Tuesday through Sunday 8:30 am to 2:30 pm; admission Drs 800,* whose collection mostly comprises religious icons and other bits and pieces rescued from churches wrecked in 1953, including several finely carved iconostaseis, along with some 19th-century paintings.

The 16th-century **Agios Nikolaos tou Molou Church** (Saint Nicholas of the Mole), *open daily; admission free,* is restored, but still seemingly falling down, and so called not because Nicholas had a melanin problem, but because it's on the mole – it was originally on an islet that was later joined to the shore by infilling the gap between them. If you're here at Easter you can follow the procession with Christ's bier, the *epitaphios,* on Good Friday.

From the square you should turn south along the harborside Odos Lombardou, with a fine view of the harbor and its fleet of fishing boats, tour boats, yachts, and cabin-cruisers. It's about a kilometer beside the blue water to the south mole where the ferries from Kilini dock. Opposite

DEAD POETS SOCIETY

*Famous poets are a-drachma-a-dozen on Zakynthos, or at least they used to be. Local hero Dionysios **Solomos** (1798-1857), wrote the **Hymn To Freedom**, which was set to music by the Corfiot composer Nikolaos Mantzaros and chosen as the Greek national anthem in 1864. A statue of the poet stands in Plateia Solomou, and a bust on Strani Hill overlooking Zakynthos town, at the spot where he is said to have penned the Hymn.*

*Then there is **Andreas Kalvos** (1792-1867), who for some reason practiced his art in Lincolnshire, England (his English wife may have insisted); and **Hugo Foscolo** (1778-1827), who chose Italy instead, and is remembered there as a great national poet.*

So walk softly should you happen on a local bohemian gazing pensively at pen and paper.

the mole is the basilica-style **Agios Dionysios Church**, *Odos Agiou Dionysiou; open daily; admission free.* This is named for Zakynthos's other Dionysios, the sainted one, who died at Anafonitrias Monastery in the north of the island in 1622, having been Bishop of Aegina in the Saronic Gulf near Athens, and whose earthly remains are kept in the ornately decorated church inside a silver casket.

On the saint's festival days (August 24 and December 17) Dionysios gets a new lease of life when he is carried in procession through the town, his feet fitted with slippers. If you notice a faint echo of Venice's Piazza San Marco here, it's because the church tower is a smaller replica of the *campanile* in Venice.

Walk inland (west) for 300 meters or so, then north along the main shopping street, Odos Alexandrou Roma and its continuation, Odos 21 Maiou, to handsome and in summer bustling **Plateia Agiou Markou**. This has been quite a bit of walking up to now, especially if it's hot, and with more in the way of spiritual reward than anything else. Maybe it's time to sit at one of the square's cafe terraces and sip something cool and refreshing.

274 GREEK ISLANDS GUIDE

Feel better? If you're still with me, you can visit the nearby **Dionysios Solomos Museum**, *Odos 21 Maiou 6; open daily 9 am to 2 pm; admission free,* where the great man is entombed among memorabilia of his life and work, sharing the mausoleum and some of the limelight with another departed poet, Andreas Kalvos (see sidebar, *Dead Poets Society,* below). Close by is the **Church of Saint Mark**, *Plateia Agiou Markou; open daily.; admission free,* serving the island's Venetian-origin Roman Catholic community, and which originally dated from 1518 but went the way of all Zakynthos in the great shake of 1953. It was probably a more interesting place in 1952.

Now it's time to get high, by climbing to the ruined Venetian Kastro (Castle) overlooking the town, *Tel. 0695/22714; open Tuesday to Sunday 8:30 am to 3 pm; admission Drs 500.* There are two routes, one along a gravel footpath from behind the town, past the prominent belltower of **Panagia Pikridiotissa Church**, and the other from the north, passing cafe-lined Plateia Bochali and the **Church of Panagia Chrysopigi** (Our Lady of the Golden Spring). Three sets of gates, the first surmounted by a plaque with the Lion of Saint Mark, the symbol of Venice, lead to the inner *enceinte,* which was the site of the ancient acropolis of Zakynthos, and maybe also of the elusive Mycenaean-era Psophis. Pine trees shade this place, and a truly splendid view of over the harbor to the Peloponnese coast can be had by climbing up to the wall.

ROOTIN' TOOTIN' TRADITION

The Venetians, with their typically Italian love of pageantry, left behind a tradition of fanfare that survives to this day, and even the smallest village on Zakynthos has its own brass band – or knows where to find one. The island even has a philharmonic orchestra.

Around Zakynthos

As you drive around the island watch out for the old thatched-roof structures on stilts, called kaleva, which can be seen in the fields and at some beaches around Zakynthos and look like houses for giant birds. They were used in the past by fieldhands as a place to escape from the heat of the day by getting into some shade and off the ground where a cooling breeze blew. Some are still in use today.

From Zakynthos town take the coast road northwest, skirting Cape Krioneri, through a 10-kilometer succession of purpose-built, family-oriented beach resorts whose main asset is their stretch of fine sand, on either side of **Planos** and **Tsilivi**, until you come to **Alikanas**, which has the novelty of being based on an old village (or at least a village that was old before 1953). Nearby **Alikes Beach** is one of the best on the island, with a little arched bridge connecting two parts of the resort across a small river.

From here you turn your back on the beaches and head inland to **Katastari**, the biggest village on the island, at the northern end of the agricultural plain. The road begins to climb into more rugged country around the foothills of **Mount Vrachionas**, past **Agios Ioannis Prodhromos Monastery**, to **Orthonies** and **Volimes**, which is actually a trio of villages, known respectively as Kato, Meso, and Ano Volimes, and where making handmade lace and handwoven carpets of moderate quality, and fine honey and goat's cheese are cottage industries.

Continue through **Korithi** to **Cape Skinari** at the northernmost tip of the island, and the nearby harbor at **Agios Nikolaos**, from where a car ferry makes a 1 1/4-hour crossing to **Kefallonia**. Don't miss the tour-boat excursion from Agios Nikolaos to the exceptional, mystic-blue waters of the **Kianou** (Blue) **Caves**. A little way south, near **Spiliotissa Monastery**, is picturesque little **Mikronisi**, occupying the tip of a headland (if you want a remote beach, albeit shingle) walk to the one at nearby **Makris Gialos**.

Backtrack through Volimes to **Anafonitria**, a village with a fine square shaded by plane trees, and on to **Anafonitria Monastery**, a kilometer or so from the west coast, *open daily; admission free*. The monastery has a medieval tower and Saint Dionysios's cell, with some icons and vestments that apparently belonged to him.

If you haven't had enough of monasteries yet, follow the sign in Anafonitria square a few kilometers north to **Agios Georgios Kremon Monastery**, whose name means "of the cliff," not far from one of the most rugged spots on the west coast. Rugged enough that a boat ran ashore here in the early Seventies on a sandy, cliff-lined cove while apparently smuggling cigarettes and liquor, and is now partly swallowed by the sand. To reach **Smuggler's Cove**, park beyond the monastery for the final leg on foot over a rough track to the spectacular clifftop overlooking the scene. From here you need a parachute or hang-glider, or some pretty good rock-climbing skills to get down to the inviting beach. An alternative is to take a tour-boat excursion from **Porto Vromi** on the coast near Anafonitria.

You can either retrace your steps to Zakynthos town, or keep to the wild and scenic road that runs southwest between Mount Vrachionas and the sea. It rises and plunges through **Maries**, near which are some Mycenaean tombs, and **Exo Chora**. Take the right fork here alongside the coast to **Kambi** and nearby **Skiza**, where there are more Mycenaean tombs. Beyond **Agios Nikolaos** (a different one from the ferry terminal mentioned above) the road begins a curving descent into the plain, through **Macherado**, whose **Agia Mavra Church** has an ornately decorated interior, and back to Zakynthos town.

Another excursion from Zakynthos town is southeast along the coast road, through the straggly resort of **Argassi** and past 485-meter **Mount Skopos**, into the beach-lined tip of the **Vassilikos Peninsula**. The beaches here are mostly very good and don't have much in the way of development other than a few tavernas and beach bars, loungers, umbrellas and pedalos for hire. Sheltered **Gerakas Beach** is one of the best places to see the endangered **loggerhead turtles**, and is partly protected from development for that reason, but still has beach umbrellas and pedalos.

It's a different story when you backtrack through **Ambelokipoi**, past the airport, then along the **Gulf of Lagana**. The beaches here are the ones most favored by the loggerhead turtles and – wouldn't you know it – are occupied by the full panoply of modern Mediterranean beach resorts. **Laganas** itself is the "star" here, with vast numbers of restaurants, fast-food joints, bars, discos, supermarkets, bodies toasting on the sand, and such like. Watersports are ostensibly limited in the area, though there's not much evidence of this. The important loggerhead beach at nearby

Kalamaki is, however, off-limits at night. Two small islets in the gulf are also loggerhead sanctuaries.

Keep gong southwest past **Lithakia** and, nearer the sea, **bituminous springs** referred to by Herodotus and Pliny the Elder. Finally the road reaches to **Keri** village, which has a few old houses that survived 1953, beyond which is a lighthouse beside **Cape Marathia**.

ENDANGERED LIST

*Life is hard for the **monk seals** that used to be a common sight in the waters around Zakynthos. They don't much care for tourists, and local fishermen don't much care for the seals, which eat fish and octopus that by rights ought to end up on tourists' plates. Between being frightened away from their breeding grounds by tourism and being killed by fishermen if they do venture inshore, the seals have been put off their stroke in the mating game. They're literally living like monks.*

The World Wildlife Foundation runs a conservation project in the area, trying to restore the seals' numbers. You might see seals along the rugged west coast of Zakynthos – but from binocular range only, unless you want to be part of the problem.

***Loggerhead turtles**, too, find their survival at loggerheads with intense human beach activity, especially since female loggerheads like to haul themselves up on the best beaches when it comes time to lay their hundred or so eggs in a pit dug in the sand. The beaches, of course, are already occupied by sun loungers so the turtles mostly stay away. If you see one of these impressive creatures, or one of their nests, leave it alone.*

NIGHTLIFE & ENTERTAINMENT

There are wall-to-wall discos and bars in all the resorts.

SHOPPING

Volimes in the northwest is noted for the handmade lace and crocheted rugs made by local women and on sale in the village. The honey and goat's cheese made and sold here also has a good reputation.

EXCURSIONS & DAY TRIPS

Tour boats leave regularly from the harbor at Agios Nikolaos near Korithi in the north of the island to the Blue Caves and Smuggler's Cove. Tickets cost Drs 1,500 and Drs 2,000 respectively.

PRACTICAL INFORMATION

• **Banks & Currency Exchange** – The **Ionian Bank** in Zakynthos town at *Plateia Agiou Markou* is open Monday through Thursday from 8 am to 2 pm, and to 1:30 pm on Friday. There are bureaux de change in all the resorts, usually open from 9 am to 6 pm. Hotels, some travel agencie,s and the post office exchange most convertible foreign currencies and traveler's checks, but at a poorer rate than the banks.

• **Doctors** – Your hotel may have a list of English-speaking doctors. **Zakynthos Hospital**, is in the western foothills, *Tel. 0695/22514.*

• **Maps** – A map of the island can be bought from most news vendors, souvenir shops and hotel shops for Drs 500.

• **Police** – The main police station is at *Odos Tsoulati 5, Zakynthos town, Tel. 0695/22550.* The tourist police are at *Tel. 0695/30265.*

• **Port Authority** – *Tel. 0695/22417*

• **Post Office** – The main post office in Zakynthos town is at *Odos Tertseti 27.* This and other post offices are open Monday through Friday from 7:30 am to 2 pm.

• **Telephone** – The area code for all of Zakynthos is *0695.* The Greek Telecommunications Organization (OTE) office in Zakynthos town is on *Odos Vassileos Georgiou,* beside Plateia Solomou. Open daily from 7 am to midnight.

• **Tourist Information** – There is no Greek Tourist Organization (EOT) office on Zakynthos. You can get some information, however, from the tourist police, travel agencies, and from the bigger hotels.

13. THE CYCLADES ISLANDS

The Cyclades Islands

There are 56 islands, big and small, in the **Cyclades** group, which lies off the southeast coast of Attica and stretches southwards towards Crete. The origin of the name is uncertain, but the most likely explanation is that the islands form a *kiklos,* a circle, around the ancient sacred island of **Delos**.

One of the early centers of European civilization, the Cyclades Islands hosted a flourishing culture as early as 3200 BC, which has left behind a rich legacy of art, and which merges with the Minoan culture of Crete by around 2100 BC, a fusion that produced the marvelous **Thira** frescoes to be seen at the National Archeological Museum in Athens.

Nowadays they are the most popular Aegean islands with tourists. This is partly due to their proximity to Athens and its ports of Piraeus and Rafina, to the extensive ferry links between them, which make getting around in summer fairly easy (if you ignore the crowded ferries), and partly due to their own fascination, which keeps the crowds coming back time after time.

CYCLADES FINDS & FAVORITES

• *Ano Mera*. *A tiny inland village on Mykonos that has escaped, at least partly, the tidal wave of touristic hype that has washed over the island, and has retained some elements of its original character (see Mykonos).*

• *Mount Knythos*. *You need to be sure you have time to climb this 112-meter hill on Delos. It has no outstanding monuments at its summit, but the view of the ancient religious zone, not to mention of the islands beyond, is superb (see Delos).*

• *Buried Minoan town*. *Excavations at Akrotiri in the south of Thira (Santorini), may be uncovering the real Atlantis, a Minoan town whose houses were decorated with fabulous mosaics, and which was abandoned just before the cataclysmic eruption of the island's volcano in about 1470 BC (see Thira).*

MYKONOS

This island has taken 3,000 years of Greek history to make any kind of a splash, and now that it has, the ripples have spread far, wide, and yonder. Mykonos has become an international cultural icon, its very name a byword for hedonism, excess, gaiety in all senses of the word, and a too-self-conscious-by-half form of sybaritic hipness that makes some people want to throw up everything and live this way for ever, and other people to just throw up. Mykonos, in short, isn't everybody's cup of Greek coffee.

And that's exactly how those who love the place and its scene prefer it. If you can't stand the heat, they would tell you, stay out of this particular island kitchen, where every dish is overdone, variety is the spice of life, and what's sauce for the goose won't necessarily do for the gander.

In Mykonos, myth and reality swirl around each other like gypsies dancing flamenco, if that isn't mixing too many cross-cultural metaphors. Is it or is it not a typical, traditional Cycladic island? Well, it is and it isn't. The maze of whitewashed houses that constitutes much of Mykonos town dates back to the days of piracy – being pirates themselves, Mykonos folks knew that pirates were all at sea on land, and that they could hide from

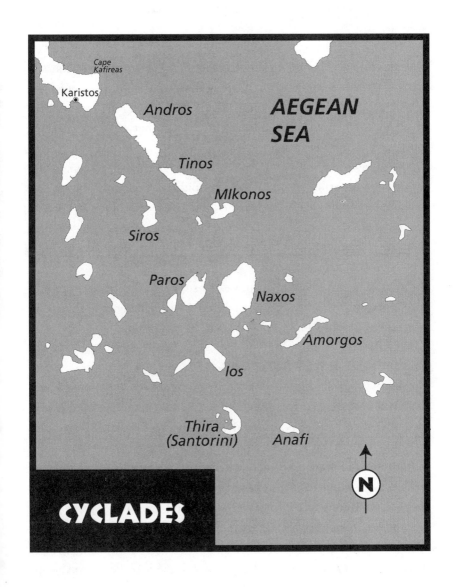

Cape
Kafireas

Karistos

Andros

**AEGEAN
SEA**

Tinos

MIkonos

Siros

Paros

Naxos

Amorgos

Ios

Thira
(Santorini)

Anafi

N

CYCLADES

raiders among the narrow labyrinthine streets and make faces at them when their backs were turned. They might still be doing the same to the throngs of tourists who get lost in this seductively beautiful place every year.

However, in the past, a traditional Cycladic village didn't have a Tex-Mex restaurant, or serve up bacon-egg-sausage-'n'-tomato breakfasts – just two of many for-instances. By going there, tourists have changed the place irrevocably. There's no return to the past; the egg can't be put back in its shell; Mykonos can't unlearn the lessons that 40 years of taking money off tourists has taught it.

So the age of innocence is dead. Few visitors to Mykonos seem to care overmuch about such recondite speculations. They come for the fun, the cool breeze in a hot place, the beaches, the 57 varieties of sex, to shop, to see the latest incarnation of Petros the Pelican, because people tell them their life will have a big empty space at its core if they don't, and because they get on the wrong ferry.

Finally, be advised that an abundant supply of drachmas is the only sure remedy for "Mykonosis," defined in the medical literature as "excessive overindulgence in everything under the sun."

ARRIVALS & DEPARTURES
By Air

Mykonos Airport, *Tel. 0289/22237*, lies 2.5 kilometers southeast of Mykonos town. At peak periods, **Olympic Airways** operates seven scheduled return flights a day to Mykonos from **Athens**, flying time 40 minutes. In addition, there are two flights a week from **Thessalonika**, flying time 1 hour; two a week from **Heraklion** on Crete, flying time 1 hour; three a week from **Rhodes**, flying time 1 hour; and one a day from **Thira** (Santorini), flying time 40 minutes.

For current departure flight times and ticket prices, contact Olympic in Mykonos town at *Plateia Agios Loukas, Tel. 0289/22490*. Travel agents on the island can also book onward flights.

Taxi fare from the airport to Mykonos town is around Drs 1,200.

By Sea

Between Mykonos and **Piraeus**, there are two to three car ferries a day in summer, *Tel. 0289/26167, 0289/24819, or 0289/26846.* Direct journey time is 5 hours 45 minutes; one-way deck tickets cost Drs 4,500. Most ferry, hydrofoil, and catamaran connections, however, are to **Rafina**, a closer port on the east coast of Attica 28 kilometers from Athens. In that direction, there are two to four car ferries a day, *Tel. 0289/22853 or 0289/22242*; journey time is 4 hours; one-way deck tickets cost Drs 3,800. Theoretically (because bad weather and other factors play hell with the timetables), there are two to five hydrofoils and two jet-catamarans a day, with the larger number of sailings clustered around the weekend; journey time is 2 1/2 hours; one-way tickets cost Drs 7,900.

Mykonos has good ferry connections with other islands of the **Cyclades** group. In summer, there are car ferry, hydrofoil or catamaran sailings a day, *Tel. 0289/26167, 0289/26846, 0289/22853 or 0289/22242*, to the following islands: two a day to **Amorgos**; four a day to Andros; one a day to **Ios**; one to two a day to **Naxos**; two a day to **Paros**; three to six a day to **Syros**; six a day on average to **Tinos**; four a day to **Thira**; and stops at other islands of the group depending on the ferries' variable timetables and route networks. As examples, journey time by car ferry to Syros is 1 hour 25 minutes, and one-way deck tickets cost Drs 1,500; journey time by hydrofoil is 40 minutes, and one-way tickets cost Drs 3,000.

There is one car ferry a week in summer, *Tel. 0298/24819*, between Mykonos and **Crete**; journey time is 4 hours 40 minutes, and one-way deck tickets cost Drs 3,200. On alternate days there is a car ferry to **Samos**, *Tel. 0289/26167 or 0289/26846*; journey time is 5 hours, and one-way deck tickets cost Drs 3,600.

ORIENTATION

With an area of 85 square kilometers and an 81-kilometer coastline, Mykonos lies in the northern half of the Cyclades group, and has a population of around 6,000. It is 133 kilometers southeast of **Rafina**, a more convenient starting point than Piraeus. **Mykonos town** (aka Chora), nestles on low-lying land at the heart of a wide bay, and the inland village of **Ano Mera** sits in the middle of the island, with hillier country to its west, east and north, reaching up to a less-than-dizzy 372 meters in the north near **Agios Stefanos**.

Otherwise there isn't a lot to the place, geographically speaking at any rate, apart from beaches – but what beaches! The best of them line the south coast, with another stretch of good ones north of Mykonos town.

GETTING AROUND THE ISLAND
By Bus

Surprisingly for such a small place, there are two bus stations in Mykonos town, although calling them "stations" may be stretching a point. The **South Station**, *at Plateia Platis Gialos,* serves the airport and the beaches directly south of Mykonos town. From west to east along this stretch of coast, there is one bus an hour to **Agios Ioannis Beach**; two an hour to **Ornos Beach**; one an hour to **Platis Gialos beach**; and two an hour to **Paradise Beach**. Five buses a day run to and from the **airport** between 8 am and 7 pm.

The **North Station** is opposite the OTE office at the beginning of *Odos Agios Ioannou.* Northwards to **Agios Stefanos**, there are buses every 45 minutes; eastwards to **Ano Mera**, there are buses every half hour or so, half of which turn south at that point to **Elia Beach**, with the other half continuing east to **Kalafatis** and **Kalo Livadi Beach**.

All buses are operated by **KTEL**, *Tel. 0289/23360.*

By Caïque

There are regular caïque departures in summer from the south end of the harbor to **Platis Gialos**, and equally frequent departures to various beaches eastwards between there and **Elia Beach**.

By Car

Among many firms on the island, rental cars are available for around Drs 15,000 a day for a small car from:
• **Kosmos**, *Paralia. Tel. 0289/24013*
• **Motospeed**, *Odos Vrysi. Tel. 0289/23854*

By Moped & Scooter

Mopeds, scooters, and off-road bikes are available for rent throughout the island for from Drs 3,000 to Drs 5,000 a day. At the top of the price range, it may make more sense to share the cost of renting a small car.

By Taxi

Taxis on Mykonos even have a square named after them – at any rate Plateia Mavrogenous, *just behind the middle of the harbor, is commonly called* Taxi Square. To call a taxi, dial *0289/23700.*

WHERE TO STAY

In summer Mykonos is expensive, and its hotels and other accommodations fill up fast; in the spring and autumn shoulder seasons it is just as expensive. Even with 134 registered hotels, apartment hotels, and bungalow complexes, plus campsites and rooms in private houses, it is mostly a seller's market. The trick is either to reserve in advance or to arrive on an early ferry, and try to sort out the wheat from the chaff of offers from accommodation touts who meet the ferries. If you delay too long in making up your mind, the chaff will be gone as well as the wheat.

The **Mykonos Accommodation Center**, *Odos Matoyanni 46, Mykonos town, Tel. 0289/23160, Fax 0289/24137,* can also help.

PRINCESS OF MYKONOS, *Agios Stefanos. Tel. 0289/23806, Fax 0289/23031. Rates (with tax): Drs 45,000 single; Drs 50,000 double. Breakfast Drs 2,000. 38 studios. American Express, Diners Club, Visa, MasterCard.*

If money is no object, and you want to keep away from the throngs wearing thongs, this is about as good and as far away as you can get. The only problem with Agios Stefanos is that the north coast gets smitten by the *meltemi* wind in summer, so this is cooler temperature-wise than most places on Mykonos. Having said that, the Princess puts you in the lap of luxury, a shade below royalty perhaps but not so much that you would notice. The studios are air conditioned, and furnished and equipped in a highly chic rendition of local style, with satellite television. Facilities include swimming pool, à la carte restaurant, fitness center with gym, sauna and jacuzzi. The hotel even has a conference room, but despite

Mykonos's freewheeling reputation this is in fact no more than a boring old room for holding conferences in.

ANO MERA, *Ano Mera village. Tel. 0289/71230, Fax 0289/71276. Rates (with tax): Drs 20,000 single; Drs 22,000 double. Breakfast Drs 1,200. 67 rooms. American Express, Diners Club, Visa, MasterCard.*

Out on a limb in a way, one kilometer from the village of the same name in the middle of Mykonos, the Ano Mera is a deluxe hotel that offers a different kind of Mykonos experience, at least in so far as it is neither beside a beach nor embroiled in the fevers of Mykonos town. Its location in a relatively quiet area is the Ano Mera's strongest suit, as otherwise it is a comfortable though not especially memorable place. It does have a swimming pool.

NAZOS, *Odos Rohari, Mykonos town. Tel. 0289/22626, Fax 0289/24604. Rates (with tax): Drs 13,000 single; Drs 18,000 double. Breakfast Drs 1,500. 14 rooms. No credit cards.*

If you want to be away from the water's edge, if only because that is often the noisiest location, the Nazos is a good bet. One of a cluster of hotels in the hilly eastern edge of town, it offers a slightly higher standard of comfort and service than the others, and charges a bit more for the privilege. The big, comfortable rooms have a good view of the town, the sea, and the Mykonos landscape.

PHILIPPI, *Odos Kalogera 32, Mykonos town. Tel. 0289/22294, Fax 0289/24680. Rates (with tax): Drs 9,000 single; Drs 16,000 double. Breakfast included. 13 rooms. No credit cards.*

This is one of the gems of Mykonos for budget travelers who want as much access to character and quality as those whose pocketbooks are fatter. It's in a busy part of Mykonos town, but the rooms look out on an interior garden so it is a lot more restful than it might otherwise be. Rooms are cosy and colorful in a flowery way, and mercifully free from chic.

APOLLON, *Paralia, Mykonos town. Tel. 0289/22223. Rates (with tax): Drs 9,000 single; Drs 14,000 double. Breakfast included. 20 rooms. No credit cards.*

Right in the middle of the waterfront, this oldest swinger in town was already a hotel when Mykonos was just a kid trying on its first pair of swimshorts. The building itself dates from the last century, and many of its simply furnished rooms look out on the dark-wine sea of the *Paralia's* evening taverna shuffle.

ILIOVASSILEMA, *Tourlos village. Tel. 0289/23013. Rates (with tax): Drs 9,000 single; Drs 14,000 double. Breakfast included. 17 rooms. No credit cards.*

Tourlos is on the coast only a kilometer north of Mykonos town, and the Iliovassilema is beside the beach, with a shaded terrace overlooking the sea. The best rooms are those which have a seaview. There is the question of whether you want to be outside Mykonos town in the first place, and yet still so close to it. However, prices here are very reasonable as things go on this island, and the rooms are both clean and adequately equipped.

WHERE TO EAT

PHILIPPI, *Odos Kalogera 32, Mykonos town. Tel. 0289/22294. Drs 7,000 to Drs 12,000. American Express, Visa, MasterCard. Stylish Greek.*

The elegant restaurant of the same-name hotel (see above), amidst the hotel's garden in the heart of town. Philippi does Greek standards with an added touch of designer class, but the menu reaches beyond souvlaki and moussaka to continental dishes, with the accent on French.

O KOUNELAS, *Odos Zougane, Mykonos town. Drs 4,000 to Drs 8,000. No credit cards. Seafood/traditional.*

A traditional taverna whose seafood is good enough that the local fishermen go there to eat. You can't say fairer than that, and you can see your fish being cooked before your very eyes. It isn't cheap, exactly, but seafood rarely is.

SESAME KITCHEN, *Odos Dinameon, Mykonos town. Tel. 0289/24710. Drs 3,500 to Drs 7,000. Visa. Vegetarian/stylish Greek.*

Vegetarians might have found this restaurant beside the Maritime Museum to be right up their street, except that Sesame lets the street down by also serving meat dishes, particularly chicken.

NIKOS, *Kastro, Mykonos town. Tel. 0289/24320. Drs 3,000 to Drs 6,000. No credit cards. Seafood/traditional.*

A few streets inland from the western end of the harbor, Nikos maintains both the style and the substance of a typical Greek village taverna in its atmosphere, presentation, clientele, and prices. The seafood dishes are particularly popular.

SEEING THE SIGHTS

Mykonos town is a sight all by itself, and among the most emblematic places in the Aegean. There are caïques and fishing boats bobbing in the taverna-lined harbor or drawn up on the sand of the town beach, a cluster of windmills overlooking the harbor on the south side, a warren of flower-bedecked, dazzlingly white-painted houses with blue shutters and railings climbing up the gentle slope from the sea, and almost inevitably a squadron of cruise ships in the bay.

Between the harbor and the windmills is the area known as **Little Venice**, as the wood-balconied houses are actually in the water at this point. A few meters north of here is the **Church of Panagia Paraportiani**, a remarkable, trompe l'oeil kind of place that is considered an outstanding example of the Cycladic style of architecture. It comprises four chapels oriented on different axes that kind of meld into each other. Photographers and water-colorists flock here to worship at this shrine of light and shade, and try to pin the thing down on paper.

Next door is the **Folklore Museum**, *open Monday to Saturday 4 to 8 pm; admission free.* Housed in an 18th-century sea captain's house, the museum features among its range of household, fishing, and farming objects the stuffed former symbol of Mykonos, **Petros the Pelican**, whom Jackie Onassis once apparently tried to hook up with a female of the species, but who, staying faithful to Mykonos tradition, wasn't interested. In the middle of town is the **Aegean Maritime Museum**, *Odos Dinameon, Tel. 0289/22700; open Tuesday to Sunday 8:30 am to 3 pm; admission Drs 300,* which sheds some light on local nautical lore, though not on why the ferries are always late. The collection includes ship models, maps, navigation and other instruments, coins, and other maritime artifacts.

At the north end of the harbor, the **Archaeological Museum**, *Tel. 0289/22325; open Tuesday to Sunday 8:30 am to 2:30 pm; admission Drs 500,* mostly displays stuff from the nearby island of **Renia**, which itself mostly came originally from Delos: pottery, grave stelae, jewelry, and a marble statue of Hercules.

Beyond Mykonos town, you are faced with a seemingly endless vista of naked human flesh, some of it tanned an Adonis-like shade of gold and some pink tending towards livid-red; some power-gym firm, and some sagging sorrowfully in all the wrong places. When all is said and most of it done, the beaches are where Mykonos lives. Contrary to popular opinion, you don't have to be gay to sunbathe at **Paradise Beach**, **Super Paradise Beach**, and **Elia Beach** on the south coast, although it clearly helps. Yet there are beaches enough for everyone on this coast, reachable by bus or caïque from Mykonos town, and a willingness to walk will bring you to less wonderful but quieter stretches of sand. The beaches around **Kalafatis** at the eastern end of this coast tend to be quieter.

If you want to get away from the summer crowds, head to the northern beaches around **Agios Stefanos** and **Panormos**. You'll most likely have to share them with the sharp *meltemi* wind, but you might still consider that to be a fair trade.

Although **Ano Mera** village near the middle of the island is far less precocious than Mykonos town, it has only a couple of hundred inhabitants, and being the main point of interest other than beaches outside the capital, it gets easily swamped. The 16th-century **Monastery of Panagia Tourliani** at the village is on most visitors' itinerary. It has a cool courtyard, an 18th-century belltower, and some notable icons. The countryside east of Ano Mera is good for walking in, if only to get away from the beach for a while.

A kilometer or so on the coast road north of Mykonos town is the hamlet of **Tourlos**, where you have the chance of a little more peace and quiet, though not much.

NIGHTLIFE & ENTERTAINMENT

There are more hot spots on Mykonos than most people can handle, and while many of them are characterized more by a frenzied determination to have a good time than by genuine style, they are only retailing what brings many people to Mykonos in the first place. The in places come and go about as fast as the ferry boats, although some have stood the test of time. At any rate they are still standing.

The **SKANDINAVIAN BAR** near Little Venice is a bewildering and noisy watering-hole which takes the joyless clean living associated with the Nordic countries of its name and blows it out the window – in the direction of the bearby **WINDMILL DISCO**, which doesn't take to it any more than the place it came from. If you're looking for something more sedate, not to say asleep, try the **YACHT CLUB** at the north end of the harbor, or **MONTPARNASSE**, where classical music mingles with Toulouse-Lautrec paintings (as the artist's pals used to say to him: "What have you got to lose, Lautrec?"). For something a little more Greek, the **MYKONOS CLUB** in Little Venice, where you can hear bouzouki music, is the way to go.

SHOPPING

Shipping gold, silver, and jewelry, along with designer-label clothes and scents, keeps the local version of the teamsters and longshoremen busy, and it's for sure that the old-time Mykonos pirates would have had a ball with this stuff. Mykonos town is virtually choked with such places.

EXCURSIONS & DAY TRIPS

The most popular excursion from Mykonos is to **Delos**, a sacred island in ancient times and now entirely an archaeological reserve. Caïques leave from Mykonos town every half hour or so in summer; round-trip tickets cost Drs 1,500. You are not allowed to stay on Delos. (See *Delos* below.)

PRACTICAL INFORMATION

· **Banks & Currency Exchange** – The **National Bank of Greece** has a branch at the Paralia. It is open Monday through Friday from 8 am to 2 pm, and in summer from 6:30 to 8:30 pm, as well as (for currency exchange only) on Saturday from 9:30 am to 12:30 pm, and on Saturday and Sunday from 5:30 to 8:30 pm. American Express is represented by Delia Travel *at the Paralia,* Tel. *0289/22322, Fax 0289/ 24400.*

• **Doctors** – **Mykonos Health Center** is a short way out of town on the road to Ano Mera, Tel. *0289/23994 or 23996.*

• **Police** – The police station is in the southeast of town, *off Odos Ipirou,* Tel. *0289/22235.* The tourist police are at the north end of the harbor, Tel. *0289/22482.*

• **Port Authority** – Tel. *0289/23922.*

• **Post Office** The post office is on the waterfront beside the Delos Hotel, *north of Plateia Mavrogenous (Taxi Square).* It is open Monday through Friday from 7:30 am to 2 pm.

• **Telephone** – The area code for Mykonos is *0289.* The Greek Telecommunication Organization (OTE) office is at the north end of the harbor, *off Odos Agios Ioannou,* Tel. *0289/22499.*

• **Tourist Office** – The Municipal Tourist Information Office is at the north end of the harbor, *off Odos Agios Stefanou,* Tel. *0289/22201, Fax 0289/22229.*

DELOS

Delos is the sacred island of antiquity around which the Cyclades Islands form a *kiklos,* a circle. From the earliest times the small island seems to have been an important cult and trading center, dedicated to **Leto,** the mother of Apollo and Artemis, who were born on Delos, and later as the site of one of the great oracles of Apollo. In the 7th century BC the Ionian Greeks held their communal festival, the **Delia,** here.

It wasn't long before Athens, attracted by Delos's strategic position, began to muscle in, and in 478 BC Delos became the headquarters of the Athenian-dominated Delian League, a position it lost to Athens in 454 BC, when the league's treasury was transferred there and used to beautify the Parthenon and other sites in Athens. The Athenians finally expelled the entire population and "purified" the island, removing all graves and forbidding anyone to give birth or to die there (it's not clear what the punishment was for dying there).

By around the middle of the 2nd century BC, the Romans were already in evidence as traders, and under the Republic the island added to its already considerable wealth of cult sites the infrastructure of a vigorous trading station – a kind of ancient Hong Kong. Slavery was also big business on Delos, and at one time it was said that 10,000 slaves changed hands every day.

Thoroughly sacked in 88 BC and again in 69 BC, Delos went into a tailspin from which it never recovered. By the 2nd century AD, it was despoiled and depopulated, and as the Christian era wore on what remained of its magnificent temples and other monuments was looted and broken up for use as building materials elsewhere.

Today the island is a sanctuary once more, this time under the protection of the French School of Archaeology. By late afternoon it has been purified of the throngs of tourists who come to stroll through its venerable ruins. The archaeologists can then get on in peace with whatever French archaeologists get up to when there is no one around to watch them.

ARRIVALS & DEPARTURES
By Sea

Delos can only be reached by tour boat from neighboring islands, and you must return on the same day, with the same boat. So it pays to take the first sailing across and the last one back if you want to maximize your exploration time. **Mykonos** has the most frequent sailings, the shortest crossing time, and the cheapest tickets. At peak times in summer there are nine boats a day from Tuesday to Sunday, sailing usually to the west coast harbor at the Sanctuary of Delos, which takes about 40 minutes, and in poor weather to Gourna Bay on the east coast; return tickets cost Drs 1,500. There are also frequent tour boat sailings to Delos from **Naxos**, **Paros**, and **Tinos**.

ORIENTATION

With an area of less than five square kilometers and a semi-permanent population of around 20 guardians and archaeologists, Delos lies two kilometers west of **Mykonos**.

The main **Sanctuary** area is in the northern part of the west coast around the ancient **Sacred Harbor**, with the remains of such imposing monuments as the **Terrace of the Lions**, the **Sacred Lake**, the **Sanctuaries of Apollo and Artemis**, and the **Hippodrome**. South of this area is the ancient **Commercial Habor**, where the tour boats dock, and another cluster of monuments, including the **Theater**, overlooked by 112-meter **Mount Kynthos**. Yet further south is the **Asklepieion**. To the northeast, beside the alternate, poor-weather dock for tour boats, is the **Stadium**.

GETTING AROUND THE ISLAND

Walking is the only way to get around on Delos. The distances are not great, however, and in a 3- to 5-hour excursion you can see just about everything.

WHERE TO EAT

There is an expensive **cafe-taverna** beside the Museum. It is expensive not because it is of a high standard, but because it has a monopoly. Bringing your own picnic is a better idea.

SEEING THE SIGHTS

Assuming you arrive at the tour boat dock on the west coast, in what was the ancient **Commercial Harbor**, lined by ruined warehouses and other harbor installations, and you have a 5-hour exploration period, you should have time to make a circuit of most of the **Delos Archaeological Site**, *Tel. 0289/22259; open Tuesday to Sunday 8:30 am to 3 pm; admission (including entry to the on-site museum) Drs 1,500.* You will probably not, however, have the time necessary to explore it in any real depth.

From here you walk generally southeastwards through the **Theater Quarter**, the once-crowded residential area. Comparable to Pompeii as an evocation of ordinary people's homes, the quarter is also notable for the remarkable, if somewhat bizarre, mosaic of Dionysos riding side-saddle on a panther in the **House of Dionysos**, and the mosaics of a trident and a dolphin wrapped around an anchor in the rebuilt **House of the Trident**. The **Theater** itself is in a ruined state, with most its seating having been removed. Beside it is a large, compartmented water-cistern.

Look out also for the 8-meter deep **water-cistern** at the nearby **Guest House**, an ancient Delian lodging. It's hard to tell what the facilities were like, although it is fair to assume that air conditioning and minibars weren't among them. In the nearby **House of the Dolphins** is a beautiful mosaic of dolphins being ridden by a cupid.

Going eastwards from here, you can climb the slopes of **Mount Kynthos**, whose 112-meter height makes for a fairly easy ascent yet offers a superb panorama of the island and its ancient sites below, as well as of neighboring Cyclades islands. At the top are scanty remains of the **Sanctuary of Zeus and Athena**. On the way you can take a sidetrack southwards to the **Grotto of Hercules**, marked by a pointed roof made from angled granite slabs.

Back down the mountain again, and continuing northwards, you pass through an area in which are concentrated many sanctuaries dedicated to foreign gods. These include the **Temple of Hera, Temple of Isis**, and **Temple of Serapis**. A series of other houses, monuments and temples leads, with a possible short detour southwards to see the **House of Hermes**, to the path towards the **Museum**, *Tel. 0289/22259; open Tuesday to Sunday 8:30 am to 3 pm; admission included in the entry fee for the island as a whole.* Here are gathered the vast majority of finds from the excavations the French School has been conducting on Delos since 1872, dating mostly across a thousand years of time from the 7th century BC, but also including finds from as far back as the 3rd millennium BC.

There are archaic sculptures of people and animals, both real and mythical; classical-era pottery; marble, terracotta and bronze statues; sculptural elements from temples; mosaics; and a collection of Mycenaean ivory votive objects.

West of this is the main monumental zone surrounding the **Sacred Harbor**, which those who are short of time would be well advised to stick to. The **Sanctuary of Dionysos** is easily identified by the two giant, truncated marble phalluses on top of columns that guard the entrance. Beside this is the big **Agora of the Italians**, beyond whose northwestern corner is a hole marking the spot where the **Sacred Palm Tree** stood. Next to this is an oval-shaped wall marking the location of the **Sacred Lake**, where swans and geese sacred to Apollo once swam. West of the lake is the **Terrace of the Lions**, five weathered and faintly comical archaic lion sculptures on pedestals.

Recrossing the Agora of the Italians, you come to the long **Stoa of Antigonos**, bordered by five **Treasuries** leading to the **Temple of the Athenians** and the **Temple of Apollo**, at the heart of the religious zone called the **Hieron of Apollo**. Beside the ceremonial gateway to this zone is the base of the now-vanished **Colossal Statue of Apollo**, and near that the base of the equally vanished **Bronze Palm Tree**. Around it are stoas, columns, temples, agoras, shrines, cult sanctuaries, altars, and other debris from a thousand years of pagan worship on the site. The **Sanctuary of Artemis** lies closer to the harbor.

If you are moved enough by this astonishing array of ancient ruins – one of the most evocative in the world – to want to come again, you can either delve deeper into the individual sites mentioned above, as well as others in the core zone, or visit outlying areas – the **Stadium**, for example, on the northeast coast at Gourna Bay, or the **Asklepieion** on the west coast south of Mount Knythos.

THIRA (SANTORINI)

You can tell just by looking at **Thira** that something terrible has happened here: the signs and scars of a great disaster can be seen all around you – and that's only the arrival of the latest cruise ship to disgorge its horde of sightseeing passengers. However, the titanic forces that blew the island apart in a volcanic eruption around 1470 BC are still at work, assembing their strength for a repeat performance that would send the cruise ships flying all the way to Gibraltar.

Thira gets busy in summer. Even by the standards of the Cyclades this is an ultrabusy place. In compensation you get the most limpid light in Greece, one of the raciest social whirls in the Aegean, and the chance to view the scene of an awesome natural convulsion (as well as the Pompeii-like satisfaction of knowing you arrived too late to be a participant).

Thira was populated in prehistoric times, and during the Early Cycladic and Minoan periods from 3200 BC to roughly 1500 BC it hosted a flourishing civilization, as a key component of the Crete-based Minoan maritime empire in the Aegean. The evidence for this period is still being uncovered in excavations at Akrotiri in the south of the island. All that came to an abrupt end around 1470 BC when the volcano that is what Thira actually was erupted. There are signs that the Mycenaeans colonized what was left of the island a century or so later, to be replaced by Dorian Greeks led by **Thiras** around 1000 BC.

THE BIG BANG

*When the Thira volcano blew its top in about 1470 BC, it made the loudest bang ever heard on Earth in historical times. Thira went up with a force equivalent to more than a hundred hydrogen bombs going off at the same time, destroying two-thirds of the island and burying the Minoan settlement at present-day **Akrotiri** under layers of lava and black pumice.*

The tsunami (tidal wave) it caused may have reached a height of 50 meters in the shallow waters off northern Crete, 105 kilometers southwards, before slamming into the coast, along which lay Knossos and other palaces that were the main centers of Minoan life. Although it is not clear certain that the Thira eruption was the smoking gun that killed the Minoan civilization, it couldn't have done it much good, and falling ash from the explosion may have damaged the agriculture of a society that depended on a precarious surplus to support the structures of civilized life.

Thira's cataclysmic eruption gave birth to a persistent legend. The Egyptians kept records of the explosion and its effects, and a thousand years later the Greeks picked up the story from them. Plato used it in his Dialogues, but didn't believe that the fabulous drowned civilization could have been in the Aegean, so he shipped it westwards to the ocean and called it Atlantis. It has lain deep in the human imagination ever since: a vanished culture that combined high civilization and advanced technology with wisdom, happiness, and peace – exactly the combination that eludes us today.

The island played a minor role in the drama of Classical Greece, before becoming an important naval base in the Hellenistic period for the Egyptian-based Ptolemy dynasty. The Romans don't seem to have had much call for a used volcano, although they did add to the embellishment of Thira town. Under Byzantium, Thira's strategic position again made it useful but that didn't last, and after a period of Venetian occupation the Turks stepped in during the 16th century. Thiran ships played an important part in the Greek War of Independence in the 1820s.

Nowadays, it is a tourist island par excellence, for which the volcano must take most of the credit. Despite occasional mini-eruptions through the centuries, and the odd earthquake now and then, that volcano is dormant. If it wakes up while you're here, you'll at least have the consolation of going down in history at the same time as you go up in the air.

ARRIVALS & DEPARTURES
By Air

Thira Airport lies six kilometers southeast of Fira, near Monolithos on the east coast, *Tel. 0286/31525*. At peak periods, **Olympic Airways** operates between five and eight scheduled return flights a day to Thira from **Athens**, flying time 50 minutes. In addition, there are three flights a week from **Thessalonika**, flying time 1 1/2 hours; three a week from **Heraklion** (Crete), flying time 40 minutes; four a week from **Rhodes**, flying time 1 hour; and one a day (except Tuesday) from **Mykonos**, flying time 30 minutes.

For current departure flight times and ticket prices, contact Olympic in Fira at *Plateia Theotokopoulou, Tel. 0289/22490*. Travel agents on the island can also book onward flights.

Taxi fare from the airport to Fira is around Drs 2,200.

By Sea

Between Mykonos and **Piraeus**, there are from four to eight car ferries a day in summer, *Tel. 0286/23660, 0286/22127 or 0286/22958*. Direct journey time is 9 hours 45 minutes; one-way deck tickets cost Drs 5,200.

Thira has good ferry connections with other islands of the **Cyclades** group. In summer, there are car ferry or hydrofoil sailings, *Tel. 0286/*

22127, to the following islands: five a week to **Anafi**; two on most days to Amorg**os**; one on most days to **Folegandros**; from four to six a day to **Ios**; one on most days to **Kythnos**; two on most days to **Milos**; two to three a day to **Mykonos**; six a day on average to **Naxos** and **Paros**; two a day on average to **Syros**; and stops at other islands of the group depending on the ferries' variable timetables and route networks.

As examples, journey time by car ferry to Paros is 3 hours 50 minutes, and one-way deck tickets cost Drs 2,900; journey time by hydrofoil is 2 hours 20 minutes, and one-way tickets cost Drs 6,000.

There is a car ferry on most days between Thira and **Crete**, *Tel. 0286/ 23660*; journey time is 4 hours, and one-way deck tickets cost Drs 3,200.

ORIENTATION

With an area of 76 square kilometers and 69 kilometers of coastline, Thira is the southernmost island of the Cyclades group, and has a population of around 8,000. It lies 224 kilometers southeast of Piraeus, and 105 kilometers north of Crete. The shape and topography of the island is the legacy of the great volcanic eruption of circa 1470 BC. It forms a rough crescent with the open side facing west around a wide lagoon where once stood the caldera and slopes of the volcano, and which is now dotted with the volcanic islets of **Nea Kameni**, **Palea Kameni**, and **Aspro**. Three kilometers off the northwestern tip of the main island lies **Thirassia**, a pretty small island boasting all of 10 square kilometers and a population of 300.

On Thira itself, the main town, **Fira**, lies just above the middle of the west coast, with the main harbor, **Athinios**, just below the middle. Going north you come to **Oia** and the beach at **Mavropetra**. The center of the island is dominated by the main town and harbor, the airport, and the beaches at **Monolithos** and **Kamari**. South of here is 566-meter **Mount Profitis Ilias**, the ruins of ancient **Thira town**, and at the southwestern corner of the crescent, **Akrotiri** village and the nearby, ongoing excavations at the **Minoan-era town** which went under a welter of lava and pumice when the volcano blew up.

GETTING AROUND THE ISLAND

By Bus

Fira is the focus of the island's bus network, which is quite extensive for such a small place, with routes poking into most nooks and crannies. In summer, of course, they all get pretty crowded. Northbound is straightforward, there being just a single route with buses every 30 minutes through **Finikia** to **Oia**. Southwards, there are buses every 30 minutes to **Monolithos**, passing the airport on the way; every 30 minutes via **Gonia** to **Kamari**; every 30 minutes through **Pirgos** and **Emporio** to **Perissa** on the southeast coast; and hourly through Pirgos to **Akrotiri** and the **Minoan town** excavation site.

In addition, buses leave Fira an hour before the arrival of a ferry at **Athinios**, and leave Athinios an hour after the boat's arrival.

By Cable Car

This runs up and down the steep volcanic cliff between **Fira** and the **Old Harbor** 200 meters below the town. A ride costs Drs 800. The view from the car is superb, and it certainly beats walking up the 587-step, switchback stairway in the summer sun, or being carried up on muleback.

By Caïque

There are regular caïque tours from Fira, Oia and Athinios in summer around the lagoon and to the nearby islands of **Thirassia**, **Nea Kameni**, **Palia Kameni**, and **Aspronisi**.

By Car

It's hard to imagine needing a rental car here, but people on vacation do the strangest things. You're looking at about Drs 20,000 a day for a baby-sized European car. Try:

• **Alamo**, *Karterados. Tel. 0269/22070*
• **Manos**, *Fira. Tel. 0286/23592*

By Moped & Scooter

Fira might well be called Fira because all the mad moped riders that infest it will put the Fira god in you. The kids here all seem to have been born in the saddle, and many of them seem set on dying in it as well. When you add masses of summertime riders whose nearest experience appears to have been their childhood tricycle, and mopeds which look like they went through the great volcano blast, you have an experience awaiting that could easily be described as interesting.

Mopeds are available for rent in Fira, particularly in the area around the bus station, and in most of the villages, for from Drs 2,500 to Drs 4,000 a day. Check the state of the machine as best you can: breakdowns are frequent.

By Taxi

Taxis on Thira are few, far between, and not exactly what you would call cheap. The drivers don't try to cheat you, however, because they make enough money without needing to go down that road. They are based in Fira, Tel. 0286/23700.

WHERE TO STAY

So popular is Thira that in season its hotels and other accommodations fill up fast. You don't need to stay in Fira, however, as the good bus network means you can easily and quickly get to outlying villages, where rooms don't disappear quite so fast – yet disappear they do, so don't hang around in the quest for accommodation.

ATLANTIS, *Odos Ipapantis, Fira. Tel. 0286/22232, Fax 0286/22821. Rates (with tax): Drs 27,500 single; Drs 37,000 double. Breakfast included. 27 rooms. American Express, Diners Club, Visa, MasterCard.*

The Atlantis occupies one of the best positions in Fira, with an entrance beside the belltower of the Orthodox cathedral, and rooms with a superb view of the caldera and the offshore islets. Most of the rooms have a balcony allowing appreciation of the view, in addition to being equipped with private bathroom. The hotel has a bar, restaurant, and television lounge. Although it has no swimming pool, it is a more personable place and better value for money than more expensive options that do.

PELICAN, *Off Odos 25 Martiou, Fira. Tel. 0286/23113, Fax 0286/ 23514. Rates (with tax): Drs 19,000 single; Drs 23,000 double. Breakfast included. 18 rooms. American Express,Diners Club, Visa, MasterCard.*

An in-town hotel close to the main square, that is even more pretty to look at than many in Fira, being located in an old converted house. The rooms have private bathrooms and a refrigerator, and there is a television lounge. The only problem here is that the surroundings tend to get noisy at night.

FREGATA, *Oia. Tel. 0286/71221, Fax 0286/71333. Rates (with tax): Drs 15,000 double. Breakfast included. 19 rooms. No credit cards*

In Oia, where you can easily pay getting up for Drs 50,000 for a studio, you have to sacrifice something to get affordable prices. You don't sacrifice too much at the Fregata, except the ambience of an old building. This is modern, but compensates with a great view and nice rooms.

KARLOS, *Akrotiri. Tel. 0286/81370, Fax 0286/81095. Rates (with tax): Drs 11,000 single; Drs 14,000 double. Breakfast included. 20 rooms. No credit cards.*

You are within easy reach of the excavations at the ancient Minoan town, in this new hotel in the center of Akrotiri. The owners are welcoming and will collect you from the harbor if you telephone them, saving the cost of a taxi, or the hassle and delay involved in getting a bus.

WHERE TO EAT

Thira is filled with restaurants whose cuisine can best be described as international, although the word "expensive" also comes to mind. Getting out of Fira opens up possibilities for better dining in the traditional style.

NIKOLAS, *Odos Erythrou Stavrou, Fira. Drs 3,500 to Drs 6,000. No credit cards. Seafood/traditional.*

One of the tavernas in Fira that does not cater exclusively to tourists, but serves fine seafood and other Greek dishes at an affordable price. The service might give you the impression that you'd be more welcome at a tourist taverna, but that's surely only an impression.

O PSARAS, *Akrotiri. Drs 3,000 to Drs 5,000. No credit cards. Seafood.*
Unfashionable Akrotiri has some good simple tavernas, and this is perhaps the best one serving seafood.

KYKLADES, *Fira. Drs 2,500 to Drs 5,000. No credit cards. Traditional.*
A traditional kitchen, and another place where local people go, this one beingmore welcoming to tourists than Nikolas seems to be.

PARADISE, *Akrotiri. Drs 2,500 to Drs 5,000. No credit cards. Traditional.*
With a terrace in the main square of Akrotiri, this traditional taverna is easily found and not so easily forgotten.

SEEING THE SIGHTS
Fira

Thira's most interesting sight, its **volcano**, has vanished, taking most of the island with it, but what little it left behind has become one of the premier tourist attractions in the Aegean.

Fira, like the other caldera-top villages, is a surreal sight all by itself. A ribbon of white and blue buildings, it clings to the rim of the black volcanic cliff that plunges into the cobalt sea below. If the inhabitants are in no worse shape than Californians whose homes straddle the San Andreas Fault, they are in no better either, and the dreadful warning of the 1956 earthquake seems to have been too glibly ignored by the owners of all those overhanging houses, hotels, and tavernas. At the very least, the knowledge that one good shove from nature will send the whole show tumbling into the lagoon should add a frisson of excitement to your sunset drink on a bar or taverna terrace.

Assuming that everything stays *in situ*, you can haul yourself along Fira's undulating streets to admire the scene and the scenery – you and about ten thousand other people, that is.

Then there is the **Archaeological Museum** *at the north end of Odos Ipapantis, near the cable car station, Tel. 0286/22217; open Tuesday to Sunday 8:30 am to 3 pm; admission Drs 800.* The museum houses finds from excavations at the Minoan settlement near Akrotiri, and from classical-era Thira town on the east coast. Superb Minoan frescoes from the former location may one day be exhibited here, if they can first be pried from the grasp of the National Archaeological Museum in Athens.

Nearby is the **Megara Gyzi Museum**, *Odos 25 Martiou; open Monday to Saturday 10:30 am to 1:30 pm and 5 to 8 pm, Sunday 10:30 am to 4 pm; admission Drs 400.* This museum has more contemporary exhibits, including photographs of Fira taken just before the 1956 earthquake.

Beside these two museums is the **Roman Catholic Cathedral** and the **Dominican Convent**. The **Greek Orthodox Cathedral** is a richly arcaded and domed edifice with a bell tower at the southern end of Odo Ipapantis.

Outside of Fira

Going north from Fira, you pass through the clifftop hamlets of **Imerovigli**, which has ruined mansions dating from before the 1956 earthquake, **Tourlos** and **Foinikia**, on the way to **Oia** at the northwest tip of the island. This village, thoroughly wrecked by the earthquake and rebuilt around the ruins, is the location for most of the stunning caldera-and-village photographs, which have all but come to define Greece, never mind Thira – although the view, so far from being typical, is unique. You can visit the small **Maritime Museum** here, *open Tuesday to Sunday 9 am noon and 4 to 7 pm; admission Drs 300.*

At the end of a 220-step descent of the cliff face you arrive at some small beaches and a nearby harbor from where caïques cross over to **Thirassia Island**.

The best black-sand beaches are south of Fira on the gentler east coast. **Kamari Beach** is the busiest, but there are also reasonable ones at **Monolithos**, **Perissa**, and south of Akrotiri at **Red Beach** and **White Beach**, so called because of the tint of the soil in the area.

Beside the coast south of Kamari are the ruins of **ancient Thira town**, a mostly Hellenistic-era settlement, but with elements dating back to the 7th century BC and onwards into Roman and Byzantine times. You can follow the **Sacred Way** from the **Temple of Apollo Karneiros** past the **Roman Theater**, the **Stoa Basilike**, **South Agora** and **North Agora**, to the **Temple of Dionysos**, among other vestiges of the town. For more information: *Tel. 0286/22217; open Tuesday to Sunday 8:30 am to 3 pm; admission Drs 500.*

On the way here you will have passed through high-sited **Pyrgos**, a pretty inland village surrounded by a medieval wall and with a Venetian-era **fortress**. The village has no fewer than 25 blue- and green-domed churches. From Pyrgos, a track continues up 566-meter **Mount Profitis Ilias**, which has a monastery and a radar station at the top, and a marvelous view over this strange, volcanic blister of an island.

Akrotiri, at the southwest coast, may be the least spoiled of Thira's coastal villages, although the popularity of the **Minoan-era town** that is being uncovered by ongoing excavation one kilometer to the south is beginning to change that (*Tel. 0286/81366; open Tuesday to Sunday 8:30 am to 3 pm; admission Drs 1,200*). Buried under lava and pumice from the volcanic eruption, the town hides an ancient mystery: was it destroyed by some event around 1628 BC unrelated to the volcanic eruption, and its remains then covered by the eruption of 1470 BC? You won't get many answers from a tour along the roofed-over wooden walkway among the houses so far uncovered, fascinating though the passage through the ancient town is. The site's magnificent early Cycladic frescoes, including those of two youths boxing, and a fleet leaving harbor, are safely ensconced well out of reach in Athens.

Offshore Islets

Off the main island, in the middle of the caldera lagoon, and reachable by tour boat, are the islets of **Nea Kameni**, which has a 140-meter volcano that smokes like a pack-a-day man; **Palea Kameni** and its hot-springs; and tiny **Aspronisi**.

The more substantial islet of **Thirassia** off the northwest coast of the main island is like a miniature version of its big brother, but with the caldera facing east instead of west, and is a good place to get away from the latter's sometimes wearing hustle and bustle. You'll get there either by car ferry to a landing slip in the north of the 7-kilometer-long island, or by caïque to the foot of the 300-step staircase from the port below **Manolas**, Thirassia's main village. The islet is mainly notable for its calm, its view of the lagoon and Thira across the way, and the **Church of Agia Irini**, which accounts for Thira's other name: Santorini.

SHOPPING

Gold, silver, jewelry, and designer-label clothes and scents are widely available in shops on and round Odos Agiou Mina and Odos Ipapantis in Fira.

EXCURSIONS & DAY TRIPS

There are plenty of excursions offered by the phalanx of travel agencies in and around Plateia Theotokopoulou in Fira. You can take tours by bus of the island and visit its beaches and ancient sites; tours by caïque of the lagoon in the crater caldera and of the volcanic islets in the lagoon; and tours to Thirassia island. These range from 3 hours duration to all the live-long day. Try:

• **Santo Volcano Tours & Travel**, *Plateia Theotokopoulou, Fira. Tel. 0286/ 22127, Fax 0286/22955.*
• **Damigos Tours**, *Plateia Theotokopoulou, Fira. Tel. 0286/22504, Fax 0286/22226.*

PRACTICAL INFORMATION

• **Banks & Currency Exchange** – The **National Bank of Greece** has a branch in *Odos Dekigala, behind Plateia Theotokopoulou.* It is open Monday through Friday from 8 am to 2 pm. American Express is represented by **X-Ray Kilo Travel and Shipping Agency**, *Plateia Theotokopoulou, Fira,* Tel. *0286/22624, Fax 0286/23600.*
• **Doctors** – **Fira Medical Center** is on the parallel road *to the east of Odos Dekigala beside the Santorini Hotel,* Tel. *0286/22238.*
• **Police** – The police station is in the south of Fira, *on Odos Dekigala,* Tel. *0286/22649.* The tourist police are at the same address andphone.
• **Port Authority** – Tel. *0286/22239*
• **Post Office** – The post office is south of the main square, set back from the road, *off Odos 25 Martiou.* It is open Monday through Friday from 7:30 am to 2 pm.
• **Telephone** – The area code for Thira is *0286.* The Greek Telecommunication Organization (OTE) office is south of the main square, *off Odos 25 Martiou.*

• **Tourist Office** – There is no tourist information office on Thira, and the many agencies that ostensibly offer such information are actually private agencies selling tours, accommodations, and other paid-for services.

14. RHODES

Rhodes (Rodos)

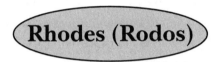

Tlepolemos, the son of Hercules, a great man and valiant, Contributed
nine ships of staunch Rhodians... From Lindos, Ialysos, and bright Kamiros.
Homer – The Iliad

Rhodes fully deserves to be one of the most popular islands of the Mediterranean, and it is. A beautiful, scented, green, diamond-shaped jewel of an island, it is the fourth biggest in Greece, and is possessed of a climate, scenery, and historical fascination matched by few others. It has superlative beaches and the backing of Helios, the sun god himself. These attractions add up to a floodtide of summertime visitors, who all but overwhelm the island's hotel space, beach space, and inner space. Rhodes has a 220-kilometer coastline: ruining it with package-tour development is a big job, but over the last 30 years it has gone a long way towards being done. Ruination of the entire island is a lot further off, thank heaven, and there are still plenty of places of escape in the interior and even at remoter parts of the west and south coasts.

In Greek mythology, **Helios** gave the island to his wife, the nymph **Rhoda**, who was the daughter of Poseidon and Aphrodite, and the sun god made the gift as beautiful as Rhoda was herself. The first traces of human habitation date from the neolithic period, and it is certain that the Minoans colonized the island, basing themselves at Ialysos. Later, the Achaeans took over and Homer records the Rhodians' contribution of ships and men for the war with Troy, mentioning the three main cities of Lindos, Ialysos, and Kamiros. The island fought, no doubt under duress, on the Persian side during their two great invasions of mainland Greece, and later backed Sparta in the Peloponnesian War against Athens.

It wasn't until Athens and Sparta were in decline, however, that Rhodes entered upon its golden age. In 408 BC, the three Rhodian cities united to found the city of Rhodes at the northernmost tip of the island, bringing in the top-rated architect Hippodamus of Miletus to design the city from the ground up. By all accounts it was among the most beautiful of the Greek world, adorned with many sculptures and crowned by the great **Temple of Helios**. With a powerful navy, the city exercised a thalassocracy, maritime control of the Aegean Sea.

In 305 BC came Rhodes's biggest test, when it was besieged by the Macedonian general Demetrius with an army of 40,000 and an array of awesome siege machinery, including the giant Helepolis which needed more than 3,000 men to move it. The Rhodians resisted valiantly and in the end Demetrius gave up the attempt, leaving behind all his siege equipment as a token of admiration for the defenders. These were sold to finance the building of a 35-meter bronze statue of Helios. Set up perhaps at the harbor, or perhaps in the grounds of the Temple of Helios, the **"Colossus of Rhodes"** became one of the seven wonders of the ancient world. It was toppled by the earthquake of 227 BC, and its giant fragments lay where they had fallen until the 8th century AD, when they were gathered up and sold for scrap metal.

Other than an occasional thorough devastation – Mithridates, Cassius, Arab and Ottoman raiders – not much happened in Rhodes until 1309, when the island was surrendered by the Byzantines to the Knights of Saint John of Jerusalem. These were a bunch of failed Crusaders who had been chased out of the Holy Land, and finally washed up on Rhodes. In their hands, Rhodes town became little more than a war machine, even if an

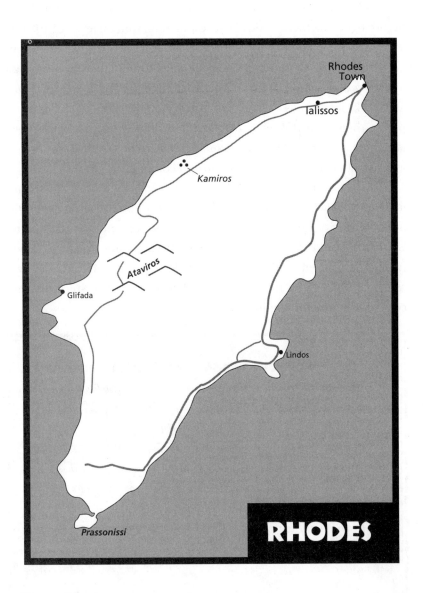

admittedly handsome one, a Christian fort deep in the territory of the expanding Ottoman empire.

The Turks knocked on the knights' gates unsuccessfully in 1480, before battering them in dead earnest in 1522 with an army of 100,000 against 650 knights and a thousand allies. Still, it took them six months to get inside and force the knights to capitulate. Rhodes then went through its four-century share of Greece's occupation by the Turks, an experience all Greeks look on as a collective historical nightmare. Unlike in other places, though, the Ottoman heritage has not been dug out by its roots, and there are surviving mosques and other signs of it in Rhodes town, as well as a small remaining ethnic Turkish community.

In 1912, Rhodes was signed over to the Italians. Under Mussolini's fascists, old buildings were restored and new ones built, each in the comic-opera style favored by the strutting would-be recreators of the Roman Empire. In 1944-45, the island underwent yet another siege, as Allied troops hammered its Nazi occupiers. Finally, in 1948, Rhodes was returned officially to the homeland it had never left in spirit through centuries of foreign domination – Greece.

RHODES FINDS & FAVORITES

• *Rhodes Old Town*. As marvelous a medieval spectacle as you will see anywhere in Europe, the Old Town attracts more as an ensemble than as a series of individual sights (see Rhodes Town).

• *Statue of Helios*. This is more of a try-to-find. Where did the great colossal statue of the sun god that was one of the seven wonders of the ancient world stand? Even the experts don't know for sure, so this is your chance to do some historical detective work (see Rhodes town).

Prassonissi Lighthouse. It marks the marvelously isolated southern tip of Rhodes and in summer you can walk to the tiny islet on which it stands (see Eastern Rhodes).

ARRIVALS & DEPARTURES
By Air
Rhodes's **Diagoras Airport** lies near Paradisi on the coast 16 kilometers southwest of Rhodes town, *Tel. 0241/91771.* At peak periods, **Olympic Airways** operates between four and six scheduled return flights a day to Rhodes from **Athens**, flying time 50 minutes. In addition, there are two flights a week from **Thessalonika**, flying time 1 hour 15 minutes; four a week from **Heraklion** (Crete), flying time 45 minutes; three a week from **Mykonos**, flying time 1 hour; between two and four a day from **Karpathos**, flying time 1 hour 10 minutes; one a day from **Kasos**, flying time 40 minutes; four a week from **Kastelorizo**, flying time 45 minutes; three a week from **Kos**, flying time 30 minutes; and three a week from **Thira** (Santorini), flying time 1 hour.

Rhodes makes a good alternative to Athens as a starting point for an island tour, particularly of the Dodecanese Islands, as it has very good connections within this group, making it none-too-risky to rely on being back on Rhodes in time for your return flight. International connections are one flight a week in summer from **Rome**, flying time 1 1/2 hours; one a week in July and August from **Larnaka** (Cyprus), flying time 55 minutes; and one a week in summer from **Beirut**, flying time 2 hours 5 minutes. There are masses of charter flights from all over northern Europe to Rhodes, from April through October. You book a charter flight from a travel agent in Europe, with the return set for between one and six weeks after departure. This will cost in the region of $200 to $300, depending on where you fly from and when.

For current departure flight times and ticket prices, contact Olympic Airways in Rhodes town, *Odos Ierou Lochou 9, Tel. 0241/24555.* Travel agents on the island can also book onward flights.

Taxi fare from the airport to Rhodes town center is around Drs 2,500.

By Sea
Between Rhodes and **Piraeus**, there are from one to three car ferries a day in summer, *Tel. 0241/23000 or 0241/77070.* Direct journey time is 14 hours; one-way deck tickets cost Drs 8,200.

Rhodes's best ferry connections are, naturally enough, with other islands of the **Dodecanese** group. In summer, there are car ferries, *Tel. 0241/23000 or 0241/77070*, to the following islands: two a week to **Astypalea**; two on most days to **Kalymnos**; between two and five a day to **Kos**; between one and four a day to **Leros**; one on most days to **Nissiros**; between one and four a day to **Patmos**; one on most days to **Symi**; between one and four a day to **Tilos**; and stops at other islands of the group depending on the ferries' variable timetables and route networks. As examples, journey time to Kos is normally 3 1/2 hours, and one-way deck tickets cost Drs 3,400; journey time to Patmos is around 9 hours, and one-way deck tickets cost Drs 5,250.

In addition, there are hydrofoil sailings in summer between Rhodes and these islands. These can be delayed or canceled by poor weather, and they typically cost more than twice as much for journeys that are about twice as fast as the ferries. **Samos**, **Ikaria**, and **Fourni**, to the north of the Dodecanese, have one hydrofoil connection a week, *Tel. 0241/24000*; journey time to Samos is 5 1/4 hours, and one-way tickets cost Drs 13,200.

Ios and **Thira** in the **Cyclades** group have connections with Rhodes twice a week, while **Paros** and **Syros** have connections once a week. There are two car ferries a week to **Crete**, *Tel. 0241/23000*; the ferry route is via the neighboring small island of **Halki**, and **Karpathos**. Journey time to Crete is 11 hours; one-way deck tickets cost Drs 6,300.

International car ferries sail between **Piraeus**, Rhodes, Limassol in **Cyprus**, and Haifa in **Israel** twice a week, *Tel. 0241/27900*. Journey time from Cyprus is 18 hours; one-way deck tickets cost Drs 15,000. There is also a daily service between Rhodes and **Marmaris** in Turkey, *Tel. 0241/27900*; journey time is 1 hour, and one-way tickets cost Drs 11,000.

ORIENTATION

With 1,400 square kilometers, Rhodes is the fourth biggest Greek island, and has a population of around 100,000, joined by as many as 900,000 tourists a year. It lies 11 kilometers off Turkey's southwest coast, and apart from tiny Kastellorizo is the easternmost Greek island, closing off the southeast corner of the Aegean.

The climate is about as perfect as you could hope for, with 300 days of sunshine annually, warm summers and moderate winters, and a rainy season that usually leaves enough precious liquid behind to fill the island with trees, plants, and flowers. In recent years, however, the rains have been uncertain at best, and water shortages threaten. Apart from the armies of your fellow-tourists, wind is the only problem you should encounter, with the breeze on the western side being notably stiff at times.

The island seems to hang suspended from **Rhodes town** at its northern tip, and stretches 78 kilometers to **Prassonissi Islet** at the southern tip. A mountainous spine runs along the island, more on the west side, but rising in waves fom either coast and culminating in 1,215-meter **Mount Ataviros** in the west center.

From Rhodes town, roads extend southwards along either coast. On the east side, it runs down through a line of resorts to **Faliraki**, **Archangelos**, and **Lindos**, an unbelievably busy resort that is also one of Rhodes's historical gems, and then on through quieter resorts to the southern tip. On the west side the road quickly hits what little is left of ancient **Ialysos**, then on past the airport at **Paradissi** to ancient **Kamiros**, and a series of smaller resorts and Byzantine and Crusader castles to the south.

The rugged interior is where you are more likely to find the real Rhodes, in farming and mountain villages that have not been taken by storm as the coast has been by the tourism boom.

GETTING AROUND THE ISLAND
By Bus

There are two bus stations in Rhodes town, and both lie within a few meters of each other. **East coast buses**, including those for Faliraki and Lindos, are operated by KTEL and run from Plateia Rimini outside the city wall to the north, *Tel. 0241/27706 or 24268*. **West coast buses**, including those for the airport and Kamiros, are operated by RODA and run from Odos Averof across the street from Plateia Rimini, *Tel. 0241/ 26300*. Tickets to the airport cost Drs 250, while those to more distant Lindos cost up to Drs 800, and the furthest points on the route network up to Drs 1,200.

There are ten buses a day to Kallithea, 13 to Faliraki, six to Lindos, 14 to Ialysos, 14 to the airport, two to Kamiros, and one or two a day passing through the main villages of the interior.

By Car

Among the many firms on the island, rental cars are available from:
• **Alamo**, *Rhodes Airport. Tel. 0241/81690; and Odos Mandilara 64, Rhodes town. Tel. 0241/38400*
• **Budget**, *Rhodes Airport. Tel. 0241/95103*
• **Hertz**, *Rhodes Airport. Tel. 0241/25888*
• **Europcar**, *Rhodes Airport. Tel. 0241/9310; and Odos 28 Oktovriou 18, Rhodes town. Tel. 0241/21958*

It's worth shopping around for good rates, bearing in mind that the cheapest cars and jeeps may be poorly maintained and lack vital fixtures and fittings, such as seatbelts that work. Some local firms give almost as good service as the international majors and are liable to charge less. One place I'd recommend is **Roderent**, *Odos Diakou 64, Rhodes town, Tel. 0241/ 31381.*

By Moped & Scooter

Mopeds, scooters, and off-road bikes, often in a more-or-less poorly maintained state, are widely available for rent throughout the island for between Drs 3,000 to Drs 4,000 a day. For fair dealing, go to **Kiriakos Rent-a-Moto**, *Odos Afstralias 2, Rhodes town, Tel. 0241/36047.*

By Taxi

You can pick up a cab in Rhodes town at the main taxi stand in Plateia Rimini, just outside the city wall, or call a radiocab, *Tel. 0241/27666.* There are usually taxis hanging around at the ferry terminal and outside major hotels, and always at the airport. All the resorts and some bigger villages have taxis.

RHODES TOWN

Rhodes town is really two separate towns, the **Old Town** and the **New Town**, separated by the impressive circuit of the **City Wall** built in the 15th and 16th centuries by the Knights of Saint John of Jerusalem. In the depths of summer both are frenetic places, though in different ways: the Old Town wears its Byzantine, Crusader, and Latin history on its sleeve and sells it as fast as it can in souvenir shops and on atmospheric taverna terraces in the shade of towering medieval battlements; the new part doesn't care overmuch for history, beyond maybe a red-eyed breakfast resumé of last night's riotous assembly at the disco.

In either case this town of 45,000 souls is the least "Greek-looking" of Greek towns, a curious confection of Crusader-era Christendom and Blackshirt-era Italy, through both of which expressions of foreign zealotry the Greek life of the place moves like a shadow on alien walls.

WHERE TO STAY

GRAND HOTEL ASTIR PALACE, *Akti Miaouli 1. Tel. 0241/26284, Fax 0241/35589. Rates (with tax): Drs 24,500 single; Drs 33,300 double; Drs 85,000 suites. Breakfast included. 378 rooms and suites. American Express, Diners Club, Visa, MasterCard.*

On the beach at the western end of the New Town, the Astir Palace is the top Rhodes town resort hotel, although there are comparable places on the beaches a few kilometers down the coast. If your definition of "characterful" has no place for the old and true, but instead revolves around service and plushly modern surroundings, then this may be for you. As these things go, you won't be paying overmuch for the privilege either. Air conditioned throughout, the hotel has a casino, bars, restaurants, 24-hour room service, and three swimming pools, and the rooms are equipped with all necessary facilities – necessary in a deluxe category hotel, that is.

SOTIRIS NIKOLIS, *Odos Ippodamou 61. Tel. 0241/34561, Fax 0241/32034. Rates (with tax): Drs 16,500 single; Drs 19,800 double. Breakfast Drs included. 10 rooms. American Express, Diners Club, Visa, MasterCard.*

In the western part of the Old Town, this is a well-equipped lodging in a characterful old building whose outside walls are covered with greenery and bordered with flowers. The rooms are furnished in a kind of rustic style, but also have telephone, minibar, private bathroom, and air conditioning. Breakfast is on the rooftop terrace, which has a magnificent view of the town and harbor, while in the interior courtyard there is a bar-restaurant.

KAMIROS, *Odos 25 Martiou 1. Tel. 0241/22591, Fax 0241/22349. Rates (with tax): Drs 14,400 single; Drs 19,800 double. Breakfast included. 48 rooms. American Express, Visa, MasterCard.*

At the begining of a street that runs westwards from Mandraki Harbor in the New Town, the Kamiros has a good position and backs this up with a recently renovated interior that offers comfort, though without much in the way of charm. The big air conditioned rooms all have a balcony and private bathroom.

PARIS, *Odos Agiou Fanouriou 88. Tel. 0241/26356. Rates (with tax): Drs 8,000 single; Drs 13,000 double. Breakfast included. 18 rooms. No credit cards.*

In the heart of the Old Town, the Paris has modern rooms, a friendly ambience, and good quality at a reasonable price.

CAVA D'ORO, *Odos Kisthiniou 17. Tel. 0241/36980, Fax 0241/77332. Rates (with tax): Drs 5,000 single; Drs 8,000 double. Breakfast included. 13 rooms. No credit cards.*

The youthful owners of this 14th-century building just inside the city walls on the east side are more than happy to share their knowledge of the town with you. White-painted, and with red shutters and a wooden balcony above the entrance, the Cava d'Oro is among the most characterful of Rhodes town hotels, settling you into the atmosphere of the Old Town from the moment you arrive. All rooms have private facilities. If you hear someone talking about a dead parrot or singing the praises of Finland, it may be due to the lingering influence of Monty Python's Michael Palin, who stayed here while filming his *Pole to Pole* series for the BBC.

TEHERAN, *Odos Sophocleous 41b. Tel. 0241/27594. Rates (with tax): Drs 6,600 double. Breakfast included. 7 rooms. No credit cards.*

More or less typical of the budget hotels in Rhodes town, and with the added frisson of its name, the Teheran has a central location, isn't too noisy, and has sparely furnished but comfortable rooms.

WHERE TO EAT

FOTIS, *Odos Menekleous 8. Tel. 0241/27359. Drs 3,000 to Drs 6,000. No credit cards. Seafood/traditional.*

In a sidestreet off Odos Sokratous in the Old Town, Fotis is a touch more upmarket and genuinely Greek than the general run of Rhodes tavernas. The seafood dishes are especially recommended, although meat is also on the menu.

SYMPOSIUM, *Odos Archelaou 3. Tel. 0241/37509. Drs 3,000 to Drs 5,000. No credit cards. Seafood/traditional.*

A fairly calm place in what can be a frantic part of the Old Town. You eat outside in the garden in summer. Though not exclusively serving seafood, the fish dishes are the best on the Symposium's menu.

KOSTAS HADJIKOSTAS, *Odos Pythagorou 62. Tel. 0241/26217. Drs 2,500 to Drs 5,000. No credit cards. Traditional.*

A slightly chaotic kind of place in the Old Town, where you can never be exactly sure if what you order will actually appear on your plate, or when. Still, the atmosphere is jovial and welcoming and whatever food does appear is usually fine.

LINDOS, *Plateia Vasileos Pavou. Tel. 0241/24421. Drs 2,500 to Drs 5,000. No credit cards. Traditional.*

One of the better budget choices in the New Town, and about as far north as you can go on Rhodes without actually eating your seafood in the water. Greek standards like moussaka join hands on the menu with a variety of more familiar dishes, such as spaghetti.

SEEING THE SIGHTS

Sailing into **Rhodes town** can be a little disappointing, because the ferry glides past lovely little **Mandraki Harbor**, where you would ideally like to land, and ties up at the nondescript commercial port to its east (the big ferries, that is: hydrofoils, tour-boats, and inter-island caïques use Mandraki). Still, a couple of minutes walk brings you back to Mandraki and you can see what you missed on the way in. What you missed are a line of windmills on the east mole, the 15th-century **Fort Saint Nicholas**, a bronze sculpted doe and stag, each one standing atop a stone column at either side of the harbor inlet, and a harbor filled with fancy yachts. Somewhere in this area may have stood the ancient **Colossus of Rhodes**, the 35-meter statue of Helios, the sun god, but exactly where it was, your guess is as good as mine – apparently not astride the harbor entrance as medieval tradition imagined.

The Old Town is where you'll arrive first on foot from the boat, although you likely won't want to go exploring it until you've disposed of your luggage somewhere. You'll notice the walls first, and if you want to clamber around the battlements you have to do this on a **guided tour**, *Tel. 0241/35945*. These leave every Tuesday and Saturday at 2:45 pm from the **Grand Master's Palace** (aka Palace of the Knights) in the northwest corner of the old town, *Plateia Kleovoulou, Tel. 0241/23359; open Tuesday to Sunday 8 am to 7 pm; admission Drs 1,200*. It takes the best part of two hours to do the 4-kilometer circuit, and you get a good view of the town and the harbor and, if you have a particularly vivid imagination, you might be able to imagine thousands of Ottoman troops charging wildly at you while you sight your arquebus on the whites of their eyes. In any case you'll get your fill of battlements, bastions, fosses, fortified gates, ravelins, and other such delicate expressions of the military art.

The vast 14th-century palace itself, with its 300 rooms and turreted battlements, is well worth a visit. While you're in the imagining business, you might also imagine the vanished Temple of Helios which once stood on this spot, perhaps watched over by the colossal statue of the sun god, and ask yourself if the trade was a good one. The palace was totally rebuilt during the 1940s after having been blown to bits in 1856 by the explosion of an unsuspected powder store. The Italian rebuilders even "improved" on the original by embellishing the floors with ancient Greek mosaics lifted from the neighboring island of Kos – wasn't that downright thoughtful of them? Part of the palace is devoted to an exhibition on Rhodes's history.

Running down from Plateia Kleovoulou is **Odos Ippoton**, otherwise known as the Street of the Knights. You may think yourself transported back in time on this street, or at any rate to a medieval film set. It is lined with the "Inns" that were once the headquarters of the knights' various national groups, called "Tongues." These are now occupied by modern offices, but you'll see the heraldic arms of the Inn of the Tongue of France, the Inn of the Tongue of Spain, the Inn of the Tongue of Italy, etc. You can, as a matter of fact, speak in tongues as you stroll along this long and narrow cobbled street, which is one of the most perfect and extravagant examples of the Gothic style anywhere.

At the bottom end you arrive at Plateia Moussiou and the cluster of places of interest in and around the square, the most notable being the **Archaeological Museum**, *Tel. 0241/27657; open Tuesday to Sunday 8 am to 7 pm; admission Drs 800*. Formerly the Hospital of the Knights, there are exhibits dating from the Homeric to the Crusader eras on Rhodes. There is a sculpted **head of Helios**, the sun god, perhaps similar to that of the long-vanished Colossus. One of the most beautiful pieces is a small sculpture dating from the 1st century BC, called the **Bathing Aphrodite**, of a crouching nude woman arranging her hair. Lawrence Durell, who named his book on Rhodes *Reflections on a Marine Venus* in the statue's honor, wrote: "She sits in the Museum of the island now, focused intently upon her own inner life, gravely meditating upon the works of time."

Adjacent to this building is the solidly built (everything is solidly built around here) 13th-century Church of Our Lady of the Castle, which the Turks transformed into a mosque and the Italians retransformed into a church, and which now houses the **Byzantine Museum**, *Tel. 0241/27674; open Tuesday to Sunday 8:30 am to 3 pm; admission Drs 600*. Icons glow in the gloomy interior along with other works of religious art.

A little north of here, on Plateia Symis beside the **Eleftherias Gate** in the city wall, are the fragmentary remains of the 3rd-century BC **Temple of Aphrodite**. You can see all there is to see of it by looking over the fence.

Parallel to Odos Ippoton, to the south, is Odos Sokratous, which runs into Odos Aristotelous, these two streets forming the Old Town's main commercial axis. In Plateia Martiron Evreon at the eastern end of Odos Aristotelous, is a fountain with bronze seahorses. This square is dedicated to Rhodes's victims of the Holocaust: of some 2,000 Jews who lived on the island, most of them in the Jewish Quarter around the square, only about 50 survived the war. Off the square, further along Odos Dossiadou, is the restored **Synagogue**, *Tel. 0241/27344*, which is usually closed except when a service is being held.

In the other direction, at the top end of Odos Sokratous, is the magnificent **Süleiman Mosque**, dedicated by the victorious Ottoman Sultan Süleiman the Magnificent to his magnificent self. Originally dating from 1522, it was rebuilt in 1808. Its minaret would offer a fine, muezzin's-eye-view of the city if only you were allowed in. Opposite is a **Turkish Library** dating from 1793, with a 16th-century illuminated Koran among its collection of books.

In the New Town, beyond the walls on the north side, you get to see what Italians, inspired by fascism and Mussolini's fantasy of a recreated Roman Empire, got up to in their spare time. "Bombast" is the word that springs to mind to describe the edifying edifices they built here. As you walk north through the harborfront Plateia Eleftherias, and on to Odos Vasileos Konstantinou (marked as Odos Papanikolaou on some maps), you pass in succession the arcades of the **New Market**, the **Bank of Greece**, the **Palace of Justice**, the **Church of Saint John the Evangelist**, with a campanile overlooking the harbor, and the **Town Hall**.

At the corner of Odos Vasileos Konstantinou is the Turkish **Mosque of Murad-Reis**, with the little **Villa Cleobolous**, where Lawrence Durrell lived, in the grounds, and an Ottoman cemetery. Rhodes town's **Casino** stands at the western end of Odos Papanikolaou, while if you turn north into the tip of the point which marks the end of the island, you arive at the **Aquarium**, in the basement of the **Hydrobiological Station of Rhodes**, *Tel. 0241/27308; open daily April through October 9 am to 9 pm, November through March 9 am to 4:30 pm; admission Drs 600 adults, Drs 400 children.* One of the main themes of the exhibits is the threatened survival of many Mediterranean species such as the green turtle. There are display tanks showing typical habitats and the fish and other marine creatures that depend on them.

West of the town lies a low green hill called **Monte Smith** after some obscure British admiral or other, which is about as ordinary a name as you could imagine for the hill that was ancient Rhodes's acropolis, and on which Italian archaeologists clumped together bits and pieces of broken columns to "recreate" part of the vanished **Temple of Pythian Apollo**. In this area are also a restored **stadium** and **theater**, and nearby, scant remains of the **Temple of Zeus and Athena**.

Other Sights

- **Municipal Art Gallery**, *Plateia Simi. Tel. 0241/35945. Open Monday to Saturday 8 am to 2 pm. Admission Drs 500.* Features works by local artists.
- **Decorative Arts Museum**, *Plateia Simi. Tel. 0241/27674. Open Sunday to Saturday 8:30 am to 3 pm. Admission Drs 500.* Folklore and crafts exhibits from Rhodes and other Dodecanese islands, including costumes and a recreated room in a traditional house.

NIGHTLIFE & ENTERTAINMENT

- **Moustafa Baths** (Turkish Hamam), *Plateia Arionos. Open Tuesday to Saturday 7 am to 7 pm. Admission Drs 900 on Tuesday, Wednesday, and Friday; Drs 300 on Thursday and Saturday.* Always wanted to try a Turkish bath but never had the opportunity? Here's your chance. You can experience the marble floors and basins and the domed chambers of this 18th-century hamam by taking a Turkish bath. The sexes are segregated inside.
- **Nelly Dimoglou Dance Theater**, *Old Town Open-Air Theater, Odos Andronikou (near the Süleiman Mosque and Turkish Baths). Tel. 0241/ 20157 or 29085. Performances at 9:20 pm. May 10 to June 20 Thursday only, June 20 to October 30 Sunday to Friday. Admission Drs 1,000.* Top-quality traditional Greek folk dancing at this fun an charming venue in the Old Town.
- **Sound-and-Light Show**, *Municipal Garden, Plateia Rimini. Tel. 0241/ 21922. Performances between April 1 and October 31 three times daily from Tuesday to Saturday and twice daily on Sunday and Monday, beginning at 8:15 pm (from mid-May to end-July the performances start at 9:15 pm).* Tells the story of Rhodes at the time of the Knights of Saint John.
- **National Theater**, *Odos Vasileos Konstantinou. Tel. 0241/29678.* Music, opera, and dance are on the bill here, in addition to theater. Call to find out what's playing when you're in town.

WESTERN RHODES

The west coast in summer is flayed by the *meltemi* wind from the Aegean, which cools things more than most beachhounds appreciate, so they mostly congregate on the east coast. This means that if you don't want to be part of a mob on the beach you should go west, young man. Of course, most of the young women will be going east to perfect their topless tans.

See *Getting Around The Island*, above, for transport options to Western Rhodes.

WHERE TO STAY

NYMFE, *Salakos. Tel. 0241/22206. Rates (with tax): Drs 18,000 double. Breakfast included. 4 rooms. No credit cards.*

Salakos is in the hills behind Kamiros, some 39 kilometers southwest of Rhodes town. The Nymfe is as small as it is special, and claims to be the second oldest hotel on Rhodes. Dating from the turn of the century, it brings a tiny touch of belle époque splendor to an island awash with concrete monstrosities. Its rooms are furnished in period style, and in the tree-shaded garden is a small cafe terrace.

THOMAS, *Monolithos. Tel. 0246/61291, Fax 0246/28834. Rates (with tax): Drs 6,000 single; Drs 8,000 double. Breakfast included. 9 rooms. No credit cards.*

In a part of the island where accommodation is scarce other than in private homes, the Thomas's nine comfortable rooms stand out as a valuable resource. Monolithos is three kilometers from the nearest beach, but peope come here more for the mountain scenery and the peace and quiet than for the beaches.

WHERE TO EAT

JOHNNY'S, *Skala Kamirou. Tel. 0246/31342. Drs 3,500 to Drs 6,000. No credit cards. Seafood/traditional.*

Just outside the tiny fishing village of Kamiros Skala, Johnny's takes advantage of the fish coming ashore to make some reasonable seafood dishes.

GREEK TAVERNA, *Monolithos. Tel. 0246/61245. Drs 2,500 to Drs 4,000. No credit cards. Traditional.*

An odd name for a restaurant, yet accurate enough, as it sure is a taverna that sells Greek food. It's no more special than many other such places, but then there aren't many other such places on this part of the coast. The taverna also has a few room for rent.

SEEING THE SIGHTS

The coast from Rhodes to beyond the airport can be fairly described as one big hotel complex. **Trianda** has a long beach, and the frequent strong winds in his area makes the sea here a tough test for windsurfers.

You can turn inland at Trianda towards the 267-meter rocky hill called **Philerimos**, for the superb view, and the ruins of ancient **Ialysos** at the top, (*Filerimos Hill, Tel. 0241/27674; open Saturday, Sunday and Monday 8:30 am to 3 pm; Tuesday to Friday 8 am to 7 pm; admission Drs 800).* The problem with the ruins of ancient Ialysos is that there aren't many of them, although the foundations of a 3rd-century BC **Temple Athena Ialysia** and a 4th-century BC **Doric fountain** decorated with four lion heads, are among the bits and pieces that have been identified.

In possible compensation, there are the four chapels of the Knights' of Saint John's **Church of Our Lady of Philerimos**, with the order's eight-pointed cross a prominent symbol, as well as the frescoes of the underground Byzantine **Chapel of Agios Georgios**.

Further south, 25 kilometers from Rhodes town, you'll find the **Petaloudes Valley**, otherwise known as the **Valley of the Butterflies**, *open 9 am to 6 pm; admission Drs 300.* The valley is populated by a dense throng of gaily colored creatures flitting constantly from one spot to another and filling the air with a tremulous flutter – and that's only the tourists. They are here to see masses of moths, which local publicists would really prefer to have been butterflies, filling their probosces with scented stuff from the many styrax trees in this lovely little valley traversed by a stream with a series of tiny waterfalls. The hapless moths probably wonder what they've done to attract all this attention, as the Petoulades Valley is now an essential fixture on all summertime tour-group itineraries.

On the main bus route out of Rhodes town, and some 35 kilometers south of there, along a coast dotted with pebble beaches and little in the way of beach accommodations, are the ruins of ancient **Kamiros**, overlooking the sea, *Tel. 0241/27674; open Tuesday to Friday 8:30 am to 5 pm; Saturday and Sunday 8:30 am to 3 pm; admission Drs 800.*. This city has weathered the turbulent centuries far better than Ialysos, and you can see the remains of houses, one of which has a partly restored colonnade, the agora, a stoa, and the **Temple of Athena**.

Southwards, after another 15 kilometers is the small port of **Kamiros Skala**, from where caïque tours leave for **Halki** island, a desolate and dried-up little place that presents a surprising contrast with lushly covered Rhodes across the water. Kamiros Skala is a good place to turn inland if you're driving, to climb the foothills of **Mount Ataviros**, passing through **Embona**, a village noted for its costumed folk dancing on summer evenings, and on to the monastery-flecked slopes of **Mount Profitis Ilias**. A few kilometers beyond the port is **Kastellos**, a small outlying castle of the Knights of Saint John.

Beyond this, there are few landmarks on the rugged coast – although there is an isolated beach on **Glifada Bay** – until the small village of **Monolithos**, near which is another Crusader castle, atop a 160-meter cliff with a magnificent view of the west coast and across to the distant haze of Turkey. This is as far as the bus goes. If you are driving, you can continue around the wide sweep of **Apolakia Bay**, maybe stopping at deserted pebbly beaches on the way to the far south of the island.

EASTERN RHODES

The more sheltered east coast with its fine sandy beaches is Rhodes's resortland. It is hard to blame it for being so, considering its natural advantages, but you could wish that it was a bit less so to allow you to enjoy it more. Fact is that most of this part of the island gets so packed in the depths of summer with package-tour visitors that you'll be hard put to find hotel accommodation unless you reserve well in advance.

See *Getting Around The Island*, above, for transport options to Eastern Rhodes.

WHERE TO STAY

ATRIUM PALACE, *Kalathos, near Lindos. Tel. 0244/31601, Fax 0244/ 31600. Rates (with tax): Drs 23,000 single; Drs 32,000 double; Drs 72,000 suite. Breakfast included. 171 rooms and suites. American Express, Diners Club, Visa, MasterCard.*

Close to the beach at Kalathos, 6 kilometers north of Lindos, the Atrium Palace is the ultimate Rhodes resort hotel. It surely goes without saying that it is air conditioned throughout, has an outdoor swimming pool with adjacent children's pool and a heated indoor pool, interior and poolside restaurants and bars, 24-hour room service, health and fitness center, tennis, table tennis, volleyball and sea sports facilities, games room, children's playroom, hairdresser and shops, and that all rooms have telephone, radio, satellite television, minibar, balcony, and private bathrooms with bath, shower and hairdryer – doesn't it?

ELEKTRA, *Lindos. Tel. 0244/31266. Rates (with tax): Drs 13,000 double. No breakfast. 10 rooms. No credit cards.*

Possibly the best of the many small pensions in Lindos, and certainly the biggest, the Elektra makes quite a contrast to the Atrium Palace. Cosy and intimate, with plainly furnished but clean rooms, it has a verandah and its own small garden. There are facilities for preparing your own breakfast.

WHERE TO EAT

In **Lindos** there are more than 30 tavernas, most of them entirely tourist-oriented, and none of them contrives to stand out much from the others. Some that are alright are **STEFANI**, which has a good view of the town and the sea from its terrace; **DIONYSOS** and **MAVRIKOS**, both seafood specialists; **MARIA'S**, where the local people go; and the busy but well-placed **TRITON**, on the beach.

SEEING THE SIGHTS

You can essentially trip from beach to beach here, stopping at the more interesting sights on the way. The first of these is **Kalithea**, an Italian spa resort built in the 1920s and whose mineral springs are now closed, but still notable for their bizarre architecture. The underwater sea-caves here make a popular target for diving excursions.

Continuing south, **Faliraki** is one of the biggest and busiest beach resorts anywhere, with nightlife every bit as hot as the summer sun. You need a stronger word than "crowded" to describe the beaches: count yourself lucky to find space to lie down. A couple of kilometers south of this beach, around rocky **Cape Ladiko**, are some smaller, tree-shaded, and very nearly deserted beaches.

The picture is crowded down through **Afandou Beach**, which has a fine golf course, to **Kolimbia** and the busy **Tsambika Beach**. At Kolimbia you can drive or ride a moped (or even walk) inland for five kilometers to **Epta Piges**, "Seven Springs," a cool green place focused on a lake fed by the aforementioned seven springs. **Archangelos** and **Haraki** both have pretty villages at their cores and are further distinguished by their Crusader-era **castles**.

Finally, 55 kilometers south of Rhodes, you arrive at **Lindos**, a town that was famed in ancient times for its superb acropolis, second only to that of Athens, and that is renowned throughout the spaced-out universe today as the place where Pink Floyd has a villa. If you know the tune to "Money," from the *Dark Side of the Moon* album, you might want to hum it here on the bright side side of the sun, because you'll need plenty of that commodity in Lindos. The town specializes in legally picking visitors' pockets clean.

To be fair, it is handsome beyond easy description, a cluster of white village-Cubist houses trailing in narrow, traffic-free streets above the beach, along the flanks of a steep, rocky hill topped by a stout 13th-century **castle** of the Knights of Saint John, and the ancient **Acropolis of Lindos**, *Tel. 0244/31258; open Monday to Friday 8 am to 7 pm, Saturday and Sunday 8:30 am to 3 pm; admission Drs 800.* You can hire a donkey for Drs 1,000 to make the 125-meter ascent in comfort, if you can consider riding a donkey comfortable. Partway up is an ancient relief of a Rhodian trireme sculpted into the hillside. Considerable parts of the great **Doric Stoa** and **Temple of Athena Lindia**, an important place of pilgrimage dating from the 6th century BC, have survived.

To get into more tranquil parts, you can turn inland into the hills studded with monasteries and sleepy villages where all the young folk with get-up-and-go have got up and gone to the towns and resorts – "How you gonna keep 'em down on the farm?" is a question with as much relevance in Rhodes as in Nebraska.

In fact, if you just keep going south on the coast road things get more tranquil by degrees. This is notable at the beaches along **Lardos Bay** and **Gennadi Bay**, down to **Cape Lahania** – that has a nice Hawaiian sound to it, don't you think? An 8-kilometer rough track favored by the 4-wheel-drive crowd leads to isolation personified by the **Prassonissi Lighthouse** at the island's southern tip. In summer you can walk across a narrow sandy neck to the the tiny islet at land's end on which the lighthouse stands. On its east coast you can soak up the sun in relative isolation.

PRACTICAL INFORMATION FOR ALL OF RHODES

- **Banks & Currency Exchange** – There are plenty of banks and currency exchanges. Most banks are open Monday through Friday from 8 am to 2 pm (1:30 pm on Friday). A few in the resorts operate an extended tourist service in summer from 5 to 7 pm on weekdays and 8 am to 2 pm on weekends. The **National Bank of Greece** has a branch at *Plateia Kyprou, Rhodes town, Tel. 0241/27031*. American Express is represented by **Rhodes Tours Ltd**, *Odos Amochostou 23, Rhodes town, Tel. 0241/21010, Fax 0241/74025*. Thomas Cook has offices at *Odos Sofokli Venizelou 6, Rhodes town, Tel. 0241/27482, Fax 0241/35672*. Hotels will exchange most convertible foreign currencies and traveler's checks, but at a poorer rate than the banks. German marks, British pounds, US dollars, French francs, and Italian lire are the currencies favored by owners of small hotels, tavernas and shops.
- **Bookstores** – In Rhodes town, a reasonable selection of English-language books can be found at the **Academy Bookstore**, *Odos Dragoumi 7, Tel. 0241/20254*.
- **Churches** – Services are held in English every Saturday and Sunday at the **Saint Francis Roman Catholic Church**, *Odos Dimokratias 28, Rhodes town, Tel. 0241/23605*.

- **Doctors** – Your hotel should have a list of local English-speaking doctors. In an emergency, phone *100* for an ambulance. In less urgent cases, contact **Rhodes General Hospital**, *Odos Erithrou Stavrou, Rhodes town, Tel. 0241/22222 or 25555.*
- **Maps** – A good tourist map of the island, with a street map of Rhodes town on the back can be bought from most news vendors, souvenir shops, and hotel shops for Drs 500.
- **News & Information** – Day-old British newspapers are widely available. The *International Herald Tribune, USA Today,* and the international editions of *Time* and *Newsweek* can be bought at newsstands. The local English-language weekly *Rodos News* is free and available at hotels and in the tourist information office, while the daily *Athens News* is on sale for Drs 250.
- **Police** – In emergencies call *100*. The main police station is on *Odos Ethalondon Dodekanission, Rhodes town, Tel. 0241/23294.* The tourist police, for lost property, general assistance and reporting complaints against service providers, are on *Plateia Moussiou, Rhodes town, Tel. 0241/27423.*
- **Port Authority** – *Tel. 0241/28666*
- **Post Office** – The main post office in Rhodes town opposite Mandraki Harbor, *off Plateia Eleftherias.* It is open Monday through Friday from 7 am to 8 pm, Saturday 8 am to 2:30 pm, Sunday 9 am to 1:30 pm. Local post offices are open Monday through Friday from 7:30 am to 2 pm.
- **Telephone** The area code for Rhodes town and surroundings is *0241*; from Kolymbia southward on the east coast *0244;* from Kalavarda southwards on the west coast *0246.* The main Greek Telecommuni- cation Organization (OTE) office in Rhodes town is at *Odos Amerikis 91, Tel. 0241/24499.*
- **Tourist Office** – The Greek Tourist Organization (EOT) office for Rhodes is at the corner of *Odos Makariou and Odos Papagou, Rhodes town, Tel. 0241/23255.* Rhodes town's own Tourist Information Office is at *Plateia Rimini, Tel. 0241/35945.*

ANYONE FOR RHETORIC?

*No one in ancient Rhodes would ever have dreamed of saying: "Is that a rhetorical question, or is there a point in there somewhere?" Everyone was a rhetorician on an island that housed the Mediterranean world's most famous school of rhetoric. Founded by the Athenia orator **Aeschines** around 330 BC, the school later taught some of the noblest Romans of them all, including Cicero and Julius Caesar, how to speak proper.*

15. CYPRUS

I will sing of stately Aphrodite,
gold-crowned and beautiful,
Whose dominion is the walled cities
of all sea-set Cyprus.
There the moist breath of the West Wind
wafted her over the waves
of the loud-moaning sea.
Homeric Hymn to Aphrodite

Cyprus is "Aphrodite's Island" because it is where in Greek mythology Aphrodite, the goddess of love, was born, drifting ashore on a seashell from the wine-dark sea, as the Homeric *Hymn to Aphrodite* tells it. Cyprus has taken "laughter-loving" Aphrodite to its heart ever since, and who can blame it?

Sunshine, blue skies, beaches, fields of grapes ripening in the sun, orange and lemon groves, a multicolored carpet of flowers in spring, wild mountain ranges, cedar forests, remote villages, Stone Age tombs, Persian palaces, Greek temples, Roman mosaics, Byzantine monasteries,

Crusader castles, Gothic abbeys, Arab mosques, Turkish bath-houses, Imperial British hill stations – where else but Cyprus?

The island has always been a crossroads of civilization, and even if some of the civilizations that passed through this busy intersection weren't all that civilized they left the signature of their passing in ruined historic sites without number. Enough marvels have been brought to light all over the island to make scrambling around ancient ruins a major component of any visit.

Much blood has flowed across the rocky landscape and periods of absolute chaos have been common. Yet Cyprus has enjoyed long periods of peace. Between its incorporation into the empire of **Alexander the Great** in the 4th century BC, through the Roman and early Byzantine period, until devastating Arab raids began in the 7th century, Cyprus knew almost a thousand years of peace.

Cyprus is not Greece, although many of its people are of Greek origin and consider themselves to be Greek – kind of. The **Republic of Cyprus** is an independent country and has a seat at the United Nations. However, more than one-third of the island's territory has been occupied by Turkey since 1974 in contravention of UN resolutions, and the **UN Peacekeeping Force in Cyprus** (UNFICYP) mans a thin blue line (actually referred to as the green line) across the island between the Turkish and Cypriot armies.

Despite this sad background, and ill-informed opinion to the contrary, Cyprus is neither a dangerous nor a violent place. The reverse is true. It is a holiday island par excellence that extends a warm welcome to visitors and offers them much in return. True, it suffers from overdevelopment along parts of its coastline, but that is not exactly unusual in the Mediterranean. The political situation does have certain practical effects, the most important of which is that entry to the occupied north of the island is considered illegal by the Cypriot government and can result in denial of permission to enter that part of Cyprus under government control, as well as Greece.

Nicosia is the capital, a city divided between Greek Cypriots and Turkish Cypriots and lying in the middle of the island, at the heart of the agricultural Mesaoria Plain.

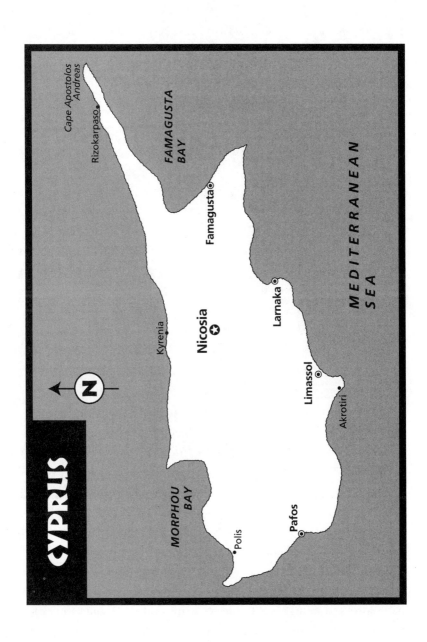

CYPRUS FINDS & FAVORITES

• **Akamas Peninsula.** *A wild and scenic area, almost untouched by the hand of man, which may become a national park (see Pafos).*

• **Greek Theatre, Kourion.** *It was a pretty stunning place to see a Greek play performed more than 2,000 years ago, and it still is today (see Around Limassol).*

• **Yiangos and Peter.** *A very traditional Cypriot restaurant at Latsi where the folks are downhome and you eat freshly caught seafood beside the fishing harbor (see Pafos).*

• **Lefkara.** *The village gets busy in summer but it is well worth seeing the women sitting outdoors creating their superb handmade lace – some pieces take a year and more to finish (see Larnaka).*

• **Panagia tou Kykkou.** *All the pride of the Orthodox Church in Cyprus, which guarded the flame of Hellenism and the memory of Byzantium through centuries of foreign domination, can be experienced at this mountaintop monastery (see Troodos Mountains).*

• **Forest Park Hotel.** *You can't do better than take yourself away from the beaches up into the cool, scented air of the Troodos Mountains to this excellent hill station hotel at Platres (see Troodos Mountains).*

• **Panagia Angeloktistos.** *For its spellbindingly beautiful and vanishingly rare early Byzantine mosaic of the Virgin and Child (see Larnaka).*

• **Kolossi Castle.** *Stride around pretending to be a Crusader knight at this Commandery of the Knights of the Order of the Hospital of St John of Jerusalem (see Limassol).*

The south coast around **Agia Napa** and **Protaras** exists purely to offer the place of escape that many sun-starved north Europeans crave (and has done so to such an extent that it is running into trouble, as holidaymakers resist the heaped-up hotels it offers). Further west **Larnaka** and **Limassol** have sprouted "wings," in the hotel strips that reach out either side of them along the coast. In the far west, **Pafos** is fast developing as a big resort area but has some way to go before it gets as "spoiled" as the others.

North of Pafos lies the even smaller and more homely resorts of **Polis** and **Latsi** leading to the **Akamas Peninsula** wilderness area which is slated to become a national park. The coast east of Polis is remote and almost untouched.

Just a little way back from the hard commercial carapace along the shore you enter a different Cyprus, a place of timeless villages and rugged scenery, reaching up to the windy heights of the **Troodos Mountains** in the west and the **Pentadaktylos Mountains** in the north. There are Byzantine monasteries and churches, Crusader castles, and hard-working farmers who turn out a cornucopia of fruits, vegetables, and grapes for wine.

As well as the Pentadaktylos Range, the Turkish-occupied north has the historic walled city of **Famagusta** on the eastern coast and the harbor town of **Kyrenia** on the northern, as well as most of the Mesaoria and Morfou Plain. The long thin finger of the **Karpas Peninsula** pointing towards Syria and Turkey ends at rocky **Cape Apostolos Andreas**.

NICOSIA

The capital of Cyprus, **Nicosia** (known to Greek Cypriots as **Lefkosia**), located more or less in the middle of the island, is the world's last divided city. Ringed by the perfect circle of **Venetian Walls** that failed miserably to protect it in 1570 when the Turks came calling, the old city retains much Ottoman grace along with relics of Byzantine and Crusader times. The government buildings are here, including the **Presidential Palace**, the even more impressive **Archbishop's Palace**, and some of the island's finest mosques.

Beyond the city in the great agricultural area of the **Mesaoria** and the **Morfou Plain** there is less of tourist interest, although the rustic charm and tranquility of the place have their own attraction and there is a scattering of isolated historic churches and monasteries. One of the astonishing things is the number of rough trails that go seemingly nowhere and take their own sweet time getting there. They are ideal for mountain bikes or off-road bikes, even if in the withering heat of a Cypriot summer most people prefer to go by jeep.

ARRIVALS & DEPARTURES

Nicosia International Airport has been closed since 1974 and is presently the main UN base in Cyprus. This situation could change, as reopening the airport is one of the "confidence-building measures" regularly proposed by the UN as a means of moving the Cyprus problem forward. Nothing has ever come of this in the past, so don't hold your breath.

You'll likely arrive in Nicosia from **Larnaka International Airport**, either by private taxi, hotel bus, or hired car. No public buses, airline coaches (other than those for package-tour visitors with pre-booked accommodation), or service (shared) taxis run to or from the airport.

By Bus

The inter-city bus stations are at Leoforos Leonidou, Constanza Bastion and Plateia Dionysou Solomou.

Larnaka to Nicosia: Kallenos Buses, Monday through Friday 6:30, 8, 9, 10:30 am, 1, 2:30, 4 pm; Saturday 7, 9, 11 am, 1 pm.

Nicosia to Larnaka: Kallenos Buses, Monday through Friday 8:30, 10:30 am, 1, 2:30, 4, 5:45, 6:30 pm; Saturday xxxx.

Limassol to Nicosia: Costas Buses, Monday, Tuesday, Thursday, Friday 9:30, 10:30 am; Wednesday, Saturday 9:30 am. Kemek Transport, Monday through Friday 6:30, 9 am, 2, 4 pm; Saturday 7 am, noon, 2:30 pm.

Nicosia to Limassol: Costas Buses, Monday, Tuesday, Thursday, Friday noon, 4 pm; Saturday 1 pm (buses continue to Pafos). Kemek Transport, Monday through Friday 6:30, 7:30, 9 am, noon, 2, 4 pm; Saturday 7, 10 am, 2:30 pm.

By Service Taxi

These are shared taxis that run at approximately hourly intervals between Nicosia and Larnaka and Nicosia and Limassol. Other services connect Limassol and Pafos. The "taxis" are actually minibuses which collect and pick up within the urban center or can be boarded at the dispatch office, and drop off either within the urban center of the destination or at the dispatch office.

Service Taxis: Nicosia to Larnaka
• **Acropolis Taxis**, *Leoforos Stasinou 9. Tel. 02/472525*
• **Kyriakos Taxis**, *Leoforos Stasinou 27. Tel. 02/444141*
• **Makris Taxis**, *Leoforos Stasinou 11. Tel. 02/466201*

Service Taxis: Nicosia to Limassol
• **Karydas Taxis**, *Leoforos Omirou 8. Tel. 02/462269*
• **Kypros Taxis**, *Leoforos Stasinou 9a. Tel. 02/464811*
• **Kyriakos Taxis**, *Leoforos Stasinou 27. Tel. 02/444141*
• **Makris Taxis**, *Leoforos Stasinou 11. Tel. 02/466201*

ORIENTATION

The first thing to know about Nicosia is that the heart of the old city is cut in two from west to east, along a line traced on a map in 1964 by a British UN officer using a green chinagraph pencil, to separate the city's warring pro-Greek and pro-Turkish factions. Ever since it has been called the **Green Line**. That sounds nice and ecological but in fact it is an ugly scar of ruined buildings, and oildrum-and-sandbag barricades. Greek Cypriot and Turkish soldiers occupy fortified positions that are sometimes only a few meters apart, with a UN post in the middle.

Otherwise it's a pretty normal place.

Streets running north-south eventually run into the barrier. West-east is easier. The old city within the Venetian Walls is mostly calmer and more shaded from the sun than the brashly modern Mediterranean capital outside where traffic tends to get frantic. If you're a tourist you'll be driving with a distinctive red plate with a "Z" prefix. You'll be allowed some tolerance by other drivers and maybe by the police, but not much.

GETTING AROUND TOWN

Taxis are the easiest way to get around; bus routes can be confusing at first. The **Urban Bus Station** is at *Plateia Dionysou Solomou (west of Plateia Eleftherias), Tel. 02/473414*. If you're planning to stay for more than a few days it may make sense to rent a moped or motor-scooter – no parking problems, get through the traffic easy, and a nice cool breeze.

Car Rental

- **Andy Spyrou Rentals** (for Europcar), *Odos Armenias 11. Tel. 02/338226*
- **Ansa International**, *Plateia Eleftherias. Tel. 02/47352*
- **A. Petsas**, *Leoforos K. Pantelidi 24. Tel. 02/462650*
- **Carop Cyprus**, *Plateia Eleftherias. Tel. 02/472333*
- **Hertz**, *Odos Metochiou 66, Egkomi. Tel. 02/477411*

Walking Tours

Guided walks through old Nicosia within the Venetian Walls (Greek Cypriot sector only) leave daily in summer from the tourist information office on Odos Aristokyprou. They offer a good introduction to the city, with access to historic churches which are usually locked, and a well-informed commentary. Leaflets listing times and itineraries are available from the tourist office.

WHERE TO STAY

Nicosia gets hot and dusty in summer, so you might want to make sure that your hotel has a swimming pool, or if you need a budget choice, that it is near one of the excellent municipal swimming pools.

CYPRUS HILTON, *Leoforos Archiepiskopou Makariou III, Nicosia. Tel. 02/377777, Fax 02/377788. Rates (with tax): CY£105-112 single; CY£126-143 double. Major credit cards.*

Given that Nicosia is a relatively small city, there is not a lot of competition in the deluxe stakes, and the Hilton is undoubtedly the city's top hotel as well as its most expensive. The facilities are excellent, including both heated and outdoor swimming pools and a well-equipped fitness and sauna center, tennis and squash courts and a mini-basketball. Top-flight Cypriot and international cuisine is served in the Fontana dining complex, which incorporates no fewer than five eateries. Ordinary rooms – known as "Superior" rooms here – are superbly equipped and instead of the usual boring top-hotel look, are brightly outfitted and stylish, with patterns on bedspreads and curtains picking up traditional Cypriot motifs. Executive rooms have no fewer than three telephones, a direct fax connection, and in some rooms a computer modem link-up.

PHILOXENIA, *Leoforos Aglangias, Nicosia. Tel. 02/499700, Fax 02/498038. Rates (with tax): CY£36 single; CY£50 double. Major credit cards. Cyprus International Conference Center.*

The Philoxenia offers many of the services provided by the Hilton, although perhaps not quite so refinedly, and does so at a considerably lower price. A disadvantage for vacation travelers may be its location beside the busy conference center.

CLASSIC, *Odos Rigainis 94. Tel. 02/464006, Fax 02/360072. Rates (with tax): CY£26 single; CY£36 double. Breakfast included. 57 rooms. American Express, Diners Club, Visa, MasterCard.*

The Classic is a new and welcome addition to the Nicosia scene, offering attractive mid-level accommodation with a touch of class and character. It is located near the Pafos Gate and Plateia Solomou, not far from the Odos Lidra shopping street. Air conditioned throughout, the hotel has a spacious and welcoming lounge and its rooms, though relatively small, are fully equipped, with the exception of a minibar.

VENETIAN WALLS, *Odos Ouzounian 42, Nicosia. Tel. 02/450805, Fax 02/473337. Rates (with tax): CY£18-21 single; CY£26-29 double; breakfast CY£2. Inside the Venetian Walls.*

Not only inside the Venetian Walls, but right beside them, the hotel has a good position near the Pafos Gate. Room service and an in-hotel restaurant lift it out of the "basic" category. It is still a straightforward kind of place though, with a Cypriot character that may be more welcome for holidaymakers than the business-orientated style of the Hilton and Philoxenia.

REGINA PALACE, *Odos Rigainis 42, Nicosia. Tel/fax. 02/463051. Rates (with tax): CY£15-17 single; CY£21-23 double; breakfast CY£2. Visa and MasterCard. Inside the Venetian Walls.*

The Regina Palace's location just inside the Venetian Walls near the popular Odos Lidras shopping area and the Laïki Geitonia restaurant district, along with its low rates, go a long way towards compensating for fairly minimal facilities. Proprietor Ms. Nedi Papageorgiou ensures that her guests get a friendly welcome and a hotel that is clean though simple.

WHERE TO EAT

ABU FAISAL, *Odos Klimentos 31, Nicosia. Tel. 02/360353. Credit cards accepted. Lebanese. Moderate-expensive.*

A fine and chraming restaurant serving excellent Lebanese cuisine in an old mansion with a garden terrace for warm summer evenings.

KONATZIN, *Odos Delfi 10, Nicosia. Tel. 02/446990. Credit cards accepted. Traditional. Moderate-expensive.*

While not purely a specialist in vegetarian food, Konatzin does a great vegetarian meze in the fine setting of a converted mansion with a garden.

PLAKA TAVERNA, *Plateia Archiepiskopou Makariou III, Egkomi. Tel. 02/446498. Credit cards accepted. Traditional. Moderate-expensive.*

The restaurant occupies the center of the old village square of now suburban Egkomi, spreading its terrace among the flowers and bushes. It can be a superb place for meze, my only reservation being that popularity has maybe dulled its edge. In particular the meze dishes might come too fast for comfort, and the bill too, unless you tell the waiter to slow down.

ARCHONTIKO, *Odos Filokyprou 27, Nicosia. Tel. 02/450080. Credit cards accepted. Traditional. Moderate.*

Some locals, and tourists too, can get sniffy about the renovated Laïki Geitonia district just inside the Venetian Walls, with its twee boutiques and tavernas that are just a little too perfect-looking to be really Cypriot. There is some truth in this, but the fact is that on a summer evening it is a romantic kind of place to eat, enveloped in the warm glow from lantern lights and serenaded by Greek music. Archontiko is one of the best.

AXIOTHEA, *Odos Axiotheas 14, Nicosia. Tel. 02/430787. No credit cards. Traditional. Moderate.*

There can be few more surreal eating experiences in Cyprus – or possibly anywhere – than in this superbly traditional restaurant a few steps away from the barricaded ruins along the Green Line. But the food is good and not aimed at tourists and the tables outside in the narrow street make for a convivial evening.

ERENIA, *Leoforos Archiepiskopou Kyprianou 64a, Strovolos. Tel. 02/422860. No credit cards. Traditional. Moderate.*

Specializes in the multi-dish meze menu and serves it with unpretentious charm. You'll have to go a little bit out from the center to Strovolos, a former village now swallowed up by Nicosia, but the trip is worth it.

SEEING THE SIGHTS

The best place to start in Nicosia is **Plateia Eleftherias** (Freedom Square). Despite its grand-sounding title it isn't much of a square, but it is conveniently located at the Venetian Walls and near the **tourist information** office, *Odos Aristokyprou 35,* in the nearby Laïki Geitonia trendy shopping-and-restaurants enclave.

A walk from here straight into the old city center along Odos Lidras brings you eventually to the **Green Line** at a Cyprus National Guard barricade, with the UN buffer zone beyond, and beyond that the Turkish army. Everybody seems to want to see this symbol of Europe's last divided city – an ordinary shopping street that ends in the shattered buildings of an old war-zone – so you may as well do it now and get it over with.

Now to pleasanter things.

Going west from Plateia Eleftherias, outside the walls on Leoforos Omirou, brings you to the American Cultural Center. Beyond that, turn right into Leoforos Mouseiou for the neo-Classical **Cyprus National Museum,** *Tel. 02/302189; open Monday to Saturday 9 am to 5 pm, Sunday 9 am to 1 pm; admission CY£1.50.* Much of Cyprus's cultural heritage has been collected by foreigners – okay, looted – over the last couple of centuries. The best of what remains can be seen in this fairly small museum. The nude marble **Aphrodite of Soloi** is here, watched over from the other end of the hall by an equally nude larger-than-life bronze of the Roman Emperor **Septimius Severus**. Even minus her arms and legs, Aphrodite still seems to have worn well. What the two get up to at night nobody knows. Perhaps they try to decipher the many tablets in Minoan-influenced Cypro-Archaic script, a variant of Cretan Linear A.

There are bits and pieces in the museum ranging from Neolithic flint tools to delicate Roman glassware, and including thousands of terracotta votive offerings from the island's many temples, as well as sculptures, bronze utensils and statues, funerary stelæ, and marble statues such as those of Asclepius and Isis.

Across Leoforos Mouseiou from the museum are the **Municipal Gardens**, a tree-shaded patch of greenery that is a welcome place of escape from the sun. The **Municipal Theater** stands in the gardens, as does Cyprus's **House of Representatives**. Opposite them, beside the Cyprus National Museum, is the British Council.

Pass the **Pafos Gate** on Leoforos Markou Drakou, watched over by Turkish and Turkish Cypriot flags flying on the bastion above you, and after the Goethe Institute you arrive outside the old **Ledra Palace Hotel**, now United Nations peacekeeping force headquarters. The checkpoint for crossing to Turkish-occupied Nicosia on a single daytime-only pass is here.

Back at Plateia Eleftherias you could have walked down Odos Solonos to visit the 17th-century **Agios Michaelis Trypiotis Church** (Saint Michael Trypiotis), and the 19th-century **Agia Faneromeni Church** (Saint Faneromeni), in which lie the remains of Archbishop Kyprianou, the ethnarch of the Cypriot Church executed by the Ottoman Turks in 1821 on the off-chance that he might have been thinking of rebelling against Turkish rule – which he may well have been. Both churches are more often closed than open.

Going east inside the walls on Leoforos Konstantinou Palaiologou, takes you past the **Bayraktar Mosque** (usually closed), named for the Turkish standard bearer who was the first soldier to scale the walls in 1570. He was killed in the battle and buried in the specially built mosque. A left turn past the bus station on Odos Areos leads to the **Ömeriye Mosque**, formerly a 14th-century Augustinian Church. For a CY£1 "donation" you can climb the minaret and get a muezzin's-eye-view of the divided city; *open Monday to Saturday 10 am to 12:30 pm and 1:30 pm to 3:30 pm.*

Keeping straight ahead on Leoforos Konstantinou Palaiologou brings you to the **Liberty Monument** in the Podocatoro Bastion. The marble and bronze sculpture group honors the successful struggle of the Cypriot guerrilla organization EOKA against British colonial rule in the 1950s.

A left turn on Odos Agiou Antoniou brings you to the **Hadjigeorgakis Kornesios House**, the mansion of the "Dragoman" Georgakis Kornesios, an intermediary between the Greek Cypriots and the ruthless Turkish authorities, who was executed by the Turks in 1809 for failing in this delicate balancing act. Still, while he lived he lived well as this Ottoman-style mansion shows. It is now the **Ethnological Museum**, *Odos Patriarchou Grigoriou. Tel. 02/302447; open Monday to Friday 8 am to 2 pm, Saturday 9 am to 1 pm; admission CY75¢.*

Further along, on Plateia Archiepiskopou Kyprianou, you arrive at a close-packed monumental zone which includes the neo-Byzantine **Archbishop's Palace**, *open daily 9 am to 5 pm; admission CY75¢*, where the private apartments of the late Archbishop Makarios III, first President of the Republic of Cyprus, can be visited.

Beside it is **Agios Ioannis Cathedral**, *open daily 8 am to noon and 2 pm to 4 pm, also Mass times; admission free,* an Orthodox transformation dating from 1662 of a centuries older Benedictine abbey church. Inside Saint John's, which is small but magnificent, are icons and murals, a pulpit decorated with the double-headed eagle emblem of Byzantium in gold, and thrones for the Archbishop and the President. Also within the archbishopric is the **Byzantine Museum and Art Gallery**, *Tel. 02/456781; open Monday to Friday 9 am to 1 pm and 2 pm to 5 pm, Saturday 9 am to 1 pm; admission CY75¢. No photography.* The museum houses a valuable collection of icons.

Other Sights

• **Famagusta Gate Cultural Center**, *Pyli Ammochostou, Leoforos Athinon. Tel. 02/430877. Open daily 10 am to 1 pm and 4 pm to 7 pm, 5 pm to 8 pm July and August. Admission free.* Venue for modern art exhibitions and other cultural events, located in the award-winning refurbishment of the Famagusta Gate in the city wall.

• **Panagia Chrysaliniotissa**, *Odos Odysseos. Open irregularly. Admission free.* Our Lady of the Golden Flax dates from the 15th century and is extraordinary in its atmosphere, dimly lit but with icons glimmering on the beautifully carved iconostasis.

• **Leventis Municipal Museum**, *Odos Ippokratous, Laïki Geitonia. Tel. 02/451475. Open Tuesday to Sunday 10 am to 4:30 pm. Admission free.* Memorabilia of Nicosia, particularly from pre-partition days.

- **National Struggle Museum**, *Plateia Archiepiskopou Kyprianou. Tel. 02/ 302465. Open daily 7:30 am to 2:30 pm and 3 pm to 5:30 pm. Admission CY50¢.* Records the war waged by EOKA against the British in the 1950s.
- **Folk Art Museum**, *Plateia Archiepiskopou Kyprianou. Tel. 02/463205. Open Monday to Friday 9 am to 1 pm and 2 pm to 5 pm, Saturday 9 am to 1pm. Admission CY75¢.*
- **Municipal Arts Center**, *Odos Apostolou Varnava 19. Tel. 02/447310. Open Tuesday to Saturday 10 am to 3 pm and 5 pm to 11 pm, Sunday 10 am to 4 pm.*
- **State Art Gallery**, *Leoforos Stasinou and Odos Kritis. Tel. 02/302951. Open Monday to Friday 10 am to 5 pm, Saturday 4 pm to 7 pm. Admission CY50¢.*

NIGHTLIFE & ENTERTAINMENT

Entertainment information is available from the monthly *Time Out* tourist guide, the Cyprus Tourism Organization's free *Monthly Events* and the free *Nicosia This Month*, produced by the municipality. All are available from tourist offices and usually from hotels, conference centers, and tour operators. During summer, CyBC radio broadcasts on 498m *Welcome To Cyprus*, giving a news summary and including "what's on" information.

For classicial music and opera, check the schedule at the **Municipal Theater**, *Leoforos Mouseiou, Tel. 02/463028.*

SPORTS & RECREATION

- **Nicosiana Ice Skating Center**, *Odos Makedonitissis.* Ice skating can be a fun thing to do in the broiling heat of a Nicosia summer.
- **Municipal Swimming Pool**, *between Leoforos Louki Akrita and Odos Agiou Pavlou.* A big outdoor complex that is a joy in summer.
- **Fishing** – you can fish at several fresh-water reservoirs in the Nicosia area, and throughout Cyprus. Information about locations and mandatory permits are obtainable from the *Head Office, Fisheries Department, Odos Aiolou, 1101 Nicosia, Tel. 02/303526.*

SHOPPING

Odos Lidras, Odos Onasagorou, and the nearby Laïki Geitonia district are the main downtown shopping areas, although the last-mentioned is very touristy. Leoforos Archiepiskopou Makariou III is also good for shopping, while some of its sidestreets have specialty boutiques.

There are many shops claiming to sell traditional Cyprus products and not all the claims are genuine, as you will see from "Made in China" stamps on some. For traditional handmade Cyprus products you should head straight for the branches of the government foundation, the **Cyprus Handicraft Service**, which aims to preserve the endangered folk-arts of earlier times. Its products are labeled "CHS" and include pottery, wood-carvings, handmade lace, loom embroidery and cotton work. Visit their headquarters, *Leoforos Athalassis 186, Tel. 02/305024*. It's in the southern suburbs, close to the Larnaka motorway access. This is not just a shop but a workshop and exhibition center as well, where traditional craftsmen and women can be seen in action. There is also a CHS shop in the Laïki Geitonia district.

WHAT'S IN A NAME?

In Cyprus there may be more to a name than meets the eye. Old spellings are being replaced by a new system of transliterating Greek characters to Roman characters. Some of the changes are straightforward enough: **Paphos** *becomes* **Pafos,** **Larnaca** *becomes* **Larnaka,** *and* **Ayia Napa** *becomes* **Agia Napa.** *Even* **Panayia Khrysorroyiatissa** *changing to* **Panagia Chrysorrogiatissa** *is just about managable. But how about* **Khirokitia** *changing to* **Choirokoitia,** *or even just* **Latchi** *changing to* **Latsi?** *The problem is made worse by the fact that implementation of the new system is patchy at best, and many Cypriots – and many Cypriot road signs and maps – have never heard of it.*

EXCURSIONS & DAY TRIPS

From Nicosia the best day excursions are those into the **Troodos Mountains** and down to the coast around **Larnaka**. You'll just about trip over agencies willing and able to sell you everything from a tiny 800cc car for a three-day rental, through jeep excursions to the **Akamas Peninsula** and the Troodos Mountains, to a mini-cruise to Israel and Egypt, and all possible variations in between.

Some addresses to try:

• **Aeolos Cyprus Travel**, *Odos Prigkipissis Zinas de Tyras 6. Tel. 02/44522*
• **Groutas Tourist Agency**, *Leoforos Homeros 31. Tel. 02/473172*
• **Honeywell Travel**, *Odos Armenias 11. Tel. 02/338226*
• **Paradise Island Tours**, *Odos Romanos 8. Tel. 02/374699*

PRACTICAL INFORMATION

• **Nicosia Tourist Information**, *Odos Aristokyprou 35, Laïki Geitonia, 1011 Lefkosia. Tel. 02/444264*

THE SOUTH

Following the loss of the tourist areas around Kyrenia and Famagusta to the Turkish invasion of 1974, the south coast was developed rapidly to replace them. This was a case of force-feeding places that had not the same natural advantages in terms of beaches or scenery and of over-exploiting those natural advantages that did exist.

In a word, much of the South is overdone. This is far from being a rare state of affairs in the Mediterranean these days, and it has to be said that the majority of visitors to Cyprus seem perfectly happy with it. The main centers here are **Larnaka**, **Agia Napa**, and **Limassol**.

LARNAKA

Most visitors to Cyprus arrive at **Larnaka** through the International Airport on the shores of Larnaka Salt Lake. They come not so much for the town itself, although it has its interesting points, but more to use it as a base for exploring the coast and the inland villages, and of course to head off to holiday resorts all over the island.

By the 9th century BC the town, known as **Kition** (and supposedly founded by Noah's grandson Khittim), was the most important Phoenician city in Cyprus and its loyalties were always suspect in the eyes of the Greek-leaning majority. During the Persian invasion of Greece it sided with the bad guys and the Athenian general Kimon took it under siege in 450 BC, dying heroically in the failed attempt to capture the city. Zeno, a Cypriot of Phoenician origin who founded the Stoic philosophy, was born at Kition in about 336 BC.

It wasn't until the 16th century that Larnaka got its present name. In 1879, the British took all the best bits and pieces of ancient Kition and used them for construction materials in Egypt.

ARRIVALS & DEPARTURES

A taxi from the airport is the best way into town as the distance is short, taxis cheap, and their drivers honest. After that a car is a necessity for anyone wanting to do much exploration. Frequent bus services are restricted to those operating within the town, or serving the coastal development strip and a few of the bigger villages roundabout. See under Nicosia for inter-city services. Other places may be served by just a single bus per day. Larnaka has a population of 60,000 and its town center is small enough to do on foot.

By Bus

Nicosia to Larnaka: Kallenos Buses, Monday through Friday 8:30, 10:30 am, 1, 2:30, 4, 5:45, 6:30 pm; check for Saturday schedule times.

Larnaka to Nicosia: Kallenos Buses, Monday through Friday 6:30, 8, 9, 10:30 am, 1, 2:30, 4 pm; Saturday 7, 9, 11 am, 1 pm.

Limassol to Larnaka: Kallenos Buses, Monday through Friday 8, 9:30, 10 am, 2, 4 pm; Saturday 8 am, 1 pm.

Larnaka to Limassol: Kallenos Buses, Monday through Friday 8, 10 am, 1, 4 pm; Saturday 8 am, 1 pm.

By Service Taxi

These are shared taxis which run at approximately hourly intervals between Larnaka and Nicosia and Larnaka and Limassol. The "taxis" are minibuses which collect and pick up within the urban center or can be boarded at the dispatch office, and drop off within the urban center of the destination or at the dispatch office.

Service Taxis: Larnaka to Nicosia
• **Acropolis Taxis**, *corner of Leoforos Grigori Afxentiou and Leoforos Archiepiskopou Makariou III. Tel. 04/655555*
• **Kyriakos Taxis**, *Odos Ermou 2. Tel. 04/655100*
• **Makris Taxis**, *Odos Vasileos Pavlou 13. Tel. 04/652929*

Service Taxis: Larnaka to Limassol
• **Acropolis Taxis**, *corner of Leoforos Grigori Afxentiou and Leoforos Archiepiskopou Makariou III. Tel. 04/655555*
• **Makris Taxis**, *Odos Vasileos Pavlou 13. Tel. 04/652929*

ORIENTATION

Larnaka is a coastal town that has developed too fast for its own good to accommodate refugees from northern Cyprus and a fast-burgeoning tourist industry. The coastal strip and streets for a block or two behind it are easy to follow and fairly pleasant. Beyond that things can get a bit chaotic and busy.

GETTING AROUND TOWN

The old Turkish quarter around the fort in the south is particularly narrow and hard to negotiate by car. Walking there and in the seafront zone is the best option.

Urban and local bus services run from the Bus Station, *Odos Karaoli & Demetriou 36. Tel. 04/650477.*

WHERE TO STAY

GRECIAN BAY, *Leoforos Kyrou Nerou, Agia Napa. Tel. 03/721301, Fax 03/721307. Rates (with tax): no single rooms; CY£82-96 double.*

If what you want is the classic beach holiday with all the style Cyprus can muster, you'll find it hard to do better than this top-flight hotel with its own beach.

SUN HALL, *Leoforos Athinon, Larnaka. Tel. 04/653341, Fax 04/652715. Rates (with tax): CY£38-45 single; CY£49-55 double.*

A downtown hotel in Larnaka that although not especially attractive to look at has all the facilities you should need, and a good location near the main shopping and taverna district.

LARCO, *Odos Umm Haram, Larnaka. Tel. 04/657006, Fax 04/659168. Rates (with tax): CY£17 single; CY£22 double.*

A mid-size hotel with a swimming pool in the atmospheric old Turkish quarter of Larnaka.

HARRY'S INN, *Odos Thermopyles 2, Larnaka. Tel/fax. 04/654453. Rates (with tax): CY£9 single; CY£15 double.*

With only nine rooms and 15 beds, Harry's is nothing if not small. Proprietress Charalambia Sampson keeps things simple and nice.

WHERE TO EAT

MONTE CARLO, *Odos Piyale Pasha 28. Tel. 04/653815. Credit cards accepted. Traditional. Moderate-expensive.*

A stylish restaurant with a balcony overlooking the Mediterranean in the old Turkish quarter of Larnaka.

ARCHONTIKO, *Leoforos Athinon 71. Tel. 04/655905. Credit cards accepted. Traditional. Moderate-expensive.*

Situated in a picturesque old building beside the seafront Foinikoudes Promenade, its Cypriot food is very good. The Archontissa is an associated steakhouse.

APOVATHRA, *Seafront, Zygi village. Tel. 04/332414. Credit cards accepted. Traditional. Moderate.*

In a village where seafood tavernas are common, but not always good, Apovathra stands out for quality.

POTAMOS, *Harborside, Potamos Creek near Xylofagou, (no telephone). No credit cards. Traditional. Inexpensive.*

Gets its seafood straight off the boats and prepares it in simple family fashion.

SEEING THE SIGHTS

You'd do well to stay in the central strip of Larnaka extending along and a little way behind the seafront on Leoforos Athinon with its palm-tree lined Foinikoudes Promenade, and a few streets back from the sea along Odos Zinonos Kitieos.

Start by picking up a map and some brochures at the **tourist information** office in Plateia Vasileos Pavlou. Little more than a stone's-throw away is the **Pierides Foundation Museum**, *Odos Zinonos Kitieos 4, Tel. 04/622345; open Monday to Friday 9 am to 1 pm and 3 pm to 6 pm, Saturday 9 am to 1 pm, Sunday 10 am to 1 pm; admission CY£1,* housed in an elegant 19th-century mansion with a balustraded balcony. Demetrios Pierides was a classical scholar and archaeologist who in 1839 began rescuing important pieces of Cyprus's cultural heritage at a time when stealing and spiriting away priceless treasures was rampant. The foundation's collection ranges from neolithic to classical times and covers pottery, ornaments, sculptures and everyday objects. Its Roman glassware is particularly fine and there is a superb funerary monument of a lounging nobleman from 750 BC.

From here it's best to backtrack through Plateia Vasileos Pavlou, past the **Marina** to the **Foinikoudes Promenade**. A bust of the Athenian hero **Kimon** who died in the Greek siege of Kition in 450 BC stands in a post of honor on the promenade. "Though he died he was victorious," reads the inscription: a slight rewriting of history since Kimon died and got beaten both. His bust is traditionally "consulted" by people with problems. The beach here is usually pretty busy, while across the way upmarket hotels and chic restaurants are slowly easing out the pubs, fast-food joints, and cheap tavernas that once dominated what is now a prime piece of real-estate.

At the southern end of the promenade is the Larnaka **Cyprus Handicraft Service** shop for traditional handicrafts. Keep going in this direction until you get to **Larnaka Fort**, which dominates the harbor, *open daily 7:30 am to 5 pm, Thursday 6 pm; admission CY75¢.* The view you get is an attacker's-eye view. Ottoman gunners who once manned the walls must have prayed for someone like you to stray within range. The 16th-century fort's lower level has been partly landscaped into a garden where open-air theater performances and concerts are held in summer. Upstairs there is a medieval museum.

A few meters west of the fort stands the 16th-century **Al-Kebír Mosque**, which is still in use and whose cool undecorated interior can be visited on payment of a small "donation." Don't forget to remove your shoes before entering.

You can now get a chance to compare Islamic with Christian religious styles by going west about 100 meters on Odos Dionysos to **Agios Lazaros Church**, *open daily; admission free.* The 17th-century Orthodox church, built over a 9th-century one, has a beautiful gilt iconostasis and a slightly mismatched baroque tower. Its most important possession is the sarcophagus of **Lazarus**, whom Jesus raised from the dead and who is said to have died again in Cyprus – this time for keeps. Lazarus is not actually in the sarcophagus (if he ever was), for the saint's remains were removed to Constantinople on the orders of Byzantine Emperor Leo VI. There is a small **Ecclesiastical Museum** on the grounds, *open daily; admission CY75¢.*

Other Sights

- **Larnaka District Archeological Museum**, *Odos Kalograion. Tel. 04/ 630169. Open Monday to Friday 7:30 am to 2:30 pm, also Thursday 3 pm to 6 pm except in July and August. Admission CY75¢.* Suffers a bit in comparison with town's Pierides Foundation collection but still has some interesting objects, including terracotta figurines, jewelry, and bronze weapons.

- **Municipal Park**, *Leoforos Grigori Afxentiou.* A small yet welcome patch of green on a hot and dusty day. Larnaka's **Natural History Museum** is inside.

- **Ancient Kition**. *Reached from Odos Leontiou Machaira. Open Monday to Friday 7:30 am to 2:30 pm, also Thursday 3 pm to 6 pm except in July and August. Admission CY75¢.* Achaean and Mycenaean Greeks had a hand in this jumble of stones, but most of the remains are Phoenician, including straggly remnants of a Temple of Astarte.

HOW STOIC CAN YOU GET?

Zeno of Kition (c.336-c.265 BC) would need all his stoic self-control to get over what time and fate have done to his home town. Most of it lies under Larnaka and what remains above ground adds up to a few pathetic scraps of stone and marble that even experts probably have trouble deciphering. Still, Zeno didn't linger long in Kition. He packed his bags and headed for Athens, where philosophers got more respect, and spent his time taking on all comers at the Stoa Poikile (Painted Portico). Hence Stoicism.

Zeno taught – excuse me while I oversimplify – that all things are predetermined and there is no point in struggling against fate. Emotions are only so much useless baggage on the road to death and should be suppressed in favor of conscientious fulfillment of duty. A modified version of Zeno's ideas appealed to Republican-minded senators during the Roman Empire, particularly those who stood up to tyrants like Nero.

*Ironically, Stoicism reached its peak of power from 161-180 AD during the reign of **Emperor Marcus Aurelius**, a kind of Stoic saint, whose **Meditations** on his life of duty are still widely read today. "Misfortune nobly borne," wrote Marcus as he fought to stem a torrent of barbarian invaders, "is good fortune."*

Christianity also found much to its liking in Stoicism, once it had been suitably sanitized by pious hands.

Around Larnaka

You can make a wide chord of a circle by car or motorbike from Larnaka, first going inland to the Troodos foothills and returning from the south along the coast road.

Leaving southwest on the Limassol Road, you pass the **Salt Lake** to your left. Between the road and the lake you will see the 33 remaining arches of the ruined **Kamares Aqueduct**, built by the Turks in the 18th century to bring water to Larnaka. If you feel like doing some rough-road driving you can turn off about 10 kilometers (6 1/4 miles) out of town towards Klavia, from where a dusty track leads across country to Pyrga and the **Royal Chapel of Agia Ekaterina**, a ruined Lusignan-era church which may have a monk in attendance supervising what seems likely to be a decades-long renovation effort.

From here turn southwest towards the coast again, turning left when you see the signs for **Stavrovouni Monastery**, *off the Nicosia-Limassol road; open daily from sunrise to sunset, except between noon and 3 pm; admission free.* From its 700-meter perch you have a superb view over a desolate piece of landscape, all the way to Nicosia in one direction and to the sea in the other. The "Mountain of the Cross" Monastery was apparently founded in 327 AD by Saint Helena, the mother of Constantine the Great, to house a relic of the True Cross which is covered in gold leaf and set in a silver-chased crucifix beside the iconostasis. The site was previously occupied by a shrine to Aphrodite. Such feminine-inspired origins are ironic, as women are not allowed in.

Stavrovouni's present structure dates from the 17th century. You have to backtrack from this remote place to the main road and continue southwest for 12 kilometers to a junction where you turn north for **Lefkara**. This village is actually two villages – **Kato** (Lower) **Lefkara** and **Pano** (Upper) **Lefkara**, separated by a few hundred meters. In both, grandmothers, mothers and daughters sit outdoors in good weather, which means almost all the time, painstakingly threading superb hand-made **Lefkara lace**. Kato Lefkara is less touristy than Pano Lefkara, but both are pretty villages. Although the object of making these lace pieces is to sell them, the sales-pitch is so low-key as to be almost non-existent.

Head south and west through Kato Drys and the flower-bedecked convent of **Agios Minas** beyond, where the nuns sell icons and honey, before turning south to Choirokoitia (it may also be signposted as Khirokitia). The **Neolithic Settlement** here dates from 5800-5200 BC, *open Monday to Friday 7:30 am to 5 pm, weekend 9 am to 5 pm; admission CY75¢.* A cluster of round rock foundations straggles up the steep hillside, indicating the houses where stone age families lived, and buried their dead hunched up fetus-style beneath the floors. .

Keep going in this direction until you reach the sparkling blue of the Mediterranean at **Zygi**, a fishing village whose day's catch ends up on the plates of happy diners at a slew of seafront restaurants. The coast from here to Cape Kiti is almost undeveloped as these things go in Cyprus, and it is worth diverting along any of a number of tracks leading to the sea.

At **Kiti** village about five kilometers south of Larnaka is the **Church of Panagia Angeloktistos**, *open daily; admission free; visitors must be respectfully dressed.* "Our Lady Built by the Angels" was rebuilt in the 12th century on the foundations of a 5th-century church. In the apse behind the iconostasis is a marvelous mosaic of the Virgin and Child flanked by the Archangels Gabriel and Michael. This is one of only seven 6th-century Byzantine religious mosaics to survive in the Orthodox world. It stands comparison with those of Justinian, Theodora, and the Byzantine court at Ravenna in Italy.

Once again, Christian worship can quickly be compared with Muslim, as the next stop, on the western shore of Larnaka Salt Lake, is the **Hala Sultan Tekke**, also known as the **Umm Haram Mosque**, *open daily 7:30 am to 7:30 pm in summer, 5 pm out of summer; admission free, but a donation is appreciated.* This is like a piece of *The Arabian Nights* set down in a dusty Cyprus oasis and is famed for its tomb of an aunt of the Prophet Mohammed who fell from her mule and died here in 649 (28th year of the Islamic era). The stone that protects her sepulcher is said to have flown miraculously from Mount Sinai. Muslim ships sailing within sight of the shrine used to lower their colors as a mark of respect. The grandmother of King Hussein of Jordan is also entombed here.

The **Salt Lake** itself is an interesting place, particularly in winter when pink flamingoes are among the bird species that flock to its waters. By summer it has dried out to a crystalline sheen and you can walk across it. In the past the salt was collected commercially but pollution from jetliners using the nearby international airport has made it unfit for human consumption.

Leaving Larnaka on the coast road northwards takes you around hotel-lined Larnaka Bay through the British military's Sovereign Base Area at Dhekelia. Apart from an occasional police checkpoint and an armed sentry at the main base gateway there are no formalities – except maybe sticking to the speed limit – when passing through the base. Coming out the other end you are in the **Kokkinochoria** district, whose rich red soil can produce three potato crops a year so long as it is well irrigated. In the past, water was drawn from underground aquifers with the help of windmills. Now, alas, the rusting windmills turn idly in the breeze and noisy diesel generators do the work instead.

The fishing harbor at **Potamos Creek** near Xyloufagou is a typically colorful Mediterranean scene, with brightly painted boats heading in and out from the fishing grounds, or tied up at the dock. Beyond this you come into hotel-land again. A mass of tourist developments fills the sandy bays and the rocky shores through **Nissi Bay**, **Agia Napa**, **Protaras**, **Fig Tree Bay** and **Pernera**, just about all the way to the United Nations buffer zone beyond Deryneia, from where the ruined Famagusta suburb of **Varosha** can be seen through binoculars.

Boat trips from the eastern resorts of Agia Napa and Protaras sail north along the coast to just offshore from the UN buffer zone. Beyond it, in the Turkish zone, you can see the surreal site of a modern town crumbling into the sand. Famagusta's once bustling resort suburb Varosha had a population of 40,000 before the Turkish invasion. It has been abandoned since 1974, its houses and hotels falling down through neglect.

Roads going northwards in this area eventually run into a Cyprus National Guard or UN Peacekeeping Force (UNFICYP) roadblock. I must stress that there is no problem in being in the Agia Napa-Pernera area and no danger. Millions of tourists since 1974 can testify to this. The usual military profile along the buffer zone is one of suffocating boredom. Confrontations, usually but not always more symbolic than serious, do occasionally take place along the line here. In the summer of 1996, two Greek Cypriot protesters were killed by the Turks.

Apart from hotels and beaches, and villages that are rapidly losing their traditional character, there is not much in this whole area except for a few forlorn-looking Orthodox churches, the 16th-century **Agia Napa Monastery**, *open daily,* and ruggedly scenic **Cape Gkreko**, whose point is sadly inaccessible due to the presence of military and civilian communication facilities.

SPORTS & RECREATION

Fishing is possible at several fresh-water reservoirs in the Larnaka and Agia Napa areas. Information and mandatory permits are available from the *Larnaka District Office, Fisheries Department, Leoforos Piale Pasha (at Fishing Harbor), Tel. 04/630294.*

All manner of **water sports** may be enjoyed along the coast: swimming, diving, snorkeling, paragliding, sea-fishing. Several **boat charter** operators can be found at the Old Harbor.

SHOPPING

• **Cyprus Handicraft Service**, *Odos Kosma Lysioti, Tel. 04/630327.* The only Larnaka branch of the government-operated handicrafts foundation.

EXCURSIONS & DAY TRIPS

The best trips are to Lefkara village to see its handmade lace, and into the Troodos Mountains. There are any number of agencies. Try:
• **Salamis Tours**, *Leoforos Grigori Afxentiou 7, Tel. 04/656464*

PRACTICAL INFORMATION

• **Agia Napa Tourist Information**, *Leoforos Kyrou Nerou 12, 5330 Agia Napa, 03/721796*
• **Larnaka International Airport Tourist Information**, *Arrivals Hall. Tel. 04/643300*
• **Larnaka Tourist Information**, *Plateia Vasileos Pavlou, 6023 Larnaka. Tel. 04/654322*

LIMASSOL

This city of 140,000 inhabitants, the second biggest in Cyprus, calls itself the "Paris of Cyprus." A slight exagerration – okay, a gigantic exagerration. Even allowing for the city's fine seafront location overlooked by the Troodos Mountains, **Limassol** (Lemesos in Greek) really is not much more than a port city – one that has developed too fast in the last two decades to accommodate refugees from the Turkish-occupied north as well as from Lebanon and that has tried to replace Famagusta as a mercantile center. It does, however, have a lot of the vibrancy usually associated with harbor towns.

Its shopping and nightlife are attractions and it is a good, though not exactly tranquil base for exploring the southwest. It is at the heart of some spectacular scenery and historical treasures.

ARRIVALS & DEPARTURES

Unless you arrive by ferry from Greece, in which case you will begin at the harbor, you will most likely arrive by road from Nicosia, Larnaka, or Pafos. If you are able to you should do so by hired car, as you will certainly need one to explore the surrounding area in any reasonable period of time.

Buses are not a good option, but "service taxis" – minibuses that run every half-hour between Nicosia, Larnaka, Limassol, and Pafos, and will pick up and drop off within the towns – are fast and convenient, though not exactly comfortable.

By Bus

Nicosia to Limassol: Costas Buses, Monday, Tuesday, Thursday, Friday noon, 4 pm; Saturday 1 pm (buses continue to Pafos). Kemek Transport, Monday through Friday 6:30, 7:30, 9 am, noon, 2, 4 pm; Saturday 7, 10 am, 2:30 pm.

Limassol to Nicosia: Costas Buses, Monday, Tuesday, Thursday, Friday 9:30, 10:30 am; Wednesday, Saturday 9:30 am. Kemek Transport, Monday through Friday 6:30, 9 am, 2, 4 pm; Saturday 7 am, noon, 2:30 pm.

Larnaka to Limassol: Kallenos Buses, Monday through Friday 8, 10 am, 1, 4 pm; Saturday 8 am, 1 pm.

Limassol to Larnaka: Kallenos Buses, Monday through Friday 8, 9:30, 10 am, 2, 4 pm; Saturday 8 am, 1 pm.

Pafos to Limassol: Kemek Transport, Monday through Friday (check schedule). Costas Buses, Monday, Tuesday, Thursday, Friday 8, 9 am; Wednesday, Saturday 8 am (buses continue to Nicosia). **Limassol to Pafos**: Kemek Transport, Monday through Friday 9:30 am. Costas Buses, Monday, Tuesday, Thursday, Friday 1:30, 5 pm; Wednesday, Saturday 2 pm.

By Service Taxi

These are shared taxis that run at approximately hourly intervals between Nicosia and Larnaka and Nicosia and Limassol. Other services connect Limassol and Pafos. The "taxis" are actually minibuses which collect and pick up within the urban center or can be boarded at the dispatch office, and drop off either within the urban center of the destination or at the dispatch office.

Service Taxis: Limassol to Nicosia
• **Kypros Taxis**, *Odos Chris Hadjipavlou 193. Tel. 05/363979*
• **Kyriakos Taxis/Karydas Taxis**, *Odos Thessalonikis 21. Tel. 05/361114*
• **Makris Taxis**, *Odos Ellados 166. Tel. 05/365550*

Service Taxis: Limassol to Larnaka
• **Acropolis Taxis**, *Leoforos Spirou Araouzou 49. Tel. 05/366766*
• **Makris Taxis**, *Odos Ellados 166. Tel. 05/365550*

Service Taxis: Limassol to Pafos
• **Kyriakos Taxis/Karydas Taxis**, *Odos Thessalonikis 21. Tel. 05/361114*
• **Makris Taxis**, *Odos Ellados 166. Tel. 05/365550*
• **Nea Pafos Taxis**, *Odos Vragadinou 1. Tel. 05/355355*

ORIENTATION

Unless you have business or shopping reasons for being in Limassol, or you want a taste of bright lights at night, you're better off outside the city and won't need to get oriented. There seems little point in being in a beautiful place like Cyprus and spending your time in busy, smoggy

Limassol. Sorry, Limassol tourist office, but there it is. Well, okay, there is the colorful **pre-Lenten Carnival**, an **Arts Fair** in June, and the **Limassol Wine Festival** in September, all of which are "don't misses" – but you don't have to stay here or hang around much otherwise.

GETTING AROUND TOWN

In some respects Limassol is a bigger and busier version of Larnaka. There is the seafront promenade, and the old Turkish quarter, harbor, fort and mosque in the south. In all this area and for a few blocks inland walking is pleasant. Urban and local bus services run from the Bus Station, *Odos Themistokleous, Tel. 05/370592.*

WHERE TO STAY

FOUR SEASONS, *Amathous Seafront, Amathous). Tel. 05/310222, Fax 05/310887. Rates (with tax): CY£95-120 single; CY£120-150.*

A superb beach resort hotel.

CONTINENTAL, *Odos Spirou Araouzou 137, Limassol. Tel. 05/362530, Fax 05/373030. Rates (with tax): CY£14-16 single; CY£24-28 double.*

The Continental is a reasonably priced family-oriented hotel, with a good location in town and with a sea view.

LE VILLAGE, *Leoforos Archiepiskopou Leontiou I 242, Limassol. Tel. 05/ 368126, Fax 05/348044. Rates (with tax): CY£9 single; CY£14 double; breakfast CY£1.*

An owner-operated small hotel deep in the heart of Limassol with rates that are hard to beat.

WHERE TO EAT

PORTA, *Odos Genethliou Mitela 17 (Limassol Castle area). Tel. 05/ 360339. Credit cards accepted. Traditional-international. Moderate.*

A touch of designer class and good taste in an authentically renovated donkey stable (I kid you not) in the old Turkish quarter.

GALLO DE ORO, *Odos 28 Oktovriou 232. Tel. 05/343382. Credit cards accepted. Traditional-international. Moderate.*

A tourist-oriented taverna whose owner Theo knows how to make his guests feel at home.

SEEING THE SIGHTS

Start at the tourist information office in Odos Spirou Araouzou, just around the corner from **Limassol Castle**, behind the Old Harbor. The castle dates from the Crusader era in the 13th century but was later strengthened and altered by the Venetians, Turks, and British. Inside is the **Cyprus Medieval Museum**, *open Monday to Friday 7:30 am to 5 pm, Saturday 9 am to 5 pm; admission CY£1.*

You might want a look at the fishing boats and tour boats crowding into the **Old Harbor** before returning to Odos Spirou Araouzou and on to the seafront promenade. which runs alongside this street and Odos Christodoulou Chatzipavlou which follows it. There isn't much else until you come to the **Municipal Gardens** on Odos 28 Oktovriou. Here you will find an Open-Air Theater and the Zoo, neither of which are much to look at. The Gardens burst into life in September, when they are the venue for the **Limassol Wine Fair** and an ocean of free wine is dispensed in a modern Dionysiac revelry.

That's about it for Limassol city, apart from a couple of other small museums that are worth visiting: the Folk Art Museum and the archaeology museum. The **Folk Art Museum**, *Odos Agiou Andreou 253, Tel. 05/ 362303; open Monday to Saturday 8:30 am to 1:30 pm, Monday, Tuesday, Wednesday and Friday 3 pm to 5:30 pm, except from June to September when it is 4 pm to 6:30 pm; admission CY75¢,* features ornaments, costumes, including wedding costumes, and everyday objects used or worn by Cypriots in the old days. The **Limassol District Archaeological Museum**, *corner of Odos Kanningos and Odos Vyronos, Tel. 05/330132; open Monday to Friday 7:30 am to 5 pm, Saturday 9 am to 5 pm, Sunday 10 am to 1 pm; admission CY75¢,* has some interesting finds. With the ancient cities of Amathus and Kourion on its doorstep, the museum had easy access to some interesting pieces, including a bust of Aphrodite and statues of Phoenician and Egyptian gods.

Outside Limassol

Leave the city eastwards on the coast road past a maze of hotels until after about six kilometers you arrive at the site of ancient **Amathus** on the left side of the road – the road signs say "Amathounda," *open daily 7:30 am to 7:30 pm*. Founded by the Phoenicians about 1000 BC, Amathus backed the Persians in the Greek wars 500 years later but wisely changed sides when Alexander the Great arrived on the scene. There are remains of the Agora, as well as temples to Aphrodite, Adonis, and Hercules, an early Christian basilica and Roman bath-house. You'll see more if you don a face-mask and flippers and cruise the waters offshore.

Keep going on this road for another six or seven kilometers, then turn right towards the sea and **Agios Georgios Alamanos Convent**, where the nuns will sell you honey and icons. Back eastwards on the coast road again you might want a swim off **Governor's Beach**, whose black sand soaks up heat until it is scorching, so watch out for your bare feet!

If you leave Limassol by the Pafos road going westwards, after about 10 kilometers you arrive at magnificent **Kolossi Castle**, *open daily 7:30 am to 5 pm, 7:30 pm from June 1 to September 30; admission CY75¢*, which became the base of the Knights Hospitaller after the Crusaders were driven from the Holy Land in 1291 – though not without some jousting over owner-ship with the rival Knights Templar before the latter were proscribed by the Pope in 1311. The existing structure dates from 1454.

Further west is Episkopi and the small but superb **Kourion Museum**, *open Monday to Friday 7:30 am to 2:30 pm, also Thursday 3 pm to 6 pm except July and August; admission CY75¢*. Here you will find all kinds of objects taken from excavations at ancient Kourion and the Sanctuary of Apollo Hylates, including pottery, oil-lamps, coins, ornaments, amphorae, sculp-tures and votive offerings. A poignant group of three skeletons – almost certainly a husband, wife, and their small child – huddle together as fate left them when they perished in the earthquake that demolished Kourion in 365.

Water is scarce in Cyprus and nobody likes to see it wasted, so the British military personnel at the **Episkopi Barracks**, which you must pass through, keep their dazzlingly green cricket and polo fields irrigated by reusing water from the base sewage system.

Kourion itself occupies a stunning clifftop setting overlooking the Mediterranean a little further west. The city reached the peak of its elegance under the Romans, who called it Curium, and also transformed its magnificent **Greek Theater** into an arena for gladiators and wild beasts, *open daily 7:30m to 5 pm, 7:30 pm from 1 June to 30 September; admission CY£1.* It has been retransformed and plays by Aristophanes and Euripides are once again performed here. Other excavated areas include an early Christian basilica, the Roman Forum, the House of Eustolios which has Christian inscriptions and a mosaic symbolizing the Creation; a house with a mosaic showing Odysseus unmasking a hiding Achilles before the Siege of Troy; and another showing gladiators in combat. Yet further west is the ruined city's Stadium.

Finally, a few kilometers westwards again, is the **Sanctuary of Apollo Hylates**, *open daily 7:30m to 5 pm, 7:30 pm from 1 June to 30 September; admission CY75¢.* The Greek geographer Strabo, writing in the 1st century, told of a promontory near Kourion "from which they hurl those who have touched the altar of Apollo." The foundations of the altar are still there so you can try touching it and see what happens. This is one of Cyprus's best-preserved ancient sites.

Return to Kolossi then turn south towards the British Royal Air Force base at Akrotiri. You pass **Akrotiri Salt Lake**, dried out in summer, on your left. If you go too far you will be turned back at the base entrance, but just before there turn left for the **Monastery of Agios Nikolaos ton Gaton**, "of the Cats," *open daily.* This is where descendants of the snake-fighting cats introduced to Cyprus by Saint Helena in the 4th century still bask in the glow of victory, watched over by the nuns.

NIGHTLIFE & ENTERTAINMENT

In summer, theater, music and dance performances are held at the 2,000-year-old clifftop **Greek Theater** at Kourion (Curium), west of Limassol.

The **Curium Drama Festival** takes place on various days during July and August, using the theater for performances of ancient Greek plays, as well as works by Shakespeare and other dramatists. Take a cushion along and something warm to wear in the evenings.

SPORTS & RECREATION

Fishing is possible at several fresh-water reservoirs in the Limassol area. Information and mandatory permits are available from the **Limassol District Office of the Fisheries Department**, *Old Harbor, Tel. 05/330470.*

All manner of water sports are practised along the coast: swimming, diving, snorkeling, paragliding, sea-fishing. Several boat charter operators can be found at the Old Harbor.

For golf, try the **Elias Golf Club**, *c/o Elias Beach Hotel, Limassol. Tel. 05/325000.*

SHOPPING

Cyprus Handicraft Service, *Odos Themidos 25, Tel. 05/330118*, is where you'll find the only Limassol branch of the government-operated handicrafts foundation.

EXCURSIONS & DAY TRIPS

The best trips are those going west to Pafos and north into the Troodos Mountains. There are any number of agencies. Try **Paradise Island Tours**, *Odos 28 Oktovriou 227, Tel. 05/368428.*

PRACTICAL INFORMATION

· **Limassol Tourist Information**, *Odos Spyrou Araouzou 15, 3036 Limassol. Tel. 05/362756*
· **Limassol Harbor Tourist Information**, *Pasenger Terminal. Tel. 05/343868*

THE WEST

This is Aphrodite country, boasting the rock called **Petra tou Romiou** where the Goddess of Love is supposed to have been wafted ashore on a seashell. Maybe she was and maybe she wasn't, but romantic couples gather there every evening to watch the sunset in the expectation that some of the goddess's magic will rub off. There is also the emblematic **Sanctuary of Aphrodite**.

More than romantic legends though, the West is perhaps the most beautiful part of Cyprus, not overwhelmed by tourist development – at least not yet – as some other areas have been. Visitors who want to get away from everything and everyone can do so in the wild West – the ruggedly beautiful **Akamas Peninsula**, which is supposed to become a National Park. Be careful with whom you visit **Fontana Amoroza** in the Akamas. Legend has it that anyone who drinks from the pool will fall head-over-heels in love with the first person they see – but legend must first deal with the fact that the "pool" is more of a muddy swamp today.

Saint George of the **Agios Georgios Church** at Cape Drepanon spends half his time dispensing advice to lovers about their relationship and the other half searching for sheep who have strayed. Makes you wonder, doesn't it?

The **Polis** district was once noted for its thieves and cutthroats. Don't be afraid to go there today: a nicer bunch of thieves and cutthroats you couldn't hope to meet – just kiddng!

PAFOS

It may not look much like it now, but **Pafos** was once the capital of Cyprus. In Greek and Roman times pilgrims arrived in its harbor from all over the Mediterranean. They were decked out with garlands of flowers and colorful robes then went dancing and singing along the processional way to the **Sanctuary of Aphrodite**, where Cypriot virgins performed the sacred rites of the goddess of love. I can't guarantee that anything remotely similar will happen today.

The Roman proconsul (governor) set up shop here and the remains of his **palace** along with those of adjacent rich folks' villas have yielded a remarkable harvest of ancient **mosaics**.

There are no fewer than three Pafoses. One is the old town, which used to have a big Turkish Cypriot population. This is either just called Pafos, or **Ktima**, to distinguish it from **Kato Pafos**, the main tourist district round the old harbor, and Palaea Pafos, now marked **Kouklia** on maps, the site of the Sanctuary of Aphrodite. This seems confusing, but isn't really. It's easier to think of three separate places: Kato Pafos beside the sea for tourism, Ktima a little way inland for the old town, and Kouklia 17 kilometers away for Aphrodite.

Nowadays Pafos is the most pleasant of Cyprus's main tourist areas, but it won't stay that way for long if the present pace of development is sustained.

ARRIVALS & DEPARTURES

Pafos has one of Cyprus's two international airports so it is quite possible that you will arrive here. Take a taxi the short distance into town. If you are coming from Limassol you have the choice of bus, service taxi, taxi, or hired car. Buses are cheap but slow; service taxis are frequent and they will pick up and drop off within Limassol and Pafos; taxis are reasonably priced but the distance is 65 kilometers; hired car may be best but take it easy on the narrow coast road (a new expressway is gradually being extended from Limassol).

By Bus

Limassol to Pafos: Kemek Transport, Monday through Friday 9:30 am. Costas Buses, Monday, Tuesday, Thursday, Friday 1:30, 5 pm; Wednesday, Saturday 2 pm.

Pafos to Limassol: Kemek Transport, Monday through Friday xx. Costas Buses, Monday, Tuesday, Thursday, Friday 8, 9 am; Wednesday, Saturday 8 am (buses continue to Nicosia).

By Service Taxi

These are shared taxis that run at approximately hourly intervals between Pafos and Limassol. The "taxis" are minibuses stopping within the urban center or can be boarded at the dispatch office, and drop off within the urban center of the destination or at the dispatch office.

Service Taxis: Pafos to Limassol
- **Karydas Taxis/Kyriakos Taxis**, *Leoforos Evagora Pallikaridi. Tel. 06/ 361114*
- **Makris Taxis**, *Odos Ellados 166. Tel. 05/365550*
- **Nea Pafos Taxis**, *Odos Vragadinou 1. Tel. 05/355355*

GETTING AROUND TOWN

A half-hourly bus service runs along the seafront from Kato Pafos to **Coral Bay** and an hourly service to the same place from the market in Ktima. Connections to nearby villages range from one a day in winter to four a day to more popular places in summer. An hourly service runs between the bus station and **Polis**.

WHERE TO STAY

CORAL BEACH, *Coral Bay, Pegeia (12 kilometers north of Pafos). Tel. 06/621601, Fax 06/621156. Rates (with tax): CY£72 single; CY£89-122 double.*

Occupies a prime position on one of the best beaches on the west coast and offers unrivaled luxury. The Coral Beach has a full range of sports and fitness facilities.

VENUS BEACH, *Leoforos Tafon ton Vasileion, Kato Pafos. Tel. 06/ 249200, Fax 06/249224. Rates (with tax): CY£54-59 single; CY£78-88 double.*

These are reasonable prices considering the facilities at the Venus Beach, which is just a little way out of Kato Pafos center, near the Tombs of the Kings archaeological site.

DROUSHIA HEIGHTS, *Drouseia village (37 kilometers north of Pafos). Tel. 06/332351, Fax 06/332353. Rates (with tax): CY£27-38 single; CY£36-50 double.*

A different kind of experience in a hilltop hotel amidst excellent hiking country. The Droushia Heights has won awards for its environmental awareness.

KINGS, *Leoforos Tafon ton Vasileion, Kato Pafos. Tel/fax. 06/233497. Rates (with tax): CY£20-23 single; CY£26-28 double; breakfast CY£2.*

An excellent-value, small and friendly hotel and one that is bright and cheerful. The Kings is very popular and with only 27 rooms gets filled up well in advance.

SOULI, *Latsi to Neon Chorion Road. Tel. 06/321088, Fax 06/322474. Rates (with tax): CY£16-18 single; CY£24-27 double; breakfast CY£2.*

A beautifully sited, isolated hotel overlooking the sea on the scenic and scarcely developed northwest coast. The Souli is within easy striking distance of the beautiful Akamas Peninsula and makes an ideal place for getting away from it all. It also has an excellent seafood restaurant supplied by the fishing boats at nearby Latsi.

PARK MANSIONS, *Odos Pavlou Melas 16, Ktima. Tel. 06/245645, Fax 06/246415. Rates (with tax); CY£15-19 single; CY£26-30 double; breakfast CY£2.*

This is a gem of a place, a converted old Venetian mansion hidden out of sight behind a garden. It's worthwhile making the discovery for a characterful and reasonably priced hotel away from the tourist zone.

AGAPINOR, *Odos Nikodemos Mylonos 26, Ktima (Nea Pafos). Tel. 06/233927, Fax 06/235308. Rates (with tax): CY£13-15 single; CY£21-23 double; breakfast CY£2.*

While not an especially charming place, it has reasonable prices and facilities and is good for people who prefer to be in the middle of a real Cypriot town rather than in a tourist zone.

WHERE TO EAT

In addition to the hotel restaurant at Souli above, try the following:

NOSTALGIA, *Leoforos Tafon ton Vasileion 8, Kato Pafos. Tel. 06/247464. Credit cards accepted. Russian/expensive.*

A different kind of Cyprus dining experience, in a Russian restaurant catering for the many well-heeled Russian tourists and businessmen. Just hope that none of your fellow diners think you're with the FBI!

YIANGOS AND PETER, *Fishing Harbor, Latsi. Tel. 06/321411. Credit cards accepted. Traditional. Moderate-expensive.*

If you only eat at one place in Cyprus, this should be it. A superb family-operated seafood restaurant right on the harbor at Latsi, it never lets its standards slip, even on the busiest summer day.

DOVER, *Leoforos Poseidonos, Kato Pafos. Tel. 06/248100. Credit cards accepted. Traditional. Moderate-expensive.*

An excellent seafood restaurant.

PELICAN, *Leoforos Apostolou Pavlou 102 (Pafos Harbor). Tel. 06/246886). Credit cards accepted. Traditional. Moderate.*

Probably the best of a line of harborfront tavernas that are popular because of their atmosphere and location, but where quality is often indifferent.

SEEING THE SIGHTS

The best place to start is at the **harbor** in Kato Pafos. **Pafos Fort** on the harbor wall, *open Monday to Friday 7:30 am to 2:30 pm, also Thursday 3 pm to 6 pm, Saturday and Sunday 9 am to 5 pm; admission CY75¢,* was built by the Ottoman Turks after 1570 on the foundations of an earlier Lusignan castle. If you look across the harbor from here you will see the remains of the ancient breakwater on the other side.

Some of the former Customs sheds lining the harbor have been transformed into restaurants. These are mostly OK but none are really special cuisine-wise, although they all look good and have a fine atmosphere.

Behind them is the main excavated area of the ancient city. The Roman governor's palace is here and three other partly excavated villas. You reach them through a single entrance to see the dazzling **Mosaics of Pafos**, *open daily 7:30 am to 7:30 pm from June 1 to September 30, daily 7:30 am to 5 pm from October 1 to May 31; admission CY£1.50.* The mosaics are a Unesco World Heritage site. The mosaics cover big swaths of floor with beautifully executed depictions of Greek myths.

You will thrill to Narcissus infatuated with his own reflection; be amazed by Dionysus in procession; stunned by the boy Ganymede being abducted by lecherous Zeus. It really is an ancient cinema in there: the romantic tales of Pyramos and Thisbe, Neptune and Amymome, and Apollo and Daphne; Orpheus enchanting wild animals with his lyre; Heracles fighting the lion of Nemaea; Theseus battling the Minotaur; Poseidon and Amphitrite riding the waves on a sea-monster; Zeus in the shape of a swan whispering heavenly sweet nothings to Leda; Apollo condemning the upstart flute-player Marsyas to death, and much much more, all in glorious technicolor.

After that the reconstructed **Odeion**, outside the Mosaics zone, *permanent access; admission free,* seems pretty tame. Plays and concerts are performed here in summer. On Odos Kyriakou Nikolau is the ruined

Crusader Castle called the **Saranda Kolones**. The Crusaders had only just got the thing finished when an earthquake knocked it down.

Several blocks behind the seafront off Leoforos Poseidonos are the ruins of the early Christian basilica of **Panagia Chrysopolitissa**, which are closed while excavations continue. Through the fence you can see **St Paul's Pillar**, where the evangelist was said to have been scourged in 45 AD. St Paul retaliated by converting the Roman governor Sergius, a feat that, if true, makes Sergius the first ever Christian ruler (on Earth at any rate).

Walk, or drive, back to the main road leading to Ktima and turn left on Leoforos Tafon ton Vasileion. This leads to the **Tombs of the Kings**, another World Heritage site, *open daily 7:30 am to 7:30 pm from June 1 to September 30, daily 7:30 am to 5 pm from October 1 to May 31; admission CY75¢.* There were no Cypriot kings by the time this seaside cemetery came into use in about 300 BC, but you probably had to have a good positive bank balance to get in. It now makes for a somber sight, its gloomy underground vaults contrasting with the shining blue of the Mediterranean not much more than a stone's throw away.

Other Sights

• **Pafos District Archaeological Museum**, *Odos Griva Digeni. Tel. 06/ 240215. Open Monday to Friday 7:30 am to 2:30 pm, also Thursday 3 pm to 6 pm, Saturday and Sunday 10 am to 1 pm. Admission CY75¢.* Bits and pieces from excavations in and around Pafos, including a marble sculpture of Aphrodite.

• **Byzantine Museum**, *Odos Agios Ioannou. Tel. 06/232092. Open Monday to Saturday 9 am to 5 pm. Admission CY75¢.* Houses an ecclesiastical collection that includes 12th-century icons.

• **Ethnographic Museum**, *Odos Exo Vrisis. Tel. 06/232010. Open Monday to Saturday 9 am to 5:30 pm, Sunday 10 am to 1 pm.* Smallish museum that crams in stuff ranging from prehistoric fossils to 19th-century bridal gowns.

Around Pafos

First let's get romantic. In Cyprus that means Aphrodite. Leave Pafos going south on the Limassol road and drive for about 17 kilometers, then head inland for a kilometer following the signs to the **Sanctuary of Aphrodite** at Old Pafos, now called **Kouklia**, *open daily 7:30 am to 7:30 pm July and August, otherwise Monday to Friday 7:30 am to 6:30 pm, Thursday 6 pm, Saturday and Sunday 9 am to 5 pm; admission CY75¢.* The temple was in business from the 12th century BC until boring old Emperor Theodosius the Great (the Great Spoilsport?) abolished the pagan cults towards the end of the 4th century.

Herodotus wrote that every Cypriot woman was obliged to give herself once to visiting pilgrims at the Sanctuary – which may have been no more than wishful thinking on his part. Yet sacred prostitution was undoubtedly a part of the rites. You'll need a pretty fertile imagination to recreate in your mind's eye the ancient scene of youthful handmaidens giving themselves willingly to every pilgrim.

The temple's remains are scanty, yet somehow the fact that they are there at all seems astonishing. An on-site museum housed in an Ottoman manor-farm, the **Chiftlik**, has finds from the Sanctuary, including a conical stone which is thought to have been the archaic cult idol of Aphrodite.

At nearby **Old Pafos**, excavation work is continuing and there is not much to see. One of the city's gates, Marcello Hill, has been uncovered, revealing a dramatic scene from the Cypriot revolt against Persia in 498 BC. A Persian siege mound reaches up to the walls, the defenders tunneled desperately to undermine it and there must have been heavy fighting. Pafos fell, Herodotus wrote, and the fate of its inhabitants can only be guessed at.

Back on the coast road towards Limassol, after another six or seven kilometers you reach an unusual rock formation in the sea called **Petra tou Romiou**. It's better known as **Aphrodite's Rock**, the place where the goddess is supposed to have been wafted ashore on a seashell. She was received joyously by the Horae (Hours), who draped her with precious jewels, set a crown of gold upon her head, and gave her earrings of gold and copper. Quite a reception. Star-crossed couples watch the sunset here every evening in summer.

Get back to Pafos, and this time leave town on the coast road going northwards. You'll pass one of the best beaches in the area at **Coral Bay** and finally arrive in **Agios Georgios** where a modern church stands beside an old Byzantine chapel at Cape Drepanon. To the north is **Lara Bay**. The beach here is a turtle hatchery, a protected area for endangered green turtles. Elsewhere in Cyprus, baby turtles have been hatching at night and heading instinctively for the nearest light source, which more often than not turns out be a disco rather than the luminescent glimmer of the sea.

You can carry on from here on a rough track leading up to and across the mountainous spine of the **Akamas Peninsula**. This wild area is supposed to become a National Park and is a Mediterranean cause célèbre among environmentalists. There is opposition to the National Park idea from local people who want the jobs and profits that tourist development would bring. Astonishingly, the British army and Royal Air Force exercise on the peninsula, so be careful you don't get blown to pieces (red warning flags are flown when the military are playing games, and there are signs warning you not to pick up things that might explode and kill you!).

The **Baths of Aphrodite**, at the northern entrance to the Akamas, *open permanently; admission free,* is a fresh-water pool where guess-who is supposed to have bathed after her amorous adventures. The waters confer eternal youth – so you're not allowed to go in, of course.

You come now to the old sponge-diving center **Latsi**, and **Polis**, two resorts that appeal to Cyprus's "alternative" tourists. Latsi is the jumping-off point for hiking expeditions into the Akamas. There are no big hotels (but one furiously disputed such development was building at the time of writing) and the coast is mostly undeveloped, particularly if you head east from Polis around sweeping Chrysochou Bay, which looks like the whole Mediterranean probably did once, before tourism got started.

Go far enough on this road, past **Pomos**, and you'll eventually be forced into the mountains to go around the Turkish army's military enclave at Kokkina. Back on the coast road you come to **Kato Pyrgos** and the main UN buffer zone.

If you have time and are willing to be jolted about a lot, you can return to Pafos by an inland route through the wild and scenic **Pafos Forest**, where the island's once extensive forest cover is being recreated, tree by tree. The rare and extremely shy **moufflon** wild sheep has a protected reserve in the forest. A remote forest station at **Stavros tis Psokas** is best reached by four-wheel-drive vehicle and makes a superb base for wilderness hikes.

Other Sights

• **Agios Neofytos Monastery**, *near Tala village. Open daily 9 am to 1 pm and 4 pm to 6 pm in summer, daily 9 am to 4 pm in winter. Admission CY75¢.* Important shrine of the 12th-century hermit Saint Neofytos, who carved a sanctuary *(enkleistra)* into the cliffside.

• **Panagia Chrysorrogiatissa Monastery**, *Pano Panagia village. Open daily. Admission free.* In addition to a dramatic location in the rugged foothills of the Troodos Mountains 40 kilometers northeast of Pafos, the monastery, founded in the 12th century, is noted for its award-wining Monte Royia wine.

NIGHTLIFE & ENTERTAINMENT

In summer, theater, music, and dance performances are held at the ancient **Greek Theater** in Pafos, behind the harbor. Take a cushion along.

SPORTS & RECREATION

Fishing is possible at three fresh-water reservoirs in the Pafos area: **Asprokremnos**, 16 kilometers east of Pafos; **Mavrokoloympos**, 11 kilometers northwest of Pafos; and **Evretou**, 10 kilometers south of Polis. A permit is needed, obtainable from the **Pafos District Office of the Fisheries Department**, *Pafos Harbor, Tel. 06/240268.*

All manner of water sports are practised along the coast: swimming, diving, snorkeling, paragliding, sea-fishing. Several boat charter operators can be found at the Old Harbor.

For golf enthusiasts, try the **Tsada Golf Club**, *Tsada village (10 kilometers north of Pafos), Tel. 06/642774.*

SHOPPING

Cyprus Handicraft Service, *Leoforos Apostolou Pavlou 64. Tel. 06/ 240243*, is where you'll find the only Pafos branch of the government-operated handicrafts foundation.

EXCURSIONS & DAY TRIPS

The best trips are those going north to Polis and the Akamas Peninsula and east into the Troodos Mountains. There are any number of agencies. For trips that get you closer to the environment or add an extra spice of adventure go to **Exalt Tours**, *Odos Agias Kyriakis 24, Pafos, Tel. 06/243803*. American David Pearlman and his "excursion alternatives" team are committed to high-level, sensitively planned trips, by Land Rover and on foot, into Cyprus's remotest and most rugged areas. Contact with nature and interaction with local culture are Exalt's watchwords. If you go on a hiking trek with them be prepared to sweat a little (actually a lot).

For mainstream excursions, try **Salamis Tours**, *Leoforos Giorgiou Griva Digeni 44, Pafos, Tel. 06/235504*.

PRACTICAL INFORMATION

• **Pafos Tourist Information**, *Odos Gladstonos 3, 8046 Pafos. Tel. 06/ 232841*
• **Pafos International Airport Tourist Information**, *Arrivals Hall. Tel. 06/ 422833*
• **Germasogeia Tourist Information**, *Odos Georgiou Afxentiou 35, Germasogeia (opposite Dasoudi Beach). Tel. 05/323211*

THE TROODOS MOUNTAINS

Cyprus's own rocky mountain high, the **Troodos Mountains**, make for a different kind of Mediterranean experience. In winter you can even ski up here in the morning before heading to the beach for an afternoon swim. In summer the cool air scented with eucalyptus and pine is an irresistible draw for many otherwise beachbound tourists.

All across the western and southern foothills are vineyards from which come Cyprus's wines, and villages for which "remote" would be a mild description. Hard hiking brings you to nature reserves and forest stations, and to Byzantine-era monasteries and churches whose founders chose the Troodos as the perfect refuge from the worldly and at that time often perilous coastal towns.

The forests which vanished into Bronze Age copper smelters and into the fleets with which Phoenicians, Persians, Greeks, Romans, Byzantines, Arabs, Crusaders, Venetians and Turks vied for Mediterranean hegemony are being recreated. This process was begun by the British and continues via the Cyprus Forestry Department which maintains signposted trails, information centers, and picnic sites with barbecue facilities around the mountains.

ARRIVALS & DEPARTURES

You won't get around too easily without a hired car, motorbike, or scooter up here. There are bus services from Nicosia and Limassol.

By Bus

Nicosia via Troodos to Platres: Zingas Buses, Monday through Friday 12:15 pm. Clarios Bus Company, Monday through Friday 11:30 am.

Platres via Troodos to Nicosia: Zingas Buses, Monday through Friday 6 am. Clarios Bus Company, Monday through Friday 6:30 am.

Limassol to Platres : Kyriakos/Karydas Buses, Monday through Friday 11:30 am. Kemek Transport, Monday through Friday 2 pm.

Platres to Limassol: Kemek Transport, Monday through Friday 5 am. Kyriakos/Karydas Buses, Monday through Friday 7 am.

ORIENTATION

The Troodos is the big lump of rock in the middle of government-controlled Cyprus – one with hardly any good roads and some of the most stunning scenery on the island. The main north-south roads are good. Anything going east-west will run into something rough after a while.

It can get cool up there even on a summer evening, but it's a clear sharp-edged tangy cool, the kind that gives you a hearty appetite and a taste for one of those crisp Cyprus wines. Just the same, if you're planning on staying overnight take something warm. Taxis are scanty and buses are few and far between in the mountains, apart from tour buses that is.

The main resorts like **Platres**, **Troodos**, and **Kakopetria** can become traffic choke-points, as can the approaches to **Mount Olympus**, at the busiest times in summer. There is plenty of room to escape the crowds if you avoid these places.

GETTING AROUND THE MOUNTAINS

Watch out for Cypriot farmers driving pick-ups on the narrow, ditch-lined mountain roads. They can easily recognise tourists' rental cars by their distinctive red license plates and "Z" prefix, and they've learned that by driving straight at them they can, magically, get the whole road to themselves. This is the kind of surprise you could easily do without.

Buses really are few and far between here. Count on no more than one a day between the smaller villages even in summer. Even taxis are in short supply, so a hired car or a coach-tour is the only sensible way.

You can hire mountain bikes at Platres, but you shouldn't do any serious mountain-biking in this terrain unless you're really up to it. The heat alone is enough to knock most people off the saddle. If you can hack it, however, there is no better way to see the mountains. An alternative to going off-road is to stay on the roads and map out a route through some of the surrounding villages. If you do this it may make sense not to have a final uphill stretch to Platres to return your bike. The downhill from **Trooditissa Monastery** is a pretty good one.

WHERE TO STAY

FOREST PARK, *outside Pano Platres. Tel. 05/421751, Fax 05/421875. Rates (with tax): CY£40 single; CY£66 double.*

The top-rated resort hotel of the mountains, set in a forested location outside the village. It has a heated outdoor swimming pool.

CHURCHILL PINEWOOD VALLEY, *Prodromos to Pedoulas road, outside Pedoulas. Tel. 02/952211, Fax 02/952439. Rates (with tax): CY£38 single; CY£50 double.*

As its name implies, the Churchill occupies a secluded pine-forest location. It has an unheated outdoor swimming pool.

EDELWEISS, *Pano Platres. Tel. 05/421335, Fax 05/422060. Rates (with tax): CY£2 single; CY£33 double.*

A quite small and welcoming hotel in the village.

STAVROS TIS PSOKAS REST HOUSE, *Stavros tis Psokas Forest Station, Pafos Forest (10 airline kilometers northwest of Panagia tou Kykkou Monastery). Tel/fax. 06/722338. Rates (with tax): CY£10 double.*

Set amidst the wild and hard-to-cross Pafos Forest, far from roads and "civilization," near the moufflon wild sheep reserve and the cedars of Cedar Valley, this is only for the adventurous. With just seven rooms and a few chalets, Stavros tis Psokas gets filled up way in advance – so book early or forget it.

WHERE TO EAT

MARYLAND AT THE MILL, *Kakopetria village. Tel. 02/922536. Credit cards accepted. Traditional. Moderate-expensive.*

A very popular high-quality restaurant. Its mountain trout is particularly good.

PHINI TAVERNA, *Foini village. Tel. 05/421828. No credit cards. Traditional. Moderate.*

A delightful village taverna in one of the prettiest mountain villages, serving good traditional food.

KALEDONIA, *Pano Platres. Tel. 05/421404. No credit cards. Traditional. Moderate.*

An unpretentious kind of place where Cypriot food tastes great on a cool summer evening.

CIVIC, *Troodos village. Tel. 05/422102. No credit cards. Traditional. Inexpensive.*

A scenically situated small restaurant just outside Troodos village to the north. Makes a good place for an al fresco lunch away from the summer crowds in the village.

SEEING THE SIGHTS

Platres (altitude 1,230 meters) is the main Troodos Mountain resort both in summer and in the winter skiing season. The tourist information office is here, but as there is not much specifically mountain-related information produced you could easily pick it up at offices in Nicosia or the coastal resorts before heading for the hills. Still, there is a map and some booklets on signposted mountain trails worth having.

Further up the mountain is a diminutive waterfall called **Kaledonia Falls** and close by, out of sight among the trees, the President of Cyprus's summer residence (it used to be the British governor's). While on the back road to Prodromos is **Trooditissa Monastery**.

The higher resort of **Troodos** (1,920 meters) is a purpose-built eateries-and-souvenirs place for tourists. It is on the way to Cyprus's highest mountain, **Mount Olympus** (not to be confused with its namesake in Greece), at 1,951 meters. In winter you can ski the snows of Olympus and in summer hike its nature trails. You cannot reach its summit, however, which is occupied by the geodesic dome of a British military radar station.

From Troodos the main road north winds downhill to Prodromos and Pedoulas, through the cherry orchards of the Marathasa Valley to the great Orthodox monastery of **Panagia tou Kykkou**, *open daily; admission to grounds and church free; to the Treasury CY75¢,* the wealthiest and most influential in Cyprus. Don't try taking pictures in the monastery church of the celebrated icon of the Virgin, said to have been painted by St Luke and presented to Kykkou by the 12th-century Byzantine Emperor Alexius I. Enclosed in tortoise-shell and mother-of-pearl it stands on the iconostasis. The merest hint of a camera will get the hinter bundled unceremoniously out the door.

On **Throni Hill**, two kilometers from Kykkou, is the **Tomb of Archbishop Makarios**, first President of the Republic of Cyprus, *open daily from dawn to dusk; admission free. The tomb is* watched over by an honor guard of the Cyprus army. The view from the little chapel above the tomb stretches across the mountains to the distant Mediterranean.

BYZANTINE CHURCHES

No fewer than nine Byzantine-era churches in the Troodos Mountains have been designated Unesco World Heritage sites, for their rare and disarmingly simple architecture and especially for their magnificent religious frescoes. They are:

*• **Agios Ioannis Lampadistis** (Saint John Lampadistis), near Kalopanagiotis. The monastery church is three churches, with three roofs, in a single building, one from the 11th century, one from the 12th and one from the 15th. Each is covered in frescoes.*

*• **Agios Nikolaos tis Stegis** (Saint Nicholas of the Roof), near Kakopetria. An 11th-century church with a double roof and magnificent frescoes.*

*• **Archangelos** (The Archangel), near Galata. A small timber roofed church with post-Byzantine frescoes.*

*• **Panagia tou Asinou** (Our Lady of Asinou), near Nikitari. Perhaps the most beautiful frescoes of all the Troodos churches, some of them dating from 1150. The Christ Pantokrator is particularly fine but look out also for those of the Last Supper and the Ascension.*

*• **Panagia tis Podythou** (Our Lady of Podythou), near Galata. A 16th-century church noted for its frescoes of the Crucifixion and Our Lady as the Queen of Heaven.*

*• **Panagia tou Araka** (Our Lady of Araka), near Nikitari. A 12th-century church with the finest of the Troodos frescoes, including those of the Last Supper and the Ascension painted by artists from Constantinople and a superb Christ Pantokrator (Ruler of the Universe) gazing down from the dome.*

*• **Panagia tou Moutoullas** (Our Lady of Moutoullas), Moutoullas. A tiny place filled with colorful frescoes.*

*• **Stavros tou Agiasmati** (Holy Cross), near Platanistasa. The church's 15th-century frescoes, many by the Lebanese master Philippe Goul, are reckoned to be among the best anywhere in the Orthodox world. There is a particularly fine representation of Our Lady attended by the Archangels Gabriel and Michael.*

*• **Timios Stavros** (The True Cross), near Pelendri. A 14th-century church with a suite of fine biblical frescoes.*

Going eastwards from Troodos then north leads eventually down through the scenic **Solea Valley** on the main road back to Nicosia. East from Troodos leads into the remote and wildly beautiful **Pitsilia** district, where most of the roads seem to disappear into the wilderness. One that doesn't quite leads to **Machairas Monastery**, a scenically sited stronghold of the Orthodox faith and Hellenism.

South from Troodos brings you through a broad swath of villages in the grape-growing **Commandaría Region**. Vineyards here produce the sweet red dessert wine called Commandaría, which originated with the Crusader Knights Hospitaller, who once controlled these lands from their Commandery at Kolossi Castle. Off the southwestern edge of this area is another wine district, the **Krassochoria**, whose villages are up to their knees in grape juice come autumn – or at least they would be if the whole process hadn't by now been automated.

Troodos Villages

The Cypriot government is almost obsessive about the health, or otherwise, of its villages and has a variety of schemes in place to arrest the drift of their young people to better-paying jobs in the towns and coastal resorts. This is mostly a vain effort. Some villages are hanging on, and all are a taste of a Cyprus far removed in spirit from the resorts.

A selection of some of the more interesting ones:

• **Agios Amvrosios** – "Green" wines are produced in this southern Troodos village at the Ecological Winery.

• **Agios Theodoros** – A picturesque artists' haven in the Pitsilia district and noted for the silver-chased icon of Our Lady in the village church.

• **Agros** – A pretty village in Pitsilia which produces rose-water, mineral water and wine (not necessarily in that order of preference).

• **Arsos** – Noted for its fiery spirit – *zivanía*, which they call "Cyprus whisky." It is distilled from grape remnant after wine fermentation in a copper pot known as a *kazani*.

• **Foini** – Numerous workshops in the village produce fine pottery. Sadly, hardly any of them now are the big old hand-thrown pots called *pitharia*. A small Folk Art Museum features this and other traditions.

- **Kaliana** – Most notable for its simple agricultural tranquility in the heart of the fertile Solea Valley.
- **Kampos** – Village in the middle of nowhere, off the northwestern edge of the mountains.
- **Koilani** – A wine-making village that keeps one foot in heaven's camp with an Ecclesiastical Museum.
- **Omodos** – Shrewdly cashing in on the tourist boom by reinventing itself as a resort. You can even get to see the villagers' houses – but only for a fee!
- **Palaichori** – Its white houses look like an avalanche frozen in the act of tumbling down the steep hillside on which it stands.
- **Pano Amiantos** – An object lesson in environmental catastrophe. The nearby Amiantos asbestos mine has closed but the mountainside hereabouts will be a long time recovering – if it ever does.
- **Pedoulas** – Cherry blossoms and cherries, and the Holy Cross of Pedoulas.
- **Vasa** – Wine and mineral water are produced and bottled in this red-roofed village.

SPORTS & RECREATION

Fishing is possible at several fresh-water reservoirs in the Troodos area. Information about locations and mandatory permits are obtainable from the **Pafos District Office of the Fisheries Department**, *Pafos Harbor, Tel. 06/240268.*

Pano Platres is the best base for buying camping, hiking, and mountaineering equipment.

Mountain-biking is one of the great sports and is pretty challenging in the Troodos. Bikes can be hired at several locations in Pano Platres and Kakopetria.

In winter, skiing is possible on **Mount Olympus**, where there are four lifts and runs on both the North Face and in Sun Valley. Skis and boots can be hired at the resort.

SHOPPING

Troodos, Pano Platres, Kakopetria, and Pedoulas are the main shopping "centers" in the mountains, with craft products on display in many shops. Foini village is noted for its pottery. The villages of the wine-producing area off the southern and western edge of the mountains are great places for buying village wines – take your own bottles or bigger containers. A good souvenir is a bottle of Commandaría wine or fiery *zivanía* liqor.

PRACTICAL INFORMATION

• Platres Tourist Information, *Village Square. Tel. 05/421316*

THE NORTH

You have to decide for yourself whether it is right and proper to visit Turkish-occupied northern Cyprus – the Republic of Cyprus government does not think so.

The Republic of Cyprus authorities do allow tourists to pass through the UN Green Line in Nicosia to the Turkish sector at the Ledra Palace checkpoint, on single daytime passes only. This facility is occasionally withdrawn. Except for special categories, such as diplomatic and UN personnel and pre-1974 foreign residents of Cyprus, no one may pass freely in the opposite direction. Pride of place in the northern half of Nicosia (Lefkosha in Turkish) goes to the magnificent Selimiye Mosque, formerly the 13th-century Gothic Cathedral of Santa Sophia, converted after the Ottoman conquest in 1570. The Mevlevi Tekke was the monastery of Cyprus's dancers of the Muslim Sufi sect, the famed "whirling dervishes;" it is now a museum.

Two 16th-century caravanserai, the Büyük Han and the Kumarcilar Han, are impressive examples of Ottoman inns, while the Büyük Hamam is ditto for Turkish baths. Ottoman graces can be further seen in the Dervish Pasha Mansion and the Library of Sultan Mahmut II.

As negotiations promoted by the UN, the US State Department, and the European Union have at least a chance of ending Cyprus's division, it may one day again be possible to travel freely throughout the island. That would open up, among other beauties, **Kyrenia**, situated around its old harbor and dominated by the Venetian **Kyrenia Castle**; the cool, forested heights of the **Pentadaktylos Mountains**, crowned with Crusader castles and the Gothic **Abbey of Bellapais**; the walled city of **Famagusta**, jewel of the Levant in the Crusader era, when it was a source of wonder for its wealthy merchants, Gothic churches, and sumptuous villas; remote **Apostolos Andreas Monastery**, at the rocky tip of the Karpaz Peninsula, formerly a place of mass pilgrimage to its healing spring said to have been brought forth by the Apostle Andrew.

In the meantime, remember that an entry stamp in your passport from the illegal "Turkish Republic of Northern Cyprus" may result in denial of permission to enter the part of Cyprus under government control, and possibly also Greece.

IMAGES OF CYPRUS/1

Plenty of writers have turned their pens on Cyprus ever since Homer's ground-breaking reference to "Kypros," where laughter-loving Aphrodite had her incense-burning altar. Among the best books are:

• Lawrence Durrell's Bitter Lemons. Set during the 1950s as Cyprus was beginning its descent into communal tragedy, Durrell's book is a portrait of the people that is by turns riotously funny and hauntingly sad. He lived at Bellapaix village outside Kyrenia in what is now Turkish-occupied Cyprus, in "a house made for some forgotten race of giants." His fellow drinkers at Dimitri's cafe, lounging under the "Tree of Idleness, whose shadow incapacitates one for serious work ... were mostly grandfathers wearing the traditional baggy trousers and white cotton shirts ... a splendid group, gray-bearded, shaggy-haired, gentle of voice and manner."

The high school students, burning to gain freedom from British rule and for union with Greece, whom he taught English in Nicosia, "were admirable children, each wrapped in the bright silken cocoon of a dream."

• Colin Thubron's Journey Into Cyprus. Like Durrell's book, Thubron's is an image of Cyprus at a turning-point. The author walked for a thousand kilometers through Cyprus just before the Turkish invasion that split the island in two. Thubron writes: "This six-hundred mile walk through Cyprus in the spring and summer of 1972 traversed an island which is now no longer recognizable. The world it depicts – a mosaic of Greek and Turkish villages interknit – has seemingly gone forever, and such a journey, wandering at will among the two communities, is now impossible ... this is the record of a country that will not return."

IMAGES OF CYPRUS/2

• *Reno Wideson's* **Cyprus: Images of a Lifetime.** *A superb coffee-table picture book of the author's photographs of Cyprus and its people, many taken before the island's division. Of Famagusta's abandoned and decaying resort suburb Varosha he writes: "It is difficult to believe and accept that this happy, busy, blossom-scented small town I have known, where visitors came in their thousands and where the sound of Orange Festival songs filled the air is now an uninhabited ghost town. I hope and pray that sanity will prevail in the not-too-distant future and that Famagusta will be restored to its previous happiness and glory."*

• *Michael Jansen's* **The Aphrodite Plot.** *Was the CIA behind it all? A fictionalized but factually parallel account of the 1974 Greek-inspired coup in Cyprus which led directly to the Turkish invasion. Among the victims was the U.S. ambassador, killed during a violent protest by Greek Cypriots. Jansen is an American journalist who covered the events.*

• *Claude Delaval Cobham's* **Excerpta Cypria.** *First published in 1908 and republished in 1969, Cobham's work excerpts some 80 writers on Cyprus dating from the 1st century to the 19th century.*

16. WHO WAS WHO IN ANCIENT GREECE

THE GREEK GODS & THEIR HANGERS-ON

Aeolus God of the winds.

Alastor Demon.

Amphitrite Goddess of the sea.

Aphrodite* Goddess of love.

Apollo* God of music and poetry. Source of prophecy at the Oracle of Delphi.

Ares* God of war.

Arethusa Nymph.

Argus Watchman with a hundred eyes

Aristaeus God of farming.

Artemis* Goddess of the Moon.

Asclepius God of medicine.

Athena* Goddess of wisdom.

Atlas Titan who rebelled against the gods and was punished by being made to hold up the sky.

Attis God of vegetation.

Callisto Nymph of Artemis.

Castor and Pollux Children of Leda, fathered by Zeus. After their death they became the constellation Gemini.

Cerberus Many-headed dog that guarded the entrance to the Underworld.

Charon Ferryman who took the souls of the dead across the River Styx to the Underworld.

Cronus Father Time. A Titan and son of Uranus, he ruled the universe before the Age of the Olympians and devoured his children.

Cybele Goddess of nature. The Corybantes were her eunuch priests.

Daphne Daughter of the river god Ladon. She was turned into a laurel tree, a symbol of Apollo.

Demeter* Goddess of agriculture. Associated particularly with corn and the Eleusinian Mysteries enacted at Eleusis near Athens.

Dionysus God of wine and orgiastic merrymaking. His festivals were called "Dionysia", or "Bacchanalia" after his followers the Bacchae.

Echo Nymph who loved Narcissus but was spurned by him. She faded away to only a voice.

Eos Daughter of Helios. Goddess of the dawn.

Eris Sister of Ares and daughter of the night.

Eros God of love. Son of Aphrodite and Ares.

Eurydice Wood-nymph and wife of Orpheus.

Fates Three goddesses who controlled human destiny. Lachesis decided on the span of life, Clotho spun the thread, and Atropos cut it.

Furies Three avenging demons: Alecto, Megaira and Tisiphone. They were called the "Eumenides" after they had settled down and changed their character.

Gaia Earth Goddess and wife of Uranus.

Galatea Sea-nymph. The Cyclops Polyphemus fell in love with her.

Ganymede A beautiful boy who became a favorite of Zeus.

Gigantes Sons of the Earth who warred with the Olympians and lost.

Gorgons Monsters with snakes in place of hair. The Gorgon Medusa was killed by Perseus.

Graces Three daughters of Zeus and Hera who embodied feminine beauty and charm.

Graiae Three ugly old sisters of the Gorgons. The opposite of the Graces.

Hades King of the Underworld, the land of the dead. The Elysian Fields, a kind of heaven, were said to lie near the Underworld.

Halcyone Daughter of Aeolus. She married Ceyx, son of the morning star.

Harpies Bad-tempered monsters with women's faces and birds' wings and talons.

Hebe Goddess of youth and beauty.

Hecate Goddess of the magic arts.

Helios Sun-god.

Hephaestus* God of fire.

Hera* Daughter of Cronus and wife of Zeus.

Hermaphroditus Son of Aphrodite and Hermes. A god with male and female attributes.

Hermes* Messenger of the gods.

Hesperides Daughters of the evening star who guarded the Golden Apples of the Sun.

Hestia* Goddess of hearth and home

Horae The Hours, handmaidens of Aphrodite.

Hydra Many-headed monster slain by Heracles.

Hygeia Daughter of Asclepius.

Hymen God of marriage.

Hyperion Titan and father of Eos, Helios and Selene.

Iapetus Titan, father of Prometheus.

Io One of Zeus's many passions, she was transformed into a cow to save her from Hera's jealousy.

Iris Rainbow-goddess.

Ixion Father of the Centaurs, he tried to rape Hera and was bound eternally to a wheel of fire.

Leto Titaness and mother of Apollo and Artemis.

Medea Witch who helped Jason capture the Golden Fleece.

Medusa One of the Gorgons, killed by Perseus.

Mnemosyne Titaness, mother of the Muses.

Muses Nine daughters of Zeus and Mnemosyne. Inspiration of story tellers.

Nemesis Goddess of retribution.

Nike Goddess of victory.

Nymphs Nature spirits. Dryads: wood nymphs; Naiads: fresh-water nymphs; Nereids: sea-nymphs; Oceanides: sea and water nymphs.

Oceanus Titan. Symbol of the Ocean.

Olympians Top gods, and goddesses, who lived on Mount Olympus.

Pan God of goats and sheep, and sower of panic.

Pasiphae Daughter of Helios and mother of the Minotaur.

Pegasus Winged horse.

Persephone Daughter of Zeus and Demeter. Queen of the Underworld who returned to the land of the living for half of the year.

Phoebe Titaness and Moon goddess.

Pluto God of wealth, but also of death.

Poseidon* God of the sea.

Prometheus Titan. Stole fire from heaven and gave it to mankind. Zeus punished him by having an eagle eat his liver every day. He was freed by Heracles.

Proteus Sea-god.

Rhadamanthus Judge of the dead.

Rhea Titaness. Mother of Zeus who saved him from being eaten by his father Cronus.

Satyr Lustful followers of Dionysus.

Selene Goddess of the Moon.

Serapis Politically convenient god in the Hellenistic Age, who combined attributes of Egyptian Osiris and Apis with Zeus and Dionysus.

Semele Mother of Dionysus.

Silenus Demigod who taught Dionysus everything he knew about drunkenness and debauchery.

Syrinx Nymph. She was transformed into a reed from which Pan made his pipes.

Themis Goddess of justice.

Thetis Nereid who was the mother of Achilles.

Titans Earlier gods supplanted by the Olympians.

Titania Titaness and Moon deity.

Triton Son of Poseidon and Amphitrite.

Tyche Spirit of Fortune or Luck. By Hellenistic times she had become an important goddess for private, rather than public, worship.

Uranus First god. Father of the Titans and God of the sky.

Zeus* The Boss God. Father of Olympus, whose libido was out of control and who struck down transgressors with his thunderbolt and aegis.

* The 12 principal gods, the Olympians, who lived on Mount Olympus.

WHO ELSE WAS WHO IN GREEK MYTHOLOGY & LEGEND

Achilles Son of Peleus and the goddess Thetis. When he was a baby she held him in the waters of the River Styx by his heel, making him invulnerable everywhere but there. A hero of the Siege of Troy, he killed Hector to avenge the death of his friend Patroclus. Paris killed him with a poisoned arrow which struck his heel.

Actaeon Hunter who saw Artemis, goddess of chastity, naked. She turned him into a stag and he was killed by his own hounds.

Adonis Hunter who was the lover of the goddess Aphrodite. He was killed by a wild boar sent by her husband Hephaestus but was restored to life by Persephone.

Aegisthus Lover of Clytemnestra, wife of King Agamemnon, while Agamemnon was leading the Greeks at the Siege of Troy. When he returned Aegisthus persuaded Clytemnestra to murder him.

Aeneas Trojan hero. The son of Anchises and the goddess Aphrodite. He escaped from the fall of Troy and went on to found a line of kings in Italy from whom Romulus and Remus were descended (or so the Romans said).

Agamemnon Leader of the Greeks at the Siege of Troy. Killed by his own wife Clytemnestra when he returned from the war.

Ajax Son of Telamon. Killed himself during the Siege of Troy when he could not inherit the armor of Achilles.

Ajax Son of Oileus. Killed by Poseidon as he stepped ashore in Greece after the Siege of Troy.

Alcestis Having offered to die in her husband's place she was saved by Heracles who fought off the messenger of death.

Alcmaeon Killed his mother to avenge his father's murder and was pursued by the Erinyes (Furies).

Alcmene Mother of Heracles. Zeus took her husband Amphityron's form to sleep with her and be the father.

Andromache Wife of the Trojan hero Hector.

Andromeda Perseus saved her from Poseidon's wrath by using the Gorgon's head to turn a sea monster to stone.

Antigone Daughter of Oedipus. When her brother Polynices was killed while attacking Thebes she defied the orders of Creon and buried his body. For this she was condemned to death by starvation but hanged herself instead.

Arachne Weaver who challenged Athena to a contest. She won and was turned into a spider.

Argus Odysseus' dog, which recognized his master on his return from Troy.

Ariadne Daughter of King Minos who helped Theseus find his way out of the Labyrinth with a ball of thread.

Atalanta A swift runner. Men who wanted to marry her first had to win a race with her. Those who lost were killed. Hippomenes succeeded by throwing three golden apples at her feet, and winning the race while she picked them up.

Atreus Father of Agamemnon and Menelaus. Fed his brother Thyestes' children to him after a quarrel.

Autolycus Grandfather of Odysseus, and a famous thief.

Bellerophon Hero who was given impossible tasks to bring about his death, but who succeeded in carrying them out.

Calchas A Greek seer at the Siege of Troy.

Cassandra Daughter of King Priam of Troy. She had been given the gift of prophecy by Apollo but it was her fate never to be believed.

Cecrops First King of Athens, born from the earth.

Centaur A creature half man and half horse. Many were of uncertain temper, but one, Chiron, taught princes wisdom.

Chimaera Fire-breathing monster with a lion's head, goat's body and serpent's tail.

Circe Enchantress who turned Odysseus' men into swine.

Clytemnestra Wife of King Agamemnon. With her lover Aegisthus, she killed him on his return from Troy and was killed by her son Orestes.

Creon Ruler of Thebes who confirmed Oedipus as king of the city.

Cyclopes One-eyed giants. The Cyclops Polyphemus was blinded by Odysseus.

Daedalus Inventor who created the labyrinth in Crete for King Minos. He then flew from Crete to Sicily on wings he made himself.

Damocles Discovered how precarious is earthly success when he found himself seated at a banquet in the court of the Tyrant Dionysius of Syracuse with a sword suspended above his head by a single hair.

Danae Daughter of King Acrisius and mother of Perseus by Zeus.

Daphnis Shepherd blinded by a nymph. He created pastoral poetry.

Deianira Wife of the hero Heracles who poisoned him by mistake.

Deucalion Son of Prometheus. When Zeus flooded the world Deucalion and his wife Pyrrha survived by building an ark that came to dry land on Mount Parnassus.

Diomede Greek hero of the war with Troy.

Electra Helped her brother Orestes avenge their murdered father Agamemnon.

Endymion Shepherd who was loved by the Moon goddess Selene. He was also said to have conducted the first Olympic Games.

Epigoni Sons of the Seven Champions, who succeeded in capturing Thebes where their fathers had failed.

Erechtheus One of the first Kings of Athens.

Eteocles King of Thebes who was killed by his brother Polynices, one of the Seven Champions who attacked the city.

Europa Zeus consorted with her in the shape of a bull and she gave birth to King Minos of Crete.

Gordus King of Phyrgia who tied the intricate Gordian Knot that no one was unable to untie and so claim the prize of becoming ruler of Asia. Alexander the Great cut it with his sword.

Hector Favorite son of King Priam of Troy and a hero of the Trojan defence of the city. He killed Achilles' friend Patroclus and was in turn slain by Achilles.

Hecuba Queen of Troy and wife of King Priam.

Helen Beautiful wife of King Menalaus of Sparta and sister-in-law of King Agamemnon. It was her abduction by Paris that sparked the Trojan War.

Hellen Son of Deucalion and father of the Greek peoples – the Hellenes.

Heracles (aka Hercules) The "caveman" of Greek legend. A strong man who took on the Twelve Labors, which included capturing Cerberus; killing the Hydra; gathering the Apples of the Hesperides; and cleansing the Augean stables.

Hero and Leander Tragic lovers. Hero committed suicide when Leander drowned while swimming from Abydos to Sestos to meet him.

Hippolytus Son of Theseus and Hippolyta. He was falsely accused by his stepmother Phaedra of attempted rape and Theseus summoned Poseidon to cause his death.

Hyperboreans Prosperous race living beyond the North Wind.

Icarus Son of Daedalus. He was killed during their flight when he flew too close to the sun and the wax of his wings melted.

Idomeneus King of Crete. Led the Cretan contingent at the Siege of Troy and sacrificed his son on his return.

Iphigenia Daughter of Agamemnon and Clytemnestra. She was saved by Artemis as she was about to be sacrificed to guarantee favorable winds for the Greek fleet sailing for Troy.

Jason Led the Argonauts to Colchis aboard the ship *Argo* on the quest for the Golden Fleece.

Jocasta Mother of Oedipus who unknowingly becomes his wife and bears him four children then kills herself when she finds out what she has done.

Laius Father of Oedipus who was killed by his son.

Laocoön Trojan hero who tried to stop the Wooden Horse being brought within the walls. He and his two sons were crushed by a giant serpent sent by Apollo.

Lapiths Humans who shared Thessaly with the Centaurs.

Leda Mother of Castor and Pollux as well as Helen and Clytemnestra. Zeus seduced her disguised as a swan.

Lotus-Eaters A race encountered by Odysseus who ate a flower that made men forget their duty and live in a state of bliss.

Lycurgus King of Thrace blinded by Dionysus.

Meleager The Fates prophesied his death when a wooden brand was consumed by fire. His mother killed him by throwing it on the fire.

Memnon Ethiopian prince who fought for Troy and was killed by Achilles.

Menelaus King of Sparta and brother of Agamemnon. The abduction of his wife Helen caused the Trojan War. With his wife restored, he was one of the few heroes who survived to settle down again at home.

Midas King of Phyrgia. Everything he touched turned to gold, a talent which proved to be a curse.

Minos King of Crete. Ordered the creation of the Labyrinth to hold the Minotaur.

Minotaur Monster, half man and half bull, who lived in the Labyrinth on Crete.

Myrmidons Warriors from Thessaly who followed Achilles to the Trojan War.

Narcissus Handsome boy who fell in love with his reflection in a pool of water.

Nausicaa Daughter of King Alcinous of Phaeacia. She found the near-dead Odysseus on the beach and took him home to be cared for.

Neoptolemus Son of Achilles. Killed King Priam of Troy and took his daughter Andromache, wife of the dead hero Hector, as his slave. He was killed at Delphi.

Nestor King of Pylos. An elderly Greek leader at the Siege of Troy. None of the young heroes listen overmuch to his sensible advice.

Odysseus King of Ithaca. Hero of both *The Iliad* and *The Odyssey*. His return to Ithaca involved ten years of adventures and he slew the suitors of his wife Penelope on his return.

Oedipus King of Thebes. He killed his father by mistake and unwittingly married his mother with whom he had four children. He blinded himself when he found out what he had done.

Orestes Son of Agamemnon and Clytemnestra. He killed his mother to avenge her murder of his father and was pursued by the Furies.

Orion Hunter. The favorite of Eos, he was killed by Artemis.

Orpheus Poet. His lyre-playing could charm wild animals.

Pandarus Trojan hero killed by Diomede.

Pandora The first woman. She released all the evils when she opened a box given to her by Zeus.

Paris Son of King Priam. He caused the Trojan War when he responded to Aphrodite's offer of the most beautiful mortal woman by abducting Queen Helen of Sparta and taking her back to Troy.

Patroclus Friend of Achilles who took up the latter's armor when Achilles sulked in his tent during the Siege of Troy. He was killed by Hector and avenged by Achilles.

Peleus Husband of Thetis and father of Achilles.

Pelops Son of Tantalus and father of Atreus and Thyestes whom he caused to be cursed after murdering his way to marriage.

Penelope Wife of Odysseus.

Pentheus Torn to pieces by the Maenads when he played peeping-tom at their rites.

Perseus Son of Zeus and Danae. He killed the Gorgon Medusa.

Phaedra Second wife of Theseus. She falsely charged her stepson with attempted rape when he rejected her advances and later hanged herself after his death.

Phaethon Son of Helios. He drove the chariot of the sun too close to the Earth and was killed by Zeus.

Philomelma and Procne Philomelma was raped by Procne's husband, the King of Thrace, so Procne fed him their children.

Philemon and Baucis Elderly couple who alone were hospitable to Zeus and Hermes when the gods tested the human race. They were saved when Zeus flooded the world.

Philoctetes Inherited the bows and arrows of Heracles. Odysseus and Diomede took him to the Trojan War when the Greek cause seemed hopeless and he killed Paris with a poisoned arrow.

Pleiades Seven sisters who became a constellation at their death.

Polynices Son of Oedipus. Led the Seven Champions against Thebes and was killed.

Polyphemus Cyclops blinded by Odysseus.

Priam King of Troy. Killed by Neoptolemus as Troy fell to the Greeks.

Procrustes A robber in Attica who cut or lengthened his victims to fit his bed.

Pygmalion King of Paphos (Pafos) in Cyprus. He fell in love with a statue of a beautiful woman and Aphrodite brought it to life.

Sarpedon Hero of the Siege of Troy who commanded the Trojans' Lycian allies. He was killed by Patroclus.

Scylla and Charybdis Scylla was a sea-monster with six heads; Charybdis a dangerous whirlpool. Odysseus had to navigate between them.

Sirens Half-human female creatures who lured men to their deaths at sea by their singing.

Sisyphus Having tricked death he was condemned in perpetuity to roll a stone up a hill from whose summit it always rolled down again.

Tantalus Punished for crimes against the gods by never being able to touch the grapes and water he reaches for.

Telemachus Son of Odysseus. He helped his father slaughter the suitors of his mother Penelope.

Theseus Athenian hero. He killed the Minotaur in the Labyrinth of Crete and engaged in numerous other adventures. The husband of Hippolyta and Phaedra.

Tiresias Blind prophet who was said to have lived the life of both a man and a woman.

BIG NAMES AMONG THE ANCIENT GREEKS

More Greeks of the classical age are known by name than the total number in the whole of previous history. As each individual was believed to possess a special excellence which it was their own and society's duty to call forth, it seems reasonable to list some of the more prominent Greeks of ancient times, reaching out on either side of the classical age, along with their achievements – or lack of them.

Aeschines (c390 BC-?) Athenian politician and orator. He argued for peace with Macedon, earning the enmity of Demosthenes.

Aeschylus (c525-c456 BC) Dramatist, born at Eleusis. He wrote some 60 plays, of which seven survive, including the *Oresteia* trilogy.

Aesop (6th century BC) Traditional name for the Greek writer whose *Fables* use animals to make moral points.

Agesilaus (444-360 BC) King of Sparta. An initially able ruler, his crushing defeat by Thebes at Leuctra in 371 BC broke Spartan power.

Alcaeus (c600 BC) Lyric poet. He wrote of the good life, but only fragments of his works survive.

Alcibiades (c450-404 BC) Athenian general in war with Sparta. An Athenian Benedict Arnold, he changed sides several times and helped defeat Athens in Sicily.

Alcmaeon (c500 BC) Physician and medical researcher who first practiced dissection and located the center of sensation in the brain.

Alexander the Great (356-323 BC) King of Macedon. Pupil of Aristotle. One of the great captains of military history, he conquered the Persian Empire and led his army to the gates of India. Founded Alexandria in Egypt.

Anacreon (6th century BC) Lyric poet from Asia Minor. Only fragments of his work survive.

Anaxagoras (500-428 BC) Philosopher. He taught Pericles and argued that all matter is infinitely divisible.

Anaximander (610-547 BC) Philosopher. He held that there were many worlds and that the cosmos was boundless and had been created by natural forces.

Anaximenes (c570-526 BC) Philosopher. He held that air was the origin of earth, fire and water.

Antenor (6th century BC). Early Athenian sculptor.

Antigonus I (?-301 BC) Macedonian general who took the title of King of Macedon after Alexander the Great's death.

Antiochus I (324-261 BC) Hellenistic King of Syria. Founded Antioch.

Antiochus III (223-187 BC) Hellenistic King of Syria. He was defeated by the Romans at Magnesia in 190 BC.

Antipater (398-319 BC) Macedonian general. He became regent of the empire after Alexander the Great's death.

Antiphon (c480-411 BC) Attic orator. He was condemned to death for his political views.

Antisthenes (444-370 BC) Philosopher. Pupil of Socrates. He founded the Cynic philosophy which held that true happiness did not depend on material well-being.

Apollonius Dyskolos (2nd century AD) Grammarian. A tetchy scholar who first systematized Greek grammar, to the distress of all subsequent students.

Apollonius of Perga (280-210 BC) Mathematician. He made the first major study of conic sections.

Apollonius Rhodius (3rd century BC) Epic poet. He wrote the tale of Jason and the Quest for the Golden Fleece, the *Argonautica*.

Archilochus (c650 BC) Lyric poet who shunned the heroic "do or die" tradition.

Archimedes (c287-212 BC) Scientist, inventor and mathematician. Born at Syracuse, Sicily. He made big advances in mechanics and hydrostatics, developing Archimedes' screw for raising water and Archimedes' principle: that a body displaces its own weight in water. He was killed by a Roman soldier at the storming of Syracuse, apparently while working on some problem of geometry.

Aristarchus of Samos (c310-230 BC) Astronomer. He measured with tolerable accuracy the distance from Earth to the Moon and Sun, and proved that the Sun is the center of the solar system.

Aristarchus of Samothrace (c215-145 BC) Grammarian. He revised the Homerian epics and was Librarian at Alexandria.

Aristides (unknown-c468 BC) Athenian politician and soldier of the Persian wars. He organized the Delian League, which developed into an Athenian Empire.

Aristippus (410-350 BC) Philosopher. Student of Socrates. He founded the Hedonistic strand of Cynicism, arguing that having fun is OK.

Aristophanes (c448-c388 BC) Great comic playwright, 11 of whose 50-plus works survive.

Aristotle (384-322 BC) Philosopher: often known simply as The Philosopher. A Macedonian, he was a student of Plato and later tutor of Alexander the Great. He founded the Lyceum in Athens and wrote on logic, the arts, astronomy, biology, metaphysics, ethics, politics and many other subjects. His was probably the most profound secular influence on human thought down to the Renaissance.

Aristoxenos (4th century BC) Mathematician and musicologist. He studied the basis of music in tones, semitones and microtones, and also invented a form of logarithms.

Arrian (c95-180AD) Historian and administrator. He wrote a history of Alexander the Great's campaigns. Hadrian appointed him governor of Bithynia in Asia Minor and he led an expedition to circumnavigate the Black Sea.

Callicrates (5th century BC) Architect. He was joint designer of the Parthenon with Ictinus.

Callimachus (5th century BC) Sculptor. He was credited with inventing the Corinthian capital.

Callimachus (299-210 BC) Poet and librarian.

Cleisthenes (6th century BC) Politician. He reformed the Athenian constitution, laying the groundwork for democracy.

Clement of Alexandria (c150-c215AD) Theologian of the early Christian Church.

Cleon (?-422 BC) Athenian politician and general. He captured a Spartan army entire during the Peloponnesian War.

Democritus (c460-370 BC) Philosopher. He proposed that atoms were the constituent parts of nature, combining according to natural laws.

Demosthenes (c383-322 BC) Politician. Renowned for his oratory, he persuaded the Athenians to go to war with Macedon. Athens was totally defeated at Chaeronea in 338 BC.

Diogenes Laërtius (3rd century AD) Author. He excerpted the Greek philosophers, thus enabling some of their writings to survive.

Diogenes of Sinope (412-323 BC) Philosopher. A Cynic, he lived an austere "natural" life.

Dion Chrysostom (c40-c112AD) Philosopher. Banished by the Roman Emperor Domitian, he was later favored by Trajan.

Dionysius of Halicarnassus (1st century BC) Historian. He wrote an early history of Rome.

Dionysius the Areopagite (1st century AD) Churchman. An early convert to Christianity and the first Bishop of Athens.

Dionysius Thrax (2nd century AD) Grammarian. He wrote a seminal textbook on the subject.

Diophantus (c200-299AD) Mathematician. He wrote an early work on algebra.

Draco (7th century BC) Politician. His legal system introduced in Athens in 621 BC specified the death penalty for almost every offence. The Athenians decided it was too "draconian" and abandoned it.

Empedocles (c490-c430 BC) Philosopher. He held that the universe consisted of four eternal elements: earth, air, fire and water.

Epaminondas (c418-362 BC) Soldier. A brilliant Theban general, he totally defeated Sparta at Leuctra in 371 BC but lost to a Greek coalition at Mantinea a decade later.

Epictetus (c50-c130AD) Philosopher. A Stoic thinker and creator of maxims.

Epicurus (c341-270 BC) Philosopher. He founded the Epicurean philosophy, which argued that happiness is dependent on being free from pain and anxiety.

Erasistratus (3rd century BC) Physician and medical researcher. He studied the nervous system and blood circulation.

Eratosthenes (c276-c194 BC) Geographer. He measured the circumference of the Earth.

Euclid (around 300 BC) Mathematician. He developed the system now known as Euclidean geometry.

Eudoxos of Cnidos (c408 BC-c353 BC) Astronomer and mathematician. He did groundbreaking work in geometry and tried to explain the motion of the planets.

Euripides (c480-406 BC) Dramatist. He produced 80 or so works, of which 19 survive, including *Orestes* and *Electra*.

Galen (c130-201AD) Physician. He compiled an influential reference work on medicine.

Gorgias (c483-376 BC) Philosopher. Downbeat thinker who argued that sensation and observation are both unreal, that nothing exists, that even if it does we know nothing about it, and that even if we did we couldn't communicate it.

Hecataeus (c550-489 BC) Historian. He can be considered the founder of historical studies.

Heraclitus (?-460 BC) Philosopher. He held that all things are in a constant process of change and consist of opposites such as hot and cold.

Hero of Alexandria (1st century AD) Mathematician and inventor. He made advances in optics and mechanics. His "machines" included a mechanical organ and automatic puppet theaters.

Herodotus (c485-425 BC) Historian. His *Histories* covered the Greek wars with Persia.

Herophilus (c335-c280 BC) Medical researcher. He conducted studies of anatomy.

Hesiod (8th century BC) Poet. His *Theogeny* tells of the origins of the Greek gods.

Hipparchus (c190-125 BC) Astronomer. He cataloged more than a thousand stars and worked out the length of the solar year.

Hippocrates (c460-c377 BC) Physician. Regarded as the "father of medicine", he worked at Cos and developed the Hippocratic Oath of medicinal good conduct.

Homer (9th century BC) Poet. One of the great figures in world literature. He is credited with writing *The Iliad* and *The Odyssey*, but not the later *Homeric Hymns*.

Ictinus (5th century BC) Architect. He was joint designer of the Parthenon with Callicrates.

Isocrates (436-338 BC) Orator. He taught rhetoric.

Kimon (?-449 BC) Military commander. He defeated a Persian army and fleet on the same day in 469 BC, and was killed beseiging Kition in Cyprus.

Leonidas (?-480 BC) King of Sparta. He died famously at Thermopylae with his 300 Spartans, defending the pass against the entire Persian army.

Leucippus (5th century BC) Philosopher. A shadowy figure who may have developed the atomic theory put forward by Democritus.

Longinus (c213-273AD) Philosopher. A Neoplatonist who lost his head for rebellion against Rome.

Lycurgus (uncertain) Statesman. He was said to have promulgated the constitution that made Sparta a permanently militarized state.

Lysias (c450-380 BC) Orator. He contended against the Thirty Tyrants of Athens.

Menander (c343-291 BC) A comic dramatist.

Milo (6th century BC) Athlete. He was twelve times winner at wrestling in the Olympian and Pythian games.

Miltiades (c550-489 BC) Soldier and statesman. He was primarily responsible for the Greek victory over Persia at Marathon in 490 BC.

Myron (5th century BC) Sculptor.

Pappus of Alexandria (4th century AD) Mathematician. He compiled the teachings of the ancient mathematicians.

Parmenides (c515-c445 BC) Philosopher. A pre-Socratic philosopher and founder of the Eleatic school.

Pausanias (2nd century AD) Travel Writer. His *Description of Greece,* based on a journey made in 160AD, remains one of the primary sources for descriptions of the country's ancient monuments.

Pelopidas (c410-364 BC) Soldier. He commanded with Epaminondas the Theban army which defeated Sparta at Leuctra in 371 BC.

Pericles (c495-429 BC) Statesman. One of the great democratic politicians of all time. He led Athens through its 5th-century Golden Age and promoted democracy as the best possible political system. He also founded an Athenian Empire in the Delian League and provoked the ultimately disastrous, for Athens, Peloponnesian War against Sparta.

Phaedrus (1st century AD) Macedonian slave at Rome. He translated Aesop's *Fables* into Latin.

Phidias (5th century BC) Sculptor. He was responsible for some of the greatest works on the Acropolis in Athens, including the statue of Athena in gold and ivory.

Philip II (382-336 BC) King of Macedon and father of Alexander the Great. He unified Macedon and led it to dominance over Greece.

Philolaos of Croton (6th century BC) Mathematician and astronomer. He first suggested that the Earth moved through space and was not the center of the universe.

Pisistratus (c600-527 BC) Politician. A Tyrant of Athens, he ruled with sense and moderation as a benign dictator.

Phryne (4th century BC) Courtesan. She was said to have been the model for Praxiteles' statue of Aphrodite.

Pindar (c522-c440 BC) Poet. A celebrated writer of odes.

Plato (c427-347 BC) Philosopher. Student of Socrates. He founded the Academy at Athens. His *Dialogues* outline Socrates' thinking and Plato's own extension of it. One of the most influential thinkers of all time, particularly through works like *The Republic*.

Plotinus (205-270AD) Philosopher. He founded Neoplatonism, a philosophy that greatly influenced early Christianity.

Plutarch (c46-c120AD) Historian. He published a biography of 46 prominent Greek and Roman figures.

Polybius (c200-118 BC) Historian from Megalopolis. He wrote histories of Republican Rome.

Polyclitus (5th century BC) Sculptor from Samos.

Polycrates (6th century BC) Politician. Tyrant of Samos. An able and moderate ruler who was also a patron of the arts.

Polygnotus (c475-447 BC) Sculptor. He depicted men as "better than they are".

Porphyry (c233-304AD) Philosopher. He extended Neoplatonist thinking.

Praxiteles (4th century BC) Sculptor. He is credited with the great works of ancient Greek sculpture, although many of the originals have vanished and are known to us only through copies.

Proclus (c412-485AD) Philosopher. He was the last head of Plato's Academy.

Protagoras (c490-421 BC) Philosopher. A Sophist, he held that all beliefs are true and that "Man is the measure of all things."

Ptolemy (c100-168AD) Astronomer and geographer. A great astronomer, his view of the earth at the center of the universe held sway for fourteen hundred years.

Ptolemy I Soter (c366-c283 BC) King of Egypt. One of Alexander the Great's generals, Ptolemy ruled the Hellenistic kingdom of Egypt after Alexander's death in 323 BC. He founded the Museum and Library at his capital Alexandria, which became the greatest center of ancient learning.

Pyrrho (c360-c270 BC) Philosopher. His idea system is a form of scepticism: that we know nothing and should not jump to conclusions.

Pyrrhus: (c318-272 BC). King of Epirus. He tried to help Greek colonies in Italy against Rome. He defeated three Roman armies but heavy losses forced him to withdraw – he won "Pyrrhic victories".

Pythagoras (6th century BC) Mathematician and philosopher. Much of his philosophy was based on numbers, which led to important advances in mathematics.

Pythias (4th century BC) Mariner. He sailed past Spain and France to Britain and possibly as far north as Iceland or northern Norway inside the Arctic Circle, and then south to the Baltic.

Sappho (c610-c580 BC) Poet from Lesbos. She wrote odes, but only two of her works survive in full.

Simonides (c556-468 BC) Poet. Said that "poetry is painting that speaks."

Socrates (470-399 BC) Philosopher. The most influential ancient philosopher although he never wrote anything. We know of his ideas mostly through Plato's *Dialogues*. He so irritated the Athenians with his constant questioning of everything that he was condemned to death for impiety and corrupting the young. He drank hemlock and died.

Solon (7th-6th century BC) Statesman. An Athenian magistrate who modernised and moderated the constitution, paving the way for democracy.

Sophocles (c496-406 BC) Dramatist. Only seven of his 123 plays survive, including *Oedipus Rex* and *Antigone*.

Strabo (c60 BC-21AD) Geographer. His *Geographica* is a vital source for the Mediterranean in ancient times.

Thales (c620-555 BC) Philosopher. Born in Miletus. He is considered to be the world's first natural philosopher and apparently held that water was the "first principle", the basis of all things.

Themistocles (c523-c458 BC) Soldier and statesman. The Athenian commander who led the victorious Greek forces at Salamis in 480 BC, foiling Persia's ambition to conquer Greece.

Theocritus (c310-250 BC) Poet. He wrote pastoral idylls.

Theophrastus (c372-286 BC) Philosopher. A student of Aristotle and Plato, he headed the Peripatetic School after Aristotle's death and laid the foundations of botany.

Thucydides (c460-c400 BC) Historian. He wrote the history of the Peloponnesian War between Athens and Sparta.

Xenophanes (c570-c480 BC) Philosopher. He critiqued the Greek pantheon of gods.

Xenophon (c435-354 BC) Historian. A mercenary who led 10,000 cut-off Greek soldiers out of Persia and wrote the story of their escape.

Zeno of Citium (c336-c265 BC) Philosopher. A Cypriot of Phoenician origin, and one of the greatest "Greek" philosophers. He founded Stoicism, teaching it at the Stoa Poikile, or Painted Portico, in Athens. Stoicism taught that striving against fate is useless and that conscientious pursuit of duty is the road to virtue.

Zeno of Elea (c490-c420 BC) Philosopher. One of the Eleatics, he created logical paradoxes as a way of refining the technique of thought.

Zeuxis (5th century BC) Painter. None of his works survive, only some descriptions of them.

INDEX

THINGS CHANGE!

Phone numbers, prices, addresses, quality of food, etc, all change. If you come across any new information, we'd appreciate hearing from you. No item is too small! Write us at:

Greek Islands Guide
*Open Road Publishing, P.O. Box 20226
Columbus Circle Station, New York, NY 10023*